THIS COPY OF

WORKS TRIUMPHS
IN DETAIL

IS SIGNED BY THE AUTHOR

GRAHAM ROBSON

H&S

WORKS TRIUMPHS
IN DETAIL

WORKS TRIUMPHS IN DETAIL

By Graham Robson

Photography by Simon Clay

Herridge & Sons

Published in 2014 by
Herridge & Sons Ltd
Lower Forda, Shebbear
Devon EX21 5SY

Design by Ray Leaning, MUSE Fine Art & Design.

ISBN 978-1-906133-59-7
Printed in China

CONTENTS

INTRODUCTION & ACKNOWLEDGEMENTS 6

PROLOGUE: 8

WHERE WERE THE CARS PREPARED?

CHAPTER 1: 15

TR2, TR3 AND TR3A (1953–61)

CHAPTER 2: 59

TR2, TR3S AND TRS RACING CARS (1954–61)

CHAPTER 3: 77

HERALD AND VITESSE (1959–63)

CHAPTER 4: 93

TR4 (1962–64)

CHAPTER 5: 114

THE 2000 (1963–67)

CHAPTER 6: 132

SPITFIRE AND GT6R (1964–66)

CHAPTER 7: 167

THE 2.5 PI (1967–72)

CHAPTER 8: 192

DOLOMITE SPRINT, RACE AND RALLY (1972–78)

CHAPTER 9: 217

TR7 AND TR7 V8 (1976–80)

CHAPTER 10: 250

STANDARD EIGHT, TEN AND PENNANT (1955–59)

CHAPTER 11: 265

STANDARD VANGUARD III (1956)

APPENDICES: 269

1 ENGINES USED IN WORKS STANDARDS AND TRIUMPHS (1953–80)

2 FOUR-WHEEL-DRIVE 1300 RALLYCROSS CAR (1968–69)

INTRODUCTION

With its post-war partner Standard, Triumph has an illustrious motor sporting record. From 1953, when Ken Richardson in a TR2 prototype scorched up and down the dual carriageway at Jabbeke, Belgium, to 1980, when Tony Pond won several major international rallies in the thundering TR7 V8, the marques were always prominent, usually competitive and often extremely successful.

The general story of the works Triumphs has been told before, but in many cases the most outstanding individual performances, and some of the most successful cars themselves, have not been documented in any great detail. Not until I began digging deep in research for this book did I realise just how much was still to be covered.

Triumph and Standard enthusiasts alike should be proud of the number of different models that won events, both on the track and in rallying, the latter encompassing events as varied as rallycross and intercontinental marathons. It was not only the TR sports cars that achieved success: consider, too, the performance of Dolomite Sprint racing cars in touring car racing, Standard Eights and Tens in rallying, Spitfires and TRS prototypes at Le Mans, and 2.5 PI saloons in the World Cup rally and East African Safari. As all of these works cars were unique and memorable in some way, I set out in this book to record the activities of each and every example campaigned in that 40-year period.

Between 1953 and 1980, Standard-Triumph became one of the most respected, consistent and successful brands in motorsport, and to many enthusiasts the cars have never lost their sparkle. Cars built by the works team won events all over the globe. In several cases they remained competitive, and successful, after international regulations changed or the production versions had been discontinued.

Although books have been written about the nuts-and-bolts specifications of some of the cars, no previous author has had the chance, the scope or the space – with encouragement from his publisher! – to go into great detail about the individual histories of all the works cars, nor to examine the myths and legends surrounding them. Until now, that is, for this book sets out to survey each and every one of the authentic works cars, and their often complex lives.

This is also the right time to point out why certain other cars, supposedly entered in major events as works cars, were nothing of the sort – for there have been several cases in recent years where the rather shadowy career of such a car has been hyped beyond all reasonable bounds, probably in the hope that its value would skyrocket accordingly.

I have been digging into the history of works Triumphs and Standards cars for many years, but this is the first time I have been able to list every event – international, national and sometimes even club-level status – tackled by every car, and to find time to list the political events, and even the unspoken deals, involving every example. Not only that, but I believe I have even been able to follow the rather mysterious ways in which some cars seemed to evolve from one identity to another, or where a new car took on an old identity.

Why did some worthy drivers never get the chance to drive regularly in the works team? Why did one or two drivers who were not of the highest standard turn up repeatedly in factory cars and not shine? Why were some palpably unsuitable cars entered for certain events? Why did some cars not appear on events that would have suited their capabilities? The answers are all here.

Here, finally, is the complete motorsport history of all the works Triumphs and Standards.

WHEN IS A WORKS CAR NOT A WORKS CAR?

Over the years I have repeatedly wrestled with the status of some cars that have appeared in long and complex motorsport histories.

What follows will no doubt start as much discussion as it settles other queries. With the admission that the term 'works' should perhaps be 'works-entered', this is how several categories of entry in this book can be explained:

• The true definition of a works car is one that was prepared by a factory's competitions department, driven by individuals who were invited to do so by the factory, and supported on events by factory technicians.

• A 'works-loaned' car is one that technically lines up as above, but was loaned to another organisation or favoured individual for a particular event. Usually such cars are/were not supported by the team on events though – just to confuse the issue – sometimes they were!

• 'Works replicas' are structurally and technically the same as true works machines. Originally they might even have been prepared by the competitions department, but they were never retained by the team.

• 'Ex-works' cars are precisely that – cars that have been sold on by the competitions department but still seen on major events.

ACKNOWLEDGEMENTS

Over the years since the first Triumph TR2 went on sale – and when I first began to take an interest in motorsport – a lot of people have helped me to get to know the Triumph (and Standard) marques. Without them, and without the knowledge gained as a co-driver, team manager, event organiser, observer and – now – historian, I would never have been able to tap into the character and charm of the teams and the cars, or to understand why the programme evolved in the way it did.

Over the years, I have interviewed, and often befriended, virtually all of the important characters whose experience and insight have made my task so much easier.

Although many of the 'old stagers' have now passed on, I would like to list the most significant of them among those staff, managers, engineers and consultants whose personal support helped enormously:

Ray Bates, Gordon Birtwistle, Ralph Broad, Peter Browning, John Davenport, David Eley, Den Greene, Ray Henderson, 'Kas' Kastner, John Lloyd, Lyndon Mills, Brian Moylan, Jim Parkinson, Simon Pearson, Bill Price, Richard Seth-Smith, Basil Wales, Harry Webster and Alan Zafer.

Naturally, too, I have used previous experience, research and interviews to bulk up the detail included in these pages, and I am also particularly grateful to the following for their reminiscences:

Keith Ballisat, Roger Bell, Gordon Birtwistle, Peter Browning, Mike Cook, Willy Cave, Brian Culcheth, John Davenport, Tony Dron, Vic Elford, Roy Fidler, Fred Gallagher, Maurice Gatsonides, Brian Horrocks, Paddy Hopkirk, Ray Hutton, 'Kas' Kastner, Simo Lampinen, Ian 'Tiny' Lewis, Mike Otto, Tony Pond, Jimmy Ray, Andy Rouse, John Sprinzel, David Stone, Jean-Jacques Thuner, Stuart Turner, Johnny Wallwork and Brian Whitaker.

As for the mass of illustrations that help to bring these pages to life, I want to start by thanking those enthusiasts who have preserved some magnificent works Triumphs to this day, and for allowing Simon Clay to photograph them again in their historic glory:

David Wenham, Neil Revington, Mark Field, Patrick Walker, Stuart Anderson, Steve Rockingham.

Apart from delving into my own archive, which has accumulated during the past 40 to 50 years, archive information and pictures also came from the British Motor Industry Heritage Trust, the Modern Records department at the University of Warwick, the Coventry Transport Museum, the Kithead Trust, and many other private sources including:

Gordon Birtwistle, John Carlton, John Clancy, Peter Collier, Mike Cook, Ian Cornish, Brian Culcheth, Chris Cunnington, Peter Darley, Dave Hill, Phil Homer, Ray Hutton, Bill Piggott, Tony Pounder, Pascal Quirynen, Neil Revington, Brian Sparrowhawk, Brian Whitaker and Mike Wood.

Much of the detailed motorsport information in the chapter about the TR7 and TR7 V8 rally cars has been made available to me over the years by Bill Price, the acknowledged expert on these cars. Without Bill's cheerful advice and guidance, the information about these cars would not be as accurate or as complete as I hope it now is.

My grateful and humble thanks to all.

GRAHAM ROBSON
January 2014

6 VC, the works TR4 now owned by Neil Revington of Revington TR.

PROLOGUE:
WHERE WERE THE CARS PREPARED?

Over the years, the works Standard and Triumph competition cars were prepared and maintained at a variety of sites. To show that pedigree is everything, that continuity (personal or technical) is vital but location sometimes meaningless, I thought it worth itemising and describing the six sites at which race or rally cars were built, maintained and modified between 1953 and 1980.

BANNER LANE, COVENTRY

The story of works Standards and Triumphs really began at the rambling ex-government 'shadow' factory at Banner Lane, Coventry. As re-armament gathered pace in the 1930s, the authorities had set up a network of 'shadow' factories that would expand the production of military hardware – aircraft, engines, tanks and guns – in parallel with (i.e. 'shadowing') existing plants. Most of these 'shadow' factories would be managed, though not financed, by companies in the British motor industry.

Standard's original 'shadow' factory was built at Canley, close to the existing car manufacturing buildings, and began operations in 1937 with the manufacture of sections of Bristol Mercury VIII radial aero engines. This factory, however, was soon dwarfed by an enormous new complex set up at Banner Lane, on the western outskirts of Coventry. Completed in 1940, the Banner Lane plant was originally built as a massive centre for the manufacture and testing of Bristol Hercules aero engines, which were air-cooled, radial, 14-cylinder mammoths displacing 38.7 litres and eventually producing 1,800bhp.

By 1945, more than 20,000 Hercules engines had been produced on this site alone, and when the war was over the lease of this vast plant was taken over by Standard. Most of the site was eventually dedicated to the manufacture and assembly of Ferguson tractors, but until 1959 a considerable section was also used as Standard's corporate HQ, along with departments dedicated to the design, engineering and devel-

The very first works Triumphs were prepared in the general experimental department at Banner Lane, Coventry. This 1952 study shows the original prototype, which became the TR2, with a Triumph Mayflower and a Standard Vanguard in the background. Glamorous?

Ken Richardson (in the reclined seat) and Marshall Dorr administered the works motorsport programme in the late 1950s and early 1960s. This is a Herald that was being prepared for the 1960 Monte Carlo rally.

opment of all new Standard and Triumph products.

All Triumphs of the immediate post-war period – models such as the 1800 Roadster, Renown, Mayflower and, eventually, the original TR2 sports car – were conceived at Banner Lane. Accordingly, preparation of the very first motorsport car, the Jabbeke high-speed demonstration TR2 registered MVC 575, was carried out in a corner of the experimental department on that site, under Ken Richardson's control.

When a competitions programme was inaugurated in 1954, the first 'team' event being the French Alpine rally, preparation of the cars continued to be at Banner Lane, and the following year the work done there included build of the three experimental TR2s that competed at Le Mans in 1955. As the programme expanded, extra space was inevitably needed and the activities of the competitions department were therefore relocated a few miles away, at the factory service department at Allesley. However, when the time came to build three brand-new Sabrina-engined TR3S racing cars to compete at Le Mans in 1959, the cars were engineered at Banner Lane before being passed over to Richardson's department at Allesley for final pre-race preparation.

The Banner Lane factory no longer exists. Sold off in 1958 as a consequence of the 'divorce' between Standard-Triumph and Ferguson's new owners, Massey-Harris, it carried on making tractors until the 2000s. Then, after the assembly of tractors finally ended on the Banner Lane site, the entire factory was progressively demolished, and has now been replaced by housing.

In the mid-1950s, the works TR3s were prepared in the factory service building at Allesley, on the outskirts of Coventry. This view shows a gleaming SHP 520 receiving attention, and other cars awaiting it. The bent Vanguard was not a works car…

These three TR3s are about to leave the Allesley Service Department, en route to the 1957 Sebring 12 Hours sports car race. Ken Richardson is at the centre of the shot.

Five brand-new TR3As being delivered to the Allesley Service Department at the end of 1958, ready to begin preparation for the 1959 Monte Carlo rally.

ALLESLEY, COVENTRY

Built to the then-fashionable Art Deco architectural style in the 1930s, these premises were sold by their original owners, Peerless & Ericsson, to Standard-Triumph in the early 1950s. Although remote from the company's main Canley complex, the Allesley site was just a few miles away to the north, on the same A45 trunk road that passed in front of the two Fletchamstead buildings.

By the mid-1950s, the Allesley site had been integrated into the factory scheme of things and designated the company's service department. Among its many diverse activities was the maintenance of company cars and the press fleet, as well as cars that were to be used by private owners in motorsport events.

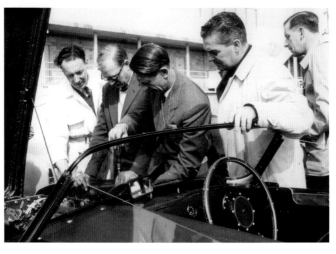

Final adjustments to a TRS before the start of the Le Mans race in 1960 or 1961. From left: Doug West (mechanic), Harry Webster, Ken Richardson, Martin Tustin and Marshall Dorr.

KEN RICHARDSON

Although Ken Richardson was not directly connected with Standard-Triumph until late 1952 and left the company in 1961, in those nine years he had considerable influence on the motorsport activities of the Standard and Triumph marques. Although he was no designer, he was an accomplished development engineer, a racing and rally driver of note, and a forceful character who managed the company's competitions department from 1954 until his departure.

Born in 1911 at Bourne, Lincolnshire, Richardson joined the ERA racing car team, which was based in his home town, soon after Raymond Mays set up the business in the 1933. Starting as a mechanic, Richardson soon became one of ERA's most respected engineers. After working on military projects during the war years, he moved on, with Mays and others, to become senior development engineer in the costly and grandiloquent BRM racing car project, which was also Bourne-based.

By the early 1950s Standard-Triumph had become a major supporter of the BRM project and people in the company knew of Richardson. So it was that in 1952, after his employment at BRM had been terminated, he was invited to test-drive the original 20TS – the predecessor of the TR2. Following his scathing dismissal of its capabilities, he was hired as the company's new sports car development engineer, and became competitions manager of a fledgling operation in 1954.

Although very effective as a manager and a shrewd picker of 'horses for courses' in terms of selecting the best cars for any particular event, he was a difficult man to accommodate in corporate surroundings. Following Leyland's financial rescue of Standard-Triumph in 1961, the competitions department was abruptly closed down and Richardson departed. In some ways it was typical of his character that he made sure none of his department's records survived.

Two vitally important characters central to getting Standard-Triumph back into motorsport in 1962 were technical chief Harry Webster (standing) and managing director Stanley Markland. None of the programmes could have run without their encouragement and, more important still, approval of budgetary funds!

Technical chief Harry Webster was the enthusiastic engineer who inspired every technical feature of the works cars between 1961 and 1968, when he moved to the Austin-Morris division of British Leyland. Here he is watching Simo Lampinen sign his contract for the 1965 season.

Graham Robson was Competitions Secretary at Standard-Triumph from 1962 to 1965. Here, seated in his spartan office at Fletchamstead North, he is discussing preparations for the 1963 Monte Carlo rally with Roy Fidler. Behind that partition, incidentally, was a row of experimental engine test beds, so the background noise was often considerable!

By 1964 the works department at Coventry was using 2000 saloons as support/service cars. This machine, in fact, had originally been the only prototype of a 1.6-litre model to be known as the Triumph 1600, which explains the unique grille.

As chairman of Standard-Triumph and then British Leyland, Lord Stokes controlled motorsport funding in the 1960s.

The works Spitfire rally cars at the factory in September 1964 before their departure for the Tour de France, with the main manufacturing buildings at Canley in the background.

Although records are sparse, it seems that Ken Richardson's works competitions department, and its fleet of TR3s and Standard Tens, moved in the winter of 1955/56 from Banner Lane to Allesley, which then became the centre of motorsport activities until 1960. As well as two batches of TR3As, work on Standard Tens and Pennants, and Triumph Heralds, and final work on the 1960 TRS Le Mans cars, all took place at Allesley before the operation moved, for a brief period, to Radford.

The service operation remained on the Allesley site for two more decades, until the factory was eventually sold off in the late 1970s and early 1980s by what had become BL. The factory continues to exist, latterly as the centre of a respected independent automotive styling/design company.

All smiles on the Shell 4000 rally – Graham Robson (left) and Kas Kastner. But this was only the first day of the event! The GM truck was full of tyres, wheels, spares and the team's luggage…

Ray Henderson (right) was the key mechanic/engineer who looked after all works cars built from 1959 to the early 1970s. With him are Denny Hulme (centre) and the author, who were to crew a prototype 2.5 PI on the 1967 RAC rally.

FLETCHAMSTEAD NORTH, COVENTRY

Originally a government shadow factory within the grounds of the Standard 'estate' and facing the A45 trunk road, the building known as Fletchamstead North – 'Fletch North' in company speak – became Ferguson's tractor engineering centre at the end of the war. In late 1959 Fletch North became involved in the business 'divorce' of the Ferguson tractor operation from the main Standard-Triumph business and, in a carefully planned swap, Standard-Triumph's entire engineering operation moved there from Banner Lane while Ferguson (which had become Massey Ferguson by then) moved simultaneously in the other direction. Amazingly, this worked well, and was achieved very rapidly indeed.

During 1960 and 1961, the 'Zoom'-shaped TRS racing cars were engineered and originally assembled at Fletch North before being taken, pre-race, to Ken Richardson's relocated competitions department at the Radford plant. Immediately after the 1961 Le Mans race, all four TRS racing cars were returned to Fletch North, where the one-off Conrero car, still untested and unraced, soon joined them on

its arrival from Italy.

After several months of hiatus, a new competitions department was then set up at Fletch North, originally managed by the author (whose title was Competitions Secretary) but under Harry Webster's direct control. Between 1962 and 1969 the works TR4s, Vitesses, 2000s, Spitfires, Le Mans Spitfires and the original 2.5 PI prototypes were all prepared in that building, although the race and rally Spitfire workshops were always separated by about 100 yards! The main department, in fact, was cheek-by-jowl with a line of raucous engine test beds, and had previously been used to house the tractor-development operation (Standard was aiming to replace Ferguson tractors with a design of its own).

After the author left the company in 1965, Ray Henderson not only carried on as chief development engineer but also became the manager of the competitions department, for a time assisted by Gordon Birtwistle. After the formation of British Leyland in 1968, it was under Henderson that liaison was first set up with the 'rationalised' competitions department at Abingdon, south of Oxford, the last 'Fletch' projects being the unique four-wheel-drive Triumph 1300 rallycross car and the prototype Dolomite Sprint rally car.

RADFORD FACTORY, COVENTRY

For a short period in 1960–61, Ken Richardson's motorsport operation was moved from the Allesley building (see above) to a corner of a newly acquired factory at Capmartin Road, Radford, a northern suburb of Coventry.

This building had originally been a 'shadow' addition to the nearby Daimler factory – yet another military-equipment operation in Coventry – and had opened for military business in 1940. Having been emptied of manufacturing equipment and fallen into disuse in the 1950s, the Capmartin Road buildings were finally separated from Daimler and leased to Standard-Triumph, which rapidly filled them with machining and assembly facilities for transmissions and engines.

One corner of the complex was then allocated to the sports car development and experimental transmission departments, and shortly afterwards also to the competitions department. It was here that the TRS Le Mans cars of 1960 and 1961 were finalised, and where the last of the TR3A and Herald works cars were based.

Standard-Triumph's finances collapsed at the end of 1960, a rescue came from Leyland early in 1961, and soon after the 1961 Le Mans race the Richardson competitions department was closed down. Capmartin Road, however, continued as a transmission and engine components production factory for another quarter of a century, one of its final specialised tasks being to machine parts and assemble V6 engines for the MG Metro 6R4 Group B project.

BANBURY ROAD, SOUTHAM, NEAR COVENTRY

During the 1970s, the renowned Broadspeed racing car operation became ever closer to British Leyland, and was soon invited to run works Triumph Dolomite Sprints in saloon car racing. Years earlier, the Broad family had been running a BMC retail car dealership in Sparkbrook, Birmingham. A son of the family, Ralph Broad, not only dabbled in race and rally car driving himself, but built up a successful tuning operation.

Broadspeed was originally set up to develop and race Mini-Coopers, but eventually expanded to run Ford Anglia 105Es, Escorts and Capris, and later BMW 3.0 CSL and Jaguar XJ5.3C coupés. Early in the 1970s Broadspeed moved its HQ to workshops situated on the A423, just south of the Warwickshire town of Southam. Conveniently, and entirely by design, this site was about halfway between Triumph's HQ in Coventry and the Silverstone racing circuit.

Starting in 1973, Broadspeed was contracted to run the works Triumph Dolomite Sprints that contested the British Touring Car Championship, and selected events in Europe, with great success. Although Ralph Broad was the team boss, the engineering boffin and the true expert when it came to 'working' the rules of homologation to his advantage, it was his engineer and race driver Andy Rouse who developed and raced the cars when they were at their height.

Broadspeed withdrew from the Dolomite Sprint programme in 1978 and shortly afterwards went into voluntary liquidation. The buildings still exist but no longer have any connection with their Triumph history.

ABINGDON, NEAR OXFORD

The works Triumphs made their final motorsport 'home' at Abingdon from 1969 to 1980, a move that would never have happened if the MG factory in which 'Comps' was situated

had not already been the home of the BMC works competition cars prior to MG becoming part of British Leyland.

Originally owned by Sir William Morris (later Lord Nuffield), MG made its home at Abingdon, south of Oxford, from 1929 and MG's race and record cars were always housed there. After MG was swept into the new British Motor Corporation (BMC), Abingdon was the obvious place at which all subsequent BMC motorsport activities should be located. Opened in the winter of 1954/55, the BMC works motorsport department grew to become dominant in motorsport in the 1960s, rallying and racing significant cars like the Mini-Cooper S, MGB and Austin-Healey 3000.

Soon after BMC became a part of the new British Leyland industrial colossus in 1968, the existing BMC competitions manager, Peter Browning, was instructed to turn his department into a 'corporate' operation and to use any or all of British Leyland's products if they could become competitive enough to win events and championships. Accordingly, for the first year or so – during 1968 and 1969 – Browning worked in harness with Ray Henderson at Triumph's Fletch North department, but eventually all works Triumph rally cars were to be developed, built and based at Abingdon.

Browning's operation produced the splendid team of 2.5 PIs that so nearly won the *Daily Mirror* London–Mexico World Cup Rally of 1970, but as victory had not been achieved British Leyland's deluded bosses closed down the operation, from which Browning had already resigned in disgust at their lack of knowledge and enthusiasm for motorsport. The profitable Special Tuning side of the old

The works Broadspeed Dolomite Sprint race cars were prepared in modern premises on the main Coventry/Banbury road during the 1970s.

Two extremely smart Dolomite Sprint race cars, identical except for their livery – one is identified 'Andy Rouse', the other 'Steve Thompson'.

Two of the original MkI 2.5 PIs being prepared at Abingdon for the 1969 RAC rally.

From 1969, following the foundation of British Leyland, works Triumphs were always prepared at the old MG building, in Abingdon, near Oxford. This shot shows preparation for the 1970 World Cup rally.

John Davenport was BL's director of motorsport when the TR7 and TR7 V8 cars were being developed at Abingdon.

department survived, to struggle on, and it was within this entity that a nucleus of enthusiasts, managed by Basil Wales, revived the team and ran Triumph Dolomite Sprints.

From 1975, the works team was officially reopened, with Richard Seth-Smith managing the operation for a short time, but with long-serving expert Bill Price remaining on hand. From the end of 1976, one-time rally co-driver John Davenport was then appointed to manage the operation – a responsibility that also included control over the Broad-speed Triumphs and Jaguars – and it was under his often-controversial leadership that the works Dolomites, TR7s and TR7 V8s were campaigned until 1980, when the Triumph side of the team was wound down. It was in this period that the team moved workshops from an old part of the factory to a new building nearby.

Thereafter, the entire Abingdon factory complex was closed down after the long-running MGB finally ceased production in 1980. The site was sold off to developers, and shortly afterwards almost every building except the original 'Comps' shop was demolished. At the same time, the BL competitions effort moved to a site at the Cowley factory, a few miles away, and on to other projects, mainly surrounding the Rover 3500 (including the Vitesse) and the MG Metro 6R4.

CHAPTER 1:
TR2, TR3 AND TR3A (1953–61)

Although Triumph had been very active in rallying in the 1930s, this was when the company was still independent, when cars like the original Vitesses and Dolomites were on sale – and when no less a personality than Donald Healey was the company's technical director.

Then came the company's business traumas, its financial collapse in 1939 and eventually the purchase of its remaining bomb-blasted assets by Standard in 1944. After that, it can be stated without equivocation that Standard – and particularly its dictatorial managing director Sir John Black – were simply not interested motorsport with production cars, and nor did they make any cars that were suitable.

Thus it was that when British rallying got going again in the late 1940s, there seemed to be little chance of cars like the Standard Vanguard and the closely related Triumph Renowns and Roadsters ever being competitive. Apart from the company's lack of interest, there were various technical problems, notably the rather lumpy handling of Vanguard-based machines combined with their limited power output – only 68bhp from 2.1 litres – and three-speed column-mounted gear change.

So it was that when the world-famous Monte Carlo Rally was revived, in 1949, there were only three Standard Vanguards and two razor-edge Triumph saloons among the 225 Europe-wide entries. None of the five figured strongly in the results, and the drivers were not noteworthy. Even so, there were a few Standard-Triumph dealers who were demonstrably enthusiastic enough to enter cars in subsequent events. In the 1951 Monte, for instance, there may have been only six Vanguards and no Triumphs at all, but the factory loaned at least one of these Vanguards – we know that because of the registration number – to a dealer, Birmingham-based motor traders Ken Rawlings and Lew Tracey. That same year there was also a Portuguese-entered Vanguard that finished 19th overall.

This was a start, but no more than that. In June 1951 Britain's first-ever RAC International Rally was held, with the competitive side of the event mainly formed of driving tests rather than high-speed motoring. Five Standard Vanguards and four Triumphs started the event and still none figured strongly in the results, but there was a glimmer of hope. Two of the Vanguards were driven by Johnny Wallwork (from Cheshire) and Peter Cooper (from the Bournemouth area), both of whom were in the motor trade and had Standard connections – both would feature strongly in what was to follow during the next few years.

In those days, in fact, there was only one British works rally team, also Coventry-based. This was the Sunbeam-Talbot team, which had just been set up under the management of Rootes sales executive Norman Garrad.

This photograph was taken at a modern reunion of five ex-works TR2s at Brooklands. Three of these cars are authentic rally team cars, while the other two raced at Le Mans. The rally cars are OVC 276 (centre, first used on the 1954 Mille Miglia), PDU 20 (second from left, used on the 1954 French Alpine rally) and PKV 693 (right, used on the 1955 Tulip rally).

None of the other well-established British manufacturers – notably Ford, Austin, Morris and MG – had followed suit. For high-profile events such as the Monte, those companies in almost every case would loan out standard cars from their press fleets, and would certainly not give them any special attention.

Soon after this Standard's Sir John Black became obsessed with at least matching and if possible beating the export achievements of sports car manufacturers such as MG and Jaguar. To attempt to do this, he first made a misjudged attempt to buy Morgan, a totally fruitless quest because the Morgan family, who owned the whole thing, were quite happy to continue in their own way. Rebuffed, he then instructed his engineers to produce a sports car, a cheap-and-cheerful two-seater, to do the job for him.

As has often been told, Black's original instructions were to base the new car, coded 20TS, on the chassis of the pre-war Standard Flying Nine because stocks were still available. The result combined cobbled-up running gear – Triumph Mayflower independent front suspension grafted to an unsuitable chassis frame – with an underpowered version of the Vanguard engine, all covered in a two-seater body style that lacked flair. It was not a success.

However, it just so happened that Ken Richardson, recently eased out of his long-serving job in the BRM racing team at Bourne in Lincolnshire, was known to Sir John Black and was invited to test the single completed prototype. After

pronouncing it a 'death-trap', Richardson was invited to join Standard-Triumph as sports car development engineer. Over the winter of 1952/53, the Herculean efforts of engineers Harry Webster, John Turnbull and their colleagues, along with Richardson as a capable and persistent development engineer (though not a designer), turned the hapless 20TS into a competent sports car – the TR2.

The styling of the definitive car was right and the price seemed to be attractive. The company appeared to have a real contender to do battle not only with MG but also with Austin-Healey, which had also joined the battlefield with its new 100 model.

At first Black was not interested in the company becoming involved in motorsport, which he regarded as an expensive and unnecessary marketing tool; he thought his sales staff could move all the cars that could be built. That situation might have persisted had Sunbeam not then chosen to carry out a pair of high-speed stunts in its newly announced two-seater sports car.

Sir William Rootes was as much of a dictator as was Sir John Black at Standard-Triumph, and, seeking a gimmick to bring the new Alpine to the attention of the world's media, he instructed Garrad to produce a specially tuned version capable of 120mph; the standard car struggled to achieve more than 90mph. In March 1953 this special Alpine was taken first to the dual carriageway at Jabbeke, Belgium, and then to the banked oval track of Montlhéry, close to Paris. Thanks to the motorsport and engine-tuning expertise of Leslie Johnson's ERA concern and of Hartwell (a prominent Rootes Group dealer chain), the job was done: Stirling Moss and Sheila Van Damm both achieved just over 120mph in a straight line at Jabbeke and then at Montlhéry Johnson drove the Alpine flat-out for an hour, covering 112.2 miles.

Sir John Black decided – quickly, decisively and without discussing it with his senior Board colleagues – that his company and his new car should attempt to beat the Alpine's new figures. Calling in Ken Richardson, who frankly had better things to do with his time at this stage, Black told him that he should work a miracle, within eight weeks and with an existing prototype. Only two TR2s existed, and the one earmarked for the exercise was registered MVC 575 on 31 March 1953, immediately after Sir John's edict.

Richardson's tiny development team at Banner Lane duly delivered the miracle and on 20 May 1953 the TR2's reputation was sealed, forever (as described on pages 18–19). After that, however, it all went quiet, for Sir John still had no intention of setting up a works competitions department; the emphasis had to be on getting the car into production and for sales to begin. The first two hand-built 'off-tools' production TR2s were completed in the summer, 248 cars were delivered before the end of 1953, and a trickle turned into something approaching a flood in the first half of 1954.

After the miracle, Richardson retreated into the engi-

THE SACKING OF SIR JOHN BLACK

In January 1954 Standard's mercurial chairman and managing director, Sir John Black, abruptly stepped down from his executive position within the company, left his office at little more than a day's notice, and was never again to be involved with the empire that he had so energetically built up since joining Standard in 1929. After becoming sole managing director in 1934, he became increasingly dictatorial and, although widely admired as a businessman, he became much disliked for his irrational behaviour.

It was Sir John who decided that Triumph should enter the sports car market in 1952, Sir John who approved the increasingly expensive work that went into turning the unsatisfactory 20TS prototype into the ready-for-sale TR2, and Sir John who inspired Ken Richardson to drive the prototype at more than 120mph on the Jabbeke road in Belgium.

After quite unjustly threatening to dismiss a senior colleague, technical director Ted Grinham, Sir John was finally ousted by his disenchanted fellow directors. This final act came just weeks after he had been badly injured when the prototype Swallow Doretti sports car in which Ken Richardson was driving him crashed outside the Banner Lane factory.

By this time the TR2 was already in slow, but genuine, series production, and was poised to go on to greater things. Sir John's successor, Alick Dick, was openly enthusiastic about motorsport and the benefits it might bring to Standard-Triumph's image, so it was under him that motorsport credibility began to emerge, steadily and most satisfactorily.

neering departments at Banner Lane, there to complete the initial development of the road cars rather than get seriously involved in any further motorsport or record-breaking. However, there were two notable privateer achievements in March 1954: one was the private entry of a factory-owned car by the editor of *Autosport*, Gregor Grant, in the French Lyons-Charbonnières rally, the other the resounding success of privately prepared TR2s in the RAC Rally. The latter was an astonishing achievement: Johnny Wallwork won the event outright, Peter Cooper was second overall, Bill Bleakley was fifth overall, and Mary Walker won the publicity-worthy Ladies' Award. Nor was this a hollow victory, for the TR2s beat full factory teams from Ford and Sunbeam-Talbot.

In the meantime, things at Coventry had been developing behind the scenes. The well-connected Dutch rally ace, Maurice Gatsonides, once told me in an interview that he had a long talk with technical director Ted Grinham at the 1953 Earls Court Motor Show: 'He said that he wanted more publicity for the TR2. He wanted to enter cars for the French Alpine Rally and asked me if I would advise on preparation and test the car… Triumph asked me if I would enter a car for the Tulip Rally to test for the Alpine? I said "No"… I suggested that we should have a really good, heavy test in the Mille Miglia instead. This was agreed. Ken Richardson was then asked to come in…'

This, in fact, is not how Richardson later recalled it – perhaps the episode did not reflect well enough on his reputation and legacy – for he later commented in *Motor* magazine: 'The RAC Rally success [of 1954] made everyone at the works competition-minded and they decided to start a competition programme – much to my horror, for I'd had 18 years in motoring sport, and really wanted to get out of it…'

However, orders were orders. At Triumph Alick Dick had clearly been talking to his sales and marketing staff. Not only did he know that links had already been set up with Gatsonides, but he also knew that 'Gatso' had already expressed certain opinions about future policy. Accordingly, he told Richardson to set up a rather impromptu team at short notice.

One task was that they should immediately tackle two very different events – the Mille Miglia (the 1,000-mile open-road race around Italy) and the equally glamorous Alpine Rally in France. And if that was not enough, at the same time they should carry out some work on a TR2 to be entered privately at Le Mans by Edgar Wadsworth and Bobby Dickson. All this work was to be done at Banner Lane in a corner of the engineering/experimental department, with whatever mechanics Richardson could scrounge.

It was at about this time that two distinctly different sporting threads – rally cars and racing cars – began to emerge. This chapter will concentrate on the rally cars and those involved in high-speed record attempts, while the next chapter will cover the racing cars. Even so, this is not always a straightforward story, for the careers of certain works cars

embraced rallying and racing, and these will be covered in this chapter. An example is the trio of TR3s that competed in the 1956 French Alpine Rally and later crossed the Atlantic to compete in the 1957 Sebring 12 Hours race.

As described in the Prologue, the team workshops moved several times over the years, so there were times when continuity was lacking. But there was one continuous thread when Ken Richardson ran the operation from 1954 to 1961. It was towards the end of 1954 that he officially became competitions manager, with his own small but dedicated team.

It was in this period that he evolved the most astonishing – and inexplicable – policy of picking drivers for the works cars, his approach being quite unlike that of his rivals at BMC, Ford and Sunbeam. He also chose an interview in a motoring magazine to state this blatant untruth: 'We are in the fortunate position of having a consistent works team who have vast experience of continental events…' In fact the brutal truth is that drivers were only invited to drive on an event-by-event basis, and sometimes had unfamiliar co-drivers imposed upon them. Over many years, I knew many of the personalities involved, and can state with confidence that some of the best and most faithful Triumph drivers in the country were treated very badly, getting only occasional calls from the works team, while other cars were doled out to inferior drivers. They might have been deserving cases in terms of publicity, they might have had motor trade connections with the factory, they might have been close friends with Richardson – but they could not drive as well as those who had been overlooked. In many cases, the individual histories of cars, described from page 18 onwards, make this clear.

In the whole of those seven years, the department looked after not only a whole series of 'side-screen' TR rally cars – TR2, TR3 and TR3A – but also Standard Eights, Tens, Pennants and Vanguards, and Triumph Heralds. Even so, it was really not until 1958 that factory cars tended to be worked hard for their living – quite a number of them were either 'one-event wonders' or were used perhaps only two or three times before being sold. In 1955, however, it did not help that the competition programme for three brand-new TR2s fell apart when most of the events for which they were entered were cancelled in the aftermath of the Le Mans tragedy, when a Mercedes-Benz 300SLR went into the crowd, killing 88 spectators as well as its driver.

Even so, the pace of technical progress made on the TRs in that time could best be described as glacial. In seven years, front disc brakes were standardised, engines were enlarged from 1,991cc to 2,138cc, and peak power went up from 90bhp to perhaps 100/105bhp – but that was about all. The size of engine in a particular rally car often changed, depending on the varying class structures of events.

One very low-cost change was made in the spring of 1956, when the FIA tightened up its regulations regarding eligibility in the 'Grand Touring' categories. This meant that a sports car running in those classes had to have a 'permanent' roof and fixed side screens. Richardson's department therefore fixed up a car to have the optional hard top in place together with fixed side screens and exterior door handles – and the authorities were satisfied. No all-new engineering was required; although exterior locking door handles were not at that time being fitted to TR3s, they were being developed for the still-secret facelift that would become the TR3A of 1958, so prototype kits from Wilmot Breeden were speedily brought into use on rally cars.

Although FIA regulations certainly allowed sports cars to compete with tuned engines, different transmissions and lightweight body panels, no such modifications ever appeared on the works side-screen TRs. These regulations, incidentally, altered significantly during the 1950s, particularly in 1958 when a new type of homologation requirement came into force.

The question of the existence of works TRs with aluminium bodies has passed into the realms of mythology. Although Richardson once said that more than one aluminium-bodied TR was prepared at Allesley in the mid/late 1950s, no such cars ever competed in motorsport or were ever reported upon, and none has ever been known of in private ownership. And when I asked engineers about aluminium panelling for TR4s, the reaction from them was blank.

So why were the works side-screen cars so closely related to the production variety? Richardson once said that he preferred to run virtually standard products because they were good enough to win awards and provided the company with the right sort of publicity. He also made the astonishing assertion that engines with twin-choke Weber carburettors were tried in comparison with the regular SUs, but found to give very little advantage – something that was later found to be quite untrue.

He was right about using near-standard cars at first, perhaps, but he was wrong by the late 1950s when the programme began to run out of steam. In a period when the TR3A's principal advance was a power increase of only 10–15bhp, Austin-Healey had improved its cars from 130bhp to more than 200bhp by 1962, while at the same time reducing their weight.

In the last few years of this period, the way that cars were used changed significantly. Until 1957 a new works car might do only two or three events before it was sold, but from the advent of the wide-mouthed TR3As each car had a more intensive programme. In 1954, 1955 and 1956, several works TR2s and TR3s were 'one-event wonders', whereas in 1959 and 1960 Annie Soisbault's car, WVC 248, started 12 events.

All in all, however, this was an exciting time for the Triumph works team, as the following individual histories of no fewer than 32 different cars makes clear.

MVC 575

FIRST REGISTERED	31 MARCH 1953
ENGINE SIZE	1,991cc
MODEL TYPE	TR2

The TR2 prototype that started it all – Ken Richardson achieved more than 120mph on the Jabbeke Road in Belgium in 1953 in MVC 575.

Soon after the 1952 Earls Court Motor Show, the original 20TS chassis and stubby-tail style were speedily abandoned, and a crash programme over that winter to redevelop the new two-seater sports car resulted in the definitive chassis frame, the more powerful engine and the longer tail body style of the car that became the TR2. Two prototypes of the 'real' TR2 were then created, one of which – this example – was given the experimental chassis number X519 and the Coventry registration number of MVC 575.

This car was originally set up as a totally standard road car, a left-hand-drive machine complete with disc wheels and the optional rear wheelarch covers, known as 'spats'. The car had only just started a normal development programme when Sir John Black summoned Ken Richardson to his office, discussed the rival Sunbeam Alpine's recent achievement on the Jabbeke road in Belgium, and instructed him to do an even better job.

With no previous Standard-Triumph competitions experience on which to draw, and with only eight weeks to do the job on a minimal budget, Richardson and a tiny team of mechanics, all based at Banner Lane, had to leave most of the car absolutely standard. Because there was no such thing as a Triumph works team at this time, Richardson had no choice other than to elect to drive the car himself – and he also set the specification for the car that eventually travelled to Belgium.

Compared with the forthcoming production car (series manufacture would not start for several more months), the left-hand-drive chassis was almost completely standard except for the use of Dunlop Road Speed tyres; Michelin X tyres were not yet widely available, and in any case the use of British tyres was thought to be essential for the obvious publicity and marketing reasons of the day. The all-steel bodywork of the prototype was retained, but without front and rear bumpers, and the rear-wheel covers were kept because it was thought that these would reduce drag at high speeds. Wind tunnel testing? None, of course.

Arrangements were made for the car to run either with a small plastic wind deflector ahead of the driver's face or with the normal windscreen erect. With the windscreen raised, the normal fold-down soft top and plastic side screens would also be in use; with the plastic wind deflector fitted, a rigid aluminium cockpit tonneau covered the right-hand side of the interior. To make sure that he sat as low as possible, Richardson elected to remove the standard bucket seat, and merely sat on a cushion stuck to the floorpan!

Finally, to round off the drag-reducing features as much as possible without producing an obviously non-standard-looking sports car, a full-length aluminium undershield was fitted beneath the chassis, this being neatly blended on to the bumperless front panel.

The optional overdrive transmission was fitted, but the engine was in standard tune. This was done for two reasons: firstly, the company still had absolutely no experience of producing more than the specified 90bhp from the 1,991cc engine; secondly, the company's senior engine development engineer at the time had a rooted objection even to attempt to find more power!

A substantial amount of pre-dawn high-speed testing took place on a favourable stretch of straight, open road not too far from Coventry, but otherwise there was little time for development before the car had to go to Belgium to make its timed high-speed runs, which were in both directions of a dead-flat dual-carriageway. Early in the morning of 20 May 1953 Richardson set off in the TR2 prototype, originally in full 'speed trim', knowing that if he did not beat the Sunbeam's speeds he might just incur a volcanic dressing-down from Sir John Black.

Sir John and Ted Grinham were on hand with several established members of the British press to see what was achieved, and they must all have been perturbed to see the car flash past them with the engine sounding distinctly rough. When Richardson got back to base, he was able to tell them that he had achieved 104.860mph on three cylinders – a sparking plug lead had somehow become detached at the start of the speed run. This, of course, meant that the TR2 had momentarily become a three-cylinder 1½-litre car!

With the engine immediately restored to full health, the TR2 then went out and achieved 124.889mph in speed trim –

just what had been hoped. Next the mechanics modified the car at the side of the road, removing all drag-reducing equipment except for the full-length undershield and the rear-wheel spats, refitting the standard windscreen, and erecting the soft top. Thus 'standardised', the car reached 114.890mph. Finally, Richardson set out to see what the car would manage without overdrive being used – it achieved 108.959mph and was clearly over-revving.

Here, then, is a summary of the speeds recorded on that May morning:

- In speed trim, with metal tonneau, full under-shield, tiny windscreen, and using overdrive.
  Flying kilometre: 124.889mph
- In touring trim, complete with windscreen, and with soft-top and side screens, using overdrive.
  Flying kilometre 114.890mph
- In touring trim, complete with windscreen, and with soft-top and side screens, but not using overdrive.
  Flying kilometre 108.959mph

The car was then driven back to the UK and briefly shown around to publicise its record before returning to normality as a regular test and development machine.

The very first image ever published of a works TR2, showing Ken Richardson at the wheel of MVC 575 as it was finally ready to tackle speed tests on the Jabbeke Road, in Belgium, in May 1953.

COMPETITION RECORD
1953 Jabbeke run
Ken Richardson
124.889mph for the flying kilometre

OHP 676

FIRST REGISTERED	31 OCTOBER 1953
ENGINE SIZE	1,991cc
MODEL TYPE	TR2

This was a works car that only qualifies for inclusion on a marginal basis, because it was the first factory-owned car on which some preparation work was done before it was unleashed into motorsport. It carried Commission number 8, making it the eighth 'off-tools' machine to be assembled in Coventry, and had right-hand drive.

Even before the first true works car, MVC 575 (see pages 18-19), had been made ready to run in Belgium, Standard-Triumph had been approached by the persuasive editor of the weekly magazine *Autosport*, Gregor Grant, to provide him with a TR2 in which he could compete in the Lyons-Charbonnières rally in France in March 1954.

Unlike Maurice Gatsonides, Grant was never likely to be the winner of such an event, but as the mouthpiece of one of Britain's two most influential motor sporting magazines (Motor Sport was the other) he certainly had clout. A competent if not outstanding driver, Grant was an extrovert Scot whose record for story-telling – no, let us change that to tall-story-telling – was absolutley unmatched, so when he told Standard-Triumph that Peter Reece, an established rally co-driver at international level, would accompany him, he was

Gregor Grant drove OHP 676 in the 1954 Lyons-Charbonnières rally.

taken seriously and the car was made available.

There was no established competitions department at this stage, so pre-event preparation of OHP 676, which had already done much work as a factory-owned test and development car, was limited and it could only be worked on in a corner of Banner Lane for a short period. Like some early examples of the TR2, this car had steel disc wheels and Laycock overdrive, along with standard soft-top bodywork – which meant that in the wintry conditions around Charbonnières and Grenoble the crew ran with the top erect at all times. Extra Lucas driving lamps – one fog and one long-range 'Flamethrower' type – were fitted neatly inside the recess for the radiator grille, but this was the only way in which OHP 676 could be visually identified as a rally car.

On this important inaugural occasion, Grant and Reece made a serious effort and were rewarded by being one of only 16 entrants out of 139 to complete the 800-mile road route without lateness. At the close of the event, in Charbonnières, they brought home an undamaged car in sixth place overall, with second place in the class for sports cars over 1,600cc. It was a remarkable result for a novice crew in a still-unproven car.

The same car/driver combination then took part in the Tulip Rally. Even at this stage there was no official works team so Gregor Grant effectively stood in, this time with Stan Asbury as his co-driver. With no fewer than six far-flung starting points, and with many high-speed tests (mainly hill-climbs) ending up at the GP circuit at Zandvoort in Holland, this was a serious event that attracted many works cars.

Yet another excellent result followed, despite two problems: the TR2 wore out its tyres, but Vredestein, the tyre company, came to the rescue; and a front wheel bearing gave up the ghost towards the end of the event but was speedily replaced by Asbury, an experienced mechanic. Grant finished 17th overall and took second place in the 2-litre sports car category, behind a Ferrari!

However, this was the end of OHP 676's life of rallying fame, as Grant, who repeatedly praised it in print, was obliged to hand it back. During its tenure as a test and development car at Banner Lane, Kit Heathcote, Ken Richardson's assistant, used it to contest the MCC National Rally of November 1954. Before being sold by the factory, in 1955, its bodywork was converted to the definitive short-door specification.

COMPETITION RECORD	
1954 Lyons-Charbonnières	
Gregor Grant	6th overall, 2nd in class
1954 Tulip Rally	
Gregor Grant	17th overall, 2nd in class
1954 MCC National Rally	
Kit Heathcote	Finished

OVC 262

FIRST REGISTERED	10 MARCH 1954
ENGINE SIZE	1,991cc
MODEL TYPE	TR2

This was an absolutely standard production car, with right-hand drive but apparently without overdrive. Carrying Commission number TS 369, it was immediately allocated to Dutch rally ace Maurice Gatsonides, who won the Monte Carlo Rally in 1953 in a works Ford Zephyr and was later hired by Standard-Triumph as its 'continental technical and sales representative'.

This meant that he was to become the leading light in the works team, although by no means on an exclusive basis. In motorsport terms he was still a freelance driver – effectively a 'gun for hire' – and he continued to drive Fords and even Aston Martins in motorsport until 1955.

OVC 262 was only used on one international rally, the rather light-hearted Rallye Soleil-Cannes in the south of France in April 1954. On that event Gatso took the car to second place in the 1,600cc–2,000cc class, and distinguished himself by spinning the car through 180 degrees on the very last corner of the very last speed test, completing his run by driving the car across the line in reverse gear! The organisers originally sought to disqualify him for this manoeuvre, but were eventually persuaded that no particular regulation had been broken.

Gatso then continued to use the car for his day-to-day transport, and for rally route surveys, but does not appear to have used it for any more serious competition motoring.

COMPETITION RECORD	
1954 Rallye Soleil-Cannes	
Maurice Gatsonides	2nd in class

The superstar who got away! Pat Moss, still known only as 'Stirling's little sister' in those days, bought her own new TR2, VFM 377, which she affectionately christened 'Fruity'. On delivery of 'Fruity', at Canley in late 1954, a rather special Standard Eight on wire wheels sits alongside, bearing a registration number that suggests it was intended for Stirling's use.

Ken Richardson at the wheel of OVC 276, which was just about to tackle the Mille Miglia race in 1954.

OVC 276

FIRST REGISTERED	5 APRIL 1954
ENGINE SIZE	1,991cc
MODEL TYPE	TR2

Although this is the fourth car listed in this chapter, it was the first TR2 to have been intended for motorsport and it was prepared seriously as a result.

Built in January 1954 and carrying Commission number TS403L, this left-hand-drive car was prepared in haste, but with great thoroughness, for Maurice Gatsonides and Ken Richardson to drive in the Mille Miglia.

The Mille Miglia was a 1,000-mile race in Italy that started and finished in Brescia and went as far south as Rome in a great loop on public roads during the first weekend in May. It was open to all manner of two-seater racing sports cars, and even some saloon cars. This TR2 stood no chance of recording a high finish because it faced very strong competition – including the might of Ferrari, Maserati, Lancia and Aston Martin racing cars – but it could compete with honour and prove that a near-standard sports car could carry on all day at high speeds. This is what Standard-Triumph set out to achieve by entering OVC 276.

Gatsonides had only agreed to take part if he could drive the car every inch of the way, so Ken Richardson's role alongside him was to act solely as co-driver and cheerleader – and

Start-line variety on the Zandvoort circuit at the close of the 1955 Tulip rally, with Ken Richardson's TR2 alongside a works Ford Zephyr and John Gott's works-loaned AC Ace.

to be ready to drive if the Dutchman faltered. For Richardson, that was one piece of the bad news, and another was that the car was due to roll off the starting ramp in Brescia at the unearthly time of 5.28am.

Mechanically this car was standard in many ways, but it had a number of special touches. The steel bodywork was unaltered, although the front and rear bumpers were removed and two small plastic screens replaced the windscreen. Two extra Lucas driving lamps – one for fog, the other for long-range penetration – were added, along with a pair of extra-loud horns!

Hidden away was an overdrive whose wiring was altered so that it operated on all four forward gears, and it also featured an operating switch on the gear lever knob. Gatsonides, who had strong connections in Holland, insisted that he acquired from Koni, a Dutch company, some telescopic dampers for the rear suspension, and these required special mounting brackets to be welded to the chassis frame. He recommended 16in wire-spoke wheels (a standard TR2 had 15in wheels) so that the best possible Dunlop racing tyres could be used, and Alfin brake drums were also fitted. Gatso was also allowed to use up to 5,500rpm (instead of the usual 5,000rpm), although this was rarely necessary as the car could not reach its maximum speed – at least 120mph – in overdrive top, which was the ratio used for the high-speed sections of the race.

Gatsonides, who was in his mid-40s, must have been exhausted before the start as he had just competed in the Tulip Rally, in a Ford, and had flown to Italy overnight, but he put in what was afterwards described as a copybook performance. The TR2 completed the 1,000-mile route in

13hr 52m 31s, averaging 71.82mph. By so doing, the car finished seventh in the 2,000cc sports car class and took 27th place overall.

Back at Banner Lane there was jubilation – but no rest for this car. In a matter of weeks OVC 276 had to be returned to a more normal rallying specification, for Ken Richardson and Kit Heathcote to drive in the French Alpine Rally in July. This meant fitting the normal windscreen along with side screens and foldaway soft-top, although rally regulations meant that the bumpers did not have to be fitted.

Although Richardson had a running battle with a Frazer Nash driven by John Gott and Colonel O'Hara-Moore throughout this very fast, hot, gruelling event, a series of mishaps put him back to fourth place in the class. Not only did he suffer a puncture on one particularly tight section, but in consequence he also went off the road and damaged the car. Later the car also suffered a broken rear leaf spring, so it was definitely one of the 'walking-wounded' by the time it reached the finish in Cannes.

During the winter of 1954/55, the works team concentrated on developing and running Standard Tens (see Chapter 10), enabling OVC 276 to have a rest for the winter apart from one minor outing, when Richardson competed in a British club speed trial organised by the Combined Universities Motor Club. After that the car was returned to a settled road-rallying specification.

OVC 276 was not used again at International level until May 1955, when it tackled the Tulip Rally along with four other works TR2s, three of which were new for the occasion. Richardson, who was on top form at this stage in his career, again fought a battle from flag to flag with John Gott and

Colonel O'Hara-Moore, who this time were driving an AC Ace, and finished just 41sec behind them, and second in their capacity class.

Standard-Triumph expected to enter the same full line-up of TR2s for the French Alpine rally in mid-summer, but, in common with several major events, it was cancelled at very short notice following the horrible Le Mans accident in June. This meant that there was only one more chance for the TR2 fleet to shine before the model was rendered obsolescent by the soon-to-be-announced TR3. This came in August, when OVC 276 was sent out for Ken Richardson to contest the gruelling Liège-Rome-Liège, a marathon that ran over four days and nights.

An earlier Triumph history, by another author, stated that OVC 276 had just completed a major rebuild before the Liège, but that is incorrect as the car had actually been in storage since Richardson's fine drive in the Tulip. For the Liège two extra Lucas SFT 576 driving lamps were added and carefully angled to provide a better spread of light to the edges of the roads.

On the Liège, Richardson and Kit Heathcote, his close friend and regular co-driver, produced a gritty performance, winning their class and finishing fifth overall, and beating Gatsonides' TR2 (RHP 557) by a significant margin. Could Richardson have done even better? Only if he had been able to defeat two Mercedes-Benz cars (one a 300SL 'Gullwing'), a Lancia and a Salmson…

Apart from being just one minute late at the time control at the end of the 32.5km Passo di Vivione test in the Italian Dolomites, Richardson set a clean sheet in a very demanding schedule. The eventual winner, Olivier Gendebien, was quoted as saying that this had been much the most strenuous

Liège so far organised. Richardson had one stroke of good fortune on the final night, in the French Alps, when his engine dynamo broke away from its mounting; the TR2 was able to continue only because of the generosity of Prince Paul Alfons Fürst von Metternich-Winneburg (later the President of the FIA) in donating a suitable bolt from his BMW's steering column!

To quote that rallying policeman, John Gott, in his post-event report: 'The performance of Ken Richardson/Kit Heathcote in their TR2 was also outstanding as they were new to the event, although they had practised over a lot of the course before the start. Their fifth place represented the best-ever performance by a British crew and they easily won the special prize for the best newcomer to the rally…'

And with that, this famous works car came to the end of its four-event career, having performed with great honour and distinction on every outing. It still exists to this day, although it is rarely seen in public.

COMPETITION RECORD
1954 Mille Miglia
Maurice Gatsonides   27th overall, 7th in class
1954 French Alpine Rally
Ken Richardson   4th in class
1955 Combined Universities Rally
Ken Richardson   Did not finish
1955 Tulip Rally
Ken Richardson   2nd in class
1955 Liège-Rome-Liège
Ken Richardson   5th overall, 1st in class

Maurice Gatsonides (at the wheel) and Rob Slotemaker crewed PDU 20 in the 1954 French Alpine rally, winning a Coupe des Alpes for an unpenalised run.

PDU 20

FIRST REGISTERED	4 JUNE 1954
ENGINE SIZE	1,991cc
MODEL TYPE	TR2

This early TR2, Commission number TS1927LO, was a left-hand-drive car equipped with overdrive and wire wheels, and was especially prepared for Maurice Gatsonides to drive in the French Alpine Rally with co-driver Rob Slotemaker, who would later achieve fame in Triumph Spitfires at Le Mans and in rallies.

A variety of media reports later praised Gatso's Alpine drive to the skies, one at least calling it a copybook performance. Apart from not quite being able to match the pace of the Gott/O'Hara-Moore Frazer Nash, the TR2 put in a peer-

All 'side-screen' TRs of the Ken Richardson period looked, and were, surprisingly standard when kitted out as works cars. Except for the roundels placed here for PDU 20's use in a modern classic event, the car looks exactly as it did when built 60 years earlier.

Even though it has had a long and hard life (it was, and is, still used in classic motorsport), PDU 20 is still remarkably original, and looks the part.

The first batch of works TR2s – of which PDU 20 was a pioneer – had totally standard bodywork; although the rear bumper over-riders were removed, a reversing light was not fitted.

PDU 20 was new for the 1954 French Alpine rally, where Maurice Gatsonides and Rob Slotemaker finished sixth overall and captured a Coupe des Alpes award for an unpenalised run on the road sections. Gatsonides had his own preferred array of auxiliary lighting, together with extra-loud horns, and the regulations for that event allowed the front bumpers to be removed.

Standard-Triumph might have had a contract with Joseph Lucas to use that company's electrical equipment at all times, but Gatsonides took no notice of that and fitted French Marchal auxiliary lights instead. He was duly admonished, but laughed it off...

Looking well used but remarkably original in all details, this works TR2 shows how the cars were prepared in the 1954/55 period. At that time it was company policy to run the engine in standard form, and there was neither time nor inclination to equip the cars with upgraded wiring and hydraulic lines; there was also no brake servo as the standard drum brakes were retained.

The wiring looks 'stone-age' by later standards, but this was as complicated as it ever got on works TR2s. The starter button was in place close to the regulator box, and at that stage there was no attempt to install extra fuses or spare coils.

This commission plate on PDU 20, a 1954 works car, shows that it was only the 1,921st car to be produced, and that it always had left-hand drive with overdrive transmission.

When PDU 20 was built and first prepared for rallying, its left-hand-drive dashboard and instrument display looked exactly like this. The standard sprung-spoke steering wheel was retained, and the only extra equipment fitted to keep the co-driver happy were two aviation-standard clocks and a map-reading lamp with a flexible stalk.

During the 1950s works 'side-screen' TRs always ran with their engines in standard form, although carefully built. The drivers were told sternly not to exceed 5,000rpm but from my experience as a co-driver I can state categorically that this instruction was widely ignored!

For years there was controversy within Standard-Triumph over the type of wheels to use on works TR2s, TR3s and TR3As. Supporters of wire-spoke wheels pointed out the speed with which a wheel could be changed, but critics insisted that steel disc wheels were stronger and more robust. The result was that both types were often used at various times during a car's works career.

Gatsonides and Slotemaker in PDU 20 at the end of their successful Coupe-winning run in the 1954 French Alpine rally.

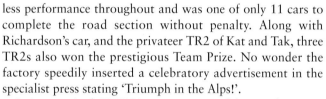

In later years, Maurice Gatsonides was reunited with PDU 20, the car in which he tackled the 1954 French Alpine rally.

less performance throughout and was one of only 11 cars to complete the road section without penalty. Along with Richardson's car, and the privateer TR2 of Kat and Tak, three TR2s also won the prestigious Team Prize. No wonder the factory speedily inserted a celebratory advertisement in the specialist press stating 'Triumph in the Alps!'.

As it transpired, PDU 20 was not entered for another event as a works car, so it became another 'one-hit' wonder.

COMPETITION RECORD	
1954 French Alpine	
Maurice Gatsonides	6th overall, 2nd in class

PDU 21

FIRST REGISTERED	4 JUNE 1954
ENGINE SIZE	1,991cc
MODEL TYPE	TR2

Although this car was one of three prepared to contest the French Alpine Rally in mid-1954, it was one of only two new machines. Although mechanically the same as OVC 276 and PDU 20, it was also the only one of the three to have right-hand drive.

For the Alpine it was allocated to Jimmy Ray, a confectioner from Lancashire and an accomplished rally driver who had won many events in his TR2-engined Morgan Plus Four, including a recent success in the International Scottish Rally. Against his stated wishes, Ray was told that his co-driver would be Lyndon Mills, a sales executive in the Standard-Triumph hierarchy who had started rallying in a privately

owned TR2 and had recently competed in the Circuit of Ireland, but was nonetheless inexperienced.

Although the team 'lost their Coupe' (Alpine-speak for 'incurred lateness at a time control') in the early hours of the event, they kept plugging on, Ray and Mills sharing the driving, until a wheel bearing failed; in the absence of service assistance, which was still officially banned at that point in the event's history, they were obliged to retire.

As with the other existing works TR2s of 1954, PDU 21 then enjoyed a winter's rest before being brought out of storage, refreshed and lent – still without its front bumper – to *Autosport*'s Gregor Grant for his second assault on the Lyons-Charbonnières rally. Grant's fine showing on the Lyons-Charbonnières in 1954 and his status as a much-respected journalist made such a loan logical, particularly as there was no other works presence on the event nor any support in the shape of service cars. As in 1954, Grant's co-driver was Liverpool-based Peter Reece.

This time the event started from Paris, but the truly difficult and demanding section was in the still-wintry mountains around Charbonnières and Grenoble; even so, the event was dominated by fast, limited-production sports cars. Grant's run was quite spoiled by his car being misdirected by a gendarme at an obscure road junction in the mountains, and in fact only 22 of 128 starters finished the road section unpenalised. At the end of the rally the TR2, undamaged, was fourth in the over 1,600cc sports car category.

Only weeks later, the car was refurbished and allocated to Jimmy Ray to drive in the Tulip Rally, this honour coming shortly after his outright win in the RAC Rally with a works Standard Ten (see page 257). This was also when John Waddington, who was sweeping all before him in British rallying in his own TR2, joined the works Standard-Triumph team as Ray's co-driver.

All went well until Jimmy met with an accident on a road section in the Vosges mountains, as he recalled many years later: 'I think we were already in about third position, and we thought we could win. But we were going through a village in France and there was this Citroën 2CV with a parish priest in it. We went one way, then he went the same way – and we did this down the street until we hit each other, and that stove in my radiator and we were out of the rally.'

The car was recovered, taken back to Coventry and made ready for the French Alpine rally, but that event was cancelled and therefore the works career of PDU 21 came to an end.

Although this was not strictly a works TR2, OKV 72 received a great deal of unofficial support in 1954 – it was owned by Leslie Brooke, a prosperous scrap-metal dealer from Coventry.

A pause for relaxation at the side of an autobahn in the 1955 Tulip rally, with all five works TR2s in the line-up. Jimmy Ray is checking up on the lead car, PDU 21, and Ken Richardson is taking a photograph. Gregor Grant (ahead of Richardson's lens) appears to be the butt of the joke…

COMPETITION RECORD	
1954 French Alpine Rally	
Jimmy Ray	Did not finish
1955 Lyon-Charbonnières	
Gregor Grant	4th in class
1955 Tulip Rally	
Jimmy Ray	Did not finish
1955 London Rally	
Jimmy Ray	1st overall

PKV 693

FIRST REGISTERED	25 MARCH 1955
ENGINE SIZE	1,991cc
MODEL TYPE	TR2

This was one of three brand-new TR2s made ready for the 1955 rally season, the intention being that they would take part in the Tulip and Alpine rallies before being sold to one of the long queue of private owners anxious to buy an ex-works TR2. Preparation work began early in 1955, regis-tration followed in March, and the three new cars were ready for use in May.

Like its sisters, PKV 693 was a right-hand-drive car with overdrive, wire-spoke wheels and Alfin brake drums. Regulations for the Tulip meant that the front bumpers now had to be fitted and, as usual, two extra Lucas driving lamps were added within the grille recess. For the Tulip it was allocated to Gregor Grant – a real honour for him.

Although not as fast as Jimmy Ray and Ken Richardson, Grant put up a brave show. At Zandvoort circuit he managed to dice with other TR2 drivers, including the experienced track driver Bobby Dickson, and he was especially quick on the speed hillclimbs where he now thought he had the measure of the TR2's sometimes wayward handling – until, that is, the route returned to Luxemburg and a special section rather cynically nicknamed the 'Route of the 1,000 Curves'. In the middle of this section, which was not entirely closed to other traffic, Grant met a truck coming the other way and it hit the rear end of the TR2, spinning it round and quite unnerving its intrepid driver. In spite of having a total handicap penalty just 96sec more than that of team leader Richardson, Grant finished 42nd overall to Richardson's 17th.

As the French Alpine rally was cancelled, the Tulip was the only event on which PKV 693 was used as a works car and it was also Grant's last outing in a competitive TR.

COMPETITION RECORD	
1955 Tulip Rally	
Gregor Grant	42nd overall

PKV 697

FIRST REGISTERED	28 MARCH 1955
ENGINE SIZE	1,991cc
MODEL TYPE	TR2

Mechanically identical to PKV 693 and PKV 698, this TR2, like its sister cars, was prepared early in 1955 in the expectation of competing in the Tulip and French Alpine rallies that year.

After one of those inexplicable decisions for which Ken Richardson became known, it was allocated for the Tulip to a new all-ladies' crew. There was more news in the crew members than in the car itself: Lola Grounds was the co-driving wife of Frank Grounds, a prosperous motor trader from Lichfield, while Cherry Osborn was a talented amateur TR2 driver who happened to be married to Standard-Triumph's company doctor. In the nicest possible way it would be reasonable to dub them 'Little and Large', for Lola was tiny – her nickname was 'pocket rocket' – while Cherry was at least as tall as some of the team's larger male drivers, such as Maurice Gatsonides, John Waddington and Bobby Dickson.

This female crew made a brave start on the 1955 Tulip, with Cherry particularly fast on the early speed hillclimbs. Unhappily, towards the end of the event and when in Germany crossing the Eifel Mountains, close to the Nürburgring, the TR2 suddenly shed its bonnet, which lashed open and cracked the windscreen. Shocked and dispirited, but still determined to make it, they did complete the event but well down the lists.

As with PKV 693 and PKV 698, this was the only time PKV 697 appeared as a works car.

COMPETITION RECORD	
1955 Tulip Rally	
Cherry Osborn	Finished

PKV 698

FIRST REGISTERED	28 MARCH 1955
ENGINE SIZE	1,991cc
MODEL TYPE	TR2

This was the third of three 'new-for-1955' works TR2s and, like PKV 693 and PKV 697, it took part only in the 1955 Tulip rally.

Bizarrely, Ken Richardson chose to allocate PKV 698 to motor trader Bobby Dickson, who had been involved with the racing side of the works team at Le Mans and the Tourist Trophy in 1954. There were far better rally drivers available: why, for instance, was Johnny Wallwork not invited, and why was John Waddington given a run as a co-driver rather than lead driver, and why could John Gott not be persuaded to remain within the team instead of defecting to BMC? No neutral observer, at the time or later, could understand Richardson's loyalty to Dickson and it is interesting to be able to quote Jimmy Ray, who was later poached by the Sunbeam 'works' team, on the matter: 'There was no such thing as a steady works driver. Ken, well I don't think he was really a rally driver, and Bobby Dickson certainly wasn't a rally driver…'

The proof came on the Tulip, where Richardson and Ray both outpaced Dickson. The lesson may have got home to Richardson; this was the end of Dickson's involvement with the Triumph organisation, although he later drove TR2 racing cars at Le Mans and in the TT.

COMPETITION RECORD	
1955 Tulip Rally	
Bobby Dickson	34th overall

RHP 557

FIRST REGISTERED	25 MAY 1955
ENGINE SIZE	1,991cc
MODEL TYPE	TR2

Although three all-new works TR2s had already been built for the 1955 rally season, a fourth new car was then added, amazingly, to the fleet. The registration date for what became RHP 557 is interesting, and proves, I believe, that this car was taken on board immediately after the Tulip rally a few weeks earlier. Originally intended for Maurice Gatsonides to drive in the 1955 French Alpine rally, which was cancelled, this car finally made its début – and in fact its only appearance – in the Liège-Rome-Liège marathon of the same year.

Gatsonides was desperately unlucky on the Liège. He and Ken Richardson, both in TR2 team cars, were extremely well-matched throughout, but on the one near-impossible special section in the Italian Dolomites, where Richardson was penalised by just one minute, Gatso somehow lost four minutes, which dropped him by two places to seventh overall. No reason was ever given by the driver.

COMPETITION RECORD	
1955 Liège-Rome-Liège	
Maurice Gatsonides	7th overall

RHP 557 only tackled one event as a works TR2 – the 1955 Liège-Rome-Liège in which Maurice Gatsonides finished seventh overall.

SRW 410

FIRST REGISTERED	5 APRIL 1956
ENGINE SIZE	1,991cc
MODEL TYPE	TR3

Although this beige TR3, complete with a red hard top, carried a slightly earlier identity than its 1956 team-mates (SRW 990, SRW 991 and SRW 992) and was actually registered several weeks earlier, it did not appear until mid-year, when it started the French Alpine in Maurice Gatsonides' hands. Interestingly, it had right-hand drive – interesting because Gatsonides, an important participant in the team to whom Ken Richardson often deferred on matters of strategy, preferred left-hand drive where possible. This TR3 had a short but distinguished works rally career.

Gatsonides' co-driver on the Alpine, one of his favourite events, was Ed Pennybacker, who was not only a keen amateur American race/rally driver who would drive for works team at Sebring in 1957, but also an American Forces Network (AFN) Frankfurt radio reporter – the potential for favourable publicity in his home country can be imagined.

Technically, the new team of TR3s was very similar to the last of the 1955 works TR2s, except that the cars were now running as 'Grand Tourers', complete with hard tops and exterior door handles. Like the production TR3s that would follow in subsequent months, the blueprinted but otherwise standard 1,991cc engines had the latest 'high-port' cylinder heads, as blooded on the TR2s that had contested the 1955 Le Mans 24 Hours race; although power outputs were never quoted, it is likely that they were about 10bhp more.

Wire wheels and oversize Alfin brake drums were fitted, and front bumpers and the new type of TR3 'egg-crate' front grille were retained. All three of these TR3s had two extra Lucas driving lamps mounted neatly on the front bumpers, close to the over-riders. Inside the car, seats and steering wheel were still standard, and, of course, this was years before anyone even thought of fitting safety belts.

These TR3s delivered outstanding performances in the 1956 French Alpine rally. This was an event whose route started and finished from the home of the organising club, in Marseilles, and normally went through the Italian Dolomites, but it was somewhat emasculated after the furore caused by the Le Mans tragedy previous year. The 1956 Alpine, therefore, became the first running of the event to penetrate deep into Yugoslavia, as far as Senj on the Adriatic coast, before turning back towards

France. The total distance was 2,620 miles.

Because durability and tolerance of less-than-perfect conditions were among their strong points, the new TR3s were ideally suited to this event. So suited, in fact, that no fewer than five out of six works or works-supported cars won a Coupe des Alpes, the prize for an unpenalised run on all road sections. Gatsonides, who had practised as carefully as usual, won the 2-litre GT class and finished eighth overall. With high performance an advantage, all but two of the top ten finishers were sports cars.

By definition, however, this event could not be a flat-out race around the Alps as the cars had to complete the entire route on the same set of tyres – marked at the start to prevent cheating – although inner tubes could be changed whenever necessary. On the topic of tyres, Willy Cave, co-driving for Paddy Hopkirk in the event, later commented: 'Tyres were subject to some concern… We learned the value of rotating the wheels, including the spare, to even out the wear to avoid losing our Coupe. It was enormously exciting, but there was this fear of going into Yugoslavia. If we broke down, there was no support, and we didn't know if we would ever get out again. We had visions of funny money and terrible petrol, and we expected to get heaps of punctures. In fact we had four or five, and seemed to be forever fitting new tubes…'

After that French Alpine of 1956, when three of the four works entries finished with great honour and made many headlines, all the cars were returned to Allesley, where very little other works activity took place for the rest of year. The only other official entry by the works, in fact, came in September, when SRW 991 competed in the Liège-Rome-Liège marathon.

SRW 410, therefore, had a long rest after its single event before becoming one of three TR3s – SRW 991 and SRW 992 were the others – to be prepared for the 1957 Sebring 12 Hours,

the sports car race held in Florida every March. Substantially financed by the New York-based Triumph import organisation, this outing was a real novelty for the factory team as works TRs had not previously competed in the USA and would not directly do so again.

Apart from the usual meticulous post-rally rebuild, 'race-prep' work carried out for Sebring on SRW 410, SRW 991 and SRW 992 before they left Allesley is summarised in the following list, compiled from modern information provided by Robert Johns, who drove SRW 992 in the race:

- Front bumpers and number plates were removed for the race, but rear over-riders and rear number plates were retained.
- Attachments for quick-lift jack operation were fitted, for changing wheels and tyres more quickly.
- Hard tops were standardised, even though some of the drivers asked to race the cars in open condition.
- Although engines might have been dyno-tested, Jones believes that they were mechanically standard as his own private TR3 racing car was significantly faster at high revs than the factory machinery.
- Girling front disc brakes (as used on all production TR3s from the autumn of 1956) were fitted, and centre-lock wire-spoke wheels were retained.
- A rear-axle ratio of 4.11:1 was specified, without limited-slip differential.
- Standard seats were retained (not race-type buckets).
- There was no roll-over safety protection and no safety belts.
- The fuel tank was standard, with a standard flip-open filler cap.

During the race, with James Roberts at the wheel, SRW 410 had only completed ten laps when the clutch-shaft retaining pin broke, immobilising the car. It was subsequently returned to the UK and soon sold.

THE 1956 FRENCH ALPINE RALLY

Of all the events in which works Triumphs put up a great performance, the French Alpine of July 1956 deserves special mention. Not only did the works team prepare four cars, of which three completed the 2,620-mile course unpenalised on the road sections, but two private entries – those from Joseph Kat and Leslie Griffiths – did the same.

The result was almost a drum roll for the excellence of the TR3 – five Coupes des Alpes, the top five places in the 2-litre GT class, and the winning of every possible team prize! Triumph's new problem, however, was that the company would now be expected to match this level of achievement on subsequent events. The works team was henceforth at the very top of everyone's expectations in open-road rallying…

COMPETITION RECORD
1956 French Alpine
Maurice Gatsonides — 8th overall
1957 Sebring 12 Hours race
James Roberts/Lou Heuss — Did not finish

SRW 990

FIRST REGISTERED	1 MAY 1956
ENGINE SIZE	1,991cc
MODEL TYPE	TR3

Following the shock to motorsport caused by the horrific accident at Le Mans in June 1955, Standard-Triumph concentrated on using Standard-badged cars for the next few months. Not only did this mean that the existing fleet of works TR2s could be sold, but also that another fleet of five brand-new TR3s could be prepared for use in 1956.

Like SRW 410, these were the first works TRs to be fitted with hard tops, one reason being that new FIA regulations meant that a 'Grand Touring' car had to have a so-called 'permanent' roof, along with rigid side screens and with exterior door handles.

SRW 990 was destined to tackle only one event – the Rally of the Midnight Sun in Sweden. Because the car was allocated to team manager Ken Richardson, he directed that it should have a white hard top, as was usual with TRs he drove. It

defies analysis to explain why the Triumph team was sent to contest this Swedish rally, where special stages had gravel surfaces and where local expertise was considered far more important than straight-line performance.

Richardson himself had never before competed in Scandinavia and had never previously driven a gravel special stage. He reputedly struggled to come to terms with conditions right from the start but, even so, he did reach the finish, eighth in the GT category but well beaten by Paddy Hopkirk in SRW 991. Reinforcing the fact that the TR3 was not suited to this event, eight of the top ten places in the general classification were taken by lower-powered machinery with the engine over the driving wheels.

After it returned home SRW 990 was not used again as a works competition entry, but was apparently used by Richardson as his regular road car for some time.

COMPETITION RECORD	
1956 Swedish Midnight Sun	
Ken Richardson	8th in GT category

SRW 991

FIRST REGISTERED	1 MAY 1956
ENGINE SIZE	1,991cc
MODEL TYPE	TR3

This was the second of the three mechanically identical cars shipped to Sweden to tackle the Rally of the Midnight Sun. To his great surprise and delight, SRW 991 was allocated to Paddy Hopkirk, who had just done his first events with the team, in a Standard Ten on the RAC Rally followed by a Standard Eight on the Tulip.

The car was familiar to Paddy as he was thoroughly used to rallying a TR2 in Ireland, having campaigned his own car there since the early months of 1955. There was also the novelty of a new co-driver, BBC producer Willy Cave, who was already renowned and would go on to even bigger and better things in the future. According to Willy, Ken Richardson's call of invitation included the remark: 'I've got this new whizz kid who's been winning driving tests all over Ireland. He's never been abroad, never been on the continent, and I think you're just the man with the experience to look after him and bring him home safely.'

Willy clearly did a good job, but ended his reminiscence

with this: 'The final test was on the seafront at Saltjobaden, and was actually a tie-decider. The results were announced next morning, and we had not done very well; the regulations had favoured the smaller cars...'

Paddy Hopkirk and Willy Cave drove SRW 991 to second in class in the 1956 French Alpine rally.

The same car was then returned to Allesley, where it was speedily prepared and sent out – with SRW 410, SHP 520 and SRW 992 – on the French Alpine rally with Hopkirk again the driver. This was Paddy's first entry in one of the French 'classics' and he certainly benefited from having Cave as his more experienced compatriot. As already described in my coverage of the sister TR3s, this was an all-conquering event for the works Triumphs.

Although he could not match the incomparable Maurice Gatsonides in the conditions encountered on the Alpine, Paddy put in a storming performance to finish second in class behind Gatso and was also one of the victorious team prize members. Paddy later commented about how helpful his winning team-mate had been to him in sharing experience and knowledge: 'Gatsonides was very serious about his motorsport. He was the first man ever to mention the word "reconnaissance" to me. He practised the whole route and made lots of notes. He was a sharer and didn't keep secrets to himself – at least I don't think he did. Things did change a bit when we started to go faster than him...'

During 1956 the Standard company suffered from strikes, a consequence being that budgets were cut for departments like 'competitions', resulting in the absence of a full team entry in the Liège-Rome-Liège marathon at the end of the summer. Gatsonides was certainly displeased that he did not get a chance to improve on the seventh place he had achieved in 1955. Instead, Richardson loaned just one car – SRW 991 – to Belgian driver Robert Leidgens, who had recorded sixth overall in 1955 in his own Imperia-modified TR2, complete with a metal hard top.

The 1956 event should really have been retitled Liège-Zagreb-Liège, for it went nowhere near Rome! After crossing the Italian Dolomites, the route penetrated deep into Yugoslavia, to Zagreb, diverted to the Istrian coast near Venice and then returned through the Dolomites all the way across the north of Italy, before circling the best of the 'French Alpine' routes north of the Mediterranean coast and returning to Liège. Four days and nights, without rest, was a considerable marathon by any standards.

Leidgens put up a brave show in a works car that must have been unfamiliar to him, especially as it had right-hand drive, and kept on valiantly to the end, taking a storming fifth place overall. To put that into perspective, only two Mercedes-Benz 300SL 'Gullwings', a Ferrari 250 GT and a Porsche Carrera beat him, and he was the best-performing competitor by far in a 'normal' road car.

As this was the very last event tackled by a works Triumph in 1956, the team had time to work on SRW 991 again. Immediately after its commendable achievement on the rough-and-tough Liège, the car was stripped out and prepared to 'race-car' specification before being shipped to Sebring in the first weeks of 1957. The detail changes made to this car were the same as those made to SRW 410 (see page

32) and one of the two drivers was Ed Pennybacker, who had already competed with Maurice Gatsonides in that car in the French Alpine.

At Sebring there was no chance of the car keeping up with the out-and-out racing two-seaters which dominated the event, but Pennybacker and team-mate Bob Oker circulated steadily and fast, kept the car on the road and out of the way of the ultra-fast machinery, and were rewarded with first in their class.

Not that this was the end of this hard-working car's career. It was then flown back to the UK for one final outing, in the Liège-Rome-Liège marathon of 1957. Just think of it: glitzy glory for the Triumph organisation in a 12-hour sports car race in North America followed by – to end its career – dirt, dust, endurance and out-and-out guts in the four-day-four-night Liège! This, as ever, was going to be a monumental challenge, and once again it would strike deep into Yugoslavia by way of the daunting Moistrocca Pass and Zagreb, the route measuring 3,670 miles non-stop.

For this event Triumph once again allocated SRW 991 to Leidgens, this being an event where all four works Triumphs were doled out to continental drivers, with not a Brit in evidence, not even in a co-driver's seat. After coming unscathed through the Yugoslavian section, Leidgens was running fifth overall by half distance, but towards the end, close to Forcalquier in the French Alps, the car stopped with what was reported as a combination of 'electric and bearing' trouble, which to every cynic in the journalistic rat pack sounded like a good synonym for an engine problem.

This was the end of a busy works career for this car, though not the end of its life in the spotlight. The factory sold it to the famous British racing cyclist Reg Harris, who used it successfully in British motorsport for a time.

COMPETITION RECORD	
1956 Midnight Sun	
Paddy Hopkirk	5th in GT category
1956 French Alpine	
Paddy Hopkirk	2nd in class
1956 Liège-Rome-Liège	
Robert Leidgens	5th overall
1957 Sebring 12 Hours race	
Bob Oker/Ed Pennybacker	1st in class
1957 Liège-Rome-Liège	
Robert Leidgens	Did not finish

SRW 992

FIRST REGISTERED	1 MAY 1956
ENGINE SIZE	1,991cc
MODEL TYPE	TR3

This was the third of the five brand-new works TR3s built for the 1956 season, and was originally sent out to Sweden to tackle the Midnight Sun rally. Inexplicably, but interestingly, Ken Richardson allocated the car to a young French racing driver, Annie Bousquet, who had become known within motorsport as the girlfriend of Porsche racing manager Huschke von Hanstein. Although she had already competed in Triumphs in Europe, she was unhappily out of her depth in rallying and she could only finish 13th in the GT category, although she got the car home undamaged.

Annie Bousquet was also due to drive SRW 992 in the French Alpine rally, but tragically she was killed in an accident in a racing Porsche in the Reims 12 Hours race. Since her TR3 had already been made ready for the event, it was loaned to Tommy Wisdom – of the *Daily Herald* – along with his daughter Ann, who had already joined forces with Pat Moss but was available for that year's Alpine because Pat was not scheduled to tackle it. Ann's worldwide fame as Pat Moss's co-driver would develop…

Although Tommy Wisdom was no longer in the flush of youth, he remained a formidable and safe driver. Helped along by SRW 992, he delivered a commendable Coupe des Alpes to the results board and finished fifth in a capacity class that was totally dominated by TR3s.

Like SRW 410 and SRW 991, SRW 992 returned from the Alpine in the summer of 1956, and then went into semi-hibernation before being prepared as one of the three works cars for the 1957 Sebring 12 Hours race. The detail changes and updates made to the car were the same as those described

for SRW 410 (see page 32). Driven at Sebring by Mike Rothschild and Robert Johns, the car lapped steadily and consistently throughout, finally taking second in its class, behind SRW 991, and helping to bring great publicity to the Triumph importer.

The car was brought back to the UK but the factory team did not use it again.

Five TR3s won Coupes des Alpes in the 1956 French Alpine rally, the three in the foreground of this shot – SRW 992, SRW 991 and SRW 410 – being works cars. From left, the works drivers were Tommy Wisdom, Ann Wisdom, Paddy Hopkirk, Willy Cave, Maurice Gatsonides and Ed Pennybacker.

COMPETITION RECORD	
1956 Midnight Sun	
Annie Bousquet	13th in GT category
1956 French Alpine	
Tommy Wisdom	5th in class
1957 Sebring 12 Hours race	
Mike Rothschild/Robert Johns	2nd in class

SHP 520

FIRST REGISTERED	16 FEBRUARY 1956
ENGINE SIZE	1,991cc
MODEL TYPE	TR3

This was the fifth and last of the new TR3s prepared at Allesley in the early months of 1956, but it was held back from the Midnight Sun expedition. All the evidence is that Ken Richardson wanted to allocate it to Annie Bousquet

for the French Alpine rally and pictures exist of her posing alongside it in the spring of 1956, when it was still a standard road car – interestingly it still had steel disc wheels at the time. But her tragic death in a Porsche in the Reims 12 Hours sports car race nullified that master plan and instead Richardson drove the car on the Alpine.

SHP 520 was the only works TR3 to be penalised on this momentous Alpine. Before reaching the first overnight halt, 710 miles into the event at Cortina d'Ampezzo, Richardson had to retire, the car having suffered 'transmission bothers' or a lost wheel according to varying reports. Whichever, there could be no speedy recovery from this, and the team boss was stranded. The car, although still relatively fresh, had no

further assignments for the rest of 1956.

For the return of a works TR to the Mille Miglia in 1957, Richardson sprung a real surprise by inviting Nancy Mitchell, the glamorous doctor's wife from Bournemouth, to drive SHP 520, which had not competed for nearly a year. Mrs Mitchell was already well established in rallying, but as a regular member of the rival BMC team she was more usually seen in MGAs and the like. However, with no rigid contract to tie her down and with a gap in her BMC

schedule, she accepted the challenge. Although it is thought that she had not previously driven a TR2 or a TR3 in anger, she had competed with honour in the Mille Miglia in a works MGA in 1956.

SHP 520 was prepared to similar specification to the three TR3s that had been sent out to race at Sebring in March 1957, so it now had front-wheel disc brakes. It also had a 25-gallon fuel tank, which, along with the spare wheel, virtually filled the boot. Because Nancy was determined to drive every inch of the route herself, she took along her usual rally co-driver, Pat Faichney.

Unhappily it was not a successful outing. After starting from Brescia early in the morning, Nancy had completed less than half of the course, down the east coast of Italy, when she had to retire the TR3. *Autosport*'s Gregor Grant stated that she went out at Pescara when her Triumph TR3 'hit a solid object and developed radiator bothers', but in fact she spun the car at the approach to a railway level crossing, hit a pile of straw bales and, by pure bad luck, had the wire from one of those bales puncture her car's radiator. She was lying third in her class at the time after averaging no less than 86mph up to that point.

COMPETITION RECORD	
1956 French Alpine	
Ken Richardson	Did not finish
1957 Mille Miglia	
Nancy Mitchell	Did not finish

TRW 735

FIRST REGISTERED	4 APRIL 1957
ENGINE SIZE	1,991cc
MODEL TYPE	TR3

Three brand-new disc-braked TR3s were prepared at Allesley for the 1957 rally season, each painted a rather fetching and subtle Apple Green colour scheme that was much liked by Ken Richardson. These cars were equipped with hard tops, wire-spoke wheels and the 'GT' kit of external door handles, and for the first time the works team used Dunlop's new Duraband radial-ply tyres.

The first outing for these three cars was the Tulip rally of 1957, but they would have been used earlier in the year had European motorsport not come virtually to standstill for a time as an after-effect of the Suez War of November 1956 and the short-lived imposition of petrol rationing that

followed it. Triumph, therefore, decided to make up for lost time by entering all three cars, to be driven by Paddy Hopkirk, Tom Gold and John Waddington. Surprisingly, Maurice Gatsonides, for whom the Tulip rally was really a 'home' event, was not allocated one of the cars.

As ever, the Tulip started and finished from four different locations and the routes on this occasion converged at Frankfurt, after which there was a long circuit down to the Vosges in France, then all the way across southern Germany before turning north-west, taking in a test at the Nürburgring before finishing at Noordwijk on the Dutch coast. Because the weather was most unseasonably cold – there was much snow and ice on the higher roads through the Alps – every crew member of these 1957 TR3s must have regretted that the team had removed the heaters to save weight!

To a degree this Tulip was a shadow of its former self as panic regulations imposed by various authorities after the Le Mans crash of 1955 had made several of the traditional speed hill-climbs out of bounds. Before, during and afterwards, there were complaints that, if a car could keep to time on the road sections, there were only five speed tests and a race at

Zandvoort to sort out a result. In 1957, however, the traditional handicapping settings had been changed, giving sports cars more of a chance than in previous Tulips.

Tom Gold and his wife June started well in TRW 735, and were still unpenalised on the road when everything went wrong on the Freiburg hill-climb test in southern Germany. To quote journalist Stuart Seager: 'Tom Gold and his wife had a very lucky escape in one of the hardtop TRs when they shot straight on at a corner, over the edge, to drop about ten feet. The car bounced on its roof and was arrested by a tree from a long roll down the mountainside. The two occupants were wearing crash hats, both of which were dented, but apart from stiff necks, neither was hurt, and when the car was eventually hauled up after some hours, it was found to be almost unscratched apart from the crushed top and splintered screen...'

As there was no French Alpine rally in 1957 – not all of the ramifications of the 1955 Le Mans crash had been sorted out and it was cancelled only two weeks before it was due to start – there proved to be ample time for the Golds to get the crippled TR3 back to Coventry and in fact it was possible for them to drive it home, although it was rather draughty! After several weeks of hard work, TRW 735 looked as good as new and was allocated to Gatsonides to drive on the Liège-Rome-Liège marathon, where no fewer than four works TRs took the start, all with non-British crews.

Amazingly, the proud Gatsonides had not been in the team for the previous year's Liège and the 1957 event was his only drive for Triumph that year – so he was determined to make a point. By half distance he was well-established in sixth place, and by keeping the green car securely on the road for the rest of the event, using his extensive knowledge of the Italian Dolomites and French Alps to consolidate his position, he ended up fifth overall. It is a measure of the rugged suitability of the Triumph for this event that the TR3s were only beaten by a Porsche Carrera and a Mercedes-Benz 300SL.

The icing on the cake was that three works TR3s – the other two were driven by Bernard Consten and Alain de

Three disc-braked TR3s ready to leave the Allesley building to tackle the 1957 Tulip rally. From left: John Waddington, Tom Gold, June Gold, Willy Cave and team manager Ken Richardson.

Changy – also won the Manufacturers' Team Prize, which caused the doyen of British rallying, John Gott, later to write: 'The talk at Spa was that Triumphs, after their wonderful showing, might be the first British car to win the Marathon...'

But not TRW 735, which ended its works career after just two events.

COMPETITION RECORD	
1957 Tulip	
Tom Gold	Did not finish
1957 Liège-Rome-Liège	
Maurice Gatsonides	5th overall

TRW 736

FIRST REGISTERED	4 APRIL 1957
ENGINE SIZE	1,991cc
MODEL TYPE	TR3

The second of the new-for-1957 disc-braked 'GT' TR3s was ready in plenty of time for the Tulip rally, where it was entrusted to John Waddington and Willy Cave, who were about as experienced as any other TR team in the business at the time. Except for being mistakenly docked one minute for lateness at the Schotten control, an error that was rectified by the organisers at the end of the rally, they spent the four-day event scrapping for class dominance with Paddy Hopkirk's sister car and John Patten's AC Aceca-Bristol.

The battle went down to the wire, at Zandvoort, where the fight between the two TRs and the Aceca almost boiled over, with all three contestants spinning at least once. In the end, it seems, Patten decided that he did not want to risk damaging his car, which was his own, as he was heard to mutter that Waddington and Hopkirk did not have to pay for their own rebuilds! The result was that Waddington won the 2-litre GT category with TRW 736 very narrowly from Patten, with

Hopkirk right behind them in third place with TRW 737.

After a rebuild, a more leisurely one than planned because of the cancellation of the French Alpine rally, TRW 736 was then allocated for the Liège-Rome-Liège to the rising French driver Bernard Consten, who would go on to win European Championship rallies outright, though not in TRs. Triumph's team consisted of no fewer than four of the latest disc-braked TR3s, and Consten's performance was the best among the team's drivers.

Right from the start, in Belgium, Consten battled for the outright lead with Claude Storez's Porsche Speedster and Jo Schlesser's Mercedes-Benz 300SL, and by the time the already battered survivors entered France for the last timed hill-climbs he was second to the Porsche, which led by more than eight minutes. During the night, the ultra-powerful 300SL passed him, but only just, and at the end of this formidably tiring four-day marathon Consten took a magnificent third place overall, the best finish ever achieved by a TR in the Liège. This, too, was one of the three TR3s that won the Manufacturers' Team Prize.

Liège-Rome-Liège in 1957, with Frenchman Bernard Consten on his way to a very creditable third place overall in the disc-braked TR3 TRW 736.

COMPETITION RECORD	
1957 Tulip Rally	
John Waddington	1st in class
1957 Liège-Rome-Liège	
Bernard Consten	3rd overall

TRW 737

FIRST REGISTERED	4 APRIL 1957
ENGINE SIZE	1,991cc
MODEL TYPE	TR3

For 1957, Paddy Hopkirk got the chance to drive this new disc-braked 'GT' TR3 on the Tulip Rally, where he fought an amiable but nonetheless serious battle with John Waddington's sister car and John Patten's AC Aceca-Bristol, eventually finishing third in a hotly contested capacity class.

Paddy, however, was unhappy with the new-fangled Dunlop Duraband tyres, as he later commented in his autobiography: 'They were amazing. They had a steel band in them, or something, and the roadholding was superb. But when they lost grip it was like the tyre had gone flat, and you spun. We all spun at Zandvoort... and we were all blamed for it. But we blamed the tyres. We all had big problems... They were good in one way, and not so good in another. It took us

a long time to be able to judge their behaviour and know where the limit was...'

Like the other 1957 team cars, this TR3 then enjoyed a summer of leisure before becoming one of four machines that started the Liège-Rome-Liège, this time being allocated to a new member of the team, Alain de Changy of Belgium. Like other Triumph team members in this event, he revelled in the car's great strength and reliability, and TRW 737 finally took ninth place as well as being one of the three cars that won the Manufacturers' Team Prize.

COMPETITION RECORD	
1957 Tulip Rally	
Paddy Hopkirk	3rd in class
1957 Liège-Rome-Liège	
Alain de Changy	9th overall

THE TR3A ARRIVES

This was the time when no fewer than five new-generation TR3As arrived at Allesley to be prepared for the 1958 rally season – and to open a new chapter in the marque's history. In the winter of 1957/58, every single old-style 1957 works TR3 was sold to make space for the new arrivals.

Not only were all these cars delivered in hardtop form, but they also showed off the new TR3A-type front grille and the exterior door handles that had been standardised from the last weeks of TR3 production. Four of them were painted Apple Green, one in more conventional British Racing Green.

These cars also signalled a point at which factory-prepared rally cars tended to become used more intensively than before. This was also the moment when Triumph signed a glamorous new French lady driver, Annie Soisbault, who would concentrate on events in Europe, especially in France.

This, too, was a season in which the factory cemented a relationship with Shell Motorsport employee Keith Ballisat, an extremely brave and successful race and rally driver, even though BP still officially supported Triumph. Not that it mattered in the end, for Shell-Mex and BP were both controlled by the same major marketing conglomerate. As Ballisat later commented to me, 'It was a little bit awkward, but Shell shrugged it off…'

The first five works TR3As shouldered all the hard work in an enhanced programme until the summer of 1958, when three more cars also arrived. It was a year, too, in which much thought was given to the road wheels with which the cars should run, for sometimes they appeared with conventional steel disc wheels and sometimes with centre-lock wire-spoke wheels. On occasions, surprisingly, both types of wheel appeared on the same team entry during the course of a rally – if not on the same car at the same time!

Another rally-prepared car – VHP 529 – appears in publicity photos but it was not used in competition. Instead we might call it a 'lookalike' because it was Ken Richardson's own road car that he also took on events from time to time as a chase car. One publicity shot from January 1958 shows two identical-looking rally-prepared TR3As – John Waddington's Monte TR3A and Richardson's VHP 529 – ready to cross the English Channel by air ferry, with Richardson's car also carrying on a boot rack a large case that certainly contained spare parts. It is interesting to see that both cars were running on steel wheels…

Without question, this was to be a much more concentrated effort by works TRs than in previous years.

VRW 219

FIRST REGISTERED	3 JANUARY 1958
ENGINE SIZE	1,991cc
MODEL TYPE	TR3A

This was the only original left-hand-drive TR3A on the strength in 1958, although, as Ken Richardson later confirmed and any knowledgeable TR3A enthusiast knows, a change from left-hand drive to right-hand drive could be done quite simply. The reason for left-hand drive was obvious, for this car was allocated to French drivers, first Annie Soisbault – newly crowned French ladies' rally champion – and later Roger de Laganeste. In all other respects, however, it was built to the same specification as the other 1958 team cars.

For its first event, the 1958 Monte, VRW 219 started from Paris along with two of its sister cars. Although the cars seemed to be mechanically almost standard, it was fascinating to see that they had a long hammock-like conversion to the passenger seat to allow the off-duty passenger some chance to get rest.

Like all the other TR3A team cars in this Monte, the car was equipped with a Perspex screen on the inside face of the windscreen to channel warm air upwards, with front and rear windscreen defrosting strips, a Halda Speedmaster, an Eolopress inflator/extinguisher and a radiator blind. For Annie Soisbault it was her first event as a fully fledged member of the Triumph works team, and to provide her with some obvious link with the rest of the team, and with the English language, Richardson paired her with experienced British co-driver Pat 'Tish' Ozanne.

Three works cars and a privately entered Standard Ten in the 1958 Monte Carlo rally. VRW 219 was driven by Annie Soisbault (not in the group) and Pat 'Tish' Ozanne, TRW 607 by Johnny Wallwork and John Beaumont, VRW 221 by John Waddington and Mike Wood, and TYR 598 (the privately entered Standard Ten) by Cyril Corbishley and Phil Simister.

This, unhappily, was an event about which the old hands talked for years to come, for it was run in awful blizzard conditions. Along with Paddy Hopkirk and John Waddington, Annie started from Paris but soon became enveloped by a blizzard that swept across France. In the Jura mountains, north and east of Switzerland, her TR3A gradually lost more and more time, not only because of the sheer impossibility of getting grip on icy, snow-covered roads, but also because of the frequent hold-ups encountered on narrow roads. Eventually they simply ran out of time, frustrated, but still with a healthy car.

If one can rely on registration numbers (even in those days some number-swapping took place), VRW 219 then enjoyed some time off, although it was available for practice and training. As it was one of only two left-hand-drive TR3As on the 1958 fleet, Annie Soisbault and later Roger de Laganeste had first call on its services. Strangely, it was never offered or allocated to Maurice Gatsonides, who was expected to be as versatile as he had always been.

It then ran in the French girl's hands in the Greek Acropolis, this famous event being held several weeks earlier than usual. Apart from the car having starter motor problems at one point, followed by some difficulties with navigation and timekeeping for the French crew, they put up a brave show on a hot, gruelling event. Not only did Soisbault win the Ladies' Prize, but she was also 12th overall and third in class, behind the event-winning Lancia and a Jaguar XK140.

There was then a considerable interlude before the car was refreshed for the distinguished French driver, Roger de Laganeste, to drive on the gruelling Liège-Rome-Liège. De Laganeste was one of four drivers in works TR3As on the Liège and not one was a Brit – two were French, one Belgian and one Dutch. All the cars had the newly blooded 2.2-litre engines, a development that is covered in more detail in the section devoted to VRW 220 (see below).

As expected, de Laganeste was very fast and was soon setting event-leading times on special tests in the Dolomites and into Yugoslavia, but the rough stuff – and the energy-sapping endurance – was yet to come. It was during the last gruelling night section back in the French Alps when his TR3A, which was actually battling for the lead with two Porsche Carreras and an Alfa Romeo Giulietta Zagato, suffered a sudden throttle-linkage failure on the Col d'Allos. This occurred nearly 80 non-stop hours into the toughest rally in the calendar and resulted in the team running out of time before repairs could be made.

Roger de Laganeste in VRW 219, complete with 2.2-litre engine, on the 1958 Liège-Rome-Liège marathon. He actually led the rally for a time before the car suffered a broken throttle linkage that caused his exclusion for lateness at the next control.

COMPETITION RECORD	
1958 Monte Carlo	
Annie Soisbault	Did not finish
1958 Acropolis	
Annie Soisbault	12th overall
1958 Liège-Rome-Liège	
Roger de Laganeste	Did not finish

VRW 220

FIRST REGISTERED	3 JANUARY 1958
ENGINE SIZE	1,991cc
MODEL TYPE	TR3A

This was the event on which Paddy Hopkirk first linked up with Jack Scott, a jam maker from Dublin, in what would become a lengthy rally partnership. The car itself was mechanically like others in this new batch, and of course it had right-hand drive.

As already noted, the weather on the 1958 Monte was foul, and Paddy struggled to keep going at all, never mind keep up to time. He was one of only five drivers to make it to the Dole control within their maximum lateness despite having gone off the road and ending up in a field, but fortunately with no more damage than a bent front bumper and grille. Later he ran out of time completely and was excluded, before the wintry horrors of the Common Route would bring further carnage to the field. Undaunted, Paddy and Jack took to the main roads to reach Monaco and drowned their sorrows in several glasses of Guinness before taking part in the after-rally manoeuvring test on the promenade, where they were rewarded with the fifth fastest time.

After this rather gruelling start to its career, VRW 220 then returned to Allesley, where the minor accident damage was speedily repaired and all winter equipment removed before the car was sent across the Irish Sea – along with VRW 221 and VRW 223 – for Paddy to drive on the prestigious Circuit of Ireland. It would be his seventh attempt to win his 'home' international, and this time there was to be no mistake.

The 1,429-mile event was a mixture of manoeuvring tests, speed hill-climbs and navigation sections, and took several days to unravel. It saw an intense battle between Hopkirk and Desmond Titterington – Paddy's team-mate but also his rival – and by the end, with neither car having suffered any serious problems, Hopkirk was the outright winner by just 8.9 penalty points.

Next it was Tom Gold's turn to drive the car. His outing was on the 1958 Tulip, where no fewer than five works TR3As took the start for a rally that promised to be much more of a speed event than it had been in previous years. Not that this helped, for on the very first day VRW 220 had to retire with what were officially noted as 'mechanical problems' – the detail was never spelled out. Accordingly, the stricken machine had to be towed back to Allesley to be readied for its next outing.

Along with four sister cars in the 1958 fleet – VRW 221, VRW 223, VWK 610 and VVC 672 – this TR3A was then given an early example of the enlarged-bore 2,138cc engine (see the accompanying panel) for the 1958 French Alpine rally, where the regulations merely grouped all the larger cars into the over 1,600cc category. This way it was hoped the works TR3As would be at least the equal of the works Austin-Healey 100-Six – which indeed they were. Within a year, however, that model had evolved into the Austin-Healey 3000 and moved out of reach in the power race!

Once again Paddy Hopkirk was behind the wheel. Apart from having to have deranged steering rectified after he went off the road early on, he made a good start and everything seemed to be in order. But then it all went wrong, as he explained: 'The car was 20 seconds faster up the Stelvio with the 2.2-litre engine but on the way up the pass, with its 48 hairpins, we had a puncture in the left-hand rear Dunlop Duraband tyre. I was on for a second consecutive Coupes des Alpes... and so decided to keep going to remain penalty-free. We made it to the top, but the engine overheated with the strain and we were forced to retire. It was probably a case of bad judgement on my behalf... I was very fond of Ken [Richardson] and he was quite right to sack me...'

It was rather an unhappy way for VRW 220 to end its four-event career. Triumph then sold the car to Fred Snaylam, an active and successful driver based in Lancashire, for his use in British events.

THE 2.2-LITRE 'WET-LINER' ENGINE

The famous 'wet-liner' engine had a long and successful career in TRs from 1953 to 1967, and it is no exaggeration to state that its enlargement from 1,991cc to 2,138cc in 1958 improved the performance of the works rally cars considerably. Incidentally, although the swept volume of the enlarged engine was 2,138cc, it has always been known as the '2.2-litre' unit.

Ken Richardson took all the credit for conceiving the 86mm bore that produced the '2.2-litre' engine, as he later confirmed in an interview.

'I had tried to convince the management in 1957 that we needed a new and bigger engine but to no avail due to the cost, so I toyed with an economical way... eventually organising the 2,138cc engine off my own bat.

'Although the Standard Vanguard had had a 2,088cc engine, utilising 85mm pistons, since its inception, these pistons were not strong enough for use in the TR. However, the 'Plus 0.040in' pistons used for re-boring Vanguards gave 2,138cc, as they were in effect 86mm in diameter.'

Specialloid made the pistons for the prototype 2,138cc engine but initially it could not even be run on the main factory's test bed as the whole project was unauthorised. So Richardson had the engine built privately in his department by his mechanics and tested it himself on the road. The rest, as they say, is history.

COMPETITION RECORD	
1958 Monte Carlo	
Paddy Hopkirk	Did not finish
1958 Circuit of Ireland	
Paddy Hopkirk	1st overall
1958 Tulip	
Tom Gold	Did not finish
1958 French Alpine	
Paddy Hopkirk	Did not finish

A famous – infamous? – shot of Paddy Hopkirk struggling to reach the summit of the Stelvio Pass on the French Alpine rally in 1958 in VRW 220, with a punctured rear tyre that allowed the engine to over-rev and wreck itself. Paddy was subsequently sacked – and still admits that it was all his fault.

VRW 221

FIRST REGISTERED	3 JANUARY 1958
ENGINE SIZE	1,991cc
MODEL TYPE	TR3A

John Waddington, who was already recognised as one of Britain's most successful rally drivers in his own TR2s and TR3s, had already enjoyed a class win in the 1957 Tulip rally in a works TR3 (TRW 736), so was offered a drive in the 1958 Monte, this time taking along his regular co-driver, Lancastrian Mike Wood, and having the use of a brand-new car. VRW 221 was set up and equipped like other TR3As in this new-for-1958 batch – which is to say that it was right-hand drive and ran in hardtop form with all the winter equipment already described.

Like his colleague Annie Soisbault, who ran out of time in the blizzard that followed the start of the Monte, Waddington also ran out of time and was excluded. Better news followed as John eventually brought his undamaged VRW 221 to Monte Carlo and took part, like Hopkirk, in the after-rally manoeuvring test on the promenade, achieving third fastest overall with only an Alfa Romeo Sprint Veloce and a Porsche 356 Carrera ahead of him.

Ulsterman Desmond Titterington then took over VRW 221 for the 1958 Circuit of Ireland, where all three of the right-hand-drive works TR3As took part. In a long battle Desmond and Paddy Hopkirk disputed every one of the 14

VRW 221, John Waddington at the wheel, tackles the final manoeuvring test on the promenade at the end of the 1958 Monte Carlo rally.

special tests and speed hill-climbs (and even high-speed descents), and the result was only settled by Titterington's timing error on a road section that cost him one minute, which equated to ten penalty points.

Following its great performance in the Circuit of Ireland, VRW 221 was hastily refreshed before being allocated to Ron Gouldbourn and Stuart Turner for the Tulip rally. This was a much tougher event than in previous years, and was a judicious balance between tight road sections, speed hill-climbs and even some circuit racing. Gouldbourn was a little less experienced at the high-speed stuff than Keith Ballisat and John Wallwork, who were also in the team, but his open-road skills, helped by the calm expertise of his co-driver, made up for everything.

The battle between Gouldbourn and his colleagues was consistently close until his TR3A had a coming-together with a Porsche on the 107km 'Thousand Curves' section and left the road. Undaunted, Gouldbourn got back on the road, sorted out some steering damage and continued resourcefully to the end, eventually finishing 10th overall and winning his 2-litre class, beating Lyndon Sims' Morgan and Annie Soisbault's works TR3A.

Because of his fine performance in the Circuit of Ireland, Desmond Titterington was redrafted into the team for the French Alpine rally and reunited with VRW 221, which, like the other works TR3As, was now fitted with the new 2.2-litre engine. With more torque at his disposal, Titterington,

VRW 221 in later life, an image chosen to confirm the authentic Apple Green colour of the 1958 team cars.

like the other works Triumph drivers, could match almost all that the mighty BMC Austin-Healey 100-Six crews could throw at him, on this event at least. But not quite all. At the end of a hard-fought few days, he took third place in class, beaten only by team-mate Keith Ballisat and Bill Shepherd's Big Healey. The TR3A was remarkably fresh and totally undamaged at the end of the event.

VRW 221 then took part in a prestigious event that had not been part of its original schedule – the Tour de France. The fast-talking David McKay, a self-promoting journalist and very active race driver from Australia who had already had considerable success in his own country, persuaded Standard-Triumph to loan him a car to compete in the eight-day event, and so VRW 221 was prepared afresh soon after Titterington had brought it home from the French Alpine.

By any contemporary standards, the Tour de France was a huge undertaking. In 1958 it started from Nice on 14 September and took in a complete anti-clockwise tour of France, including lengthy races at Reims, Rouen, Le Mans, Montlhéry and Clermont-Ferrand. There were also speed hill-climbs along the way and only three overnight rest halts,

at Le Touquet, Le Mans and Clermont-Ferrand.

It was asking too much for McKay, who had not previously taken part in this sort of event, to excel, particularly as he was up against dozens of much faster cars, including Ferraris and Porsches. Never near the front but learning as he went, he persevered only to suffer an accident that put him out of the event and brought this car's works career to a close.

COMPETITION RECORD	
1958 Monte Carlo	
John Waddington	Did not finish
1958 Circuit of Ireland	
Desmond Titterington	2nd overall
1958 Tulip	
Ron Gouldbourn	10th overall, 1st in class
1958 French Alpine	
Desmond Titterington	8th overall
1958 Tour de France	
David McKay	Did not finish

VRW 223

FIRST REGISTERED	3 JANUARY 1958
ENGINE SIZE	1,991cc
MODEL TYPE	TR3A

Of all the works TR3A performances in the 1958 Monte, quite the most eventful, exciting and remarkable was by – guess who – Dutchman Maurice Gatsonides in VRW 223. Brand new for the event and equipped in much the same way as its sister TR3As, this car started the event from The Hague, helping Triumph to gain useful pre-event publicity in Gatso's home country.

Setting off from The Hague with a relatively early start number enabled Gatso to run three hours ahead of team-mates Paddy Hopkirk and John Waddington in the early stages and this proved to be most fortunate. As recounted earlier (see page 40), a terrible blizzard hit central France during this event and decimated the field, but Gatso, thanks to that early start, was able to reach Monaco without running out of time.

Not that Gatso's progress was without incident, as he told me many years later: 'I was driving in the Vosges mountains. There were steep hills, and there was thick fog. I went round a fast corner and there was a DKW standing across the road. It happened to be Rob Slotemaker, he had blocked the road in the snow – I hit his car, I couldn't miss

him! The front end of the TR3A was damaged. We had a repair done by a blacksmith in the middle of the night at Saint Claude, because the chassis was damaged. We managed to get that battered car to the control but were nearly at our maximum lateness.'

And so they were, and the car's bodywork was crumpled on the left-hand side, and the headlamp on that side was inoperative. Of the 59 cars that finally clocked in to Monte Carlo a day or so later, Gatso's was 58th, with 980 penalty points lost. He was almost impossibly far behind the nine cars that had not incurred any penalties. Then came the final 20-hour, 655-mile mountain circuit over a complex route north and west of Monaco, and what occurred before the start of that was really rather miraculous, as Gatso explained: 'Before the start we had 30 minutes to fix the car. In that time I managed to fit a tractor headlamp that we had bought beforehand. With the help of the police, who allowed us to drive the wrong way up a one-way street to get to a little garage to get the work done, this headlamp was fitted, with a drill through the bonnet.'

By arrangement, Gatso then allowed his distinguished co-driver Marcel Becquart to drive the car throughout the mountain circuit, while Gatso sat alongside, in charge of the maps and being a very vocal cheerleader throughout. Having started at the back of the field, this redoubtable team fought their way so far up the order that their TR3A was the eighth car to reach the finish. Their reward was to take sixth overall and to win the 2-litre capacity class.

Ken Richardson, they say, blanched when he saw what Gatsonides had had to do to get his battered car to the finish.

Whether or not VRW 223 received a new chassis frame is not recorded, but the repair work must have been straightforward as the car looked immaculate when it turned out in April for the Circuit of Ireland. There it was driven by Ernest McMillen, a previous winner of the Circuit, but he went off the road more than once, lost a great deal of time, and finished well down the lists.

Keith Ballisat joined the team for the next event to be tackled by this car – the 1958 Tulip – and was initially rather astonished by his treatment: 'On that Tulip rally I don't remember seeing a service car at all. In the Alpine which followed, there was some support, but we were met only once every 12 hours or so. We had very little influence on the specification of the cars, we normally only picked them up the day before the event... There were no seat belts, no roll cages, no nothing... we didn't have special seats either. These were virtually standard motor cars, carefully screwed together...'

Keith's start in the works team, however, was not a sparkling success. He took time to settle in with an unfamiliar car, he had unspecified delays along the route, causing lateness penalties, and although he was as fast as any other TR3A driver on the Zandvoort race circuit that closed the

Loose going on the 1958 French Alpine rally for Keith Ballisat and Alain Bertaut in the 2.2-litre VRW 223. They took fourth place – and beat all the works Austin-Healey 100-Sixes.

event, he finished well down. As minor recompense, he then went on the German rally, a non-championship event, and took tenth place overall.

Keith, however, was now all set to deliver a remarkable performance in the French Alpine rally, which followed in mid-July. There had just been time to get the car back to Allesley to be fettled and to have the new, more brawny 2.2-litre engine fitted. Right from the start it was clear that the latest TR3A was exactly the right sort of car for this event. It was, for instance, at least 20 seconds quicker up the towering Stelvio pass than the 2-litre TR3s had been in previous years, and only some of this considerable leap in performance was due to the new radial-ply Dunlop Duraband tyres being used.

When the combination of speed hill-climbs and ultra-tight road sections had been taken into account, it was clear that the only cars that could beat the TR3As were the ultra-light, nimble Alfa Romeo Giuliettas (particularly the formidable combination of Bernard Consten and Roger de Laganeste in a Zagato-bodied coupé) and perhaps the Austin-Healeys.

In the end the original time schedule proved to be totally impossible to meet for every contestant, requiring the organisers – who were barely competent at times – to make changes as the event unfolded, with much huffing, puffing and face-saving. Conditions were so tough that only 25 of the 58 starters made it back to the finish in Marseilles after five days and 2,000 miles, and only seven drivers were without penalty – one of them the magnificent Ballisat. The highest-placed British driver, he finished fourth overall behind three twin-cam Alfas.

Clearly the TR3A remained so fresh after the French Alpine that it was turned round quickly for the Liège-Rome-Liège marathon that followed. It was typical of Ken Richardson's decision-making that Ballisat did not get the chance to drive VRW 223 in the Liège – instead it was provided to Maurice Gatsonides. Gatso persuaded the works team to rejig the car to his liking: the extra driving lamps were positioned behind the front grille, which was given a fold-away arrangement for the centre section so that the efficiency of the lights would not be reduced at night, and wire-spoke wheels replaced the steel discs that had been used in the French Alpine.

The Liège-Rome-Liège was a veritable high-speed marathon and as in previous years it went nowhere near Rome! Instead it penetrated deep into Yugoslavia, reaching Rijeka on the Adriatic coast before turning north to Zagreb, then going back to the Adriatic at Solin and striking off through the Italian Dolomites, crossing northern Italy and then attacking the French Alps.

As usual Gatsonides had carried out his own pre-event reconnaissance and his thoroughness was rewarded with fifth place overall, headed only by a Zagato-bodied Alfa Romeo (the same one that had won the recent French Alpine), two Porsche Carreras and Pat Moss's Austin-Healey 100-Six.

Only 22 of the 98 starters, including one other works TR3A, made it back to the finish.

This was the end of a very intense career – six events in eight months – for new-generation works TR3As were now on order and would be ready to go rallying in 1959.

COMPETITION RECORD	
1958 Monte Carlo	
Maurice Gatsonides/Marcel Becquart	6th overall
1958 Circuit of Ireland	
Ernest McMillen	Finished
1958 Tulip`	
Keith Ballisat	47th overall
1958 German	
Keith Ballisat	10th overall
1958 French Alpine	
Keith Ballisat	4th overall, 1st in class
1958 Liège-Rome-Liège	
Maurice Gatsonides	5th overall

VWK 610

FIRST REGISTERED	4 MARCH 1958
ENGINE SIZE	1,991cc
MODEL TYPE	TR3A

In all mechanical respects this left-hand-drive TR3A, painted British Racing Green, was the same as the VRW-prefixed cars on the fleet. Although always intended for Annie Soisbault to drive, it started its works career by being loaned to journalist Gregor Grant for the 1958 Lyons-Charbonnières rally. This was almost akin to throwing a fresh bone to a much-loved dog, for Gregor had become used to tackling this French classic in a car loaned to him by Standard-Triumph, even though, to be brutally honest, his driving abilities were not up to the standard that a factory team would normally expect.

There was an extra quirk of fate on the 1958 Lyons-Charbonnières: Annie turned up in her own privately owned TR3A and finished sixth overall and won the 2-litre capacity class! Gregor, on the other hand, suffered a puncture and could find nowhere conveniently wide enough to change the wheel at the side of the road, so he eventually ran out of time.

The car was then handed over to Annie and spent most of its works life in France, with occasional visits to Allesley for work to be done during its intensive programme in 1958. The French girl's first event with it was the Tulip rally, where she

battled in spirited fashion to finish a very meritorious third in the 2-litre class, despite at one point losing five minutes in thick fog on a very tight road section on which more than 20 competitors were 'clean'.

Soisbault won the Ladies' Prize on the German rally that followed, but this event was merely a sideshow, and Ladies' Prizes on their own had lost their sparkle to this particular lady – she was intent on matching the men.

Whatever ambitions she had for mixing it with the men seemed to be on hold during the first part of the French Alpine – and then it all went very wrong for her. When rounding one of the endless hairpin bends on the Stelvio she hit a stone wall and damaged the car, deranging its front

Gregor Grant and George Philips drove the new VWK 610 on the Lyons-Charbonnières rally of 1958, but without success.

VWK 610 was brand new for Gregor Grant to drive in the 1958 Lyon-Charbonnières rally but he did not complete the event; later it became Annie Soisbault's 'regular' car.

suspension and steering – and this happened right in front of a Shell film crew who recorded it all for posterity! The fact that a Denzel sports car followed suit soon afterwards was no consolation. A major rebuild with a replacement chassis was needed at Allesley before Annie could get the car back to compete in her home event – the Tour de France.

On the Tour de France she was joined by another works car – VRW 221 – but as this was on loan to Australian driver David McKay (see page 43) as a private exercise she had no cause to share service support with him. As expected, on this long event where pace on race circuits was at least as important as car reliability, Annie could only hope for the best. Could she, one wondered, repeat her success in winning the Ladies' Prize in 1957, when she had driven her own TR3? Unhappily she could not – Nadège Ferrier won the Ladies' Prize in the GT category driving a Porsche.

That was the last outing for VWK 610, which was sold to

the famous Olympic athlete Chris Brasher for use in the 1959 Monte Carlo and other events – but that is no longer part of our story.

COMPETITION RECORD	
1958 Lyon-Charbonnières	
Gregor Grant	Did not finish
1958 Tulip	
Annie Soisbault	3rd in class
1958 German	
Annie Soisbault	Ladies' Award
1958 French Alpine	
Annie Soisbault	Did not finish
1958 Tour de France	
Annie Soisbault	2nd Coupe des Dames

VVC 672

FIRST REGISTERED	1 APRIL 1958
ENGINE SIZE	1,991cc
MODEL TYPE	TR3A

This left-hand-drive car was completed in the spring of 1958 and registered on 1 April, which may not have been the most promising of starts for a works rally car – and indeed this car's two-event career was unhappy.

For the Tulip rally, in which no fewer than four other works TR3As took part, it was allocated to Johnny Wallwork – another strange decision by Ken Richardson. Although Wallwork had previously driven Standard Eights and Tens for the factory, and had also won the RAC Rally of 1954 in his own TR2, this was the first time he had driven a works TR3A – and a left-hand-drive one at that. Maybe this explains why it took him time to settle in, but by the time the event reached the French Alps he was up into tenth place, ahead of all the other TR3As with only three speed tests to

go. Close to the end, however, his TR3A was involved in a big chassis-bending accident, thankfully without causing injury. The incident was officially logged as 'two wheels collapsed' – true enough up to a point but the accident happened first and the wheels collapsed as a result of it!

The car was comprehensively rebuilt at Allesley and upgraded to a 2.2-litre engine before being driven by Maurice Gatsonides in the French Alpine rally. This outing ended against a rock face and Gatso was fortunate to avoid serious injury as the car was badly knocked about. According to Gatso, who wrote about this in detail in his autobiography, a damaged brake pipe had not been properly realigned during the rebuild and finally broke, rendering the car devoid of brakes.

COMPETITION RECORD	
1958 Tulip	
Johnny Wallwork	Did not finish
1958 French Alpine	
Maurice Gatsonides	Did not finish

VVC 673

FIRST REGISTERED	1 APRIL 1958
ENGINE SIZE	1,991cc
MODEL TYPE	TR3A

As Annie Soisbault had an extensive programme in 1958, mostly centred around VWK 610 and including the ten-day Tour de France, the factory team elected during the course of the season to add another new left-hand-drive car to the strength. Although it carried a registration number that had been reserved for it in April 1958, this car was not ready to take to the roads until mid-summer and its first – and, as it transpired, only – event for the works was the Liège-Rome-Liège at the end of August.

Technically VVC 673 was on a par with other works cars of the period, which is to say that it had a hard top and the still-exclusive 2.2-litre engine with overdrive on all forward gears. Unhappily for Annie, who was described by one of her co-drivers as 'rather vague', the car had to retire from the Liège-Rome-Liège. She was battling hard to keep up with her big rival Pat Moss in an Austin-Healey 100-Six when something damaged her car's radiator and the engine rapidly boiled its water away, leaving the car immobilised, many hours from assistance.

COMPETITION RECORD	
1958 Liège-Rome-Liège	
Annie Soisbault	Did not finish

WDU 712

FIRST REGISTERED	25 JULY 1958
ENGINE SIZE	1,991cc
MODEL TYPE	TR3A

Perhaps it was a coincidence, but yet another brand-new works TR3A – WDU 712 – was registered on 25 July 1958, just a few days after Maurice Gatsonides' works car had demolished itself in the French Alps during the Alpine rally. Compared with previous years, it was truly amazing that in 1958 the works rally team put no fewer than eight new cars on the road; in 1957 there had been only three.

According to the build information, this car was originally right-hand drive without overdrive and with a 2.0-litre engine, but by the time it was handed over to Robert Leidgens for the 1958 Liège-Rome-Liège it was left-hand drive! In all these cases it is best to rely on photographic evidence rather than what the 'record' says...

Leidgens, who had already excelled by taking fifth place in the 1956 Liège in SRW 991 (see page 34), was just as fast as expected in 1958. By the time the surviving cars reached the French Alps he had bustled his way into the top ten and he kept it all together through the final day to end up sixth, immediately behind the redoubtable Gatsonides.

As far as the works team was concerned, that was the end of the car's activity for the season, but it would appear again, still in 2.0-litre form, in the Tulip rally of May 1959. In one of those situations that puzzle historians, on this occasion the car was works-owned, works-prepared and driven by a sometime works driver in the form of Rob Slotemaker – but he entered the car privately.

Throughout the speed tests Slotemaker was right with his illustrious 'official' team-mates, but unfortunately he lost time on the tight road sections and was unable to challenge for the class victory when the event reached its climax in Holland at the Zandvoort circuit. Team boss Ken Richardson, however, had all bases covered, as *Autosport*'s reporter noted: 'The all-Triumph race was a demonstration by Rob Slotemaker of knowing Zandvoort inside out. The

WDU 712 was new in 1958, and is seen here on the French Alpine rally of 1959, driven by Rob Slotemaker. The Dutch driver took second place in his 2-litre class behind another works TR3A. One imagines that Slotemaker realigned the driving lamps to encourage more cooling air to enter the front air intake during daylight driving.

Dutchman led until the last lap, when he slowed down behind the pits, opened his door and yelled to Ken Richardson for instructions. Presumably there had been some pre-race natter, for Ballisat, Gatsonides and Wallwork all passed in that order, before Slotemaker crossed the line...'

WDU 712 was next sent to contest the French Alpine rally, where Slotemaker was joined by three of the 'WVC' cars. As there was both silverware and prize money to be won in the two separate classes for which the TR3As were eligible on this event, Slotemaker was entered in a 2.0-litre car. By the end of the first leg, Rob remained unpenalised and in contention for class victory, a great boost to morale, but matters got more difficult on the Austrian part of the route, and on the rough Turracher Höhe pass the car developed problems with its shock absorbers and brakes. Although these components were repaired, the class battle was over and Slotemaker had to settle for second, behind Roger de Laganeste in WVC 249.

Next, WDU 712 was made ready to tackle its second Liège-Rome-Liège. It was again entrusted to Slotemaker, who had now convinced Richardson that he was good enough to play with the big boys at all levels, not merely as a co-driver but as

a lead driver. This was a very tough event and car after car dropped out, either broken or running outside maximum lateness, but the gallant Slotemaker was competitive to the very climax of the rally. It was only after the murderously tight section around St Jean-en-Royans that he finally ran out of time and was forced to retire – one could say that it was the event that won and not the car or its driver that lost. So punishing was it that only 14 crews of the original 97 starters were classed as finishers.

A NEW TR3A FLEET FOR A BUSY 1959

Just before the end of November 1958, the works team took delivery of no fewer than six Signal Red hardtop TR3As, all of them with overdrive and centre-lock wire-spoke wheels, but only one with left-hand drive. A study of this new fleet's commission numbers shows a spread of just 176 cars, suggesting that they were all originally assembled, at Canley, in the same week of November/December 1958.

Is that significant or trivial? Who knows – but what is clear is that this was all part of an on-going progress of a real clear-out of the TRs that were being held by the works department. Eight new TR3As had contested the 1958 race and rally season and all survived the rough and tumble of the year, but no fewer than seven of them were sold off at the end of the year, with only WDU 712, a newer car that joined the fleet in mid-1958, surviving the cull.

Technically the six new TR3As were prepared almost entirely to the same specification as the 1958 cars in their finalised form, which is to say that they usually operated with the 2.2-litre engine wherever it was allowed. The 2.2-litre engine was still exclusively available to works cars at first, but it is worth noting that it became optionally available on production cars during the winter of 1958/59. Rather than using steel disc wheels, the cars usually ran with wire-spoke wheels (of 15in diameter) as the latest 60-spoke design from Dunlop was significantly stronger than the mid-1950s variety had ever been.

In some cases there were minor variations in lighting arrangements, usually by driver request. Sometimes cars had three extra driving lamps, the third one mounted on the shroud just ahead of the bonnet badge; sometimes the usual pair of extra lamps was mounted outboard of the bumper over-riders; sometimes smaller types of lamp were recessed into the front grille; and eventually the side/indicator lamps were positioned on the front wings themselves rather than in the extremities of the grille. Swivelling roof-mounted spot lamps continued to be used, although these were soon to be rendered illegal by new Construction & Use regulations. Sometimes these measures were mixed and matched, which must have made it all very confusing for the mechanics preparing the cars for events…

There was still no sign of any extra power for the engines, nor were any of the cars ever equipped with aluminium or even glass-fibre body panels, both of which were allowable as 'freedoms' by the evolving homologation regulations.

In this period it was almost as if there was a complete change in operating philosophy, as almost all of these red cars would be worked harder and more consistently than previous works TRs had been. For example, WVC 248, originally Annie Soisbault's left-hand-drive car, started no fewer than 13 events in a year and a half! Moreover, the team also had to make provision for its annual visit to the Le Mans 24 Hours race and to carry on campaigning Standard Tens and, later, Triumph Heralds. All this must have meant that the works team was under more pressure than ever before, especially when as many as four or five works TRs started a major event.

COMPETITION RECORD

1958 Liège-Rome-Liège
Robert Leidgens — 6th overall
1959 Tulip
Rob Slotemaker — 6th in class
1959 French Alpine
Rob Slotemaker — 2nd in class
1959 Liège-Rome-Liège
Rob Slotemaker — Did not finish

WVC 247

FIRST REGISTERED	31 DECEMBER 1958
ENGINE SIZE	1,991cc
MODEL TYPE	TR3A

The first of the new TR3As obtained by the works for the 1959 season, WVC 247 was made ready for the 1959 Monte Carlo Rally, where it was to be driven by Maurice Gatsonides. Like the other three new works cars on this event, it ran with a 1,991cc engine because class capacity limits made it more sensible, but the lack of power compared with the still-new 2.2-litre power unit hardly mattered on an event where grip was more important than extra torque. Unlike others in the team, Gatso chose to run on steel disc wheels rather than centre-lock wire wheels.

Unfortunately for Gatso, he chose to start this Monte from Athens, where the weather was best described as rugged, but he was still able to start out on the final classification test where strict regularity was required and was policed by checks, both declared and secret. Unhappily, it helped during this part of the competition to be a French driver, with friends who could scout ahead and provide reconnaissance notes about the location of secret checks.

That was bad enough, but the fact that the experienced Dutchman ran into a series of setbacks meant that this was a Monte to forget. He lost the use of a headlamp on the way up the Turini and went into a snowdrift as a consequence, then only an hour later he suffered his first puncture and by the end he had had two more. This was the first occasion on which studded Duraband tyres were tried, and the drivers said that the vagaries of these tyres on varying surfaces was the cause of their problems. Gatso's only consolation was that his car, suitably spruced up after the event for display on the terrace of the Casino, won the Prix d'Honneur in the Concours de Confort.

Triumph then entered the three right-hand-drive 'WVC' cars in the Circuit of Ireland, where an unfavourable performance handicap did not help them. WVC 247 was loaned to Ulsterman Brian McCaldin, who had a good run on the event, which was dominated by driving tests, to finish second in his class to Johnny Wallwork in WVC 249.

By the time of the Tulip Rally all six of the new 1959 works TR3As had been completed and they all ran in this event, still using 2-litre engines and therefore running in the 2-litre GT class. This Tulip was generally acknowledged to be more difficult than ever before, with tighter timing and more demanding speed tests. Although the start from Paris was gentle enough, the route toughened up considerably once it reached the French Alps. Only five cars in the entire entry were completely unpenalised on the road sections.

The works TR3As dominated their class and took the top three places, with the privately entered examples of David Seigle-Morris and Rob Slotemaker close behind. Gatsonides was third in WVC 247 after losing two minutes on road sections, whereas class-winning Keith Ballisat in WVC 250 made it through unscathed. This turned out to be Gatso's final appearance in a works Triumph as he deemed it time to retire after spending five years involved the team, complete with a stormy relationship with Ken Richardson.

For the French Alpine rally, where Triumph invariably shone, three of the 'WVC' cars were entered and Rob Slotemaker finally got his chance to join the big boys in WDU 712 (see pages 47-48), so WVC 247 was left at home. Instead it was made available as a back-up car to Cambridge University Automobile Club, which was making a seven-day record attempt at Monza with XHP 259 (see pages 56-58). The idea was that all the team members would drive WVC 247 on the journey to Italy, where it would be on hand to be plundered for spares as required – but it seems that no such problems occurred.

After its return from Monza, WVC 247 was made ready for competition in the Liège-Rome-Liège – with its prehistoric horrors of terrible roads in Yugoslavia – where Keith Ballisat, happily recovered from his broken jaw on the French Alpine, drove the car with Alain Bertaut alongside him. Incidentally, when Ballisat was photographed before the start of the event, he was sporting a very smartly trimmed beard that was surely connected with the need to let his fragile jaw regain strength.

Keith Ballisat (left) and Ian 'Tiny' Lewis toast themselves after WVC 247 had helped to win the Manufacturers' Team Prize in the 1959 German rally. Note the repositioned indicator lights in the front wings.

Running in 1,991cc form and with a class victory in its sights, this car put up a remarkably solid and composed performance in an event where the vast majority of starters failed to reach the finish. The time schedule in the Italian, Yugoslavian and French mountains, with their assorted rough tracks, was unrelenting and much time was lost, but in the end Ballisat brought this hard-working car home, beaten only in its class by Annie Soisbault's sister car (WVC 248).

Surprisingly, the works team then sent no fewer than three cars to contest the German rally, which started from Stuttgart and included three long road sections before finishing at Baden-Baden. Much of the route was in familiar French Alpine rallying territory, and included speed tests up Mont Ventoux and the Col du Rousset. There was a complex performance-handicapping system that favoured the small-engined cars.

As far as the GT machinery was concerned, it was only an outstanding performance by Pat Moss in – guess what? – an Austin-Healey 3000 that stopped the works TR3As from dominating the category. Driving WVC 247 once again, Ballisat, accompanied for the first time by Ian 'Tiny' Lewis, therefore took second in his class and was in one of the TR3As that won the Team Prize.

WVC 247 then had a lengthy winter's rest, not only because the works competitions department was on the move to new premises at the recently acquired and refurbished

Rob Slotemaker (at the wheel) and Ron Crellin at the end of the 1960 Tulip rally, where they took second in the class, beaten by David Seigle-Morris in his own privately prepared TR3A.

engine and hosted yet another new pairing in the form of Rob Slotemaker and Ron Crellin, who was making a name for himself as a co-driver in British rallies with Brian Harper. It was a combination that obviously gelled as they beat other team members in identical cars to finish second in the 2,001–2,500cc class, and were unpenalised on all but one of the road sections, the exception being the test up the Col de Turini to the summit that required 12km to be completed in 12 minutes and defeated all but eight of the field.

As far as Triumph enthusiasts were concerned, however, the sensation of this Tulip was that private owner David Seigle-Morris, co-driven by Vic Elford, campaigned his own 2.2-litre TR3A (registered D 20) and beat all the other TRs in the event. His reward was to be drafted into the works team for its next event, the French Alpine rally, in which he would drive WVC 248 and win a class yet again!

Slotemaker and Crellin got together again in WVC 247 for the French Alpine rally, where the car had a 2-litre engine. This outing, however, could not have ended more unhappily, for the TR3A broke a half shaft only a mile after the start on the quayside of Marseilles, on a speed hill-climb test just outside the city. With no limited-slip differentials in those days, that was that – a downbeat way for WVC 247 to end its seven-event works career.

Radford plant, but also because company motorsport policy was by then concentrated on the use of Triumph Herald Coupés (see Chapter 3) in the 1959 RAC and 1960 Monte Carlo rallies. However, although the works TR3As were now at the peak of their development, there were still opportunities for them to dominate classes and – importantly in the view of management – for their reliability to make the winning of Team Prizes very likely.

Although Standard-Triumph's company finances were becoming rocky and near bankruptcy would follow towards the end of 1960, the works team continued to spend heavily, although sporadically, as the 1960 season progressed. In January two TR3As and no fewer than five other works cars started the Monte Carlo rally and then, after a long rallying lay-off while the team concentrated its efforts on getting the restyled TRS Le Mans cars (see Chapter 2) ready for action, all four of the surviving 1959 works TR3As were prepared for the Tulip rally.

For the 1960 Tulip WVC 247 was provided with a 2.2-litre

COMPETITION RECORD	
1959 Monte Carlo	
Maurice Gatsonides	68th overall
1959 Circuit of Ireland	
Brian McCaldin	2nd in class
1959 Tulip	
Maurice Gatsonides	3rd in class
1959 Liège-Rome-Liège	
Keith Ballisat	8th overall
1959 German	
Keith Ballisat	2nd in class
1960 Tulip	
Rob Slotemaker	2nd in class
1960 French Alpine	
Rob Slotemaker	Did not finish

WVC 248

FIRST REGISTERED	31 DECEMBER 1958
ENGINE SIZE	1,991cc
MODEL TYPE	TR3A

From the outset of the 1959 programme, one works TR3A, the left-hand-drive car registered WVC 248, was reserved for Annie Soisbault's use. It was to lead a busy, eventful and often successful life until mid-1960, although Annie's moods and the fortunes of her car seemed to vary from event to event. Technically, visually and functionally, WVC 248 was prepared to the same specification as the other cars of the 'WVC' group.

Soisbault's season did not start well, for she crashed on the

Monte Carlo rally when encountering ice soon after the event left Chambéry. A month later she took the car to compete in the Rallye del Sestrière, a regularity jaunt based around the Italian ski resort north of Turin. Third in class made the exercise worthwhile in terms of the result, but it was no test of a rugged rally car – just an excuse for a motoring social weekend. Annie also tackled the Lyons-Charbonnières, finishing second in the Ladies' category behind Pat Moss, followed by a ladies-only jaunt in the Paris–St Raphael event. The Tulip rally that came next, in May, was a much more serious affair, but somewhere along the way Annie's car dropped out and did not feature at the finish.

Next, however, came a fine performance on the Acropolis rally in Greece, where weather conditions were extremely arduous and variable. The demands of the route caught out a lot of competitors in a field of formidable quality, but Annie and her TR3A – fitted for this event with a 2.2-litre engine – kept going and won the Ladies' Prize as well as the over 1,600cc class.

Then came the French Alpine, where Annie's 2.2-litre car was expected to go well, and indeed she did set sparkling times on special speed tests, especially in the rough and tumble of the Austrian back roads. Although in with a good chance of winning the Ladies' Prize, helped by the fact that Pat Moss was driving a much-modified Austin A40 Farina on this occasion, her TR3A retired after suffering a puncture on the Vivione pass. Finding space on this narrow road to effect a wheel change was bad enough, but when she extracted the jack she claimed that she found a vital part of it missing and therefore could not get the job done.

Despite this setback Annie and her refreshed car were on much better form in the gruelling Liège-Rome-Liège marathon, which took place in the first few days of September. Although the vast majority of the cars in the event were eliminated, either by mechanical bothers or by the unrelenting time schedule, Annie kept going and won not only the Ladies' award but also her 2-litre capacity class, beating Keith Ballisat along the way. She also finished fourth in the GT category, beaten only by three much more powerful rear-engined Porsches, one of which was the Carrera that won the event outright.

Although Annie then went on to compete in a TR3A in the seven-day Tour de France at the end of September, it was not in one of the works cars. Even after she had been signed to join the factory team in 1958, she had retained a privately owned TR3A, and it was in this light-coloured car with wire spoke wheels, and running with a soft top, that she won the prestigious Ladies' Prize.

Incidentally, it was in this same event that Keith Ballisat appeared in a car that one reporter described as a 'near-vintage drum-brakes TR2'. Unfortunately, the TR2 did not finish the event as it began to suffer from a failing rear wheel axle bearing in the Pyrenees section, and finally retired on the

Exhausted but happy, the two works crews who had survived the 96-hour horrors of the 1959 Liège-Rome-Liège Marathon de la Route. Annie Soisbault and Renée Wagner drove WVC 248 to fourth place while Keith Ballisat and (out of shot) Alain Bertaut brought WVC 247 home in sixth place.

This was the 1960 Monte Carlo rally, with Jean-Jacques Thuner driving the hard-working WVC 248

Clermont-Ferrand race-circuit test with that bearing totally destroyed.

Annie's usual car was then refreshed back at Allesley before being sent out to tackle the German rally, where, as noted in the WVC 247 section, all the TR3As had to battle with Pat Moss's Austin-Healey 3000. The result was that Annie finished behind Pat, as well as behind team-mate Ballisat, but was one of the victorious members of the Team Prize contest.

Finally, her ninth – and last – event of the 1959 season in WVC 248 was the British RAC rally, with the car in 2.0-litre form. She had only tackled this rally once before, and that was in 1958 in a works Standard Pennant, and this time it got off to a bad start. Annie's co-driver for this event only was Valerie Domleo, who later became Valerie Morley when she married rally driver Donald Morley. Valerie delivered her driving partner to the start of the first driving test, on the lower promenade in Blackpool, and explained that she would reconnect with her 'after the test'. Annie completed the test and drove on, but could not find Valerie. She drove on ever further and was about 15 miles out of Blackpool before she realised that 'after the test' meant precisely that – immediately after the stop line.

Valerie later gave me her side of this story: 'I'd given up on her, even before we had really started! But eventually she came back into Blackpool and drove up and down the road above the test, tooting and flashing her lights, looking for me. Obviously we were late at the first time control, and that cost us the Ladies' Prize… and it also cost Annie her chance of winning the European Ladies' Championship of 1959.'

The RAC rally created great controversy that year as a result of the route at one point in the Scottish Highlands becoming blocked by snow. Only a small number of cars managed to divert to reach the Braemar time control within their maximum time limit, the rest being docked a maximum penalty – and Annie was one who suffered a maximum penalty. Had the snow blockage not occurred, there were all manner of manoeuvring tests, high-speed hill-climb tests and even a spot of circuit racing to sort out a result, but this was all rendered meaningless by the maximum penalties applied to all but the first 13 cars to finish.

The snow blockage was shrugged off by the organisers after all manner of protests had been made, considered, rejected, readmitted and finally rejected once again by the stewards of the RAC. But for the snow Annie would certainly have been in the top ten, but in the end she was placed 24th and came second in the Ladies' contest to Ann Hall in a Ford Anglia 105E. Because there had only been one works TR3A in the event, Ken Richardson had craftily registered a 'team' that comprised Annie Soisbault along with private entrants David Seigle-Morris and Edwin Hodson – and they duly won the Manufacturers' Team Prize!

Annie did not drive WVC 248 again, although she was due to do so in the last event of the year, the Portuguese rally.

There she bailed out at the last moment, telling the world that the TR3A had 'axle trouble', which was completely false, and declining to start. This was all to do with the points situation in the Ladies' Championship after her problems on the RAC – her shambolic start and then the snow blockage – but was to no avail. In 1960 she finally left the team after using XHP 259 for two outings.

This incredibly hard-working car's next outing was the Monte Carlo rally of January 1960, where it was allocated to Geneva-based Jean-Jacques Thuner, who had already won the Geneva rally of 1959 and thoroughly deserved his place in the team. The car had a very familiar-looking specification with hard top, wire-spoke wheels, roof spotlight and – on this occasion – the 1,991cc engine, but this time there were four extra driving lamps and a luggage rack on the boot lid to carry an extra spare wheel. Dunlop's rally-specification Duraband tyres were used, sometimes in studded form when icy conditions were encountered.

Embarking from Paris, Thuner made a good start and arrived at the 'concentration' control in Chambéry – where all routes converged from the far-flung starting points –

COMPETITION RECORD	
1959 Monte Carlo	
Annie Soisbault	Did not finish
1959 Sestrière	
Annie Soisbault	3rd in class
1959 Lyons-Charbonnières	
Annie Soisbault	2nd in Ladies' Prize
1959 Paris-St Raphael	
Annie Soisbault	Finisher
1959 Tulip	
Annie Soisbault	Did not finish
1959 Acropolis	
Annie Soisbault	1st in class
1959 French Alpine	
Annie Soisbault	Did not finish
1959 Liège-Rome-Liège	
Annie Soisbault	6th overall
1959 German	
Annie Soisbault	3rd in class
1959 RAC	
Annie Soisbault	2nd in Ladies' Prize
1959 Portuguese	
Annie Soisbault	Did not start
1960 Monte Carlo	
Jean-Jacques Thuner	Did not finish
1960 Tulip	
Johnny Wallwork	3rd in class
1960 French Alpine	
David Seigle-Morris	1st in class

having lost only a solitary minute. But in the tight section that followed, through the mountains towards Monte Carlo, he finally ran out of time and had to retire.

Three months later Johnny Wallwork got one of his rare calls to rejoin the works team, and was invited to contest the Tulip rally in the newly rebuilt WVC 248, now in 2.2-litre form and converted to right-hand drive. In an event that comprised mainly road mileage with a smattering of speed tests and circuit racing, Wallwork finished close behind Rob Slotemaker's sister TR3A, while the remarkable David Seigle-Morris won the class in his privately owned 2.2-litre TR3A. Like all the other leading TR3A drivers, Wallwork was penalised one minute on the 12km ascent of the Col de Turini.

This car's last works appearance, in the French Alpine in mid-1960 with a 2.0-litre engine, started off David Seigle-Morris's very successful works rallying career with BMC and then Ford. After a huge battle against three Big Healeys, two Alfa Romeos and two Porsches on this gruelling four-day event, Seigle-Morris did remarkably well to win the 2-litre class and his showing was all the more outstanding because WVC 248 was the only works TR3A to reach the finish, the other three having had to drop out. Nevertheless, this was his only drive for the works Triumph team – so he left it with a 100 per cent success record!

The car was sold to company employee Gordon Birtwistle, who later became a very accomplished high-speed experimental test driver.

WVC 249

FIRST REGISTERED	31 DECEMBER 1958
ENGINE SIZE	1,991cc
MODEL TYPE	TR3A

The first event for WVC 249 was the 1959 Monte Carlo rally in the hands of Johnny Wallwork, a very competitive driver who had finally earned a seat in a TR after having had to slum it in Standard Tens.

On the Monte Wallwork made it through unscathed from Stockholm to Monaco and set out on the classification test in high spirits, but then dropped well down the order. A cylinder head gasket blew part way through the test and left the car on only three cylinders, while Wallwork also encountered difficulty in arriving at time checks when required – particularly the secret checks that were more secret to some competitors than to others.

After the close of the rally Wallwork took WVC 249 out to compete in the after-rally manoeuvring test on the promenade, where a good result could be a considerable boost to morale even if it could not affect placings in the rally itself. In a truly virtuoso performance by a character used to this sort of thing in British events, Wallwork set third fastest time overall, beaten only by a Mercedes-Benz 300SL and a Porsche 1600.

The next outing for this team came in the Circuit of Ireland, where all three of the right-hand-drive 'WVC' cars started. However, not even the determined Wallwork could beat the unfavourable performance handicaps, and he had to settle for a class win and eighth place overall.

The tough Tulip rally came next for WVC 249, still in 2-litre form. In the end Wallwork lost a single minute on the 23km section from Saint-Agrève to Fay-sur-Lignon in the

Haute-Loire region of France, dropping him out of the top standings into seventh place overall and second in the 2-litre class to Keith Ballisat's sister TR3A.

By this time Wallwork had hoped to become a permanent member of the works team, but, amazingly, he did not receive another invitation from Triumph for a full year! Like many, he could not understand the logic behind Ken Richardson's mix-and-match methods of selecting drivers. In fairness to him, however, the next rally was the French Alpine and it was no disgrace to be substituted by Roger de Laganeste, a recognised specialist in this event and a previous winner in an Alfa Romeo. With a class victory targeted on the French Alpine, WVC 249 again ran with a 1,991cc engine and de Laganeste duly delivered the desired result, making the advertising copywriters very happy indeed.

For the Liège-Rome-Liège that followed, Richardson allocated this car to Claude Dubois of Belgium, who had recently driven a twin-cam TR3S at Le Mans. Unfortunately Dubois got no further than the roughest part of Yugoslavia on the second day of the event after WVC 249 suffered a very damaging accident and had to retire. There were no injuries

COMPETITION RECORD	
1959 Monte Carlo	
Johnny Wallwork	73rd overall
1959 Circuit of Ireland	
Johnny Wallwork	1st in class
1959 Tulip	
Johnny Wallwork	2nd in class
1959 French Alpine	
Roger de Laganeste	1st in class
1959 Liège-Rome-Liège	
Claude Dubois	Did not finish
1960 Monte Carlo	
Marcel Becquart	Did not finish

to the crew, but it seems significant that this car was not used again for four months, this being a period when more and more emphasis in the factory effort was being placed on the new Triumph Heralds (see Chapter 3).

After its rebuild over the winter, WVC 249 was entered on the 1960 Monte in 2.2-litre form for the veteran Marcel Becquart, who elected to start from Lisbon, Portugal, in the expectation that weather conditions would be more favourable on this concentration run through Spain to southwestern France. Unhappily for Becquart his calculation misfired, for his TR3A left the road in icy conditions near Millau in France. A photograph published in *Autosport* showed the car with its nose stoved in against a telegraph pole on the outside of an ice-covered corner. The cause was almost certainly terminal understeer, the result a ruined radiator that prevented further progress.

The cost of rebuilding WVC 249 as a factory-fresh rally car after that accident was not considered viable and so it was never done, the car ending its works career after an effective life of almost exactly one year.

WVC 250

FIRST REGISTERED	31 DECEMBER 1958
ENGINE SIZE	1,991cc
MODEL TYPE	TR3A

This was the fourth of the new 'WVC' TR3As that were prepared together and it made its first public appearance on the 1959 Monte Carlo rally, driven by the formidable crew of Keith Ballisat and French co-driver Alain Bertaut.

Despite being hit by a non-competing car even before their arrival at the starting compound in Paris, they made it through the ice, snow and fog of the Massif Central and the Alpes Maritimes and looked set for a fine performance on the classification test and mountain circuit – but Keith unfortunately put the car off the road in the final hours. With help from brawny locals, the car was eventually put back on the road and made it to the finish, but all chance of a good result had gone.

This car was then loaned to Irishman Ernest McMillen for the Circuit of Ireland, but on only the second day it was eliminated in the mountains of Kerry when McMillen met a non-competing VW van head on in a timed section and had to dive off the road to avoid a severe accident. The car had to be returned to Allesley by transporter for a major rebuild before its next scheduled outing on the Tulip rally.

The rebuild was clearly done beautifully, for Keith Ballisat put in an astonishing performance on the Tulip in what was still a 2-litre car. In an event where all the difficult motoring was concentrated on tight, difficult road sections in the Massif Central and Alpes Maritimes, car after car was late, through going off the road in trying to keep up to schedule or getting lost in foggy conditions. But Ballisat and co-driver Ed Marvin kept going and were one of only five crews to reach the finish in Noordwijk unpenalised. Outright victory went to the popular Morley twins in their own Jaguar 3.4, but Ballisat's performance in taking second place overall was a splendid show too.

For the French Alpine rally that followed, Triumph shuffled its resources and entered all four 'WVC' cars, but Ballisat was again in WVC 250, now fitted with a 2.2-litre engine. There were hopes, of course, that Keith would produce another magnificent drive and indeed he did – until the closing hours. There remains some confusion as to what happened in the next few days, but what seems to be clear is that Ballisat led the hotly contested 2.2-litre class until the very last few hours, when effectively the event was all over and he was nearing the finish in Cannes. On that final leg the car crashed and Ballisat suffered a broken jaw, but, amazingly, he was fit enough to tackle the Liège-Rome-Liège marathon less than two months later.

After another comprehensive rebuild WVC 250 rejoined the works team in October for the German rally, where two other works TR3As – WVC 247 and WVC 248 – also started. John Sprinzel, who until now had campaigned Austin-Healey Sprites as a semi-detached member of the BMC team, drove the car on this event. The TR3A, of course, was unfamiliar to Sprinzel, but, as he later explained, there was a silly reason for his troubled run: 'Unfortunately… someone had filled the brake-fluid reservoir with normal oil. The result was somewhat chaotic, in that both clutch and brake seals rotted away in a very short time, and it was only through team-mate "Tiny" Lewis's help that we were able to have some sort of brakes, the clutch being unsaveable. However, Stuart and I managed to get through the rally using second and second overdrive for all the tight bits…'

The result was that Sprinzel took fourth in class, behind not only Pat Moss's Big Healey but also team-mates Keith Ballisat and Annie Soisbault. The Team Prize, however, was a small consolation.

During the winter WVC 250 was given another major rebuild back in Coventry and then provided to Keith Ballisat for the Tulip rally, the event that he had so nearly won in 1959. As described earlier (see page 50), four surviving members of the Signal Red fleet started the event, all with 2.2-litre engines, and competition between them was so close that it was very difficult to forecast who would triumph at the finish – but in the end David Seigle-Morris's private entry beat the works cars. After losing a solitary minute on the notoriously tight climb of the Col de Turini, near Monte Carlo, Ballisat was pipped by the sister cars of Rob Slotemaker and Johnny Wallwork.

It was so typical of Ken Richardson's capricious way of choosing drivers that he then offered WVC 250, in 2-litre form, to Les Leston for the French Alpine rally. Leston was a competent racing driver who had just competed in a TRS at the Le Mans 24 Hours, but he was not a rally driver of renown. His limitations were at least balanced by the experience of his co-driver, Stuart Turner, not that this helped him. Before the end of the first day the TR3A went off into a ditch on a tight section near La Mure and could not be retrieved.

With that, the works career of WVC 250, and of Leston, came to an end.

COMPETITION RECORD	
1959 Monte Carlo	
Keith Ballisat	119th overall
1959 Circuit of Ireland	
Ernie McMillen	Did not finish
1959 Tulip	
Keith Ballisat	2nd overall
1959 French Alpine	
Keith Ballisat	Did not finish
1959 German	
John Sprinzel	4th in class
1960 Tulip	
Keith Ballisat	4th in class
1960 French Alpine	
Les Leston	Did not finish

WVC 251

FIRST REGISTERED	19 NOVEMBER 1958
ENGINE SIZE	1,991cc
MODEL TYPE	TR3A

The entry of this car for Ian 'Tiny' Lewis in the Acropolis rally of May 1961 was almost a case of 'getting rid of the empties'. This was a one-off final appearance of a works TR3A in an unsuitable event, from a department that had seemingly washed its hands of TR3As months earlier. It was also the last TR3A to be sold off into private ownership.

This car was the oddball of the 1959 fleet. Although it was the first of the Signal Red cars to be completed at Canley and the first to be delivered to Allesley, in November 1958, its only event was this outing on the Acropolis in 1961. In the meantime, it seems, Ken Richardson used it as his own personal road car for two years. By 1961, of course, the TR3A had long since come to the peak of its development with the successful launch of the 2.2-litre engine in 1958/59, and had become consistently outpaced by the brutally fast and expensively developed works Austin-Healey 3000s. No new TR3As had been added to the fleet for two years, the last full team entry had taken place in the summer of 1960, and the other four surviving 1959/60 team cars had all been sold off by the works.

With Leyland now in charge of Standard-Triumph's finances and with the closure of the competitions department imminent, 'Tiny' Lewis was the only front-line driver remaining with the team and he was persuaded to tackle the 1961 Acropolis. Persuaded? Well, as all but the wilfully blind now realised, a TR chassis was not at its best on rough rally tracks and an ageing TR3A could no longer keep up with the persistently updated Big Healey, so Lewis knew he would be fighting against the odds. Seasoned driver that he was, however, he took Tony Nash with him as an able co-driver, made sure that the car had a 2.2-litre engine, and did his level best in the circumstances.

The Acropolis, an arduous event on rocky tracks, was run in relentlessly hot, dusty conditions in 1961 and the results were dominated by rugged saloons from Saab, Mercedes-Benz, Sunbeam and Volvo. Only two sports cars finished in the top ten and these were – guess what? – the TR3A and Pat Moss's works Austin-Healey 3000. With second place behind the Big Healey in the over 1,600cc class, the motorsport career of the works TR3As came to an honourable close.

That was in May 1961. The Le Mans 24 Hours race took place the following month and within a few weeks of that the entire competitions department had been closed down.

COMPETITION RECORD	
1961 Acropolis	
Ian 'Tiny' Lewis	10th overall

XHP 259

FIRST REGISTERED	24 MARCH 1959
ENGINE SIZE	1,991cc
MODEL TYPE	TR3A

This car, one of the six taken up by the works team for use in 1959 and beyond, was not used as intensively as the others in the batch of TR3As, but nevertheless it had a very varied career.

Although it had been built in November 1958, at the same time as the other Signal Red works cars, it did not make its rally début until May 1959, when Cyril Corbishley drove it on the Tulip rally, along with four other team TR3As. Not that this was an auspicious start to its career, for somewhere in the mountains around the Ballon d'Alsace the car and the scenery came together. That caused delay, and in the end Corbishley dropped out of contention completely.

There then followed a remarkable diversion. A team of enthusiastic Cambridge University Automobile Club (CUAC) members took a works Triumph TR3A – XHP 259 – to the banked oval at Monza and set out to lift every possible class endurance record up to and including seven days and nights

The car makes an unscheduled pit stop for electrical problems to be investigated.

XHP 259 was used in an ambitious seven-day/seven-night record attempt at Monza in the summer of 1959, when a team of Cambridge University Automobile Club (CUAC) enthusiasts did all the driving. The car was driven flat out all the way.

non-stop, which would have meant completing nearly 17,000 miles. They had exclusive use of the track for seven days and their ultimate aim was to average over 100mph for that duration. The driving team was Gerry Boxall, Bill Brookes, John Cumming, Graham Denby, John Gerrard, Rupert Jones, Bill McCowan and Brian Whitaker.

Whitaker told me that record-breaking had become something of a CUAC speciality as earlier teams had set records with Austin A35s and Austin-Healeys. He explained how the exercise with the TR3A came about: 'Graham Denby, whose family business was a supplier to the motor industry, used all his contacts to see who might help us set up a 1959 attempt and effectively he was the team leader. Clearly he struck gold with Triumph – and before we knew it we were all off to Monza with a 2-litre works TR3A!'

Not only did Triumph's Ken Richardson attend the exercise, along with three of his works mechanics, but there was also assistance from Shell, who provided all fuel and lubricants, and Dunlop, who provided service throughout from 'Dunlop Mac', the company's senior motorsport technician. The car's preparation details were as follows:

- The engine was standard, although the air cleaners were removed from the carburettors.
- For less mechanical strain in high-speed running, there was Laycock overdrive and a 3.7:1 axle ratio, allowing maximum speed to be achieved at a little over 4,000rpm in overdrive fourth.
- A white hard top was fitted, with holes drilled into the rear window to encourage the throughput of fresh air.
- Cambridge-based Pye was persuaded to provide two-way radio in order that the drivers could keep in touch with

the pits as they passed, so the hard top was fitted with an aerial.

- Quick-lift jacking points, as used at Le Mans with the TR3S 'Sabrina' cars, were fitted to the chassis.
- Front and rear bumpers were removed, as allowed by the regulations.
- A plastic 'bug deflector' was added to the bonnet.
- The centre-lock wire-spoke wheels carried Dunlop racing tyres.
- Padded covers were fitted over the headlamps to guard against breakage from flying debris.
- A leather strap was fitted to help hold down the front of bonnet.
- The front grille was much modified, not only by making provision for an engine oil cooler, but also by having some grille bars removed and others nipped flat to maximise air flow into the engine bay.
- To meet the regulations, all spares had to be carried on board – they included electrical items, a coil spring, plugs, an oil filter, dampers and even a steering box.

When used on its own, the banked Monza circuit officially measured 2.7 miles, which meant that the TR3A would pass the pits every 90 to 95 seconds. Clearly the lap scorers had to stay alert to tick off every passage in this relentless progress. As each of the steep stretches of banking had been designed for speeds of up to 200mph, little effort would be needed to keep the TR3A on line for hour after hour. If the steering geometry was set accordingly, with suitably strong self-centring action, it would, indeed, have been possible to let the TR3A find its own way round, without putting any side load on the tyres.

None of the members of the CUAC team had even sat in the car before they arrived at Monza, and they had had

Graham Denby started the record attempt...

nothing to do with the car's preparation and equipment. However, in one respect they did have an influence, as they refused to take Richardson's advice to run the car open rather than with a hard top. The car set off at 12 noon on 25 July.

'Each of us would do a two-hour stint,' recalled Whitaker, 'and because there were eight of us we got a lot of time off. In the end it began to feel quite slow. It was boring. We were keeping to the same path, lap after lap, at the same speed – the challenge was not to go to sleep. To stay awake, all I did was to count laps... I didn't mind driving at night, but the worst time was when we had to drive through a thunderstorm – not very pleasant. We soon found that the banking

...but a blown engine brought the run to a halt after three days.

According to regulations, all spares had to be carried on board.

was very rough indeed – before you reached the finishing straight there was an enormous bump just on the steering-neutral 100mph line!'

As the run developed, two things went wrong. First, the two-way radio only worked when the car raced past the pits during the first few hours, and then it failed completely. Second, the pistons of the SU carburettors became stuck before the end of each stint.

'That was a real shocker,' continued Whitaker. 'SUs aren't really made for steady throttle opening – the pistons should always be going up and down a bit – so at each stop Ken had to take the tops off them, put some Brasso around the pistons, and slot them back into place. It could all be done while refuelling took place.'

Whitaker confirmed that the car was driven more or less flat out all the time and in overdrive top it did 105–110mph. Everything went well until the end of the third day, when suddenly a connecting rod broke and a piston parted company with the crankshaft, blowing a big hole in the side of the block and bringing the car to a sudden and grinding halt. To meet one of the regulations for record attempts, the car had to cross the finish line and so it had to be pushed round the rest of the lap. After the event it was suggested that constant running in the 4,000–4,500rpm range had coincided with an engine vibration period, leading to the failure.

'At some time in the next 24 hours,' stated Whitaker, 'we had to do another lap to get another record! So we had to push-start the car and it staggered round for 2.7 miles at 25–30mph, after which it was pushed over the line again. We blew up the tyres as hard as they would go to reduce rolling resistance.'

Although everyone was disappointed that the 1,991cc engine had let go just before the three-day mark was reached, XHP 259 had set no fewer than eight new records in International Class E (for cars of 1,501cc to 2,000cc). The car even set a new four-day record because it was so far ahead of the old one after only three days! The precise distance covered was 6,850 miles (11,020km) and the new time/distance records were as follows:

2,000 miles	102.1mph
5,000 miles	102.5mph
5,000 kilometres	102.5mph
10,000 kilometres	102.6mph
One day	102.2mph
Two days	102.5mph
Three days	95.2mph
Four days	71.0mph

Standard-Triumph was pleased and the CUAC team was delighted, although there was an understandable sense of anti-climax afterwards. Curiously there was virtually no publicity as Britain's motoring press mostly ignored it, although a print-union strike at the time was a factor in stopping the news getting out.

The car was not used again in motorsport until May 1960, when the factory entered all four of its fleet of red TR3As in the Tulip rally. Using a 2.2-litre engine and converted to left-hand drive, XHP 259 was allocated to Annie Soisbault, who could not quite perform as well as Rob Slotemaker, Johnny Wallwork and Keith Ballisat in the sister cars, nor David Seigle-Morris in his own privately owned example, so she had to settle for second place in the Ladies' Prize, which the redoubtable Pat Moss won in a new Austin-Healey 3000.

For its last event, the French Alpine of June/July 1960, XHP 259 was given a 2.0-litre engine and Annie set out once more to beat Pat Moss, her major rival. After less than 24 hours, however, the TR3A lost a rear wheel and was stranded, out of reach of factory support. Annie did not drive again for the Triumph team.

Annie Soisbault (right) and Renée Wagner were second in the Ladies' category of the 1960 Tulip rally in XHP 259.

COMPETITION RECORD

1959 Tulip
Cyril Corbishley — 4th in class

1959 Monza record run
CUAC team — Eight records set

1960 Tulip
Annie Soisbault — 2nd in Ladies' Prize

1960 French Alpine
Annie Soisbault — Did not finish

CHAPTER 2:
TR2, TR3S AND TRS RACING CARS (1954–61)

Compared with rallying, the story of the side-screen TRs and their derivatives on the race track was remarkably different. This was a seven-year saga that started with near-standard TR2 road cars and ended with an Italian-produced prototype that was never raced.

The story starts at the Le Mans 24 Hours in June 1954 with the entry of a lone TR2 by Edgar Wadsworth, a Burnley-based businessman with a considerable sporting record. The entry was in Wadsworth's name because he had practised a reserve entry the previous year and therefore had priority for the 1954 race, but much of the race preparation took place on a very short timescale at County Motors of Carlisle, a Standard-Triumph dealership where racing driver Bobby Dickson was the senior director. Registered OKV 777 and painted British Racing Green, the car ran in near-standard mechanical specification and finished 15th overall – a remarkable start to Triumph's Le Mans career.

For 1955 things got more serious. Standard-Triumph decided to go to Le Mans with a fully-fledged team of three official works TR2s with consecutive registration numbers – PKV 374, PKV 375 and PKV 376. Compared with 1954, much more time was available to get the three new cars carefully prepared for the race: original build and preparation was carried out at Banner Lane in the spring of 1955 and

The reunion of ex-works TR2s at Brooklands: the two cars on the left competed at Le Mans, OKV 777 in 1954 and PKV 374 in 1955.

Three works TR2s ready to start the 1955 Le Mans 24 Hours – PKV 374, PKV 375 and PKV 376. As far as the organisers were concerned, PKV 374 was initially a 'reserve' entry but finally gained a starting slot, to be driven by Mortimer Morris-Goodall and Leslie Brooke. This particular car was fitted with prototype Girling front disc brakes and Alfin rear drums.

Car 29 was driven in the 1955 Le Mans 24 Hours by Ken Richardson/Bert Hadley and eventually finished 15th overall. Ken Richardson (back to the camera, close to the driver's door) is seen pointing out some detail to Lyndon Mills, who at the time was a Standard-Triumph sales executive. Note that the car was fitted with a standard driving seat.

then the three cars went to County Motors for final pre-event preparation.

Before the race only two start places were guaranteed, the third being a 'reserve', but in the end the third car did start. The cars were entered as prototypes and therefore could be fitted with disc brakes, two different systems – Girling front discs and Dunlop all-round discs – being tried. Both systems worked extremely well throughout the race, and the Girling installation, which was fitted to two of the cars, was eventually adopted on the TR3 for the 1957 model year.

Apart from their disc brakes, the specification of these

1955 Le Mans TR2s was identical to the 1954 Le Mans car in almost every detail. Even the 'Triumph' badges at the front were retained, almost certainly because of company policy! All three ran with a canvas tonneau cover above the passenger seat area and two extra Lucas driving lamps tucked inside the radiator grille recess, where they did nothing for aerodynamic efficiency or radiator cooling. As before, the three cars were painted British Racing Green, and for recognition purposes two of them had coloured surrounds to their front air intakes – one red, the other white – while the third was left in body colour.

Although the top speed of these works cars – 113mph according to official timings – was not quite as fast as the 118mph achieved by the 1954 entry, they were able to lap consistently more quickly and they could average nearly 90mph over a lap. All the same, the leading Jaguars and Mercedes-Benz cars were now hitting almost 180mph on the Mulsanne straight and were up to 40 seconds a lap faster than the TR2s, which they could therefore lap at least twice every hour!

The big contest for Triumph at Le Mans in 1955 was against three prototype MGA cars that were raced in advance of the appearance of the production version. Although these cars only had 1.5-litre engines, they benefited from special cross-flow cylinder heads (courtesy of Harry Weslake) and had ultra-light aluminium bodies.

Although the weather was dry throughout, the appalling accident in which a Mercedes-Benz car was launched into the crowd opposite the pits, killing more than 80 spectators, cast a pall over the whole event. The results, though, were important for Triumph: all three cars got to the finish, still running strongly at the end in 14th, 15th and 19th places, and the merits of their new-fangled disc brakes were confirmed. In the contest with MG one must judge that the honours were split fairly evenly: one of the MGAs beat the Triumph trio by finishing 12th, there was a second finisher in 17th place, and the third car crashed out in the early stages.

At this race it was interesting to see individuals among the works personnel who would emerge as stalwarts and bring so much to the continuity of the works efforts at Le Mans in subsequent years. For example, Ray Henderson, who went on to achieve so much with works Triumphs over the years, was much involved in the team of mechanics, and Les Makinson from the experimental department had the job of refuelling specialist, a task he would also carry out with the 'Sabrina' cars in later years.

Despite this strong outcome, however, there would be no more Triumph cars at Le Mans until 1959, and it is easy to see why. At a time when competing cars were becoming ultra-specialised, it was clear that the TR2s – or the TR3s that succeeded them – could never win anything when running in standard specification. In future Triumphs prepared for Le Mans would either need a lot more power or drastically different body styles, and in the meantime attention turned instead to the rallying scene.

But here is an oddity. Everyone from managing director Alick Dick to the humblest mechanic had witnessed the big gap between the TR2s and other cars racing in the 2-litre class, but the factory never considered developing the engine. Even though private tuners were already starting to extract much more power, and reliable power at that, from this engine, there was a deep-rooted objection at Banner Lane to any form of engine development and Ken Richardson's works cars always ran in standard condition. Indeed, there was a body of opinion at Banner Lane that the engines should never exceed 5,200rpm, and certain individuals continually harked back to an occasion when a crankshaft had failed at just over 5,000rpm. It was not until the early 1960s, when the works TR4 rally cars were developed, that power outputs rose to 130bhp and beyond, with a rev limit of 6,000rpm.

Even though the horrendous accident of 1955 had shocked the world and made high-profile manufacturers shy away from Le Mans for a time, most of them would return. The romance and magic of Le Mans had certainly gripped Standard-Triumph's management team and by 1956–57 Alick Dick, along with general manager Martin Tustin and technical boss Harry Webster, began to plan for a return on the basis that Triumph's next Le Mans car should still look like a production car even though its engine could be different. The car, and in particular a new engine for it, would be engineered in-house but could not immediately be given high priority as work on new production models (such as the Herald) and development of existing models (such as a six-cylinder engine for the Vanguard) would have to come first.

As Dick once commented about the new engine, which would be an ambitiously engineered twin-overhead-camshaft design, 'I wanted it to be able to get Triumph the team prize... and I wanted it also to be producible, even in quite small numbers, for a top-line version of the new TR...' This was a good story and senior staff always backed up the philosophy, but in the end the twin-cam design never came close to being adopted in a road car.

Webster's engineering team, led by David Eley and with most of the pencil work done by Dick Astbury, started work on the new twin-cam 2-litre engine, coded 20X (20 = 2 litres, X = experimental), during 1956 but it was not until 1957 that the new design even started test-bed running. Settling the basic layout was one thing, but deciding on important aspects such as valve timing and camshaft profiles was quite another: credit here went to Lewis Dawtrey's technical department, which worked alongside the mainstream engineering function although it was not involved in mainstream new-model development.

Every engineer in Coventry, of course, was already familiar with the magnificent achievements of the twin-overhead-camshaft Jaguar XK power unit, but now there was a new

contender in the city. The inspiration for the general layout of the new Triumph engine came from no further away than Widdrington Road, where Coventry-Climax's simple but effective FPF 1.5-litre racing unit was already cutting a swathe through the ranks of Formula 2 motor racing, and by 1959 it would be enlarged to 2.5-litres to become a World Championship-winning Formula 1 engine.

Like the FPF, the cylinder head layout of the new Triumph was simple and classic, with twin overhead camshafts and part-spherical combustion chambers, the valves being opposed to each other at 73 degrees. However, with an eye to making the engine, as Dick stated, 'producible, even in small numbers', all castings were designed to be extremely simple, there being a type of sandwich construction from top to bottom – head, water jacket, block, crankcase, sump and sump cover. The crankcase was in cast iron, the other castings in aluminium.

If peak power had been the only consideration, twin dual-choke Weber carburettors might have been chosen, but company politics dictated otherwise. At this time, in fact, Standard-Triumph itself had absolutely no experience with this twin-choke layout, and in fact no such carburettors had ever been seen inside the walls of Banner Lane. In place of Webers, therefore, Triumph instead specified for the 20X engine a pair of the special DU-coded twin-choke SU

The 'Sabrina' twin-cam engine was specially designed to run in Triumph works cars at Le Mans. With an eye to possible use as a low-production unit in later years, it was designed in a 'sandwich' manner with a cast-iron block, aluminium crankcase and aluminium cylinder head. As used in TR3S and TRS cars, two twin-choke SU carburettors were employed.

The Sabrina 2-litre twin-cam engine fitted easily in the engine bay of TR3S and TRS cars, both of which had a wheelbase 6in longer than that of the TR3A road car. In this form the engine produced a reliable 150bhp.

Flying in formation! The three TR3S cars in line astern during the 1959 Le Mans 24 Hours, with XHP 939 (Ninian Sanderson/Claude Dubois) ahead of XHP 938 (Peter Jopp/Dickie Stoop and XHP 940 (Peter Bolton/Mike Rothschild).

(199kg). In particular it was 3.75in longer, which explains why the two types of Triumph racers that used this engine – TR3S in 1959, TRS in 1960 and 1961 – both shared a long-wheelbase chassis. This chassis was 6in longer than that of the production TR3A, with the engine bay lengthened by that amount to give what the engineers thought to be adequate installation space. Subsequent experience, incidentally, showed that it would have been possible to retain the existing TR3/TR4 wheelbase, as standard TR4 road cars were run experimentally with the Sabrina engine neatly installed.

Three new cars called TR3S were built in time for the 1959 Le Mans race. Occasionally, in later years, wild rumours circulated among conspiracy theorists to suggest that there were four cars, but there is absolutely no evidence of this in company records or documents, nor in terms of hardware.

Although the TR3S cars looked almost exactly like the existing TR3A, they used hybrid bodyshells in which the main 'core' was based on a steel TR3A shell – apparently aluminium was never considered – but with outer skin panels and certain other features in glass-fibre. Once again Standard-Triumph's inexperience in certain areas of engineering showed up, as the excessive thickness of the glass-fibre panelling made it too heavy. The long-wheelbase chassis was also much stiffened, a strategy that was later admitted to have been overkill for the smooth track at Le Mans.

As fitted to the TR3S cars, the new Sabrina engine was

carburettors (as also used on the original 1.5-litre Coventry-Climax FPF), which were only manufactured to special order and never went into series production.

Industry politics? This was always complicated. It is worth recalling that Triumph was already using conventional SUs on its best-selling TR3 and TR3A road cars, in spite of the fact that SU was owned by a rival, BMC, that might one day look for an excuse to make these carburettors unavailable or prohibitively costly. It was thought to be a good thing politically to continue to use such instruments and thereby let SU know that Triumph believed in the company...

Drive to the twin overhead camshafts was by chain, and the gear wheels and adjustment mechanisms at the front of the engine were covered with two prominent castings. There were those who suggested that these castings looked like the outline of a well-developed female, which is why Norma Sykes, the blonde 1950s TV hostess employed by the diminutive comedian Arthur Askey, has a lot to answer for. Known as 'Sabrina' in show business, her only obvious asset was a startling figure with a particularly opulent bust... well, you have probably worked it out. The code '20X' was soon forgotten and 'Sabrina' took over – the word even appears in many Standard-Triumph documents of the period!

The Sabrina engine was significantly larger than the existing TR3 wet-liner engine and weighed a solid 438lb

The build-up to Le Mans in 1961 and the four TRS cars arrive at the team hotel – the Hôtel de France at La Chartre-sur-le-Loir. At the end of the decade John Wyer's Ford GT40s, twice winners at Le Mans, would also be based here.

rated conservatively at 150bhp. The non-standard rear axle was supplied by Salisbury and was very closely related to the brand-new axle used in the Daimler SP250 sports car. There were Girling disc brakes on all four wheels.

Although the new cars were much faster than the 1955 models – lap speeds tumbled by approximately 20sec to 4m 46s – they could have been even faster if they had been more aerodynamically shaped and not so heavy. Figures later published by the Le Mans organisers showed that the only prototypes heavier than the 2,143lb (972kg) of the TR3S cars were 3-litre V12 Ferraris and an Aston Martin!

One major mistake was also made – these cars were raced with engine cooling fans fitted. This made no sense in a motor race, of course, because the speeds involved provided plenty of cooling air to the engines in any case. Ken Richardson, who had much more motor racing experience than any of his bosses, fought tooth and nail against it, but top management overruled him. Predictably, on two cars the fan blades eventually came into contact with the radiators, puncturing them and causing instant retirement due to loss of coolant, after 35 laps for one car and 115 for the other, and as a result the third car lost time because it had to be called in for the blades to be removed. That car, driven staunchly by Peter Jopp and Dickie Stoop, completed 22 of the 24 hours and reached seventh place before its engine oil pump drive failed. As Richardson later explained, the fan-blade problems

on these occurred because the engine-mounting rubbers softened during the race, allowing the engines to move forward under braking.

The TR3S cars never raced again, nor appeared again in public in that form. Their TR3A-style bodies were taken off and destroyed according to the official record, although we now know that the body from XHP 939 has survived. However, the rolling chassis of the three TR3S cars, together with one further chassis, went on to form the basis of the rather different 1960 racing cars. The series of four new racing cars built up for 1960 were called TRS – not, as sometimes stated, 'TR4S' – and they used developed versions of the long-wheelbase TR3S chassis with a wider front track and rack-and-pinion steering.

The novelty this time was that the TRS cars were clothed in a glass-fibre version of the body style of the still secret 'Zoom' project road car, which was then thought likely to become the new TR4 in 1961. It is said that the works made these body panels by laying up glass-fibre matting over one of the two Zoom prototypes, thus ensuring the same style. At this stage, the TRSs did not have cooling vents in the front wings – these were adopted in 1961.

The origins of the Zoom project lay in the hiring of the Italian stylist Giovanni Michelotti as a consultant in 1957, four years after the side-screen TR first appeared. In the next three years Michelotti produced a number of new styling

In 1960 three TRS cars – 926 HP, 927 HP and 928 HP – competed at Le Mans and all of them finished, although with engines slightly afflicted by development problems towards the end. Here they are lined up ready to start the race, with mechanic Roger Sykes at the wheel of 928 HP as it is backed into place, and engine guru Ted Silver (white overalls) holding on to the screen.

TRS OR TR4S? CREATING A FALSEHOOD

In recent years people who were never close to the factory race team have attempted to rename the TRS as the TR4S. This is quite incorrect and appears to have been based on the publication of a completely spurious and ethereal results listing on the internet. It is appropriate to make the following observations:

- I joined Standard-Triumph before the 1961 Le Mans 24 Hours was run and was based, as an engineer, in the same department where the TRS cars were maintained. I can confirm that at no time did the mythical 'TR4S' title ever surface.
- When the 1960–61 Le Mans cars were in use, they were always known as TRS – both in private and in public.
- Authoritative British magazine reports from those years – *Autocar*, *Motor* and *Autosport* in particular – always reported and recorded them as TRS, which reflected the information put out by the factory, and by the Le Mans race organisers.
- The so-called 'TR4S' title never appeared at the time because the TR4 did not exist when these racing cars were in use in 1960 and 1961. The TR4 appeared in September 1961, after the career of the Le Mans cars had ended.
- The official Le Mans results sheets never stated 'TR4S' – in fact they usually just quoted 'Triumph'.

---

themes and suggestions for a replacement for the TR2/TR3/TR3A range, all of them based on evolutionary versions of the existing chassis frame.

Registered 926 HP, 927 HP, 928 HP and 929 HP, these four cars were taken to Le Mans in 1960 and 1961, and in both years three of them took part in the race. Unfortunately they were even heavier, by 155lb (70kg), than the TR3Ss and their aerodynamic performance was even worse, as confirmed by lap times at Le Mans 10 seconds below those of the previous year. Company cynics nicknamed them as 'flying rectangles' or 'Coventry-registered barn doors'.

Yet they were reliable and all three finished the 1960 race, although they were not classified in the results because they did not cover sufficient distance owing to a problem that caused power loss in their engines. A late change to engine specification, which Ken Richardson claimed not to have been told about, meant that the valve seats of the race engines had reduced Brinell hardness, eventually causing valve 'sinkage' and associated loss of timing. The TRSs were in a strongly contested class but nevertheless the only car to beat them was a highly developed 1.8-litre MGA Twin-Cam; without the valve-seat problems, they would surely have triumphed with a 1–2–3 finish.

Finally this programme all came good after a big post-mortem of the 1960 event. Long and positively leisurely rebuilds took place in the works team's new home in Capmartin Road, colloquially known as the Radford factory, and the same four cars went to Le Mans in 1961 – and again the three that took part all circulated reliably for the full 24 hours. By now the engines were delivering 155–160bhp, lap times were at least eight seconds better than those of the year before (although still no better than those of the TR3Ss of 1959), and pit work was slick. The result was that the fastest of the TRSs, driven by Keith Ballisat and Peter Bolton, averaged 98.91mph and covered 2,373.34 miles in the 24 hours.

At 4.00pm on the Sunday, in a flourish of showmanship, Ken Richardson made sure that the three cars crossed the finishing line together in formation so that the appropriate publicity pictures could be taken. Alick Dick's dream of winning the Team Prize in the world's most famous sports car race had finally been realised. The TRSs had made their point by finishing 9th, 11th and 15th overall, and in their class respectively third, fourth and fifth behind two extremely special Porsches. Harry Mundy of *Autocar* later wrote: 'The only team to finish the race intact was Triumph – an achievement indeed, and some recompense for last year's disappointment.'

As related in the previous chapter, the competitions department was closed after the 1961 Le Mans race but would reopen the following year. However, there was no more Le Mans activity until 1964, when the first of the highly developed Spitfire '70X' models appeared.

This car, 929 HP, was the spare for Le Mans in 1960 but did get to race the following year, Marcel Becquart and Mike Rothschild finishing 15th overall.

For years there was controversy over the use of wire-spoke or steel disc wheels on works TR2, TR3s and TR3As. Fans of wire wheels pointed out the speed with which new wheels could be fitted, but critics insisted that disc wheels were stronger and more robust. The result was that both types were used during a car's works career, though not at the same time...

OKV 777

FIRST REGISTERED	21 MAY 1954
ENGINE SIZE	1,991cc
MODEL TYPE	TR2

OKV 777 had a full tonneau to give some improvement to cockpit aerodynamics, a cowled 'single-seater' windscreen ahead of the driver, and a very large fuel filler neck on the tail.

The 1954 Le Mans Car, OKV 777, shows details for which Ken Richardson's team would be noted. They include padded covers over the headlamps for daylight running, extra leather holding-down straps for the bonnet and a cowled surround for the rear-view mirror. The entire bodyshell was in standard pressed steel and the engine was also standard, although carefully prepared.

Although OKV 777 was not a fully supported works car, it was certainly not a fully private effort either – and I propose to treat it as the first of the works racers.

Painted British Racing Green, this car had slightly complicated beginnings. Carrying commission number TS1730, it was a very early TR2, built in Canley in May 1954, just a month or so before the Le Mans 24 Hours. Immediately after manufacture it appears to have been sold to County Motors of Carlisle and, as related in my introduction to this chapter (see page 59), pre-race preparation was undertaken there in the limited time available before its entry at Le Mans by Edgar Wadsworth.

Although OKV 777 was not a works car, its specification was essentially the same as that of the factory-prepared TR2 that had taken part in the Mille Miglia, six weeks before Le Mans. Although preparation was meticulous, the engine was virtually standard. The steel bodywork was standard except for the removal of the front and rear bumpers, the addition of a simple wrap-around Perspex screen ahead of the driver and the use of two leather straps to help secure the bonnet.

To aid aerodynamic performance, a tonneau cover was fitted, the front badge was removed, and there was a neat fairing over the rear-view mirror. Wire-spoke wheels, overdrive and Alfin brake drums were fitted, Dunlop racing tyres were specified, and the car was equipped with two Lucas long-distance driving lamps.

Although everyone hoped that this near-standard car would perform with honour, no one expected it to beat every other 2-litre car in the race – and there were many, including some people in the engine test shops at Banner Lane, who doubted whether the engine could survive for 24 hours. The budget was strictly limited, and few of the pit crew – none of whom were from the factory – had much experience of long-distance events.

The result, however, was a complete triumph. Maybe the stormy weather conditions helped a little by making ambient temperatures unusually cool, yet this gallant car survived without noticeable drama. Using the simplest possible tactic – driving flat out! – the drivers kept going, rising to 26th place after 12 hours, 17th place after 18 hours, and 15th place by the end of the race. Overall fuel consumption was an amazing 34.68mpg.

Not that this was achieved totally without drama, for towards the end the tired transmission began to suffer from a slipping clutch, which reduced the top speed to no more than 100mph. As explained in *The Motor*, there was real panic at the close: 'The privately entered TR2... nearly stopped the hearts of the pit staff by coming to rest on the Mulsanne straight on the very last lap. The driver, however, had rightly calculated that if he went on he would have, under regulations, to do an extra lap, so he took a minute or two's respite to have a smoke before pressing the starter button and

continuing on his way... There can be no doubt that the overall performance of this, the cheapest car in the race, caused a most favourable impression...'

As no one, especially Wadsworth, expected the TR2 to win its class, there was no disappointment when the car was outpaced in the 2-litre category by three works Bristol 450 coupés and a Bristol-engined Frazer Nash. But it is certainly worth noting that the Bristols were out-and-out racing cars, their chassis having evolved from those of the ERA G-type single-seater of the early 1950s, while the Frazer Nash was a hand-built machine designed for high performance.

It was a great start for what would become a well-known individual car, although on the drive home – no transporters or trailers in those days – OKV 777 was badly damaged in a road accident in Lichfield and had to be repaired in Coventry before resuming its career.

The identity of Wadsworth's co-driver at Le Mans remains an enduring mystery. According to the entry list and Triumph's post-event advertising, OKV 777 was co-driven by Bobby Dickson. However, the race report in *Motor Sport* magazine named the co-driver as John Brown, but he later wrote to the magazine on matters of team preparation and claimed to be only 'one of the pit staff'. However, Wadsworth's son John, himself a much respected rally driver, insisted that it was Brown, a good friend of his father, who drove the car because on the day Dickson was 'not able to take part', whatever that implies. Cyril Dean of Carlisle, on the other hand, an apprentice at County Motors at the time, is sure that it was Dickson who drove the car. We will probably never know the answer.

After its rebuild the car was sent to Northern Ireland in September for the Tourist Trophy at Dundrod, where public roads were closed for a harum-scarum sports car race that counted towards the World Championship. OKV 777 was one of six TR2s entered and this time the factory supported it more overtly, with works boss Ken Richardson joining Bobby Dickson for driving duties. One of the other TR2s, incidentally, was Leslie Brooke's Coventry-registered example that had already taken part, without success, in the Mille Miglia and the French Alpine rally.

The six TR2s were organised into two team entries of three cars each and all of them finished strongly, undamaged and with great credibility, winning both Team Prize awards! In their Series Production Sports category they were beaten only by two specialised machines – a Frazer-Nash and a Porsche – and secured the next five places in the class. The fastest of the TR2s, the private entry driven by Brian McCaldin and Charles Eyre-Maunsell, took 19th place overall with a race average of 70.51mph, a very respectable pace for a 2-litre sports car although well down on the 86.08mph achieved by the winning Ferrari of Mike Hawthorn and Maurice Trintignant. OKV 777 took 23rd place at 69.63mph.

Autosport's celebrated technical editor, John Bolster, gave this verdict: 'Speaking of reliability, the performance of the TR2 Triumphs was excellent. That six of these moderately priced cars started, and that every one of them finished at a respectable average speed is beyond all praise: never has a team prize been so well deserved...'

This was the end of the short works-supported career of OKV 777, which reverted to Bobby Dickson's hands. Later in its life TR enthusiast Geoff Stamper of Penrith restored it to magnificent as-new condition and it survives to this day.

COMPETITION RECORD	
1954 Le Mans	
Edgar Wadsworth/Bobby Dickson[1]	15th overall
1954 Tourist Trophy	
Ken Richardson/Bobby Dickson	23rd overall
[1] As described in the text, John Brown may have been the driver.	

PKV 374

FIRST REGISTERED	17 MAY 1955
ENGINE SIZE	1,991cc
MODEL TYPE	TR2

This was one of three new works TR2s prepared at Banner Lane for Le Mans in 1955. Compared with 1954, much more time was available for careful preparation of the cars as they were originally built quite early in the spring of 1955.

Whereas the other two cars, PKV 375 and PKV 376, both covered 2,026 miles in the 24 hours – 234 miles more than the privately entered TR2 of 1954 – PKV 374, despite having been the fastest of the three for the first quarter of the race, was only able to complete 1,793 miles – for reasons that will be explained. Overall this was an extremely creditable performance set by what were certainly the most 'standard' prototypes in the race, and was due to a combination of several positive factors.

First, the 1955 race was held mainly in dry weather, so speeds were higher than in the previous year. Second, the use of what became known as the 'Le Mans' (or 'high-port') cylinder head and larger SU H6 carburettors gave more power, the factory claiming a test-bed output of 94bhp. Third, there was all-round determination to make these machines go as fast as possible and pit work was slicker, helped by the use of long-range, 22-gallon aluminium petrol tanks that extended the range of the cars considerably and reduced the number of time-consuming pit stops. Fourth, the

In this pre-start shot of Le Mans in 1955, with PKV 374 in the foreground, team rally driver Maurice Gatsonides – the tall figure wearing sunglasses – is visible in the centre, next to Ken Richardson's car.

However the four-disc Dunlop system, which was good enough for the Jaguar D-types that were prepared just a few miles away, would provide a telling comparison. Although cost was not a major consideration in these Le Mans cars, it was also significant that Girling was already a major supplier to Standard-Triumph, whereas the braking division of Dunlop was not. Although Triumph never adopted the four-disc Dunlop set-up, it would soon find a use at Jaguar for the XK150 and 3.4-litre saloons, and subsequently on several other high-performance cars as well.

As before, the three cars were painted British Racing Green, but for recognition purposes two had the surround to the front air intake painted in a different colour – white in the case of PKV 374. The drivers of PKV 374 were Leslie Brooke, scrap-metal dealer from Coventry, and Mortimer 'Mort' Morris-Goodall, who had just completed a year as team manager of the Austin-Healey racing team.

Early in this long race, the TR2s held station well, as planned, and did not even attempt to get on terms with the flying 140bhp 2-litre Bristols and Frazer Nashes that had beaten the TR2 in 1954. Then the Mercedes-Benz crash tragedy occurred and it must have been difficult to concentrate thereafter. Perhaps this was why Leslie Brooke put PKV 374 off the road at Tertre Rouge, at the beginning of the Mulsanne straight, where it became beached in the sand bank on the outside of the curve, undamaged but stuck.

In trying the classic first/reverse/first/reverse tactic of trying to get the TR2 out of trouble, Brooke only managed to dig the car deeper into the sand – and got the gearbox stuck in reverse too! To solve this he had to remove the special quick-release gearbox tunnel cover and loosen the extension, only to lose several bolts irretrievably in the sand! Furious but indomitable, Brook started digging – he conveniently 'found' a shovel close by – and it took him at least 90 minutes before he had shifted enough sand to get the TR2 out on the road again. There was no damage to the car, but it was a massive setback for the team itself. Having got back to the pits, Les handed over to his co-driver 'Mort' Morris-Goodall (telling him about the missing gearbox bolts!), then immediately drank pints of cooling water – straight out of a can usually used for topping up radiators.

After the race the car was purchased by King Hussein of Jordan and always retained its special features.

cars were fitted with disc brakes, which proved to be much more durable than drums had ever been.

As the factory wanted to learn as much as possible from this foray, two entirely different disc-brake installations were used, and both worked extremely well throughout the race. PKV 374, like PKV 375, was fitted with Girling front disc brakes and 11in Alfin rear drums, while PKV 376 was fitted with Dunlop discs on all four wheels. Having Girling discs on two of the three cars was almost certainly because Triumph's engineers were already homing in on the use of a Girling installation for future road cars, and it would eventually be adopted for the TR3 introduced for the 1957 model year.

Oh dear! Early in the 1955 Le Mans race Leslie Brooke put PKV 374 off the road into a sandbank. He is about to start the long job of digging it clear – which he managed eventually.

COMPETITION RECORD
1955 Le Mans
Mortimer Morris-Goodall/Leslie Brooke 19th overall

PKV 375

FIRST REGISTERED	17 MAY 1955
ENGINE SIZE	1,991cc
MODEL TYPE	TR2

The second of the three cars entered for the 1955 Le Mans 24 Hours was mechanically identical to PKV 374, as described above, and was therefore fitted with the Girling disc/drum installation. Its drivers were team manager Ken Richardson and veteran British racer Bert Hadley, who had first come to prominence in the twin-cam Austin 750 single-seaters of the late 1930s. The car's nose was painted with a red surround to the front grille aperture.

This car had what might be described as a 'routine' 24 hours, finishing 15th with a race average of 84.7mph. Although the drivers were exhausted after their ordeal, the car seemed well capable of carrying on for a long time and visually it was unscathed except for the loss of one of the extra driving lamps.

After the event the car was brought back to Banner Lane, where the behaviour – and the potential – of the Girling disc/drum braking system was carefully analysed. The 1957-model TR3 road car, as announced in October 1956, used a system directly evolved from this layout, which means that it must have been approved for manufacture before the end of

1955, less than six months after the Le Mans race itself. Like PKV 374, this car was not used again by the works and so now moves gracefully out of our story.

COMPETITION RECORD
1955 Le Mans
Ken Richardson/Bert Hadley   15th overall

Three works TR2s started the Le Mans 24 Hours in 1955, all of them in standard form except for their disc brake installations. All three cars finished, looking fresher than some of their drivers. From right, the first four drivers in the line-up are Ken Richardson, Bert Hadley, Leslie Brooke and Mortimer Morris-Goodall. Bobby Dickson and Ninian Sanderson are standing behind the furthest car in the line-up.

PKV 376

FIRST REGISTERED	17 MAY 1955
ENGINE SIZE	1,991cc
MODEL TYPE	TR2

The story of PKV 376 at the Le Mans 24 Hours is best described as 'PKV 375... ditto... ditto...', for this car looked like and performed like its sister, and had the same sort of essentially untroubled run. It finished one position ahead of its team-mate, in 14th place, and completed just 160 metres more! Bobby Dickson and Ninian Sanderson shared the driving duties.

Technically, this car was identical to the two other 'PKV' cars of 1955, except that it was fitted with Dunlop disc brakes at front and rear. The braking system was made even more efficient by the fitment of a vacuum brake servo, which gained its vacuum by being plugged in to the inlet manifold of the engine.

Three months after Le Mans, this car was a lone works entry for the Tourist Trophy, which, as in 1954, was held on the Dundrod circuit north-west of Belfast on a triangle of narrow, bumpy and inherently perilous public roads closed for the occasion. In 1955 the race was titled the Golden Jubilee Tourist Trophy, to mark the founding of the event on the Isle of Man. This was a serious motor race by any standards, for it was part of the World Sports Car Championship and attracted teams from Aston Martin, Ferrari, Jaguar, Maserati and Mercedes-Benz. But as far as Triumph was concerned the stiff competition was from the Le Mans MGAs, which would be running with the new-fangled twin-cam engines that would eventually reach production in the MGA Twin Cam of 1958.

PKV 376 was driven by Ken Richardson and Bobby Dickson, and was backed by two privately entered TR2s from Northern Ireland. In a race that was marred by several very serious accidents on the narrow roads, the works car took 22nd place overall, immediately behind the privately entered TR2 of Wilbert Todd and Ian Titterington. These two TR2s were also second and third in the 2-litre class, which was won by an out-and-out sports-racing Maserati.

COMPETITION RECORD
1955 Le Mans
Bobby Dickson/Ninian Sanderson
14th overall
1955 Tourist Trophy
Bobby Dickson/
Ken Richardson
22nd overall

XHP 938

In the 1959 Le Mans 24 Hours the TR3S registered XHP 938, driven by Peter Jopp and Dickie Stoop, sadly retired from seventh place overall only two hours from the finish.

For 1959 the works team produced three new TR3S race cars to compete at Le Mans. These were TR3A lookalikes, except that they had a 6in-longer wheelbase, many glass-fibre panels and were powered by the new twin-overhead-camshaft 'Sabrina' engine. They were numbered XHP 938, XHP 939 and XHP 940.

FIRST REGISTERED	8 APRIL 1959
ENGINE SIZE	1,985cc
MODEL TYPE	TR3S Le Mans car

As described in the introduction to this chapter, Triumph built three Sabrina-engined TR3S racing cars in 1958/59 and all three of them started the Le Mans 24 Hours in 1959. Technically and visually, all three cars were identical and the objective for them was to put in a solid performance in their 2.0-litre class. Managing director Alick Dick hoped that they would all survive 24 hours of flat-out motoring and that Triumph would win the prestigious Team Prize.

For Triumph's return to Le Mans, company policy was that the cars should look as much like production TR3As as possible. Even from the pure side view, it was difficult to pick out the lengthened wheelbase, with all six extra inches allocated to a longer engine compartment, the better to give space for the Sabrina engine. At the front end the body shape and TR3A grille looked standard, but an extra grilled aperture below the normal full-width lattice provided air to an engine oil cooler mounted up front. There were no front bumpers, while two sturdy Lucas driving lamps added to the lighting arrangements. A full-width plastic windscreen was fitted, not because it helped aerodynamic performance but because race regulations required it. Intakes behind the door openings channelled air to the outboard rear disc brakes, but otherwise the rear end looked visually the same as that of a

TR3A. The ensemble was topped off with the use of normal 60-spoke centre-lock wire wheels.

As described in my introduction to this chapter, two of the three TR3Ss were eliminated from the race when their fan blades punctured their water radiators, but this car, XHP 938, lasted for many more hours. Driven by Peter Jopp and Dickie Stoop, it was called in for the fan blades to be removed as soon as the reason for the other failures became apparent, and then went on to circulate quickly and without apparent effort for some considerable time.

When being driven by Jopp, XHP 938's fastest race lap was 4m 46.9s (104.95mph), which was 16 seconds quicker than the very special 'works-blessed' MGA that was racing against it in the same capacity class. Unhappily, after 22 reliable hours of motoring that saw the car rise to a sturdy seventh place overall, the engine oil pump failed, causing instant bearing failure. If only the car had survived the next two hours, it would easily have won its capacity class, and the only cars to beat it overall would have been the two race-winning Aston Martin DBR1s and four 3-litre Ferraris. If only...

COMPETITION RECORD	
1959 Le Mans 24 Hours	
Peter Jopp/Richard ('Dickie') Stoop	Did not finish

The TR3S of 1959, and the TRS cars that evolved in 1960 and 1961, had a chassis with the wheelbase lengthened by 6in. The rear axle was different from that of the TR3A road cars, being based on the wider-track Daimler SP250 type.

XHP 939

FIRST REGISTERED	1 JUNE 1959
ENGINE SIZE	1,985cc
MODEL TYPE	TR3S Le Mans car

In all respects except for its competition number, XHP 939 (no 25) was identical to XHP 938 (no 27). Driven by Ninian Sanderson and Claude Dubois, it also lapped at almost the same rate and survived until lap 114, when, after more than nine hours of running at an average of up to 100mph, it became the second of the TR3S cars to suffer from its engine-cooling fan puncturing the water radiator.

In a long, complicated but well-documented process, the bodyshell of this car escaped the fate of its team-mates and was not broken up, and somehow or other it was sold off. At this point, although my policy in this book is to conclude my car-by-car descriptions when their works careers ceased, with XHP 939 I am going to make an exception. This bodyshell was eventually used as part of a privately assembled long-wheelbase TR3A, complete with conventional wet-liner engine and running gear, and many years later was considered ripe for restoration as a real TR3S. At this point it was delivered to a restorer in the West Midlands, and there it languished.

Years later the Commission Plate, which was recorded as X629 in the Standard-Triumph Experimental Register, seems to have been sold off, but not by the accredited owner of XHP 939. In due course a completely new look-alike of the car took shape, carrying that commission plate and the registration number XHP 939, although naturally it did not have a twin-cam Sabrina engine and did not appear to include a single component from the original car. And there I will stop as this is as far as I am able to go in explaining what became a long-drawn-out and rather unseemly dispute…

Seen with Ninian Sanderson at the wheel, XHP 939 had to retire from the 1959 Le Mans 24 Hours, but lived on in later years, latterly with a mass-production 'wet-liner' engine.

COMPETITION RECORD	
1959 Le Mans 24 Hours	
Ninian Sanderson/Claude Dubois	Did not finish

XHP 940

FIRST REGISTERED	8 APRIL 1959
ENGINE SIZE	1,985cc
MODEL TYPE	TR3S Le Mans car

Looking very smart in the early stages of the 1959 Le Mans 24 Hours, XHP 940, with Peter Bolton at the wheel, looks exactly like a TR3A – yet the wheelbase was 6in longer with the 'stretch' all ahead of the doors.

This TR3S, driven by Peter Bolton and American Mike Rothschild, was the first of the three cars to retire from the 1959 Le Mans 24 Hours, for it had only completed 35 laps in less than three hours when a fan blade broke off, punctured the water radiator and caused almost instant disaster to the engine.

Both drivers had had one session each, but by 8.00pm on the first day their Le Mans weekend was over.

COMPETITION RECORD	
1959 Le Mans 24 Hours	
Peter Bolton/Mike Rothschild	Did not finish

926 HP

FIRST REGISTERED	31 MARCH 1960
ENGINE SIZE	1,985cc
MODEL TYPE	TRS Le Mans car

The boot of the TRS race car of 1960–61 housed a large fuel tank and the spare wheel, with a heavy 'bottle' jack for emergency use if a wheel change was needed out on the circuit. As is clear from this photograph, most of the body panels were produced in glass-fibre.

The four new TRS race cars used the rolling chassis of the 1959 TR3S race cars but with brand-new bodies constructed principally from glass-fibre and inspired by the 'Zoom' prototype. Four-wheel disc brakes were standard on this car. The location of the photograph is in the front parking area at the Allesley Service Department, on the outskirts of Coventry.

Following the 1959 Le Mans 24 Hour race, the three TR3S cars were dismantled and never reassembled again as complete twin-cam machines. Instead, and in good time for the 1960 Le Mans 24 Hours, four new Sabrina-engined racing cars, titled TRS, were built instead, all with right-hand drive.

The fascia/instrument panel of the TRS of 1960–61 was simple and starkly equipped. The rev counter was ahead of the driver's eyes and did not display a red line. Those were the days when safety belts were not fitted, and when it was fashionable to use a wood-rim steering wheel. The windscreen is yet to be fitted to this car.

Three of the four TRS cars were created by modifying and updating the rolling chassis of the dismantled TR3Ss, and the fourth was put together out of a set of spare components from 1959. These chassis were clothed in new-style bodyshells made partly of glass-fibre. To many, the finished cars looked rather 'unrace-like', as indeed they were because they were basically the same shape as the two brand-new 'Zoom' road car prototypes that had arrived for assessment and development at Banner Lane in 1959.

As 926 HP was the first of the new-shape TRS cars to be completed, in March 1960, it was also the first to shown to the press, and photographed. In that form, it had chrome-plated windscreen surrounds (the screens were of the minimum height allowable by the regulations), and there was no air scoop ahead of the base of the screen. Every cynic looked into the engine bay, and every cynic confirmed that engine-cooling fans were not being used…

However, by the time the cars had been further developed, and made ready for the race, a number of changes and updates had been applied. Extra stone guards had been moulded on to the glass-fibre rear wings behind the line of the rear wheels, leather holding-down straps had been applied to double-secure the bonnet panel, an air scoop had been added to the panel immediately ahead of the windscreen, and the screen pillars had been rendered matt black.

Keith Ballisat and Marcel Becquart, neither of whom had raced the TR3S cars in 1959, shared 926 HP on this occasion and must surely have been disappointed to find that it was both heavier and demonstrably slower around the French circuit that everyone had hoped. Reliability, however, no longer seemed to be an issue, for this car, and its two sister models, settled down to lap consistently, often running very close together. As *Autocar* noted in its race report, describing the situation eight hours into the race: 'Also extremely steady up to this stage were the three Triumphs, running like a train in 16th, 17th and 18th positions.'

Unhappily, as the race progressed, the engines fitted to all three TRSs began to suffer from a gradual loss of power, which was originally thought to because of stretched valves, but was later found to be due to valve-seat sinkage. The cumulative effect, however, was that valve clearances were lost and the engines began to suffer.

This TRS actually finished the 24 hours in 15th place but could not be classified in the results because it had not reached the minimum race distance required by the regulations. In its class the only car to finish ahead of it, narrowly, was the works-supported MGA Twin-Cam, which was running with a very non-standard 1,762cc power unit.

For the 1961 Le Mans race the same quartet of TRSs was stripped out, rebuilt and modernised to a certain degree. After a great deal of modification and test bed work, the valve and valve-seat problems of the Sabrina engines were solved. The cars themselves now had hot air outlet vents in the front wings, of similar appearance, it seems, to those that featured on one of the Zoom prototypes. All in all the cars seemed to be extremely well prepared for their second foray to France.

Ballisat shared the driving of 926 HP with Peter Bolton on this occasion and they enjoyed a faultless run to finish a magnificent ninth overall. The car covered 2,373.324 miles in the 24 hours, averaging 98.91mph, and was timed at more than 130mph on the Mulsanne straight.

All the effort was worth it: in finishing ninth, 11th and 15th the three TRS entries finally achieved Alick Dick's aim of winning the Manufacturers' Team Prize. That done, the cars were then retired from works motor racing and finally sold off through Triumph's North American import organisation – and all have survived to this day.

There was one happy little postscript for 926 HP following the race. After its return to Coventry for a clean-up and checkover, it was loaned to *Autocar*'s Midlands editor, Ted Eves, for a

Le Mans, 1960: 926 HP in the hands of Keith Ballisat and Marcel Becquart battling with the works Austin-Healey 3000 through the Dunlop Curve.

COMPETITION RECORD	
1960 Le Mans 24 Hours	
Keith Ballisat/Marcel Becquart	15th overall
1961 Le Mans 24 Hours	
Keith Ballisat/Peter Bolton	9th overall

90-minute session on public highways in Warwickshire. Although performance figures were not taken, Eves noted in the 14 July 1961 issue just how noisy this car seemed to be amid everyday traffic: '...at 3,500rpm, torque and noise come in together with embarrassing éclat. Although not recommended, it was quite possible to dawdle at 2,800rpm in top...'

A standing-start sprint to the quarter-mile mark was recorded in 16.4 seconds. Using the gearing that had been fitted for Le Mans and with a recommended engine rev limit of 6,500rpm, 76mph was available in second gear. When leaving a 30mph speed limit, stated Eves, the car just needed, 'a change up into third, and 100 was reached in 17 seconds from the derestriction sign'. Not for nothing was this reminiscence headlined 'No hollow Triumph'.

927 HP

FIRST REGISTERED	31 MARCH 1960
ENGINE SIZE	1,985cc
MODEL TYPE	TRS Le Mans car

Technically identical to 926 HP, this brand-new car was made ready for the 1960 Le Mans 24 Hour race, where Peter Bolton and Ninian Sanderson drove it. Like the other TRS racing cars, it circulated steadily throughout the 24 hours, but suffered badly from the valve problems already noted and finished 59 miles behind the Ballisat/Becquart car. Like its sister cars, therefore, it was not officially classified even though it ended up in 19th position.

For 1961 this car received the same improvements as its stable

Rob Slotemaker (scratching his head) and Les Leston (nursing a back injury) post-race with their 11th-placed TRS, reflecting on just how gruelling the 1961 Le Mans 24 Hours had been.

A routine pit stop for Rob Slotemaker at Le Mans in 1961, his TRS on the way to 11th place overall.

mates – a much-developed engine, slightly more power than before, and outlet vents in the sides of the front wings – and on this occasion it was driven by Les Leston and Rob Slotemaker.

According to Triumph's PR information service, the unfortunate Leston apparently aggravated a leg ligament injury when running across the track to the start during the traditional 'sprint/jump-in/fire-up' getaway. In fact he was already having trouble with injury as film shows him getting in and out of the car, before the start, with some difficulty! But Les was not about to let this stop him enjoying a works drive and he shared the driving with Slotemaker throughout.

In almost every respect 927 HP had a routine day-and-night run, except that at an early stage the engine suddenly faltered,

and the car was stranded at the pits for four laps until it was discovered that the engine ignition coil had failed. A change to the spare coil, which was fortunately mounted alongside the active one, solved the problem. After that single hold-up, the car continued unrelentingly to finish 11th overall.

COMPETITION RECORD	
1960 Le Mans 24 Hours	
Peter Bolton/Ninian Sanderson	19th overall
1961 Le Mans 24 Hours	
Les Leston/Rob Slotemaker	11th overall

Personalities identifiable in this study of 928 HP in 1960 are Mike Rothschild (driver), Ken Richardson (in overalls, by the open driver's door) and Les Makinson (in white overalls), who was the team refueller although his 'day' job was superintendent in the experimental department.

928 HP

FIRST REGISTERED	10 JUNE 1960
ENGINE SIZE	1,985cc
MODEL TYPE	TRS Le Mans car

This was the third of the TRS cars that started the Le Mans 24 Hours of 1960. Like its sister cars – 926 HP and 927 HP – it circulated steadily, but eventually suffered from rapidly worsening engine problems and did not qualify for an official finishing place, although it crossed the line 18th.

Although it was then fully prepared and taken to Le Mans in 1961, 928 HP was not used there, not even during practice. It could, of course, have been cannibalised for spares, or even 'cloned' in the event of one of the other three cars crashing in the pre-race qualifying sessions, but no such drastic action was ever needed. The 'cloning' stratagem, incidentally, had actually been carried out by the Healey 100 team in 1953, and the event scrutineers never found out! Accordingly, 928 HP returned to Coventry as a 'one-race wonder' and was never again used by the works team.

COMPETITION RECORD
1960 Le Mans 24 Hours
Les Leston/Mike Rothschild   18th overall

929 HP

FIRST REGISTERED	10 JUNE 1960
ENGINE SIZE	1,985cc
MODEL TYPE	TRS Le Mans car

As the fourth new TRS to be completed in the spring of 1960, this car was transported to Le Mans for potential use for 'spares on the hoof', but it was not used on the track at any stage that year. Accordingly, it was returned unused to Coventry and prepared for the 1961 race.

For much of the 1961 race, driven by Marcel Becquart and Mike Rothschild, it circulated at similar speeds to its sister cars, but during the Sunday morning the engine began to emit smoke and sound rough. A lengthy pit stop established that the problem was a failed camshaft oil seal. There was neither the time nor the freedom under the regulations to change components, so fingers were crossed while a rag soaked in jointing compound was wrapped around the housing of the seal in the hope that this would do the job – it did!

That delay, however, meant that the car could only complete 2,190 miles in the 24 hours, compared with 2,373 miles run by the leading TRS and 2,782 miles by the winning 3-litre Ferrari Testa Rossa.

COMPETITION RECORD
1961 Le Mans 24 Hours
Marcel Becquart/Mike Rothschild   15th overall

Another Le Mans pit stop in 1961 shows various personalities with 929 HP: Ken Richardson (in overcoat, bending down), chief mechanic Ray Henderson (in baseball cap, attending to the bonnet straps) and Les Makinson (at the back of the car, refuelling).

3097 VC

FIRST REGISTERED	14 SEPTEMBER 1962
ENGINE SIZE	1,985cc
MODEL TYPE	Conrero-built Le Mans car

Information about this, the most exotic of all Triumph TR prototypes, is irritatingly vague, for all the principal characters who were originally involved have now died, almost every written record has been destroyed, and the unique car that survives is held by a London-based collector who will not allow access to inspect it.

The story begins with this fascinating comment from the minutes of a Standard-Triumph board meeting on 19 September 1960: 'It was resolved that Conrero should build four Le Mans cars for the 1961 race, at the approx. cost of £25,000...'

Three of those cars were expected to race as works entries, with the fourth serving as a spare car or test car, but in the end they never appeared. So what happened? Why was only one car completed? And who was Conrero anyway?

It is easiest to answer the last question first. Virgilio Conrero ran a well-established Italian tuning house of the period, already respected for its work on special Alfa Romeos and other Italian exotica. In the same way that Cosworth became the default destination for anyone wanting engine advice in the UK in the 1960s, Conrero was the top specialist in Italy for chassis work at the time. Conrero knew Vignale, Vignale knew Michelotti, Michelotti worked for Standard-Triumph – so it is easy to see where the links were made.

If Standard-Triumph finances had not collapsed in 1960/61, three new Conrero-built cars like this would have competed at Le Mans in 1962. The tubular chassis frame was entirely special and the body was in aluminium, but all running gear was developed from the existing TRS.

The interior of the prototype Conrero TRS, which was delivered to the Triumph factory in the late summer of 1961. Note the TR3A-type overdrive switch, located just ahead of the steering wheel rim on the left-hand side.

As intended for use in the Michelotti-styled, Conrero-built race cars, the Sabrina engine used two twin-choke Weber carburettors, which increased the 2-litre engine's power output to at least 160bhp.

> **COMPETITION RECORD**
> Delivered to Coventry in 1961, but did not race.

After the 1960 Le Mans race, where the TRS effort had faltered, Triumph knew what had to be done. The TRS was too large and heavy, and had all the aerodynamic qualities of a good barn door. To produce a better racing car, the only sensible route was to swallow a bitter pill, throw away the Zoom-style visual connection and start again.

After surveying every option, Alick Dick and Harry Webster decided that the job could not be done in-house and farmed out the project to Conrero. Works team manager Ken Richardson was apparently not central to this project, for the TRS had been largely an engineering department exercise. Before the money ran out – at the end of 1960 Standard-Triumph came close to bankruptcy – Triumph sent the running gear of a TRS, but not a bodyshell, to Italy and gave Conrero a free hand to complete the job of turning out a finished racing car.

By early 1961 work had slowed down, at Triumph's request, but one right-hand-drive car was completed by the middle of the year. Not only did it have a brand-new chassis frame of mainly tubular construction – 'like a Ferrari 250 GT of the day' as one pundit assured me – but it also had a sleek, sexy, light-alloy coupé body style designed by Michelotti and built by Vignale. The completed car had many road-car-like fittings, such as chrome around the windscreen and side windows, which were not strictly necessary on a racing car.

The wheelbase was much shorter than that of the TRS, perhaps by as much as 10in – precise information is not available. There is a story that Conrero already had such a chassis from a cancelled Alfa Romeo project and, if true, this would certainly have given the company a flying start on the Triumph project.

The gearbox, axle and suspension were all like those of the TRS, and the wheels, with their Dunlop racing tyres, were certainly the same. The adoption of twin-choke Weber carburettors instead of the twin-choke SUs used on the TRS cars should have given more power, but there is no information about that.

The single prototype was delivered to Coventry later in 1961, and driven only by the favoured few. I was running motorsport activities from early 1962 and was told to keep clear, as the Conrero 'had no future'. As far as is known, full performance tests were never carried out at the factory. Given the Triumph Prototype Register number of X707 and registered 3097 VC in mid-1962, it hung around in Triumph's engineering department for some time before being sold off to the USA – along with the fleet of TRS cars – via the North American Triumph importer. Later it was returned to the UK and now lives in storage in the Home Counties, apparently needing much work to restore it completely. One day, one hopes, it will reappear.

It was a car that promised so much. With slightly more horse-power than the TRS (160bhp maybe), lighter (by at least 300/400lb) and with a far better drag coefficient, it must surely have been capable of 150mph and more. That might not have been enough to beat the Porsches in the 2-litre class, but it would have given them something serious and credible to think about.

CHAPTER 3:
HERALD AND VITESSE (1959–63)

The story of Standard-Triumph's search for a versatile replacement for the dumpy little Standard Eight/Ten/Pennant range has been told many times in great detail. To summarise, the project that was originally considered was not the car that finally went on the market, as the Herald, in 1959. Not only that, but originally there were no plans for these cars to have a separate chassis, nor for a six-cylinder Vitesse to evolve from the Herald.

Although the Herald was both larger and slightly heavier than the Eight/Ten/Pennant range that it replaced, it had two potential advantages as a rally car. The first was that it had all-independent suspension. The second was that, from Day One, there was to be a smart two-door coupé derivative in which an evolution of the twin-carburettor engine originally seen in 'GT' Standard Tens was already scheduled to be normal showroom equipment.

For marketing reasons it might have been more prudent to use Herald saloons in motorsport, but the decision to concentrate on the Coupé model was a 'no-brainer'. First of all, the Coupé's engine had 51bhp (gross) compared with 39bhp (gross) for the single-carburettor engine found in the saloons; the higher-powered engine would not become optional on the saloon until 1960. In addition, the Coupé qualified as a saloon for homologation purposes because it had four seats and its rear-seat compartment was dimensionally well within the regulations.

Nothing, unhappily, could be done about the Herald's size and bulk, but these cars could be made to handle very well indeed despite all the ill-informed jibes made over the years about the behaviour of the swing-axle rear suspension. Anyone continuing to doubt this should look ahead only a year or so to the excellent behaviour of the Triumph Spitfires (see Chapter 6), which performed so well at Le Mans and Sebring. Furthermore, it was not long before front-wheel disc brakes – a great advance on the drums previously fitted to all small cars – became available on this chassis.

There was no hurry, nonetheless, to get the new Heralds into motorsport, as 'Comps' was busy not only with the TR3As in rallying but also with the new TR3S – complete

The only time a Herald won at international level: Geoff Mabbs' privately owned car on the 1961 Tulip rally.

Had the Heralds benefited from as much homologation activity as the Mini-Coopers that were about to take over, they would have won many more awards. Outright victory on the Tulip rally, enjoyed by Geoff Mabbs in his own car, was a very special occasion in 1961.

All four brand-new Vitesses being prepared for the 1963 Monte Carlo rally. They had not then been registered, and were not in their final colour scheme.

All three works Vitesses made it to Monte Carlo, unscathed, in the 1963 rally, though the awful blizzard-like conditions foiled their every attempt to take awards. Lined up here, in the sun, on the promenade in Monte Carlo, are John Sprinzel (6001 VC), Mike Sutcliffe (6002 VC) and Vic Elford (6003 VC). One of these cars – 6003 VC – would become a 2-litre-engined prototype for the Spa-Sofia-Liège event later in the year.

with its twin-cam engine – at the Le Mans 24 Hours race. This explains why only privately prepared and entered Heralds first appeared on the international scene, with, for example, Ian 'Tiny' Lewis finishing ninth overall in the French Alpine rally of 1959 in a Coupé registered TL 5. This car had been bought, developed and prepared by 'Tiny', who always insisted that Triumph then benefited from his work by incorporating a number of his development tweaks in its works cars!

The Herald was eventually seen as a plucky but inherently underpowered machine with which to go rallying. Naturally it could not directly compete with larger-engined and more specialised saloons, and after 1961, when the original Richardson-era competitions department was closed down, it was swamped by a new generation of what are generally known as 'homologation specials'. These were cars like the BMC Mini-Cooper and the Ford Lotus-Cortina, which were limited-production machines with much higher performance and specification levels.

The Herald's greatest success as a competition car, in fact, came when the Triumph factory was just about to write it off as a worthwhile works machine. Even then, it was only the tactical experience of works driver 'Tiny' Lewis, and his expert way of reading regulations, that allowed him to usher a privately owned Herald driven by his near-neighbour Geoff Mabbs into outright victory in the 1961 Tulip rally, which was being run under a complex class-improvement formula. This was the only time a Herald won at international level.

A year later, when what I immodestly propose to call the Robson-era competitions department had opened up at Fletchamstead North, a new and potentially promising derivative of the Herald, the Vitesse, was put into production. With its six-cylinder engine and close-ratio gearbox, the Vitesse looked as if it could be a promising rally car: with further development and some imaginative homologation of performance packages, some thought that it could be rendered competitive. It could certainly be made to handle very well – factory testers Fred Nicklin and Gordon Birtwistle soon proved that – and in rally trim it might be able to match the formidably successful works Sunbeam Rapiers. But there turned out to be a stumbling block that could not be overcome.

When the Vitesse was put on sale in mid-1962, there were saloon and convertible derivatives, but no Coupé, and the only engine available was the 1,596cc unit with 70bhp. Although it was a brisk and compact little saloon, only those wearing blinkers could have thought that it might immediately have the beating of the latest fast saloons announced by Standard-Triumph's rivals. But it was not going to be easy for the Vitesse to beat the best that Alfa Romeo, Volvo, BMC (with the new Mini-Cooper) and Ford (with the imminent Cortina GT and Lotus-Cortina) could collectively put up against it.

Two rallies made this scenario abundantly clear. On the 1962 RAC rally Triumph's single entry, the white development hack registered 407 VC, broke its transmission, and then a trio of brand-new works cars struggled to remain competitive in the blizzard-like conditions of the 1963 Monte Carlo rally. It would be fair to say that the Vitesse motorsport programme was propelled more by marketing and publicity instincts than by the assumption that it might speedily be turned into a winner.

In fact the only Vitesse to be competitive in 1963 at international level was 6003 VC, the hastily developed 2-litre prototype car that Vic Elford took on the Liège-Sofia-Liège marathon in the summer. We will never know how that could have ended up, however, because a desperately unlucky fuel pipe breakage caused the whole car to be destroyed by fire at half distance.

From a range of 50 years I think it is now acceptable to speculate with a volley of 'ifs'. If Standard-Triumph had been making good money, if the product-development programme had been extended in a certain way, and if a beefed-up 2-litre Vitesse had been put on the market at the time, such a car might have been a competitive rally machine for two or three years. The legislative problem, however, was that at least 1,000 such cars would have to be built to ensure homologation. Could so many cars have been sold? And how would works cars have coped with the rough, unmade tracks that were a growing feature of rallying.

However, it was not to be. By the end of 1963 the entire Vitesse motorsport development programme had been closed down, for attention had already turned to making 2000s (see Chapter 5) and Spitfires (see Chapter 6) into more specialised motorsport machinery.

TL 5

FIRST REGISTERED	NOT KNOWN
ENGINE SIZE	948cc
MODEL TYPE	Herald Coupé

The story of the works Heralds starts with an intriguing mixture of subterfuge, private enterprise and confusion. The first car that qualifies as a works one, in my opinion, was originally bought by motor trader Ian 'Tiny' Lewis for his own use in rallying but was virtually 'adopted' by Ken Richardson's department after it won its class in the 1959 French Alpine rally. To add confusion, the registration TL 5, which had previously appeared on Standard Pennants and other cars, was used on at least two different Herald Coupés in a rather frenetic career!

'Early in 1959,' recalled 'Tiny' Lewis, 'Ken Richardson asked me if I would like to join the works team to do the Alpine rally, and said that he wanted me to use a Standard Ten. I said, "No, I'm not interested – I want to use a Herald." So Richardson replied, "OK, if you want to do it in a Herald, it will have to be in your own car", to which I replied that I was happy to do that, just as long as I could have one of the very first cars off the assembly line.'

And so it was that Lewis spent some weeks developing and preparing his new Herald Coupé, which carried the personalised registration number TL 5. Because this car was always intended to run in standard 'showroom' categories, he concentrated on preparation rather than modification, and did no more to the engine and transmission than take them down and make sure they were built up again to 'blueprint' standards.

Most of the special development concerned the handling, where the standard car's tendency to oversteer when pushed very hard needed to be addressed.

'As you would expect,' explained 'Tiny' in an interview, 'I soon discovered that the rear wheels could tuck themselves under as soon as you started to get really vicious with it. Anyway, after about three attempts, I got the rear suspension working properly. I did that by reassembling and resetting the transverse rear leaf spring, so that it had negative camber when sitting normally, but when the car tried to tuck the wheels in, the wheels couldn't get any further than upright – that was always the key.'

On the French Alpine rally of mid-1959, 'Tiny' and TL 5 virtually had to look after themselves at first, for the works team was operating no fewer than four TR3As. However, once the going got tough and the Herald kept its clean sheet – helped along by more favourable point-to-point schedules – while the TR3As struggled against more severe timing, that attitude soon changed.

In summary, as John Gott reported in *Autosport*, 'The Coupe des Alpes was handicapped to favour saloon cars... Private owners "Tiny" Lewis/Tony Nash did a wonderful job to bring the new Triumph Herald through unpenalised and win a Coupe.'

Mid-event, one result of this progress was that the Herald suddenly got some attention from the works mechanics. When they complained that they were not carrying parts for the Herald, Richardson pointed out that he had loaned two Heralds to members of the motoring press, and that these should be cannibalised if necessary. Which is exactly what happened, and it is believed that one of the reporters was left stranded for a time...

Using a combination of experience, good endurance driving and sheer rallying 'bushcraft', Lewis kept going throughout the 2,407-mile event, which used a route that

Ian 'Tiny' Lewis urging TL 5 up Prescott hillclimb, a stage on the 1959 RAC rally – by this time TL 5 was apparently YRW 268 in disguise!

things like that, I really don't know. But I think it's on the cards that they did…'

Whatever the ins and outs of this story, the fact is that TL 5 was one of four works-backed Herald Coupés entered for the RAC rally in November 1959. 'Tiny' drove the rejuvenated TL 5 (as a works-supported private entry), while the other three cars were brand-new Allesley-prepared examples (XHP 245, YRW 266 and YRW 267). The event started from Blackpool and ended at London's Crystal Palace race circuit, visiting the north of Scotland on the way – and it caused more controversy than any British rally before or since.

The main problem, as already spelt out in Chapter 1 (see page 52) concerning the works TR3As of the period, was that a complete blockage of a mountain section between Nairn and Braemar, in the Grampian mountains of Scotland, caused almost every car to get stuck for hours. This meant that the 15 crews who made an early decision to take the long way round the mountain to reach Braemar, and reached that control before being eliminated for being out of time, occupied the top positions issued at the end of the event, and no protests were upheld against the unfairness of this situation.

Not only did none of the official works Heralds get round the mountain in time, but they also lost time on other road sections. TL 5, on the other hand, was serenely on schedule at every other point and outpaced the works cars on the speed tests at other locations. In the end, Lewis's only road penalty was a whopping 300-point imposition for missing the Braemar control completely.

In a later reappraisal of the 1959 RAC rally, that doyen of rallying, BMC team captain John Gott, recalculated the results as they would have been if protests about the retention of the Nairn/Braemar section had been upheld. These produced the remarkable conclusion that 'Tiny' Lewis's Herald would have risen to fifth place overall, and that the Heralds would have won the Manufacturers' Team Prize instead of finishing second to the works TR3As! But 'if ifs and ands were pots and pans…'

This was the official end to the life of TL 5 as a works-supported car, for Ken Richardson made sure that he was provided with Allesley-built machines thereafter. However, TL 5 continued to appear in Lewis's hands in British hands for a season or so, but after the closure of the works competitions department in mid-1961 he was immediately snapped up by the Rootes/Sunbeam team on the other side of Coventry and stayed faithful to them for the next few years.

seemed to cover much of the French Alpes Maritimes and the Italian Dolomites, including all the highest passes. By the end, in Cannes, the little Herald began to feel worn out, for apart from its lack of engine power its drum brakes were also struggling. In the end, it notched up a stirring ninth place overall and third in its class, which was won by the highly modified Renault Dauphine that also won the event outright.

And this is where the mystery grew, as 'Tiny' told me in an interview: 'After the Alpine it went back to the factory for about a month. To this day I'm convinced that it wasn't the same car that came back again! The TL 5 that came back, well, it might have had my engine and transmission, but it was otherwise almost a brand-new car… Whether they used the original TL 5 as a copy for suspension modifications and

COMPETITION RECORD
1959 French Alpine
Ian 'Tiny' Lewis   9th overall
1959 RAC
Ian 'Tiny' Lewis   16th overall

XHP 245

FIRST REGISTERED	16 MARCH 1959
ENGINE SIZE	948cc
MODEL TYPE	Herald Coupé

This Herald Coupé was one of the original batch of pilot-build cars prepared for the press launch of the new range in April 1959. After fulfilling that role it was handed over to the works team for development as the very first of the Heralds to be used in rallying. It would only be used in two rallies – the RAC of November 1959 and the Monte Carlo of January 1960 – before being sold off. It was, however, the precursor to the batch of four other works Heralds (YRW 266 to YRW 269 inclusive) that followed it through the workshops at Allesley.

Cyril Corbishley and his co-driver Geoff Haggie started from Blackpool at number 122, right behind Pat Moss's Morris Minor 1000; the RAC rally entry was seeded by class in those days so all the up-to-1,000cc saloons ran close together near the back of the massive field. Cyril, however, was one of masses of drivers who got thoroughly stuck in the notorious snowdrifts on the Tomintoul mountain section of the Scottish Highlands and were forced out of time.

The money must have stretched a whole lot further in those days, for on the 1960 Monte Carlo rally the works Triumph team comprised two TR3As and no fewer than five Herald Coupés. All of the Heralds ran in virtually standard condition, all of them with the well-proven 948cc 'SC' engine equipped with twin SU carburettors.

For interest, it is worth pointing out just how much effort had gone into making each of these little cars 'winter-friendly', as *Autocar*'s comprehensive pre-event survey made clear.

'The Heralds are running in standard mechanical form. Like all other works entries, the engines have been carefully prepared and tuned to give maximum power on French petrol, or its equivalent in octane rating. Radiator blinds, controlled from the fascia panel, will be used to maintain optimum temperatures. Other weather-beating equipment includes fog lamps and a snow shield beneath the radiator.

'All the cars have roof-mounted, swivelling spot lamps, and reversing lights. Apart from the addition of a Halda Speed Pilot, two chrono-stop watches and extra switches, the fascia is normal. The standard hinged tray beneath the panel forms a useful map compartment. Visibility is assisted by defroster bars on the windscreen and back window.

'The driving seat of each Herald is a production model, but the angle of the back rest of the navigator's seat can be adjusted by altering the position of two small chains, and a

thickly padded head rest also is fitted. The luggage locker carries extra fuel, oil and water in addition to two spare wheels...'

Was this the specification of a serious rally car or of one that advertising agencies would have approved of? Your decision, I think...

Again allocated to Cyril Corbishley for the Monte, this car started from Glasgow in an event that had its usual mixture of dry roads, snow, ice and fog. In a typically gritty performance, Corbishley and Peter Roberts got through to Monte Carlo with the loss of only seven minutes as far as Chambéry, and a 'clean' run from there to the principality itself. Although they had not been able to practise the Mountain Regularity section as much as they would have liked, they converted their arrival position of 18th to 25th at the close of the event.

The car was then sold while the works team retained its red-and-white 'YRW' cars for use in the next few events.

Cyril Corbishley and Peter Roberts drove this works Herald Coupé, XHP 245, on the 1960 Monte Carlo rally and their 25th overall was a fine performance in such an under-powered machine.

COMPETITION RECORD
1959 RAC
Cyril Corbishley   Did not finish
1960 Monte Carlo
Cyril Corbishley   25th overall

YRW 266

FIRST REGISTERED	15 OCTOBER 1959
ENGINE SIZE	948cc
MODEL TYPE	Herald Coupé

After XHP 245 had started testing, Ken Richardson's team set about preparing four new Herald Coupés for use in rallying, all of them painted red and white. Although Richardson never planned to use all four new cars at once, the budgetary purse strings were relaxed sufficiently for his team to build the cars together with a view to phasing them into service when appropriate. YRW 266 was the first of this

In his 'works-replica' car Geoff Mabbs, sharing with Leslie Griffiths, battled for every second against team driver Ian 'Tiny' Lewis in YRW 266 on the 1961 Tulip rally.

By taking advantage of a complex class-improvement formula on the 1961 Tulip rally, Geoff Mabbs was gifted outright victory by works driver Ian 'Tiny' Lewis, who had been mere seconds slower than Mabbs.

batch and its specification was shared with the other cars of the type.

Because these cars were homologated as Group 1 and, where appropriate, Group 2 'saloons', they had to run in virtually showroom condition, for multi-carburettor kits, lightweight body panels, and non-standard items such as overdrive and disc brakes were all specifically banned. Although they were reasonably competitive at first, once BMC's much lighter and more nimble front-wheel-drive Minis became reliable – a process that took a great deal of time – they would be struggling for pace. Compared with its rivals, the Herald's weight was the handicap that proved most difficult to overcome.

Peter Bolton and Gordon Shanley drove this car on its first event, which was the 1959 RAC rally. Enough has already been described about this infamous rally, where a snow-blocked road caused organisational chaos, so suffice to say that Bolton's Herald became entangled in the blockage and incurred a maximum penalty through missing the Braemar control. Without that hold-up, the records show that he would have been much more competitive in the hotly contested 1-litre class. The fact that he also left the road at one point, damaging the front of the car and losing 17 minutes of road penalties, did not help, especially as he had to complete the route with rope strapped around the front end of the bodywork to keep it in place. One minor consolation was that Bolton, along with Keith Ballisat in YRW 267 and 'Tiny' Lewis in his own privately prepared Herald, finished second in the Manufacturers' Team Prize – beaten only by a team of TR3As!

Easily repaired in December and 'winter-equipped', YRW 266 was then allocated to Rob Slotemaker to drive on the 1960 Monte. Ever practical, Rob decided to start from the nearest town to his home in Holland, accordingly choosing Frankfurt in West Germany. He fought his way through all the snow and ice, reached Chambéry on time, and then set a very strong series of regularity times on his way to Monaco only to experience an extraordinary case of bad luck. On approaching Monte Carlo his car hit a large stone that had just been dislodged into the road – it punctured his Herald's water radiator, all coolant was speedily lost, and Rob's event was over.

If one believes that registration numbers explain all, YRW 266 then spent most of 1960 in storage before being brought out to compete in the 1961 Monte Carlo rally, again in 'showroom' specification. However, this was not as a full-blown works entry but as a loan arrangement to 'Tiny' Lewis, who was the only member of the 1960 team of drivers who had stayed loyal to Triumph after its rallying activities had effectively closed down following the 1960 French Alpine rally.

In retrospect, 'Tiny' should not even have bothered to turn up at the start from Glasgow, for this was a Monte where yet another storm blew up over regulations. Fifty years after the event had been conceived, this was the first Monte to include special stages, which ought to have been enough to produce a fine and fair result. But this was the Monte Carlo rally and that would have been far too simple…

Instead, a complex handicapping formula was devised, and it was applied to every competitor's special stage times. The formula was based on a car's engine size and its catalogued weight, and definitely favoured heavy, underpowered, small cars – which may explain why victory eventually went to a trio of lumbering Panhards. Success for French cars on the Monte Carlo rally? No one should have been surprised…

As expected, the weather was wintry and foul, particularly in the Massif Central that all the Glasgow starters had to face. Of the 63 cars that left from Scotland, only 16 managed to reach Monte Carlo within time limits. And only Lewis's Herald made it without any time penalties – a quite astonishing achievement.

Following this remarkable run, and his plucky performance on the special stages between Charbonnières and Monaco, 'Tiny' found himself lying fourth among the British competitors, with only Paddy Hopkirk, Peter Harper and Henry Taylor ahead of him.

All this, however, was a waste of his time, for the handicap had already ensured that he could not achieve a high finishing position, nor even a strong position in his class – which included those front-wheel-drive Panhards. It was a little consolation to him that he won the Royal Scottish Automobile Club's Cup as the best starter from Glasgow, that he was also a member of the RAC's own Challenge Cup-winning team (Pat Moss's A40 and Peter Harper's Sunbeam Rapier were the others), and that his gallant car came through the event quite unscathed.

There was still time for one outing, which came three months later when 'Tiny' was paired with YRW 266 to tackle the Tulip rally, another event where handicapping systems varied from year to year. The route stretched all the way from Noordwijk in Holland down to an overnight halt in Monte Carlo before returning to Noordwijk again, with a series of speed hill-climb tests in the French mountains along the way. As in the Monte, Lewis's car was the only factory-backed Herald in the event, but this time he was backed by his close friend and West Country neighbour Geoff Mabbs, who was competing in his own personal Herald Coupé, which was registered 111 LHW and had no links with the works team.

By trying to be as fair as possible to everyone in 1961, the Tulip's organisers made a fundamental mistake in making it possible for a resourceful competitor to manipulate the results, and 'Tiny' was able to exploit this in a way they had not considered. The organisers proposed to total up every competitor's individual test times, then to express them as a percentage of that performance in the capacity class in which he/she was running, and these percentages would then deter-

Although Triumph team boss Ken Richardson (left) played no part in Geoff Mabbs' 1961 Tulip rally victory, he was happy to bask in the favourable publicity that followed.

mine the general classification. This, by definition, meant that a competitor who proved to be outstandingly faster than all other cars in his class would have a lower numerical rating than one who only narrowly won that class. Not only that, but the spread of percentages would depend on the scope, number and general pace of each class.

So much for the theory. In practice there was a running battle between 'Tiny' Lewis and Geoff Mabbs in a class where other competitors were significantly slower. Until the very last few minutes of the event, it was clear that Mabbs was about to win his class, with 'Tiny' close behind him, but that he might only take about fourth position overall.

On the final run back into Holland, 'Tiny' and his co-driver Tony Nash had a great deal of time to consider tactics, and, after consultation with Mabbs, had carried out a number of computations. On arrival at the finish in Noordwijk, 'Tiny' firmly declined to hand in his time card at the final control and was therefore excluded from the standings, a stratagem that altered all the previous 'percentage' standings and handed outright victory to Mabbs!

To the victor the spoils – but to 'Tiny' Lewis not a thing. Not everyone, it must be admitted, was best pleased, but Standard-Triumph's advertising people were delighted…

COMPETITION RECORD	
1959 RAC	
Peter Bolton	25th overall
1960 Monte Carlo	
Rob Slotemaker	Did not finish
1961 Monte Carlo	
Ian 'Tiny' Lewis	25th overall
1961 Tulip	
Ian 'Tiny' Lewis	Withdrawn at the finish

YRW 267

FIRST REGISTERED	15 OCTOBER 1959
ENGINE SIZE	948cc
MODEL TYPE	Herald Coupé

Keith Ballisat drove YRW 267 on the 1959 RAC rally at No 127, in close company with works team-mates Cyril Corbishley (No 122) and Peter Bolton (No 125). Although Ballisat lost a total of 12 minutes in road penalties at various

Ian 'Tiny' Lewis and Tony Nash in their works Herald, YRW 267, at the end of the 1960 Tulip rally, where they won their capacity class.

locations, all three made steady progress until reaching what proved to be the decisive hold-up in the Scottish mountains – where snow blocked the route to Braemar.

All three works drivers found it impossible to extricate themselves before running out of time to reach the Braemar control. Corbishley went no further, but Ballisat, like Bolton, gamely kept going, lost no further time and ended up 23rd overall. The real consolation was that Ballisat and Bolton, because of their grit and determination, were also members of the trio who took second place in the contest for the Manufacturers' Team Prize.

Surprisingly, this car was then put in storage for six months, before being brought out for use by 'Tiny' Lewis in the 1960 Tulip rally. This, as already described in Chapter 1 (see page 50), was an event that was settled not only by a rather complex class-improvement method of marking on the speed tests, but also by the imposition of one impossible schedule, for the ascent of the famous Col de Turini. As it happened, Lewis's Herald was the best-performing car in the 1-litre category for saloon cars and his friend Geoff Mabbs in a privately owned Herald finished close behind him in the class.

This performance, and its implications for the following year's event, played a crucial part in Lewis's tactics with YRW 266 in the 1961 Tulip, as described in the previous entry.

COMPETITION RECORD	
1959 RAC	
Keith Ballisat	23rd overall
1960 Tulip	
Ian 'Tiny' Lewis	1st in class

For spectators on the Monte Carlo rally, one way to keep warm is to wave and wave: this is 'Tiny' Lewis and Tony Nash in YRW 268 on the Col du Granier in the 1960 event.

YRW 268

FIRST REGISTERED	15 OCTOBER 1959
ENGINE SIZE	948cc
MODEL TYPE	Herald Coupé

Although registered and part-prepared in the autumn of 1959, at the same time as the other new Heralds on the works roster, YRW 268 was not put into use until January 1960, when Ian 'Tiny' Lewis drove it on the Monte Carlo rally and elected to start from Glasgow.

Lewis enjoyed a faultless run all the way to Chambéry and also on the much more demanding 'Common Route' to Monte Carlo, reaching the principality as one of only nine crews to be totally unpenalised. But it all then went wrong for him on what was called the 'Mountain Regularity test', for he

COMPETITION RECORD	
1960 Monte Carlo	
Ian 'Tiny' Lewis	57th overall

was by no means 'regular' and went off the road more than once. He was rather more deserving of a good result than he actually achieved.

The factory team did not use this Herald again.

YRW 269

FIRST REGISTERED	15 OCTOBER 1959
ENGINE SIZE	948cc
MODEL TYPE	Herald Coupé

Although the works Herald was really not fast enough to shine in the French Alpine, 'Tiny' Lewis got the very utmost out of YRW 269 in 1960. Impressive in all but straight-line performance, the car looked good on the tight sections.

Like other cars in the new fleet of works Heralds, YRW 269 was registered in 1959 but not put to use until January 1960, when Keith Ballisat and Stuart Turner drove it in the Monte Carlo rally, starting from Glasgow. Even before this car reached the tightly timed sections in the Alpes Maritimes, after the route passed through Bourges, the car met with an accident.

'We were using studded tyres,' Ballisat told me. 'I was asleep at the time, and Stuart was driving. The accident was all down to the tyres and the road surface – there wasn't anyone else around at the time. We went sideways into a ditch. We both ended up in a French hospital, me with a cracked pelvis and a lot of plaster on.'

In his autobiography *Twice Lucky*, Stuart Turner added further recollections: 'It left me with a mission to tell people never to use rigid material to rest a map on, because my board broke Keith's pelvis when it jammed against the dash. I remember that the wine in the French hospital, fed intravenously, was of a very good year...' The determined and indefatigable Turner might have suffered two broken ribs, but he was back in rallying within four weeks.

The factory took time to restore YRW 269 to full health, and in the meantime had plenty on its hands with a full team entry of TR3As in the Tulip rally and the TRS racing car programme for Le Mans. Finally the Herald Coupé was made ready for 'Tiny' Lewis and Tony Nash to drive in the French Alpine rally.

The Herald was not the ideal car for the Alpine. Although it was nimble enough, and Lewis was a determined and experienced driver, what was really needed was a lot of power, which the Herald still lacked. Although he lay 13th overall at the end of the first 1,070-mile leg from Marseilles to Chamonix, Lewis's challenge faded in the long, gruelling second half, leaving a number of factory-backed Renault Dauphines in charge of his class.

COMPETITION RECORD
1960 Monte Carlo
Keith Ballisat — Did not finish
1960 French Alpine
Ian 'Tiny' Lewis — Finished

YWK 534

FIRST REGISTERED	1 JANUARY 1960
ENGINE SIZE	948cc
MODEL TYPE	Herald Coupé

Annie Soisbault was provided with a brand-new Herald Coupé for the 1960 Monte Carlo rally, naturally enough deciding to start from Paris. She monopolised the pre-event press publicity by turning up at the start with her pet cheetah curled up in the rear seat, and claimed that she and co-driver Annie Spiers would take it with them all the way to Monte Carlo. Although the poor animal was indeed seen in the cabin when the Herald finally arrived in the principality, this was, needless to say, a good stunt involving a certain amount of sleight of hand, for it had not travelled in the Herald all the way!

This event was clearly not in one of Annie's better spells for she had already lost 29 minutes on the road sections by the time she reached Monaco, and did not qualify as a finisher.

The factory team did not use the car again.

COMPETITION RECORD
1960 Monte Carlo
Annie Soisbault — Did not finish

407 VC

FIRST REGISTERED	18 MAY 1962
ENGINE SIZE	1,596cc
MODEL TYPE	VITESSE 1600

Ace mechanic Ray Henderson, later competitions supervisor, working on the original works Vitesse, 407 VC, before the 1962 RAC rally, when it ran with a Group 3 triple-SU carburettor kit.

When the six-cylinder Vitesse range was launched in mid-1962, this car, painted white with black spears along its flanks and initially absolutely standard in specification, was one of the engineering prototypes and was used for a variety of test and validation work in the spring of 1962 before being handed over in May to the newly reopened and relocated works competitions department at Fletchamstead North. Hand-built in the engineering workshops in the winter of 1961/62, some months before Vitesse series production was ready to begin at Canley, this car carried the experimental commission number of X690, and was given the registration number 407 VC just a few days after the quartet of brand-new works TR4s (3 VC, 4 VC, 5 VC and 6 VC) was also commissioned.

At first 407 VC was used by the competitions department as a service and 'chase' car, and I myself used it in 1962 to follow the TR4s around the routes of the French Alpine rally and the Liège-Sofia-Liège, including venturing into Yugoslavia, all of which provided very valuable endurance

experience. The rear seat was taken out and plywood boxes instead put in that space, the better to carry a variety of spare parts for use by other service cars if required. At this time the car had an overdrive transmission that this was arranged to work on second, third and top gears. Braking was upgraded with Ferodo competition-style DS11 front brake pads and VG95 rear brake shoes, together with competition-spec brake fluid. Standard 3.5in wheel rims were used when following the French Alpine, but 4.5in rims, as used on Herald-derived Triumph Courier vans, were substituted for the 'chase' role on the Liège-Sofia-Liège. The newly launched Dunlop SP3 radial-ply tyres were fitted instead of the standard crossplies.

After these duties, 407 VC was something of an 'old nail'. Next, as a development exercise, it was decided to prepare it as a Group 3 rally car to compete in the RAC rally, where it would run in the same category as the TR4s, although still only with a 1.6-litre engine, tuned for the occasion. Why was it not run as a Group 1 or Group 2 car? The reason was because those categories were already stuffed with well-developed cars, notably the 1.6-litre works Sunbeam Rapiers (which had been honing their craft for several years) and the new BMC Mini-Cooper (which had already won several major events outright despite having only a 1.0-litre engine).

At this time, the freedoms that existed in the Group 3 category meant that 407 VC's engine could be tuned considerably. Accordingly, a strictly one-off 1.6-litre engine was specified, with triple SU carburettors and a different camshaft profile – developments that the engineers at Fletchamstead North were dabbling with at the time. This engine was claimed to develop 95bhp, which meant that it was likely to put a heavy load on the existing transmission. It had been hoped, incidentally, that a 1.6-litre Vitesse of this specification would eventually be put on the market, but this intention was soon abandoned and instead a 2-litre twin-SU derivative came along. In addition 407 VC was given stiffer suspension settings, its chassis frame was beefed up in one or two detail areas (following pavé testing that had been carried out on other prototype cars), 4.5in wheels were fitted, and a second fuel tank was fitted (on the opposite side of the boot compartment to the standard tank) to give a total capacity of 18 gallons.

This RAC rally entry was an opportunity to give a first, tentative works drive to Vic Elford, who had hitherto been a works co-driver at BMC but was making his own way, rapidly and with great flair, in British events in privately owned machinery. Although competition in the Group 3 category turned out to be even stiffer than had been feared, Elford set off with that air of confidence that would soon become very familiar to his peers and his team-mates.

But everyone in the team, including Elford and his co-driver Mike Butler, realised that the standard gearbox – a requirement of Group 3 – might wilt, and eventually it did. By the time the car had completed 17 special stages it was already in trouble, but its crew thought they might be able to spare an hour on a subsequent road section before they had to tackle the Lake District stages, and so Ray Henderson hastily rushed down the road to the Standard-Triumph dealer in Penrith, commandeered a ramp at short notice, and prepared to change the gearbox for a spare he just 'happened' to have in his service car. As Vitesse owners know, this is a very long job because the gearbox/clutch/bellhousing unit has to come out through the front of the passenger compartment after removal of the seats, and it soon became clear that the job could not be done in an hour. In fact it took about 90 minutes, a feat that nevertheless left the dealer staff open-mouthed, but it meant that Elford was out of time and out of the event.

The morale of this story was that if a Vitesse was to go rallying with significantly more power, then a stronger gearbox was needed, and it would also be useful for the chassis to be modified to allow the gearbox to be lowered out of the car rather than hoisted out through the passenger compartment. Neither of these was other than a theoretical solution at the end of 1962.

COMPETITION RECORD	
1962 RAC	
Vic Elford	Did not finish

The very first works Vitesse was 407 VC, which the author had already been using as a works chase/service car. Vic Elford drove it with great spirit on the 1962 RAC rally – here it is seen on the open road in Scotland – but the gearbox eventually failed, and retirement was inevitable.

6001 VC

FIRST REGISTERED	1 JANUARY 1963
ENGINE SIZE	1,596cc
MODEL TYPE	VITESSE 1600

No sooner had the works TR4s completed the 1962 RAC rally than the competitions department took delivery of four brand-new Vitesse 1600s with the optional overdrive transmission. The cars came fully assembled from the production lines at Canley and were originally finished in white, but they were repainted powder blue before being made ready for rallying. The intention was to use three of them on the forthcoming Monte Carlo rally, while the fourth car would be a spare that could be used for testing or practice as necessary.

No high-performance derivative of the Vitesse had gone on sale, so to meet the particular Monte regulations of 1963 the specification of the works cars had to be Group 1 (effectively 'showroom' standard) or Group 2 ('Improved Touring Cars'). Prototype items could not be used, significant engine tuning was forbidden, and the cars could not be lightened in any way. For the Monte a form of handicap was applied to Group

Two of the brand-new Vitesses, still not registered and still not complete, being readied for the 1963 Monte Carlo rally, with 5 VC – Jean-Jacques Thuner's car in that event – sitting alongside. Competitions secretary Graham Robson is 'adjusting' the driving lamp on the Vitesse, which proves that this was a posed shot!

2 entries that required their special-stage times to be multiplied by three per cent – in other words a time of 10 minutes would be recorded as 10 minutes 18 seconds. For entrants choosing the Group 2 category this amounted to a gamble that they would have to factor into their pre-event calculations.

To spread the possibilities of success, as it were, the works Triumph team decided that two of the Vitesses would be built to Group 2 specification and one of them – this one – would be run in Group 1 condition. As such this car had Armstrong adjustable dampers, uprated springs (Courier van coils at the front, reset transverse leaf springs at the rear), Ferodo competition brake materials, a fly-off handbrake, wider Courier-type road wheels and an array of extra driving lamps up front.

Inside, the obvious visible feature of works rally preparation was the fascia panel, which was allowed by a homologation 'freedom' to be completely new. At the time, the instrument panel of the production Vitesse was boringly simple, with only a speedometer, a fuel gauge and the usual switches. A completely different layout was adopted for the works cars, using modified Smiths dials mainly from the Spitfire and the TR4. The speedometer and a typical rally clock were mounted ahead of the co-driver, while the driver was faced with a rev counter surrounded by a cluster of small dials. Microcell adjustable front seats were fitted.

Registered 6001 VC, this car had dark blue spears painted along the side of its powder blue coachwork. The driver for the Monte was John Sprinzel, who, it must be admitted, was

John Sprinzel on the 1963 Monte Carlo rally in 6001 VC – he did not enjoy the Lockheed anti-lock braking system.

no longer as happy as he had been when the department was set up a year earlier (see Chapter 4, page 95) and must have realised that this car would have to succeed through its agility rather than its performance.

In the meantime, careful scrutiny of the FIA 'Blue book', which among other things defined the 'freedoms' and the 'thou-shalt-not' aspects of a Group 1 car, had revealed the possibility of using anti-lock braking devices, if such things existed. Although this was years before Dunlop applied its own system to Jensen FF road cars, and a full decade before the first ABS systems became practical in Germany, the British Lockheed company already had its own ideas. Quoting from my book *Triumph Herald and Vitesse* (1997), this is what happened next.

'The Leamington-based Lockheed company was a long-time supplier of braking equipment to Standard-Triumph, and with a newly developed anti-lock system to publicise, it was most anxious to try the new kit out on the Monte. The Lockheed system involved the use of a sensor mounted close to the differential, belt-driven from the prop shaft. As with later but much more sophisticated electronically controlled systems, sudden changes in the transmission shaft speed (in this case, the prop shaft) resulted in the brake fluid pressure to the rear brakes (only the rear brakes....) being cut off.'

As I recall, there was little time for these installations to be tested on the practice car (6004 VC) before the event began, but it was clear that none of the drivers liked them very much, and would much rather have taken their chances with the normal system. With some justification, Sprinzel complained that there were occasions when the action 'froze' in operation, so that it took time for the rear brakes to come back into normal use.

All the usual gambles had to be taken concerning a choice of starting point. It was decided that all three Vitesses, along with Jean-Jacques Thuner's works TR4 (see page 105), should start from Paris, for two reasons in particular. First, Paris starters would be near the front of the field after the starting routes converged at Chambéry, where the cars would take up their allocated positions by competition number. Secondly, a Paris start allowed the works team's rather meagre servicing 'umbrella' to be deployed a little more effectively around France. From Chambéry, the route took in five long special stages in the French mountains before reaching Monte Carlo, where there was a final series of short races around the street circuit used for the Monaco GP.

No one could have forecast just how awful the weather was going to be in January 1963. I was team manager on the Monte and just before my journey to Paris I had been stranded in the Isle of Man, where the airport was closed because of a blanket of snow and freezing fog. On the rally itself the competitors experienced incredibly slippery and dangerous roads in the mountains and here Sprinzel lost 22 minutes, perhaps unnerved by the behaviour of the Lockheed anti-lock braking system, which, he later admitted, he did not trust. Despite his Vitesse remaining immaculate at the finish, he was a subdued and dispirited 60th overall. In the end, only 26 crews reached Monte Carlo without road penalties, and just 102 of the 296 starters made it to the finish at all.

As it transpired, this was the one and only time that 6001 VC competed at international level as a works rally car, although it was used, without success, in the inaugural 'rally-cross' event held in deep snow at Brands Hatch in February 1963, and then popped up occasionally over the next few months in the hands of other works drivers in British rallies. This was also the last time Sprinzel competed as an official member of the works team, although on several occasions in subsequent years he used his influence with the public relations department to obtain a spare Triumph of some sort for a rally, and to take along a representative of the national press to make it all worthwhile.

COMPETITION RECORD
1963 Monte Carlo
John Sprinzel   60th overall
1963 Brands Hatch rallycross
John Sprinzel   10th overall
Plus a few other appearances in British club rallies

6002 VC

FIRST REGISTERED	1 JANUARY 1963
ENGINE SIZE	1,596cc
MODEL TYPE	VITESSE 1600

Except that its engine was prepared to a Group 2 state of tune, 6002 VC looked visually the same as the other Vitesse team cars except for the use of white paint spears along its flanks. Group 2 tune meant a gas-flowed cylinder head and a different camshaft profile, endowing the car – according to the pre-event press release! – with some 20 per cent more power than standard. The car was to be driven on the 1963 Monte by Mike Sutcliffe, who had had a successful 1962 season in TR4s (see Chapter 4) and, bringing with him a quirk from that experience, specified that the Vitesse be fitted with a TR4-type steering wheel, which featured sprung spokes.

As prepared for the 1963 Monte Carlo rally, the 1.6-litre works Vitesses were virtually standard. Mike Sutcliffe and Roy Fidler drove 6002 VC, but were badly delayed by the blizzard-like weather. This was the only event tackled by this particular car.

This Group 2 Vitesse was visibly faster than John Sprinzel's Group 1 car, 6001 VC, but Sutcliffe did not figure well in the results because somewhere in the white-out blizzard he lost 42 minutes on the road sections – even more time than Sprinzel – for reasons that he never spelled out or admitted to at post-event inquests. He had started out going rather faster than Vic Elford in 6003 VC, but Elford overtook him on the final stages.

This car was not used again as a works machine in an international-status event, although it was useful as a management 'chase' car for the TR4s during 1963. Thereafter it was sold off, and somehow its identity survived over many years as a car carrying the same registration number has been seen regularly at Triumph and other classic events in recent years.

This Vitesse, 6002 VC, was used as a high-speed 'chase car' by the author on the 1963 Liège-Sofia-Liège rally. Here it is at a service point where a TR4, 3 VC, was being fettled.

COMPETITION RECORD
1963 Monte Carlo
Mike Sutcliffe   76th overall

6003 VC

FIRST REGISTERED	1 JANUARY 1963
ENGINE SIZE	1,596cc/1,998cc
MODEL TYPE	VITESSE 1600

It was typical of the thrusting young Vic Elford that he might have been the newcomer to the Triumph works team in 1963, but he was always the most determined to produce a great result. His Group 2 Vitesse, 6003 VC, was outwardly and mechanically almost identical to 6002 VC, but finished much higher up the results list of the ultra-tough Monte Carlo rally of 1963. This car, incidentally, ran with a uniform powder blue colour scheme, without a contrasting colour on its flanks.

Having started the Monte just six minutes behind 6002 VC, Elford kept a clean sheet as far as Chambéry, after which his fortunes and those of his team-mates rapidly diverged. Thereafter, by brilliant, brave and sometimes aggressive driving in awful snowy and icy conditions, Vic kept the Vitesse on the road and was one of just 26 drivers

Pre-Monte Carlo rally line-up in the snow: new recruit Vic Elford is closest to the camera, with 5 VC (Jean-Jacques Thuner's TR4) furthest away.

to reach Monte Carlo without road penalties of any type. In every good fairy-tale this would have brought him victory in his class – not victory overall because front-wheel-drive Saabs, Citroëns and Minis dominated the leader board – but Vic just failed to do this. In a tight finish, the 1.6-litre class was fought out to the very end with Peter Harper's works Sunbeam Rapier and Helge Kristiansen's Ford Cortina Super, a battle that went down 'to the wire' and finished with Elford very close behind both of these rivals in third place.

There was no doubt that a Vitesse with certain extra homologated items – such as a 'Third World' camshaft profile – could now defeat the Rapiers, if not the Lotus-Cortinas and Mini-Cooper S cars that were soon to appear. Bear in mind that Peter Harper's Rapier was running as a Group 1 car and the special-stage time comparisons given in the accompanying table make fascinating reading. Incidentally, I had been in the works Sunbeam team prior to my time with Triumph and I know just how much clever sporting homologation took place to make the Rapier as quick as it was!

It was only after the event, incidentally, that the team discovered that Elford had disliked the Lockheed anti-lock installation so much that he worked out a way of disabling it. The short belt that actuated the sensor just 'happened' to break – which made him a lot happier!

Because the team was so impressed with Elford's potential, it arranged for him to use 6003 VC in selected British events in the months that followed, despite funds being very restricted. The experience, it was thought, would help him develop as a works driver, and might teach the works department more about the car. With hindsight, however, this was a diversion. There was no success for Elford on the first of those guest appearances, in the inaugural TV 'rally-cross' event held in deep snow at Brands Hatch – on the access roads, car parks and occasionally on the track!

Under normal circumstances 6003 VC might have ended its works career before the summer of 1963, although it was to prove useful on the service fleet as a 'chase' car on the Tulip and French Alpine rallies. But with Vic Elford in the team, 'normal circumstances' never seemed to apply, for he thought that constant pressure to get his own way would eventually see him prevail!

Having started international rallying as David Seigle-Morris's co-driver, Vic was so sure of his ability that by 1963 he was already aiming to get into F1 – which he did by 1968 – and was planning his career ladder on that basis. By profession a life-assurance salesman, he was self-confident and presented himself well, so when he conceived the plan of running a 'special' car in the Spa-Sofia-Liège event the phrase 'no chance' was dismissed from his mind. On that event the regulations were very flexible and homologation rules were not enforced, so a 'special' car would be

MONTE CARLO RALLY 1963: COMPARISON OF SPECIAL-STAGE TIMES			
	Sunbeam Rapier	Triumph Vitesse	Vitesse comparison
	Peter Harper	Vic Elford	
Stage 1	48min 05sec	48min 10sec	5sec slower
Stage 2	39min 56sec	38min 00sec	1min 56sec faster
Stage 3	15min 58sec	15min 02sec	56sec faster
Stage 4	7min 36sec	7min 56sec	20sec slower
Stage 5	26min 44sec	27min 10sec	26sec slower
Stage 6	7min 21sec	7min 47sec	26sec slower
Overall	–	–	95sec faster

Oh, what might have been! After a great deal of nagging and persuasion, Vic Elford managed to get the works team to build 6003 VC as a full 2-litre prototype to tackle the Spa-Sofia-Liège marathon, where such prototypes were allowed to compete. By the time the event reached the roughest part of Yugoslavia, Elford was battling for the lead, but then a fuel pipe suddenly broke and the car was destroyed by fire.

eligible. Vic loved the handling of the Vitesse, knew all about alternative Triumph engines and transmission layouts, and decided that a more powerful, stronger Vitesse might just do the job. If it did, he reasoned, he was the man to carry out the strategy.

In July 1963 the works team had just returned from the French Alpine rally, during which all three TR4s had retired (see pages 102-103), two after crashes, one of which was by Elford himself. With the horrors of the Spa-Sofia-Liège about to unfold and funds running low, morale in the team was ebbing away. It was at this point that Elford launched his persuasive verbal campaign and approached me, as team manager, with his idea for a 'special' Vitesse.

I had to tell him that there was no chance and that he would be driving a works TR4, but this was brushed off. Nothing daunted, he then asked for, and got, an interview with technical chief Harry Webster. He went through the same persuasive presentation and was briskly turned away once again. Elford then asked if he could approach Sir

Donald Stokes, the company's chairman, and Webster was happy to let him try, thinking that he would be fortunate even to get a hearing. Vic threw himself into yet another presentation and spoke to Sir Donald in his London offices – and miraculously pulled off the deal! On the basis that Ray Henderson's mechanics would build the car, and that no one else's time would be wasted in the effort, Stokes gave the go-ahead.

The car that Vic had driven on the Monte was immediately put into a corner of the workshop and within six weeks it was completely transformed. First of all a 1,998cc version of the engine used in 407 VC for the 1962 RAC rally was produced; an engine of this capacity, complete with three SU carburettors and approximately 110bhp, was about to power the yet-to-be announced Triumph 2000. Backing up this enlarged engine was a more robust works TR4-type gearbox and overdrive assembly, a shortened propeller shaft and a chassis-mounted rear differential of 1964-model Triumph 2000 type, all mated to suitably beefed-up half shafts. Because of the greater bulk of this gearbox/overdrive unit, there was no chance whatsoever of it ever being removed through the inside of the car on the event itself – but it was thought to be bomb-proof, everyone was quite relaxed about it, and no spare was going to be carried around the Balkans in any case!

Bodily the car looked quite normal, other than at the front where a much larger radiator – a taller TR4 type – had to be accommodated. Henderson's body specialists altered the bonnet pressing and the panel under the bumper to make room for the larger radiator, and also put extra cooling slots in the lower panel. As a final touch the front end was altered to include two 7in headlamps alongside the two original Lucas headlamps – Vic was not going to have any excuse about being unable to see where he was going. Time was so short that little could be done to upgrade the chassis, but the works Vitesse was already a good-handling car and would be fitted with the latest Dunlop rally tyres, so the only crossing of fingers would have to concern the efficiency of the brakes.

The car was only just completed in time to be delivered to a cross-channel ferry to get it to Belgium for the start of the event, and no testing or development of any sort had been carried out. Nevertheless, Vic Elford and his co-driver Terry Hunter, running with competition number 34, set off in high spirits with high hopes.

Running non-stop, their special Vitesse reached the turn-around point at Sofia, Bulgaria, without problems. After a break of just one hour for a meal, Elford and Hunter tackled the first sector of the return journey towards the Adriatic. Their progress was very brisk on rocky, dusty, car-breaking roads via Skopje, Pec, Titograd and Perast, and unofficial results at Split showed that this remarkable 2-litre Vitesse seemed to be holding fourth place overall. At this point 6003 VC was led only by the Mercedes-Benz 230SL of Eugen Böhringer (the eventual victor) and Erik Carlsson's front-wheel-drive Saab 96, and probably Lucien Bianchi's front-wheel-drive Citroën DS19 as well.

Then suddenly, without warning, the engine caught fire and Elford had to stop the car rapidly on a remote rocky track close to Bribir. Despite the car having an on-board fire extinguisher, the flames were so severe that there was nothing the crew could do except abandon ship with as many of their belongings as they could rescue, and watch the car gradually burn itself to a hulk. Subsequent examination showed that a fuel supply pipe to the carburettors had fractured and spilt neat petrol on the hot exhaust manifold. Because of the stretched-out nature of the route, the nearest works service vehicle was hours away from the funeral pyre, so the car had to be abandoned. Elford and Hunter finally begged, borrowed and scrounged their way back to Liège in two different non-competing cars, leaving 6003 VC to its fate.

That, however, was not quite the end of this story. The Coventry branch of HM Customs & Excise insisted on seeing that 6003 VC really had been burned out and comprehensively wrecked, so eventually it had to be repatriated from deepest Yugoslavia. It was only after the charred remains had been exhibited to inspectors outside the competitions department in Coventry that they were able to agree that the car had not actually been 'exported'. The car was then ritually written off, its remains cut up and the parts dispersed.

How, then, could it be that many years later a Vitesse rally car turned up at British classic events, road-registered and carrying the number plate 6003 VC? Apparently there were, and are, ways and means. Be assured, however, that not one nut or bolt of the real 6003 VC, not even the original commission plate, was in this lookalike...

COMPETITION RECORD	
1963 Monte Carlo	
Vic Elford	3rd in class
1963 Spa-Sofia-Liège	
Vic Elford	Did not finish
Ran with a 2-litre engine on the Spa-Sofia-Liège	

6004 VC

Although this was the first of the powder blue works Vitesses to be completed, and was used extensively for practice and testing before the 1963 Monte Carlo rally, it was not entered for the event itself, and in fact never took part in any competitive international event.

Although factory records were not carefully kept, and certainly nothing has survived, this is the works Vitesse that was most often loaned out to Vic Elford and Roy Fidler to

FIRST REGISTERED	1 JANUARY 1963
ENGINE SIZE	1,596cc
MODEL TYPE	VITESSE 1600

contest a variety of British Motoring News Championship rallies in the first few months of 1963. It was sold off at the end of 1963, when the other Vitesses in the department were also disposed of.

CHAPTER 4:
TR4
(1962–64)

This chapter, more than any other in this book, has been written with a great deal of personal experience behind it, for I was competitions secretary for Standard-Triumph during this period. Accordingly, the major part of my introduction is a much-modified and updated version of a memoir written some time ago. I hope the reader will be understanding of the personal angle that will become obvious as the description unfolds.

When I joined Standard-Triumph in May 1961 there was no master plan, either for me or for the works competitions department. Working at first in the experimental/development department, I was on the rebound from an unhappy sojourn in the retail motor trade, and the offer of a job as a development engineer at the factory was welcome. I was already active in British rallying, as a co-driver, and had enjoyed some success. Before starting work at Standard-Triumph, in fact, I had turned down an approach to join the BMC rally team's pool of works co-drivers, essentially for financial reasons as co-drivers in those days were badly paid, if paid at all. After I had been at Standard-Triumph for some months, technical director Harry Webster asked me for my views on Standard-Triumph's potential future in motorsport, and so at his request I wrote a 'discussion paper' and submitted it. Weeks of silence followed.

In the meantime the Sunbeam rally team – a rival operation based on the other side of Coventry – had invited me to be co-driver with Peter Procter on the 1961 RAC rally as well as all of his 1962 events, starting with the Monte Carlo rally. That was when the trouble started – time, money and company politics were the enemies. In order to do four or five events in a season, with recce trips, I would need to take about ten weeks off work, which was potentially a huge problem. So Peter, a prosperous self-employed businessman without such concerns, and I decided to tackle the Monte, then worry about the rest of the year after that.

Harry Webster, of course, seemed to know exactly what was going on, and solved the problem in his own way. Just before the Monte, he called me into his office and told me bluntly that it was time I stopped indulging my hobby with a rival firm and that he was taking Standard-Triumph back into motorsport. He wanted me to become his Competitions Secretary.

In a matter of days, he promised, some of the recommendations made in my 'discussion paper' would be implemented. A new department would get four of the recently announced TR4 sports cars for the programme of rallies that I had suggested in my paper – Monte Carlo, Tulip, French Alpine, Liège-Sofia-Liège and RAC. I would manage this operation and would report to John Lloyd, Webster's workshop manager. The budget would be derisory, however, and I would be allowed only four mechanics, plus any help that could be scrounged from specialist test and development departments, particularly from the body shop.

What about secretarial assistance, I asked? None – no money. What about deals with tyre and fuel companies? Already in place with Dunlop and BP, both of which would provide free product and a small amount of funding. Could I have any permanent service cars? No – we would have to scrounge from the engineering fleet.

And so it started. Even before I disappeared off on the 1962 Monte, Harry and I had agreed on a four-event programme starting with the Tulip rally in May. Our new works team, with Ray Henderson as my foreman and chief mechanic, would operate from a spacious development workshop behind the main experimental workshops, one of which had been used to develop a new generation of Standard tractors.

Three of the four brand-new works TR4s at Canley in April 1962.

As this was going on, Peter and I finished fourth overall on the Monte in our works Sunbeam Rapier, with Sunbeam winning yet another team prize. Immediately afterwards Triumph announced its return to motorsport, and within a week Ray and I opened our doors. The workshops were spacious enough – but empty. There was one office, which we shared, with one telephone and one old-fashioned typewriter.

Ray was unconcerned by these sparse resources, for he already had a mountain of organisational experience and could achieve miracles with the very minimum of financial backing. Not only had he led Triumph's Trans-African Herald proving trip of 1958 (from Cape Town to the UK, via the Sahara and Tangier), but he had also been chief mechanic at the Le Mans 24 Hours race with the TR3S and TRS cars. He was amazingly resourceful and I soon discovered that if anything needed to be scrounged, borrowed or done as a favour, then Ray could organise it. Quite early on, I asked him how he was able to do all this. He looked at me in a way that brooked no response and said, 'Better not to ask' – so we left it at that.

Three other mechanics soon arrived, their first job being to prepare a so-called 'standard' Herald 1200 for American show-business journalist and personality Bob Halmi to drive in the East African Safari. We never saw that car again and I know nothing of its career, except that it did not finish. Soon afterwards the four new TR4s arrived, straight from the production lines at Canley. As soon as the cars had been stripped to their component parts and a start made on reinforcing their chassis frames, I realised I had a fine team that would be ideal for the job.

From our very first day Ray and I knew we had a development mountain to climb. Ken Richardson's previous competitions department had not only been closed down several months earlier, but it had operated in a different workshop several miles away. In addition, on its closure all build records and specifications had been destroyed, which was certainly wilful and secretive, if not vindictive. Our only way of knowing what had gone into one of the works TR3As was to find one such car and investigate it.

Fortunately, Gordon Birtwistle – a young road test engineer in the next-door department who would become a valuable member of our team – had recently bought one of the works TR3As and could tell us a lot; his car was WVC 248, an ex-Annie Soisbault TR3A that had enjoyed what could be called an eventful life. Gordon's eventual reward a few years later was to buy one of the TR4s, 4 VC, so he could then judge for himself the improvements we made in two short years!

Once our four TR4s had been completely dismantled, Ray and I cast around for ways to make them stronger and faster. Making them stronger was not a problem – we had reams of pavé test reports to tell us where the weaknesses were – but we wanted to make them lighter, as well as more powerful. Our problem, though, was that there was not an ounce of experience to draw upon, for Ken Richardson's cars had always had standard engines and rock-hard suspension, which was quite unsuitable for unmade roads and tracks, while lightweight panels had apparently never been used even though they were certainly allowed by the homologation regulations that Ray and I studied. Although Ray did not know one end of a homologation paper from the other when we started, he soon learned to read the rules – and the 'freedoms' – like a veteran and between us we worked up a list of what we wanted. Both of us knew that some 'wants' would never be satisfied, but we were prepared to keep nagging for the others.

Ray made one thing very clear from the start: I would have to go to all the meetings while he would build the cars and run the workshops! The meetings were interminable. I asked for more power (a lot more power), different gear ratios, a limited-slip differential, light alloy body panels, Perspex side and rear windows – and more money to tempt the best drivers to join us.

Even though Harry Webster sat in on many of the meetings, it was an uphill struggle. There was no more money and I was told to forget all about that – someone else would run the budget. Surprisingly, no one argued against the need for the Perspex or the aluminium panels, which came from the production car's press tools at a 'satellite' Triumph factory in Liverpool. I was told to forget about special gears, but Harry agreed to talk to Salisbury about limited-slip diffs; he was as good as his word but these were not made available until 12 months later.

With publicity pictures in mind, we chose powder blue bodywork because red was BMC's colour, British Racing Green did not photograph well and white seemed to get grubby very quickly – so powder blue was a compromise choice. As delivered, all four cars had overdrive, wire wheels and the two-piece hardtop, and speedy footwork secured the memorable registration numbers 3 VC, 4 VC, 5 VC and 6 VC (we were too late to get 1 VC and 2 VC).

I suspect that I spent the whole of the team's annual budget in those first weeks between March and May when all four cars were being prepared. Besides the team's regular mechanics, people working in our department during this period usually included two craftsmen from the body shop, an electrician from Lucas, and representatives from Laycock (overdrives) and Armstrong (shock absorbers), along with Fred Nicklin and Gordon Birtwistle as test drivers. It was never quiet and it was certainly never dull. There might have been a lack of money, but there was no lack of commitment.

We soon discovered that there seemed to be no one, literally, on the Standard-Triumph design or development staff who knew anything about power-tuning the wet-liner engine. Any number of privately owned TR3s and TR3As were already racing with SAH and Derrington engines, for which 135bhp and more was claimed, but such engines had never even been tested at the factory let alone fitted to a car. The best that the engine development team could offer was a different distributor curve! The traditional old stagers, about whom I had been warned, also insisted time and again that 5,200rpm should be the absolute rev limit. The fact that the racers with their privately prepared cars and engines always used at least 6,000rpm cut no ice with the diehards!

Webster, however, was ever the pragmatist and accepted my proposals. I reached agreement with Syd Hurrell, whose initials formed the name of his SAH Accessories business, that we would homologate the SAH bits and pieces – manifolds, camshaft and Weber carburettor manifolds – while he would supply the parts for free, along with suitably gasflowed cylinder heads, in return for valuable publicity. Harry agreed to find time for his engineers to test this kit and make sure it worked, and for this task they used an area located immediately behind the partition at the back of my office. Straight away the first such engine matched what Hurrell claimed of it, and no subsequent development work was ever done by the factory's engineers. This was also the first experience for these engineers of dual-choke Weber carburettors and it was weeks before they got to grips with the various adjustments that could be made to these sophisticated Italian instruments.

On the chassis side, the department's mechanics reinforced the four chassis frames in detail, with new mounting brackets for larger rear Armstrong lever-arm dampers (type DAS10). Nicklin and Birtwistle tested various new suspension settings, the final choice featuring firmer dampers but standard springs; although rear dampers were always by Armstrong, Koni telescopics were soon used at the front. A front anti-roll bar was never fitted to these cars, and the steering ratio was always standard.

The standard gearbox was retained, but Laycock rebuilt the overdrive to what was called 'BMC specification', which was stronger and allowed overdrive to be used on all forward gears! Various final drive ratios were homologated, all taken from existing production cars such as the Standard Vanguard and vans such as the Atlas Major.

Extra rally equipment, particularly the extra chassis strengthening and underbody protection needed at the time, added a lot of weight, although the use of aluminium panels and Perspex windows, together with the ruthless removal of bumpers and other trim items, took a lot away. The net result was that a works Triumph TR4 weighed about the same as a standard one!

Within weeks our TR4s were technically more advanced than Richardson's TR3As had ever been, although we could not force through every improvement at once. Memory suggests that when John Sprinzel and I took 6 VC on a British rally in April 1962, the engine was still standard, the doors were still in steel and the interior was fully carpeted. But at least the car handled better than John's TR3A had

Twin dual-choke Weber carburettors were first used in the 1962 Geneva rally, then became normal equipment on works TR4s. The 2,138cc engines then gave a dead reliable 135–140bhp.

done and the overdrive operated with a satisfying thump on all four forward gears. The car got a great deal of attention.

In those early days we received regular visits from Peter Riley, who had a car components business as well being a BMC team driver. He supplied everything from clocks to safety belts, horns to driving lamp covers, stick-on registration numbers to driving seats. He also regaled us with stories from rival works departments and usually had at least one ripe rumour to pass on. Pat Moss to leave BMC for Ford? Reliant to build Zephyr-engined Sabres? Rover to start building works 2000s? The Lotus-Cortina homologation delayed? We learned it all from Peter.

Finding a suitable team of three drivers – in those days the Team Prize competition was prestigious – was one thing, but finding ways to pay their expenses was quite another. Because we were small, new, under-financed and very late on the scene in 1962, it was not easy to build up a driving team. I first approached John Sprinzel, who agreed to join me, and it was John who passed on to me what BMC team leader John Gott had once told him about the ideal team of three rally drivers: 'You need one old lag, one overseas driver, and one shit-or-bust merchant.'

John thought he already qualified as the old lag and I was readily persuaded to use Jean-Jacques Thuner of Switzerland as the overseas driver. Thuner was a tarmac and pace-notes specialist who had already won the Geneva rally in his own TR3A, and his connections with the Standard-Triumph importer in Geneva, Blanc & Paiche, were impeccable – and, as it transpired, invaluable. For my 'shit-or-bust merchant' I wanted to entice Peter Procter but he was already tied up for the year, so in the end I took a real gamble by signing Lancastrian Mike Sutcliffe, who had several Ford and BMC works drives on his honours list. Sprinzel brought guile and experience, Thuner (and especially his co-driver John Gretener) the

Jean-Jacques Thuner (the 'overseas driver'), Mike Sutcliffe (the 'shit-or-bust merchant') and John Sprinzel (the 'old lag') in line astern, ready for the speed test on the famous Nürburgring race circuit in the 1962 Tulip rally.

Jean-Jacques Thuner (the 'overseas driver'), Mike Sutcliffe (the 'shit-or-bust merchant') and John Sprinzel (the 'old lag') in line astern, ready for the speed test on the famous Nürburgring race circuit in the 1962 Tulip rally.

invaluable continental knowhow, and Mike Sutcliffe the pace… but with him I was not so sure about the rest!

I vividly remember unleashing Sprinzel to prowl around an early TR4 in the workshops, throwing out everything that he did not think a rally car needed and that the regulations allowed him to discard. The pile of items on the floor soon included carpets, sound-deadening material, trim pads, the spare-wheel cover and other related items. The body craftsmen were horrified, complained that this was vandalism, and rushed off to tell their foreman. It was only after we had pointed out what the regulations allowed us to do – and also weighed the discarded items – that they were mollified.

We did not pay any fees but every crew member received £7 a day for his expenses – just about enough in those days – plus a petrol allowance. In the beginning one of the accountants wanted to see receipts for every penny spent and the balance of monies returned to them, but no unspent cash ever came back and soon dumb insolence on the part of my crew members – with my tacit agreement – got the better of him. Later in 1962 I got that allowance raised to £10 per day as a back-door way of providing some sort of driving fee, but it was not until 1965 that Simo Lampinen and briefly Terry Hunter became Standard-Triumph's first paid rally drivers. Later in the 1960s, incidentally, the accountant who had originally demanded receipts was jailed for theft, having started falsifying expenses claims from the rally team!

My lasting memory of those two years was that there was never any time to spare, especially as 1962 was the year in which I also elected to get married. If recces had to be made, I usually went along as co-driver and notes-maker to save the company some money. If service plans had to be drawn up, I was the typist. If hotels had to be booked, guess who made the reservations? Engineers had to be lobbied, meetings had to be attended, advertising agents had to be consulted, HM Customs & Excise had to be placated over inaccurately listed spares kits in service cars, drivers had to be briefed – and we also had to go on the rallies!

There was one problem, however, that neither Ray nor I had ever anticipated. Although it was great to have craftsmen on loan from 'experimental', it was often difficult to convince them that deadlines were deadlines. If a TR4 had to leave on Friday afternoon to catch a boat or an aeroplane, then it had to leave. Yet if the fit and finish of a bonnet panel, or the cut of a trim pad, was not perfect and to their satisfaction, the craftsman would always want to strip everything down and rectify the detail. Management, too, always insisted that recce cars received a respray, or at least a freshen-up, before they left the building on a new trip, even though they were unlikely to be seen in public.

As usually happens, that four-event programme soon expanded, with Thuner tackling the Geneva rally as well. At the end of the year we began to prepare a team of Vitesse 1600s for the 1963 Monte, which took up a lot of time but achieved very little (see Chapter 3), and for 1963 Vic Elford joined the team in place of Sprinzel and brought new urgency to our operation. This was when I realised that keeping a driver happy was one thing, but it was something else entirely to achieve that with a driver who was also a very hot property as far as other team managers were concerned. Had I not been so desperate to keep Vic in the team for 1964, I would never have allowed him to nag his way all the way up to Standard-Triumph's most influential individual – Donald Stokes – to get a special 2-litre Vitesse built for the 1963 Spa-Sofia-Liège marathon (see page 91).

The original plan was to use 3 VC, 4 VC and 5 VC as rally cars, with 6 VC as a spare/recce car until the first accidents inevitably occurred, after which the pack would have to be shuffled as necessary. There was never an occasion when fewer than three cars were available for an event, but it was close at times. As it happened, 5 VC tackled every event – 11 starts – and was always driven by Thuner, while 6 VC did six events but suffered two major accidents.

There were no other cars, no 'clones' and no spare bodies – not at the time. Chassis frames tended to be replaced after rough and tough events like the RAC and the Liège-Sofia-Liège, but the increasingly special bodyshells and running gear were worked hard, remaining unchanged from event to event. There was one major exception to this rule: following Mike Sutcliffe's serious crash in the 1963 French Alpine (see pages 110-112), the remains of 6 VC had to be used in a new chassis and bodyshell, but as many of the existing special parts as possible, together with the 6 VC identity, were transferred from the wreck to the 'new' machine.

The lack of money and resources meant that we never went testing, although we sent out recce cars wherever possible, and at first we did not even have dedicated service vehicles for the events we entered. When we needed spare chassis frames to replace those crumpled on a rough event, Ray Henderson would disappear for a while, shortly to return with complete new items, often with no questions asked or answered as to where they had come from.

Despite the financial constraints, we always tried to be as professional as possible. I believe we had limited-slip differentials in the TR4s before BMC fitted them to Austin-Healey 3000s, and we were certainly dabbling with driver/co-driver intercoms before Ford and BMC took them up. And I am certain that if we had been allowed to co-operate more closely with ace engine tuner 'Kas' Kastner from Standard-Triumph Inc of the USA, we might easily have had 150–160bhp engines by the end of 1963. The trouble was that the powers-that-be always muttered about 'Californian air' being used to claim absurd power figures from the USA, and the co-operation never came about – yet they were wrong and 'Kas' was right.

It was difficult to make the TR4s competitive at once. They always had to battle as underdogs because they started rallying when the Austin-Healey 3000s were at their peak. The figures were simple enough: the 2.2 litres of a TR4 could not beat a Big Healey's 2.9 litres and nor could 135bhp match 210bhp. And if the Healeys were absent from an event, there were Alfa Romeo TZs and 2-litre twin-cam Porsche Carreras to contend with. Although the alloy TR4s

Three works TR4s are ready to tackle the Shell 4000 rally in Canada in early 1964. Rebuilt in Coventry in December 1963 and January 1964, the cars were then shipped to Kas Kastner's workshops in California, where they received new alloy wheels and Oregon registration plates.

When he got his hands on the TR4s before they tackled the 1964 Shell 4000 rally, Kas Kastner claimed to 'tickle' the horsepower up to 150bhp. Maybe that was a slight exaggeration – but his genius at setting up race engines was never in doubt.

became much faster than previous works TR3As had ever been, too much time had passed and been wasted.

This, then, is the story of an extremely busy two-year programme that saw the cars reach their development peak in mid-1963. By that autumn everyone in authority at Standard-Triumph – Donald Stokes, Harry Webster, sales director John Carpenter *et al* – agreed that there was no longer a serious rallying future for the TR4. Rallies had become too rough for low-slung sports cars to survive, and the first 'homologation specials', the Mini-Cooper S and Ford Lotus-Cortina, were about to render series-production cars obsolete. At this time, therefore, our lobbying really started, on the one hand for a 'homologation special' of our own (the special-engined Spitfire) and on the other hand for a rough-road 'tank' (the 2000 saloon). Harry Webster and I got our way in the end, but what happened over the following two years is an entirely different story.

Early in 1964, three of the four TR4s were shipped off to Canada for the Shell 4000 rally – a 4,000-mile, five-day marathon, the longest in the world at the time – and did not return until the 1990s, by then in private hands of course. Although political correctness was not a feature of the 1960s, incidentally, Standard-Triumph USA still ensured that it kept everyone on side by arranging for the three cars to be driven by a European, an American and a Canadian!

3 VC

FIRST REGISTERED	17 APRIL 1962
ENGINE SIZE	1,991cc/2,138cc
MODEL TYPE	TR4

Completed only just in time to be run-in on the road journey from Coventry to the air ferry terminal in Southend, 3 VC in its original form had all its lightening features – aluminium skin panels, Perspex side and rear windows – but was still running a standard engine. Because of the way the class structure was laid out on the Tulip, this car and its team-mates ran with 1,991cc engines.

John Sprinzel was allocated this car, and for the first and only time in my tenure as Competitions Secretary I was his co-driver. This Tulip started from Noordwijk on the Dutch coast, had a night halt in Monte Carlo, and ended back at Noordwijk after four days.

The competition to all three works TR4s came principally from Rauno Aaltonen's MGA 1600 MkII, a model that had received several years of painstaking development and homologation at Abingdon and was already equipped with engine and transmission updates that were not yet available on the TR4s. It was no surprise, therefore, that the MGA was slightly quicker, but it was a surprise that Sprinzel himself was outpaced by the other two TR4 drivers and eventually finished fourth in class behind them as well as the MGA.

More was expected in the French Alpine rally, which followed just four weeks later. All four of the works TR4s started this event, all fitted with 2.2-litre engines equipped with a newly available SAH tubular exhaust system and a modified camshaft. At a stroke power and torque were increased by at least 20 per cent, and there was more to come. Once again Sprinzel drove 3 VC with Willy Cave as co-driver this time. The works team had high hopes.

John Sprinzel and Willy Cave take the start of the 1962 French Alpine rally in 3 VC.

As ever, the Alpine started from Marseilles, travelled all the way through the French Alps and across northern Italy to a night halt in Brescia, then circled the Dolomites and returned to the finish in Cannes. It was the sort of event that should have been ideal for Sprinzel and the TR4, so it was farcical, and galling, that on the Dolomites loop, when making good progress though thick fog, he was rammed from behind by Pierre Orsini's Alfa Romeo, the impact being enough to put both cars out of the event.

Next it was time to prepare for the Liège-Sofia-Liège marathon, which all agreed would be a daunting challenge. Funds were quite limited for the works team by this point in the year, so there was no way that a full reconnaissance all the way to Sofia, Bulgaria, and back could be tackled – and the roads, tracks and schedules were known to be more demanding than ever before. Team captain John Sprinzel had considerable 'previous' on this event, but neither Mike Sutcliffe nor Jean-Jacques Thuner had ever tackled it.

The works TR4s could only be specifically prepared for the Liège-Sofia-Liège as far as time and experience would allow, and experience was very limited because even the works TR3As had not taken part in this marathon since 1959. Two significant changes were made to the works TR4s: firstly, they were given new full-length undershields of louvred sheet steel that stretched all the way back from under the water radiator to behind the overdrive assembly; secondly, each car was treated to neatly styled hot air outlets behind the front wheel arches to compensate for the adverse effect of the undershield on the dissipation of heat from the engine compartment. There was also time to make a 'temporary' improvement to front ground clearance by fitting 1.0in alloy spacers between the top of the coil springs and the chassis turrets, a change that seemed to work well and had little effect on the handling. In addition, steel boot lids were reinstated and provision was made for each car to carry a second spare wheel on the lid by means of an external fixing.

Using the carefully modified 3 VC, Sprinzel – our 'old lag' in this otherwise inexperienced team entry – started cautiously, although helped by the fact that he had somehow managed to 'acquire' a set of reconnaissance notes from BMC! Although he got the car through the worst of the Yugoslavian rough stuff, along the Adriatic between Split and Novi the car suddenly failed, with a broken radiator – not the sort of problem that could be sorted out in a short time. Naturally, Murphy's Law ensured that there was no service car within several hours' reach, not even the flying 6 VC 'spares-on-the-hoof' machine.

For the RAC rally of 1962, the last of the season, 3 VC finally got a 2.2-litre Weber-carburettor engine and, like its sister cars, sported a new driving-lamp arrangement, with no fewer than five forward-facing Lucas lamps. This was thought to be a good idea at the time, but these lamps proved to be rather vulnerable to damage from diving into deep potholes or even occasionally ploughing into banks or snowdrifts!

This was a rally with many gravel-surfaced special stages and was expected to favour front-wheel-drive cars or those with more power and ground clearance than the TR4s – and that duly transpired. Sprinzel set out to match the times of the Big Healeys but, as was often the case, found this difficult. After the Blackpool start the route led across to the Yorkshire forests, where 3 VC briefly went off the road in the Pickering stage. Thereafter, Sprinzel judged that there was little point in wrecking a low-slung sports car on the very broken-up and sometimes potentially chassis-breaking stages of this RAC rally, and drove steadily to the finish. By the halfway halt, back in Blackpool, he was 17th, and at the finish in Bournemouth he had risen to 15th. As far as the factory was concerned, though, this RAC was not an entirely fruitless outing as the three works TR4s all finished, and took second place in the Manufacturers' Team Prize contest behind BMC, whose Big Healeys, as expected, were faster throughout.

After a somewhat leisurely rebuild over the winter of 1962/63, 3 VC was made ready for a new driver to the works TR4 strength, starting with the Tulip rally. Disappointed with his own efforts the previous year, Sprinzel had voluntarily withdrawn from this event and was replaced by Vic Elford, who had impressed us all with his efforts in a Vitesse in the 1962 RAC and 1963 Monte Carlo rallies (see pages 86 and 90).

For the Tulip, the TR4s reached their ultimate works mechanical specification, for all three cars had 135bhp Weber-carburettor 2.2-litre engines, Salisbury limited-slip differentials and the finalised three-lamp auxiliary lighting display. On an event that relied heavily on speed hill-climbs and circuit tests, together with a performance-handicapping system, the TR4s could not only hope to beat the formidable works Austin-Healey 3000s but they had also become extremely potent GT machines.

Elford, who had carried out a comprehensive recce with me (in 6 VC), was very fast from the start, the top GT scratch times in the event being shared out with the Morleys in their Austin-Healey 3000 and one or other of the rapid Porsche 356 Carreras. Vic's principal battle was with Roy Fidler in 6 VC, for even Jean-Jacques Thuner in 5 VC was not quite able to keep up this pace. At the end, the result in the over 1,600cc class was amazingly close, with the Morleys' Big Healey just beating the three works TR4s. The organisers helpfully published a 'phantom' list of results based solely on scratch times, and in this – what enthusiasts would call the 'real' rally – Fidler and Elford were third and fourth overall behind the Morleys and Henri Greder's remarkable 4.2-litre Ford Falcon Sprint.

Six weeks later, 3 VC was still in top form, while its driver, Vic Elford, was already convinced that he had become one of the fastest rally drivers in the world. Accordingly, he started the French Alpine rally confident that he could beat the

Austin-Healey 3000s on some of the speed tests, and the overall time schedule, though demanding, was just about feasible for a fast sports car. By that time the TR4s, complete with their Weber-carburettor 2.2-litre engines and limited-slip differentials, were as competitive as they would ever be.

On the very first speed hill-climb – the Sainte Baume, a few kilometres east of Marseilles, where the event started – the four fastest times were set by three Big Healeys and by Claude Buchet's Abarth-bodied Porsche 356 Carrera, with Elford fifth. A few hours up the road, on the full climb of Mont Ventoux, the order was Porsche, Healey, Healey – and Elford. To follow that, a 25km climb of the Col de la Cayolle saw the same cars dominate: Healey, Porsche, Healey – and Elford.

The pattern, it seemed, had already been set, but before the field arrived at the overnight rest halt at Chamonix Elford crashed and 3 VC was out of the event. On a tight road section high in the Alps, Elford found himself slowly catching the Morley twins' Healey and decided that he could overtake the famous combination, but went off the road in the attempt. The car was only lightly damaged but irretrievable without outside assistance, which was not available until factory service crews could finally arrive on the scene some hours later.

With Elford then committed to driving a Vitesse prototype on the Spa-Sofia-Liège (see page 92), 3 VC needed for a substitute crew for that marathon event. As a short-term experiment it was decided that this one-off opportunity should go to Don Grimshaw, a British stalwart who had won many events in TR3As and Austin-Healey 3000s, and was about to become Roy Fidler's works co-driver. Grimshaw's efforts sadly did not last that long, for on the very first rough, tough section – the Moistrocca Pass in Yugoslavia – the car suffered a puncture. The car slipped off the jack while the wheel was being changed, pinning the jack under the car and rendering things impossible for the tired crew, dealing with an unfamiliar car and in the dark too.

Parts of 3 VC, though not the car itself, then figured in the

On the 1963 Tulip rally Vic Elford drove a works TR4 for the first time. This was also the first event for which limited-slip differentials were available for these cars.

Vic Elford and David Stone at speed in 3 VC in the 1963 French Alpine rally.

Geneva rally at the beginning of October. Jean-Jacques Thuner requested the loan of a car to compete in his 'home' event, but it was decided that too much work was piling up in Coventry after the dreadful treatment handed out to the whole team by the recent Spa-Sofia-Liège. Instead, therefore, the complete engine/transmission assembly of 3 VC was hoisted out and loaned to Jean-Jacques to use in his own personal TR4.

This was a successful enterprise. Held mainly in the French Alps and featuring a speed test up Mont Ventoux, this 36-hour event included a handicapping formula that skewed the final results. On the eight long speed tests, the loaned 'heart and soul' of 3 VC helped Thuner to four second fastest times, three third fastest times and a fourth fastest. In almost every case the fastest car was his old rival, Hans-Joachim Walter, in a 2-litre Porsche 356 Carrera, but the handicapping resulted in Henri Greder's 4.2-litre Ford Falcon Sprint being outright winner. Thuner, therefore, had to be content with second place in the GT Category behind the flying Porsche – which really rubbed in the predictions that the works team had been making throughout the season.

For the 1963 RAC rally, the last European event the works TR4s would contest as a team, 3 VC was reunited with Vic Elford, who was still saying how good his 2-litre Vitesse had been on the Spa-Sofia-Liège and 'if only' he could use it on the RAC. As it turned out, the rally was a great disappointment to all concerned, for the rough, tough, gravel-strewn stages were totally dominated by a mass of Scandinavian entrants. None of the TR4s was on the pace on such stages, so that by the time they arrived at the Peebles control after 17 stages Elford was only in 18th place, although only headed in the sports car category by two works Austin-Healey 3000s. Immediately after this control, however, the engine in 3 VC suddenly blew a cylinder head gasket, something that had never previously occurred on a works TR4, and was forced to retire. Immedi-

ately after this Elford left the team, reluctantly, having been poached by a big-money offer from Ford for 1964.

Over the winter 3 VC had a thorough overhaul around a new chassis before being sent to Canada to take part in the 1964 Shell 4000 rally along with two of its sister TR4s. For this event the cars were converted to left-hand drive, and US competitions manager 'Kas' Kastner equipped them with Minilite-like magnesium alloy road wheels of American manufacture instead of the usual centre-lock wire wheels. The cars were re-registered in the US state of Oregon during their journey up the West Coast from Kastner's workshops in California to the start of the event in Vancouver, 3 VC receiving the new identity CAG 408.

As the American importers of Standard and Triumph cars were footing the bill, they chose two of the driving teams for this final event. In the case of 3 VC the chosen driver was Bert Rasmussen, a technician employed at the Toronto HQ of Standard-Triumph (Canada) who was already successful in rallying in that part of the world. Rasmussen finished steadily in 16th place overall, the highest position of the three TR4s, all of which made it to the finish, some battered and all bruised. On the speed sections Rasmussen was not as fast as Thuner, who was hampered by the marking system on the rally despite being the better, more experienced driver. Rasmussen's car survived surprisingly well, but this was the end of its works career and it was then sold off in North America – and did not return to the UK until the start of the new century.

COMPETITION RECORD	
1962 Tulip	
John Sprinzel	4th in class
1962 French Alpine	
John Sprinzel	Did not finish
1962 Liège-Sofia-Liège	
John Sprinzel	Did not finish
1962 RAC	
John Sprinzel	15th overall
1963 Tulip	
Vic Elford	4th overall GT and GT Team Prize winner
1963 French Alpine	
Vic Elford	Did not finish
1963 Spa-Sofia-Liège	
Don Grimshaw	Did not finish
1963 RAC	
Vic Elford	Did not finish
1964 Shell 4000[1]	
Bert Rasmussen	16th overall and GT Team Prize winner
[1] Re-registered CAG 408 for this event	

4 VC

FIRST REGISTERED	17 APRIL 1962
ENGINE SIZE	1,991cc/2,138cc
MODEL TYPE	TR4

Roy Fidler (left) with 4 VC before the start of the 1962 French Alpine rally in Marseilles – he and Mike Sutcliffe finished fourth overall and won a Coupe des Alpes. With him are TR4 privateer Roy Dixon (centre) and John Gretener.

This car, the only one of the quartet to be based in the UK during and after its life as a works machine, was both the most famous and the least used of the works TR4s. Although it only started four major international events, it was the car that provided Mike Sutcliffe with a Coupe des Alpes in the 1962 French Alpine rally, that Roy Fidler used to set a series of fastest times as a course-opening machine on the Manx Trophy of 1963, and that gave Roger Clark his one and only drive in a works TR4.

As one of the three TR4s that started the Tulip rally in May 1962, 4 VC – like 3 VC and 5 VC – already had its full complement of light-alloy body panels, although it had a totally standard 2-litre engine. Like the other VC cars, it had wire-spoke wheels and right-hand drive. Mike Sutcliffe, having visited the department in Coventry while this car was being built, made sure that it retained the standard sprung-spoke steering wheel, which he preferred, and began a campaign to get rid of the special light-alloy driving seat that he said he found uncomfortable.

It was not for some time, incidentally, that we learned that Sutcliffe's vision was not perfect, but there was no doubting his commitment. He chose Roy Fidler as his co-driver, for at this time Roy – a fish wholesaler in the Stockport area who was also known as 'King Cod'! – had yet to show just what a fast and predictable driver he was. It is doubtful if Mike had completed many miles in a TR4 before the event started, although, like almost every other serious club driver of the day, he had driven many TR2s, TR3s and TR3As.

As already noted in the description of 3 VC, on the Tulip 4 VC had to fight against the formidable MGA 1600 MkII of Rauno Aaltonen, and after a spirited four-day battle Sutcliffe managed to beat Sprinzel's sister car, but had to give best to Jean-Jacques Thuner in 5 VC. Like the other team cars, 4 VC got the uprated 2,138cc engine for the French Alpine that followed just four weeks later, and hopes were high. Sutcliffe also got his preferred driving seat, which apparently came from a Post Office delivery van and was retrimmed in 'TR4 blue' to keep the team happy…

The Alpine was 4 VC's finest hour. Not only did Sutcliffe retain his clean sheet on the road sections, ensuring a Coupe des Alpes for him, but he also won the 2.5-litre class and finished fourth overall. Predictably, the only cars to defeat the TR4 were two works Austin-Healey 3000s and Hans Walter's 1.6-litre Carrera-engined Porsche 356. Co-driver

Roy Fidler recalls this event with pleasure, for towards the end of the rally there were two extremely demanding sections to be completed, back to back.

'Both sections were at least 35km long,' explained Roy. 'You had to go like a bat out of hell on the first section and know the time you needed before putting the card into the printing clock. As I jumped out I remember Willy Cave standing there and screaming, "What time do you want?" I remember telling him, and he shouted back, "Don't stamp yet, your time hasn't come up". I stood there, trembling, wondering if I'd got my arithmetic right. It was the most horrendous minute or so, because I knew that Mike would kill me if I'd got it wrong. Then we set off, exactly at the right second, but we were still well into our last minute at the end of the next section…'

The car was then given a complete overhaul before Sutcliffe

On the famous 'Karussel' corner of the Mont Ventoux hillclimb test, 4 VC pushes on in the 1962 French Alpine.

Roy Fidler and Mike Sutcliffe with 4 VC at the start of the 1962 Liège-Sofia-Liège marathon.

Sadly the car was badly damaged in Yugoslavia when it went off the road in a dust cloud.

and Fidler set out to attack the Liège-Sofia-Liège, with its impossible-to-achieve time schedules and surfaces like breakers' yards. Faced with every difficulty, not least the TR4's unsuitability for a really rough rally, they got the car all the way round the Yugoslavian section and passed safely through Novi Vinodolski on the Adriatic Coast on their way back to the Italian border – but then disaster struck. Less than an hour after leaving the service point at Novi, 4 VC crashed in full daylight.

'I was pushing Mike a bit,' Fidler later explained to me, 'and we came up behind another competitor in a dust cloud. Mike wanted to know if he should sit back, but I said, "No, let's have a go, get past him." We were going through a forest, with tall trees on both sides, and following a pair of brake lights. Then there were no brake lights, no dust – and no road! The road turned sharp right, and we shot straight off into a field, and dropped 15 or 20 feet into a field. In the same place there was also a 3-litre Rover that had gone off an hour earlier…'

The car was seriously damaged, and, like the Rover, could not be retrieved from its resting place, but happily neither

crew member was hurt. Hours later, support from both Triumph and Rover service crews arrived, and each car was somehow cobbled up to make a painful journey back to Belgium and, eventually, to the Midlands. The comprehensive rebuild required by 4 VC involved a new chassis frame and substantial repairs to the bodywork, so the car was not ready for the RAC rally, in which Sutcliffe instead used 6 VC.

In fact the car's completion was further held up when priority was given to preparation of the new-generation Vitesses that were to compete in the Monte Carlo rally, so 4 VC was not finally ready for action again until February 1963. Mike was looking forward to getting his 'regular' car back for the season when, unexpectedly, I was ordered to loan a TR4 to Peter Bolton to contest the Yorkshire rally and 4 VC had to be the one.

Bolton, a Leeds-based motor trader, had driven competently at Le Mans in the twin-cam TR3S and TRS cars (see Chapter 2), but he was not a front-line rally driver. I turned down his original approach because I thought there were several more capable people who might deserve such a loan, but then he went above my head to technical director Harry Webster and somehow secured a change of mind. It was a disastrous decision. On an event that started from Ilkley on an extremely snowy night in February, Bolton got no more than ten miles down the road before he collided with a non-competing Land Rover coming the other way, severely damaging the TR4 and putting himself out of the event. His was the very first retirement of event and no amount of bluster on his part could hide the fact that it should never have happened. The overall outcome was that his effort to get a regular team drive was thwarted for good and that 4 VC went back into the workshops for repairs yet again.

Amazingly, the car was available again in three months, and as a shakedown exercise in May it was loaned to Roy Fidler to act as 'course-opening' and 'course-closing' car on the inaugural Manx Trophy rally on the Isle of Man, Roy having the role of Clerk of the Course on this event. To his great joy, Roy used 4 VC to set a whole string of best stage times while 'closing' the course, and was reportedly quite miffed that he was not allowed to publicise the fact afterwards! While making pre-event route surveys in January 1963, incidentally, Roy and I were temporarily stranded on the Isle of Man in a combination of freezing fog and falling snow (see page 88), a delay that made it very difficult to get to the start of the Monte Carlo rally in time.

Almost immediately after its return from the Isle of Man, 4 VC was used for extensive pre-event route surveys of the French Alpine rally, before then being lined up for use in the Spa-Sofia-Liège event. As has been made very clear, this was the roughest and toughest event on the TR4s' calendar and it needed an experienced crew, but at this point the team was in trouble. Not only had Vic Elford been allocated the prototype Vitesse (see pages 91-92), but Mike Sutcliffe had left the team and Roy Fidler was immobilised with a broken leg. In the end it was decided that a relatively unknown driver called Roger Clark and a youthful Brian Culcheth should get together in the works Triumph. This was a short-lived experiment, however, for in the far depths of Yugoslavia – between Pec and Titograd, on the rough tracks joining the turn-round at Sofia in Bulgaria to the Adriatic coast – the gearbox broke, and that was that.

The crippled car was stranded in such a remote spot and so far from factory assistance that it took weeks to retrieve it and get it back to Coventry, a journey done on flat-bed trucks and freight trains. In the end it was not possible for 4 VC to be used again in 1963, so it became the only one of the four works TR4s cars not to go off to Canada in the spring of 1964. Eventually it was repaired and sold to works test driver Gordon Birtwistle, and it survives to this day in the hands of a true TR enthusiast.

COMPETITION RECORD	
1962 Tulip	
Mike Sutcliffe	3rd in class
1962 French Alpine	
Mike Sutcliffe	4th overall
1962 Liège-Sofia-Liège	
Mike Sutcliffe	Did not finish
1963 Yorkshire	
Peter Bolton	Did not finish
1963 Manx Trophy	
Roy Fidler	Course-opening /closing car
1963 Spa-Sofia-Liège	
Roger Clark	Did not finish

An intriguing photo: 4 VC was crewed on the 1963 Liège-Sofia-Liège by Brian Culcheth and Roger Clark – for both this was a one-off outing in a works TR4.

With their car looking much smarter than it felt, Jean-Jacques Thuner and John Gretener brought 5 VC to the end of the 1962 Liège-Sofia-Liège, which was rough enough to inflict damage on the chassis...

5 VC

FIRST REGISTERED	17 APRIL 1962
ENGINE SIZE	1,991cc/2,138cc
MODEL TYPE	TR4

Although the popular Swiss star Jean-Jacques Thuner drove this car throughout its very busy and active works career, it was, perhaps surprisingly, originally built with right-hand drive and remained so through a series of major rebuilds that included several complete chassis frame changes. A Geneva-based motor trader, Thuner had experience of his own personal TR4 and also visited the factory in Coventry before the start of the programme, but he had very little experience of his new works TR4 before setting out in its first event, the Tulip rally, which started from Noordwijk-an-Zee in Holland.

On the Tulip's tarmac stages Thuner immediately proved to be the quickest of the works team's trio of drivers, setting several fastest times in his class, and among the sports/GT cars he was only beaten on 'scratch' times – the true times

The full-length undershield used on the roughest events took a considerable battering and had to be thrown away after just one event.

before a handicapping factor was applied – by two works Austin-Healey 3000s, a well-driven Jaguar E-type and Rauno Aaltonen's MGA 1600 MkII. To finish so close behind the works Healeys was creditable enough, but this proved to be a pattern that persisted through the two seasons. In this particular case, on the Tulip, the works TR4s had only about 100bhp from their 2-litre engines, whereas the Healeys had 210bhp...

Although the combination of the uprated 2.2-litre TR4 and Thuner's acknowledged tarmac expertise looked ideal for the next rally, the French Alpine, the Swiss driver was unlucky at the very end of the event. Having spent days swapping fast times with team-mate Mike Sutcliffe, Thuner was slightly ahead of him as the cars tackled the last of the high-speed 'selective' sections that ended at the infamous 'Quatre Chemins' junction in the hills behind Nice.

Unhappily, Jean-Jacques, walking the same timekeeping tightrope as Sutcliffe on this event (see page 101), spun on the very last of the tight sections, clipped a rock and slightly damaged the steering. To get back on track he had to do a three-point turn in a narrow section and, convinced that he had punctured a tyre, he then pulled in to change the wheel – only to discover that there was no puncture after all. The delay was enough to put him just a few seconds behind the near-impossible schedule and he dropped from fourth to sixth overall, and to second in class behind Sutcliffe.

Next came the Liège-Sofia-Liège, which Thuner and his co-driver John Gretener were to tackle for the first time. Greatly to their credit, they kept 5 VC going through all the dust, gravel and sometimes rocks, and passed through the Novi service point some way behind the Sutcliffe/Fidler car. This proved to be fortunate as they passed the scene of 4 VC's crash (see page 102) and were able to confirm that the crew were unhurt and then inform the Triumph service crew at the Italian border what had happened.

As it turned out, Thuner and Gretener themselves were extremely fortunate to survive the last gruelling 24 hours in the Italian Dolomites and the autobahn trek back to Belgium. Even before the car reached Novi, it was clear that its chassis was breaking up under the strain, so much so that the mechanics were horrified to see that the mounting pin for the forward end of the rear leaf spring on the passenger side was hammering its way up through the side member, with the definite possibility that it might break through and penetrate the navigator's seat. Little could be done but somehow the car limped home to finish in a quite remarkable ninth place overall and third in the sports car category, led by – guess what – two of the ubiquitous works Austin-Healey 3000s. That situation was getting to be monotonous...

When the car eventually returned to Coventry, the chassis engineers could not believe what they saw, and were even more perturbed when a complete strip-down of Mike Sutcliffe's crashed 4 VC showed that it too had signs of the

...as this shot of the front end of the rear suspension leaf spring makes clear! The chassis was replaced, and the design strengthened, before the car's next outing.

same sort of progressive collapse. The solution was to reinforce the mounting of the forward spring pins on all four TR4s, a fix that clearly worked as the problem never occurred again, not even on the 1963 Liège. Those engineers who had originally been sceptical about the value of motorsport eventually came to acknowledge that rallying's severity made it a good proving ground, and that made management's subsequent acceptance of a 2000 saloon car competition programme a little easier.

Nine months after this low-budget works team had come back into existence, the very first of the Weber-carburettor engines was finally ready. Test-bed development of the 2.2-litre engine began in September 1962 and peak power of more than 130bhp was soon achieved. As a trial run, it was decided to install one of these engines in the rebuilt 5 VC, which had a new chassis frame and repaired floorpan, and offer it on loan to Thuner for him to enter his own 'domestic' international event – the Geneva rally. This was an ideal enterprise, a suitably low-key event on which the Swiss driver's main competition would come from European Champion Hans Walter's Porsche 356 Carrera and where there would be nine hill-climb speed tests in the French Alps – including Mont Ventoux, the Chamrousse and the St Jean 'circuit' – to sort out a result.

Was the Weber-equipped engine better than the earlier type, which had retained SUs? No question. On all but one of the nine tests, 5 VC set second fastest time overall, and in every case it was the Porsche Carrera that narrowly beat it. After eight tests, the gap had stabilised and Jean-Jacques was ready to settle for second place overall, ahead of Erik Carlsson's works Saab and Pat Moss's works Mini-Cooper. But suddenly, on the start line of the final 'selective' test from Neyrolles to Le Piozat, the throttle linkage parted and 5 VC was immobilised for more than eight minutes before repairs could be made. The TR4 plummeted to 14th overall but, despite the gloomy faces, the overriding conclusion was delight that the new engine tune had proved to be another significant advance.

Although Thuner then completed the RAC rally safely, it was clear that on this, his very first visit to a British forest-stage rally, he did not enjoy the treatment doled out by the rough surfaces. After a steady run he finished ninth overall and third in his class, behind the Austin-Healey 3000s that came second and third overall. At Oulton Park, where five-lap sprints acted as special stages, 5 VC finished third fastest overall – behind the two works Healeys!

The hard-working 5 VC was then rejuvenated once again, this time to become the only works TR4 to start the 1963 Monte Carlo rally, an event that proved to be one of the snowiest on record. The car had the later Weber-carburettor 2.2-litre engine and a steel boot lid with a second spare wheel mounted on top of it, as on the Liège-Sofia-Liège rally. Technically, the important change was that the Dunlop studded

Twin dual-choke Weber carburettors were used on a works TR4 for the first time in the 1962 Geneva rally, where Jean-Jacques Thuner held a storming second place overall – behind Hans Walter's Porsche 356 Carrera – until the throttle linkage of 5 VC parted on the start line of the very last stage.

tyres were now based on the new SP-type carcass, which had textile bracing rather than wire bracing. These tyres were expected to be more robust than the previous Durabands and this proved to be the case.

Along with his works colleagues in Vitesse cars, Thuner started the event from Paris, a route that struck progressively more wintry weather. Even so, the gallant Swiss driver ploughed on bravely, especially considering that a sports car was far from ideal in these conditions and that, as a Group 3 car, the TR4 would have a handicap of six per cent handicap applied to its special-stage times. On the tough classification route from Chambéry to Monte Carlo the TR4 incurred just nine minutes of lateness and ended up second in class to former European champion Hans Walter's sure-footed Porsche 356 Carrera, which had the benefit of its engine being over its driving wheels.

Study of the six special-stage times showed that the TR4 was invariably faster than Vic Elford's flying Vitesse, and without the imposition of the Group 3 handicap Thuner would have finished ahead in the overall standings. Not only that, on the last competitive section of the event, a three-lap sprint around the Monaco GP circuit, Thuner's time – on road car tyres, of course – of 6min 22.2sec was beaten only by Walter's Porsche on 6min 1.8sec and Timo Mäkinen's Austin-Healey 3000 on 6min 13.9sec. With this sort of result already becoming familiar, the works TR4, though excellently developed, was regularly having to face up to more powerful opposition.

For the Tulip, which followed in May, 5 VC lined up with a different-looking team, as Vic Elford was in 3 VC and Roy Fidler in 6 VC. Thuner's familiar car was now back in full 'sprint' condition, carrying only one spare wheel and with its Weber-carburettor engine. Unlike the other two TR4s, it was not equipped with a limited-slip differential because only two such diffs were available at this time, and it was thought that Thuner's expertise on the speed tests and hill-climbs of this rally would make up for a lack of traction in certain conditions. It was only Murphy's Law that saw this strategy thwarted: when Thuner and Fidler both slid off the road at

Hard at work on the Monaco GP circuit in the 1963 Monte Carlo rally.

John Gretener gives a progress report to Graham Robson on the 1962 RAC rally, while Jean-Jacques Thuner keeps 5 VC's windscreen clean.

one particular corner, Fidler was able to motor out whereas Thuner needed some time to be extricated. Although Thuner was fast almost everywhere, he finished only tenth in the GT category – but being a member of the winning Team Prize competition was some consolation.

The performance of 5 VC on the French Alpine that followed was short but not sweet. Although Thuner started well, his TR4 second fastest to Vic Elford's on each of the first two speed hill-climbs, the car's clutch soon began to slip, and he was forced to drop out. The Alpine was one of those events where there was usually little time available for repairs, and in any case a clutch change on a works TR4 complete with skid shield was never going to be easy.

At least this left the car relatively fresh for use on the Spa-Sofia-Liège at the end of August. After the chassis problem encountered on the 1962 Liège, when the forward end of the rear spring mounting had almost burst through the floorpan and threatened to do lasting damage to co-driver John

Gretener's posterior, extra care and extra stiffening went into the chassis frame prepared on this occasion. As ever, the methodical and reliable Swiss driver kept his TR4 going while all around him fell out, and he was only hours from the Italian border, and a return to 'civilisation' after the arduous struggle around Yugoslavia, when the clutch gave way again.

The same team then competed in the British RAC rally, which, as already noted (see page 100) was a great disappointment to all concerned. Thuner, although no rough-stages expert, was as consistent and composed as ever, and by the halfway point in Blackpool he had dragged his TR4 up to 20th place overall, and was led in the sports car categories only by the Austin-Healey 3000s of Timo Mäkinen and the Morleys. He then set sixth fastest time on the stage at Oulton Park race circuit and was fourth fastest up the Porlock toll

Jean-Jacques Thuner sets out on the 1963 Tulip rally in 5 VC.

For two years this car was 5 VC, but after a thorough rebuild at the end of 1963 it went off to Canada, to become CAG 410 for the Shell 4000 rally, where it was driven by Jean-Jacques Thuner and Roy Fidler.

COMPETITION RECORD	
1962 Tulip	
Jean-Jacques Thuner	2nd in class
1962 French Alpine	
Jean-Jacques Thuner	6th overall
1962 Liège-Sofia-Liège	
Jean-Jacques Thuner	9th overall
1962 Geneva	
Jean-Jacques Thuner	14th overall
1962 RAC	
Jean-Jacques Thuner	9th overall
1963 Monte Carlo	
Jean-Jacques Thuner	2nd in class
1963 Tulip	
Jean-Jacques Thuner	10th GT Category and GT Team Prize winner
1963 French Alpine	
Jean-Jacques Thuner	Did not finish
1963 Spa-Sofia-Liège	
Jean-Jacques Thuner	Did not finish
1963 RAC	
Jean-Jacques Thuner	3rd in class
1964 Shell 4000[1]	
Jean-Jacques Thuner	21st overall and GT Team Prize winner

[1] Re-registered CAG 410 for this event

road, but still he could only finish third in his class.

Thuner's final outing in the car came in April 1964 on the Canadian Shell 4000 rally, where it carried the Oregon registration number CAG 410. Like 3 VC, his car was converted to left-hand drive and he was delighted, for he had been driving it in right-hand-drive form for two seasons. Although there were several speed tests on this event where Thuner was expected to be – and was – fastest of the entire entry, much of the event was settled by two factors alien to this team of cars. Firstly, the surfaces were generally at least as bad as those of an RAC rally and went on for much longer distances. Secondly, much of the navigation was of the North American 'Time-Speed-Distance' variety and Thuner's co-driver, Roy Fidler, who made no bones about his lack of experience in this sort of event, was guilty of several timekeeping mistakes.

Thuner was fastest of all on the first speed test, and thereafter his TR4 always seemed to be the fastest low-slung sports car. Sometimes it struggled to keep going in the muddy morasses found in the Rockies and in Ontario, but it was invariably in the top three or four times on every test. Like its two sister cars in that event, 5 VC officially ended its works career when it rolled over the finishing line in Montréal. Amazingly, it started 11 events in two years, driven on every occasion by Jean-Jacques Thuner.

Experts on the TR4 rally cars are convinced that 5 VC ended its days in North America many years ago, but a so-called 5 VC – let's call it a 'tribute car' – has subsequently appeared in Germany.

6 VC

FIRST REGISTERED	17 APRIL 1962
ENGINE SIZE	1,991cc/2,138cc
MODEL TYPE	TR4

Although it carried the highest of the registration numbers, 6 VC was the first of the quartet to be completed. It was immediately 'blooded' by John Sprinzel and me on a British rally, the Trio, a night-navigation affair held on roads and tracks in Lancashire, Yorkshire and the Lake District. This was no more than a gentle shakedown, for the schedule was not very demanding and 6 VC was one of several cars to complete the route without penalty.

After that, and with very minor updates, 6 VC was used for handling tests at MIRA and then went off with the same crew to carry out a detailed recce for the Tulip rally, the first international event to be tackled by the newly re-formed works team using its three other TR4s, 6 VC being the spare at this time. In theory the locations of the speed tests for this event

Jeff Uren (left) and Tommy Wisdom drove 6 VC in the 1962 French Alpine rally.

were not known in advance, but our fuel suppliers, BP, had managed to 'discover' the locations and pace notes were duly made. And wherever we turned up on our recce, we invariably encountered other rather furtive-looking crews from

The works TR4s always appeared to ride high, but when a full-length undershield was fitted the ground clearance was back to a normal level; front and rear bumpers have been removed from this car.

BMC, Citroën, Ford and other interested parties!

No sooner had the Tulip rally been completed than 6 VC was once again used as a recce car, for the French Alpine, and then rushed back to Coventry for a rather hasty refresh before being made available, at the request of Triumph's PR department, to Tommy Wisdom as a fourth entry for the event itself. A veteran motoring correspondent with the *Daily Herald* newspaper who had been racing and rallying other people's cars since the 1930s, Wisdom realised he was no longer fast enough and so he intended to share the driving with the man he took with him, Jeff Uren, a British Saloon Car Champion racing driver and also an ex-competitions manager of Ford. Although little was expected from

what was in effect a 'grace-and-favour' entry, the duo kept going remarkably well, with Uren doing most of the driving in a car that was unfamiliar to him. Although the crew did not match the speed-test times of the regular team members, they lost very little on the 'selective' sections and ended up fourth in class, and close behind Thuner in the GT general classification.

For a so-called spare car, 6 VC had already experienced a busy few weeks but there was more to come, for John Sprinzel convinced the team to use it as a high-speed 'spares-on-the-hoof' machine on the forthcoming Liège-Sofia-Liège, with Vic Elford at the wheel and chief mechanic Ray Henderson in the passenger seat, and a variety of spares and

The works team found that the engine bay of a Weber-carburettor TR4 became too hot when a full-length undershield was fitted, so this neat vent in the side of the front wings was devised.

Use of this permanent scoop instead of the opening flap of a production TR4 saved a little weight and complication – and it looked good!

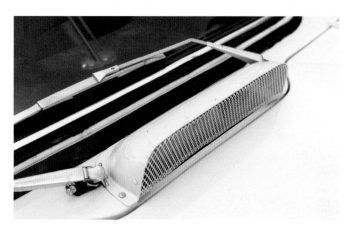

tools, including a portable welding kit, somehow crammed into the rest of the interior and the boot.

At the end of the season 6 VC was allocated to Mike Sutcliffe and Roy Fidler for the RAC rally as their usual mount, 4 VC, was still undergoing repair after its Liège-Sofia-Liège adventure (see page 102). Although they were initially the fastest of the TR4s, Sutcliffe then put the car off the road in the Wark stage, north of Darlington, and incurred a maximum lateness penalty. At half distance, when the rally returned to Blackpool, 6 VC still languished in 22nd place, but got back up to 16th by the close in Bournemouth.

Fidler moved over to the driver's seat for 6 VC's next event, the Tulip rally of 1963, as Sutcliffe was unavailable, and had

A works TR4 looked purposeful when fully developed, complete with alloy wheels, wing vents and the low-mounted auxiliary lamps; these cars always ran with hardtops in place.

Owner Neil Revington has fitted out 6 VC in its later life with divided-circuit brake lines; this was forbidden by FIA Group 3 regulations when the car was originally built in the 1960s.

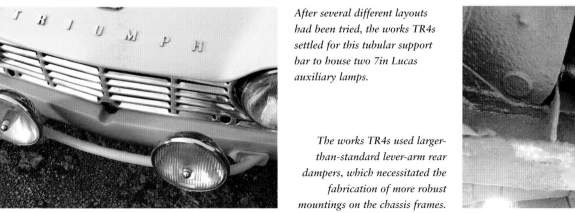

After several different layouts had been tried, the works TR4s settled for this tubular support bar to house two 7in Lucas auxiliary lamps.

The works TR4s used larger-than-standard lever-arm rear dampers, which necessitated the fabrication of more robust mountings on the chassis frames.

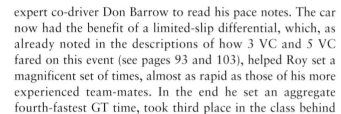

These American-made cast-alloy wheels were fitted for the Shell 4000 rally cars of April 1964, before such things were available in the UK.

The works TR4s were always neat and uncluttered at the rear: this car has the light-alloy boot lid, a stick-on number plate, a rear-mounted reversing lamp, and lacks rear bumpers – all as it would have run in 1963.

Even though the extra-large 18-gallon fuel tank is fitted to this works TR4, the wide-rim magnesium-alloy spare wheel still fits under it.

expert co-driver Don Barrow to read his pace notes. The car now had the benefit of a limited-slip differential, which, as already noted in the descriptions of how 3 VC and 5 VC fared on this event (see pages 93 and 103), helped Roy set a magnificent set of times, almost as rapid as those of his more experienced team-mates. In the end he set an aggregate fourth-fastest GT time, took third place in the class behind the Morleys' Big Healey and Vic Elford's TR4, and was part of the winning GT category Team Prize combination.

Refreshed for the French Alpine rally, 6 VC was allocated to Sutcliffe and Fidler moved back to the co-driver's seat. The crew started with high hopes of repeating their 1962 performance and were just settling in when they crashed,

very seriously, on the lower slopes of Mont Ventoux, which was only the second speed test of the event. In later years Sutcliffe conceded that the crash was his fault and that a contributory factor was his vision, which was no longer perfect. He was only shaken by the accident, but Fidler suffered a badly broken leg that put him out of rallying for several months.

'We had pace notes, of course, but Mike hadn't been up the hill since 1962,' recalled Roy. 'Vic Elford and I had done a collective recce in 4 VC just before the event and I had marked the sign for a little village on my notes. When I saw that sign I called out, "Flat Left, then again Flat Left" – and I don't remember anything after that. I woke up in hospital. I

Those air horns were bought from an accessory shop in Italy during the 1962 Liège-Sofia-Liège rally – 50 years on they still work well! The oil cooler mounted ahead and below them is a later installation.

By the 1960s, and particularly in later life when TR4s were still used in classic motorsport, fascias and instrument panels were becoming quite busy. When retrieved from Canada in the 1970s, 6 VC was still in left-hand-drive form, but was converted during the nut-and-bolt restoration that followed.

This historic rally badge dates back to the Spa-Sofia-Liège marathon rally of 1963.

The co-driver's 'office' in 6 VC is non-original, for the Twinmaster mileage recorder had not even been invented in 1962/63; note the massive horn button on the panel just below the Speedmaster.

Almost all the special stages in the 1962 RAC rally were held on loose-surfaced tracks. This is Mike Sutcliffe and Roy Fidler in 6 VC.

At the Nürburgring on the 1963 Tulip rally, with 5 VC (Jean-Jacques Thuner) and 6 VC (Roy Fidler) in a group that included Brian Culcheth's Austin-Healey Sebring Sprite.

was told that the road was narrow, Mike got his back wheels off the road into loose gravel, and immediately after the second bend there was a parapet with a concrete pole…'

The car – the original 6 VC – was written off, for it had a very badly bent chassis and an almost unrecognisable bodyshell.[1] After the usual administrative claims had been made, a new 6 VC was created from a standard new TR4 fitted with a works chassis frame that had already been prepared for it. A substantial number of components from the original car were transferred across, including the engine and rear axle, and electrical and trim items. All this took a long time, which meant that the next outing for the new 6 VC was the RAC rally. During this period Mike Sutcliffe left the team in what was really a mutual decision following his admission that perhaps he was no longer up to the task of rallying such a rapid car.

With his broken leg healed, Roy Fidler drove the effectively brand-new 6 VC on the RAC, accompanied by Don Grimshaw. Before that, however, the amazingly resilient Roy had organised the Stockport Regent Rally, which took place two weeks before the RAC, and with permission from the factory he took early delivery of 6 VC to 'run it in' as the course-opening car! Unhappily the TR4s were simply not competitive on the rough Forestry Commission stages of the RAC, and Roy, although he set off with gusto, was not quite able to keep up with his team-mates. Then, after 23 stages, the end came – suddenly and decisively.

'It happened on the way back through the Lake District towards the halfway halt,' explained Roy. 'I was tired, and I remember taking a Proplus tablet, which made me feel very confident. I thought I could do anything with the car – then I lost the back end on a left-hander. I put a wheel over the edge and the car went sideways, rolled over and slid along on its roof. I was disgusted with myself.'

It was not only Roy who was dismayed. A great deal of effort had gone into providing him with what was, effectively, a brand-new car after its French Alpine misadventure, but that is international rallying…

In fact the necessary repairs were surprisingly light, and – like 3 VC and 5 VC – 6 VC was made ready to take part in the Shell 4000 rally in Canada, complete with left-hand drive. With its sister cars it was shipped from the port of Immingham, on the Humber, to Long Beach, California, and spent time at 'Kas' Kastner's workshops on final preparation, including fitment of magnesium-alloy road wheels, before acquiring a new Oregon registration plate of CAG 409 and then going up to the rally start in Vancouver.

As the second of the TR4s for which the importers had the right to nominate drivers, 6 VC was allocated to Gordon Jennings, who was associate editor of the American monthly magazine *Car & Driver* – and would later become editor. He had little rally experience, but was expected to be a source of important after-event publicity. In his detailed report, published in his magazine in July 1964, Jennings admitted that he had been out of his depth throughout, stating that he, '…had not run in a rally for nearly ten years, and had never run in any rally of any consequence'.

[1] Following the accident, and quite unconnected with anything which was going on in the official competitions department, the old 6 VC appears to have been reborn! According to registration records preserved at the Coventry Transport Museum, the car that had been 6 VC was reborn as 5642 VC, using entirely standard parts and the same commission number as the original 6 VC. This car took shape, one has to assume, in the factory's fleet/service department, and it was officially registered on 1 November 1963. Make of this what you will…

After a sturdy performance in the 1962 RAC rally, the works TR4s won a Team Prize. From left: Mike Sutcliffe, Roy Fidler, John Sprinzel, Willy Cave and Jean-Jacques Thuner.

Humiliated on the first long special stage by Thuner, who was four and a half minutes faster, Jennings decided that his co-driver should take the wheel for the remaining slippery sections in the Rockies. On the second day, by now in the prairies, Jennings then crashed the TR4 head-on into a concrete ledge close to a bridge, distorting the chassis frame, bending the steering rack and causing the fan to puncture the water radiator. After losing two and a half hours having it all bodged up at a garage in the next town, he was able to continue. On the third and fourth days he went off several

more times, and finally crawled into Montréal in very low spirits. Amazingly, however, his co-driver's navigational skills had made up for a lot of his indiscretions, and the crew actually finished ahead of Thuner's 5 VC, which was much the quickest of the team cars on the event.

That was the end of 6 VC's works career. The car was sold in the USA to a private owner, but many years later it found its way back to the UK and in today's 'classic' motorsport it is now one of the most successful of the surviving works cars that remain active.

This shot shows why the works TR4's European rallying career was about to come to the end in November 1963, for no two-seater sports car should be expected to cope with conditions like this. Roy Fidler in 6 VC, newly 'created' after the Alpine rally crash and about to be damaged again...

COMPETITION RECORD
1962 Trio Rally
John Sprinzel — Clean sheet/class award
1962 French Alpine
Tommy Wisdom — 7th overall
1962 RAC
Mike Sutcliffe — 16th overall
1963 Tulip
Roy Fidler — 6th overall GT and GT Team Prize winner
1963 French Alpine
Mike Sutcliffe — Did not finish
1963 RAC
Roy Fidler — Did not finish
1964 Shell 4000[1]
Gordon Jennings — 17th overall and GT Team Prize winner

[1] Re-registered CAG 409 for this event

In the 1963 French Alpine rally 6 VC was written off against a large telegraph pole on the lower slopes of the Mont Ventoux speed test. Co-driver Roy Fidler was badly injured, but made a complete recovery.

CHAPTER 5:
THE 2000 (1963–67)

I can remember exactly when I decided to telephone Harry Webster to urge the development of the Triumph 2000 as a rally car. It was at the Novi control, during the Liège-Sofia-Liège rally of 1962, when I was running Standard-Triumph's motorsport efforts. Three pristine works TR4s had started this marathon event and at that point it looked unlikely that any of them would finish. Why on earth, I remember thinking, were we using low-slung sports cars to tackle such awful conditions?

Along with one exhausted mechanic, I had been slumped for hours in a Triumph Vitesse at the roadside in Novi Vinodolski, on the Adriatic coast of Yugoslavia, hoping against all reasonable hope that all three TR4s would have survived the battering handed out by Bulgarian and Yugoslavian roads in the previous 24 hours. It was a long and frustrating wait for almost everyone at this point, as only 18 of the 100 starters would eventually make it back to Belgium. A few yards away, the competent but – to me – insufferably

smug Mercedes-Benz mechanics had serviced Eugen Böhringer's big 220SE saloon and sent it on its way, to eventual victory. Ken James's works Rover P5 saloon and no fewer than three works Citroën DS19s had also sailed serenely through.

Much later, two of the TR4s arrived, looking rather sorry for themselves. There was time to give them attention – which they certainly needed. When they were jacked up, it was possible to squeeze underneath and see the appalling damage inflicted on their undersides by the rocks and ruts of the Balkans. The floorpans were pock-marked, the cooling louvres in the full-length undershields had been battered flat, and on both cars the rear suspension spring pins were steadily forcing their way through the side members. When we waved them off, with the rest of Yugoslavia and the whole of the Italian Dolomites section still to be tackled, I was not convinced that either car would survive the final day's rallying, although in the end one of them did.

From that moment I was convinced that the TR4s were no longer suited to the latest type of rough, off-road rallies that works teams had to tackle. Even though I was already so tired that I had quite forgotten what day it was – and the drivers, of course, had suffered a lot more than me – I realised there had to be a better way. I was jealous of the opposition's big saloons, which seemed to make relatively light work of such conditions. I had no doubt that Triumph needed to match them with one of its own.

That was in August 1962, when the new 2000 had reached the prototype stage. It was more than a year before the new car would be revealed to the public, and exactly two years before it could ever tackle a rally. On that hot and dusty afternoon, though, it made its date with destiny.

I had started running the works motorsport effort in February 1962, with Harry Webster in direct control, at first with TR4 sports cars and later experimenting with Vitesse saloons. There had been some success, always on tarmac and notably in the high mountains of France, Italy and Switzerland, but before the end of 1963 our works motorsport programme was at a crossroads. Although the TR4s were fast, stable and effective, they were really only suitable for tarmac rallies, and even then they were not quite quick enough to contend for outright victory. On other events, rough roads and loose-surface special stages did them no favours at all.

Webster realised, even if his colleagues did not, that there was no future for either the TR4 or the 1.6-litre Vitesse at international level. For the second time in less than three years, therefore, he told me to sit down, think things through, and have a look at Triumph's motorsport future. He was determined that Triumph should remain in top-level rallying and he also wanted to take Triumph back to the Le Mans 24 Hours race, but first he wanted to see all the options explained on paper.

Only Simo Lampinen could drive a works 2000 like this! Running in full 150bhp Group 3 trim, he was fighting for the lead of the RAC rally in his left-hand-drive EHP 78C when the engine let go.

In view of the company's rather fragile profitability at the time, he also made me a quite startling promise: 'If I agree with what you recommend, I'll try to find the money to back it.' And if I recommended an ambitious programme? 'Don't worry about that. If it looks right, I'll get the company to finance it.'

After spending hours at the keyboard of my portable type-writer, I had a document that laid out three options: to carry on rallying TR4s, to close down the department completely, or to start again with new models and redoubled effort. As an enthusiast, needless to say, I wanted the last of the three options to be chosen.

My recommendations reached Webster's desk in September/October 1963, which, significantly enough, was around the time the Triumph 2000 was revealed to the public. Every Triumph enthusiast should be grateful to Webster for accepting my proposals, which emphasised the way that two distinctly different types of international rallying had emerged in the space of only two or three years.

Some of the classic rallies remained, using all-tarmac sections where ultra-special, high-performance machines could be expected to fight it out: for such events, I suggested that Triumph Spitfires would be ideal if developed in every possible way. More and more events, though, were taking to unmade roads and tracks, some of them very rough, and to meet those challenges Triumph needed to use a big, solid, fast saloon of the type that Mercedes-Benz, Citroën, Volvo, Ford and even Rover and Humber were already using. In the Triumph range, the brand-new 2000 could be ideal.

It helped – how it helped! – that Harry Webster was a motorsport enthusiast, and a fast, capable driver. He could see exactly where the trends were pointing and to his eternal credit he agreed with the paper and took it to his Board. He came away with approval for a much more ambitious programme for 1964 along exactly the lines I suggested: we would run the new 2000 saloons and Spitfires in rallying as well as taking Triumph back to the Le Mans 24 Hours race with a team of Spitfires.

At that stage it was months before work could even begin on a motorsport development programme with the 2000. First of all the road car had to be got into production, put on sale and then homologated once 1,000 units has been built. So it was that the new Spitfires – race and rally cars – took priority for some time. In fact it was not until June 1964 that the team could begin to think seriously about the 2000s, and the first true works entry for these cars was not scheduled until late August, when the Spa-Sofia-Liège was due to start.

In line with previous practice, the competitions department built four brand-new works 2000s with the intention of using three of them regularly in events and keeping one as a spare or practice car. Painted white with powder blue roofs, the cars were collected from the production lines at Canley and, true to tradition, given the consecutive registration numbers

that we had reserved for them: AHP 424B, AHP 425B, AHP 426B and AHP 427B. By the time the cars were ready to compete in their first event, the bonnet and the tops of the front wings had been painted matt black to reduce glare on sunny days – but matt black was also in vogue and we thought it looked rather good!

Our team also scrounged the use of two old development hacks from the next-door experimental workshops for use as service cars. These 2000s were definitely tired old machines, but they were larger, faster and much more suitable as service cars than the motley selection of ex-Monte Vitesses, under-powered Atlas vans and Herald estates that had been used previously. One, 5264 VC, had started life in 1962 as the original 2000 prototype (with a 1.6-litre engine) while the other, 9081 VC, had been the second 2000 prototype. Later, when 5264 VC got too old even for this job, 5384 KV took over its duties. In all cases the rear seats were discarded and plywood boxes took their place, the better to carry mountains of spare parts – at this time, of course, the estate version of the 2000 was yet to come.

Not only were they good service cars, but they were also useful for trying out bits and pieces for the forthcoming rally cars. Heavily laden service cars soon gave us experience with springs and damper settings, although the special wheels and brakes of the rally cars were never tried out on these old machines. Careful study of prototypes subjected to the British motor industry's punishing 1,000-mile pavé test at MIRA showed that the body structure, which had been engineered

Terry Hunter was probably the fastest works 2000 driver of 1964, if not the most amenable team personality. Here he is pushing on with AHP 427B in that year's Spa-Sofia-Liège. In those days swivelling roof-mounted spotlights were still permissible.

115

by Pressed Steel, was extremely robust. Surprisingly, however, this study gave us no advance warning of the problems that were to strike the rally cars in the Spa-Sofia-Liège…

When the time came to prepare the rally cars, the intention was always to take advantage of modification possibilities allowed by FIA regulations and turn the works 2000s into rough-road 'tanks'. Near-standard Group 1 cars, it was concluded, might be strong, but would not be competitive against the Lotus-Cortinas, which were lighter and a lot more powerful, though fragile. Further-modified Group 2 versions would be little better. But if the cars were entered in Group 3 – the 'Grand Touring' category where so many other much-modified saloons had found success – they might become formidable competitors. Group 3 rules required the basic architecture of the cars to be retained – body structure, engine, transmission and suspension systems – but almost any modification within those parameters was permitted.

The biggest problem lay not in finding technical ways to solve the problems but in convincing chairman Sir Donald Stokes why these things had to be done. It was not easy to persuade a tycoon that the new model of which he was very proud was not going to be fast enough for rallying until it was modified almost out of recognition. Furthermore, while rallying enthusiasts could quite see why extrovert 2000s with Weber carburettors had to compete against Austin-Healeys and Porsches, the general public could not. If and when the cars started winning, Standard-Triumph's advertising agents

This very significant shot, dating from November 1964, shows all four works Triumph 2000s parked outside the Competitions Department at Fletchamstead North (behind the camera). AHP 426B (third from the camera) would finish sixth overall, with Roy Fidler driving.

were going to have to work hard for their fees…

In the end, though, top management agreed to our proposals. Along with leading company engineers, therefore, Ray Henderson and I sat down to discuss what was desirable and what was feasible. The limiting factor was not necessarily the cost of what we proposed but the time it would take.

In developing the Group 3 2000s, our objectives were to make them considerably faster and stronger, to give them better brakes, and to make them impervious to awful road conditions by giving them considerably more ground clearance. Fortunately there were at least three engineers at Triumph who saw this not only as a technical challenge but also as a great deal of fun. These men were Ray Bates and David Eley on engine work and George Jones on transmissions, while John Lloyd, who had responsibility for the competitions department, always took paternal interest in what was brewing. Although the design and experimental departments were told that all this specialised motorsport activity had to be achieved without disruption to the new-model programmes for the front-wheel-drive 1300, the TR4A and the GT6, no one – not even Harry Webster, who was ultimately in charge – took a great deal of notice of such edicts, and with much goodwill the works 2000s were quickly transformed into thirsty but efficient rally specials.

Well in advance of completion for their first event, the 1964 Spa-Sofia-Liège, the engines of these cars were equipped with an impressive array of three dual-choke Weber carburettors because the original twin Zenith-Stromberg carburettor/manifold layout was impossibly restricting. The Webers certainly liberated a lot of power – output was 150bhp – and the engines revved to at least 6,500rpm in this condition, with most of the torque increase at the top end. These cars made a glorious sound – service crews certainly never needed any other advance warning of their approach – and at that time we certainly did not care about their terrible fuel consumption!

The transmission used a wider-ratio gearbox with overdrive operating on top, third and second gears. With the works TR4s we had always been irritated by the fact that overdrive third and direct top were almost the same, so I asked George Jones if this could be rectified for the Group 3 2000s, which would use the same transmissions. George, whose curmudgeonly image was carefully cultivated and not at all genuine, was one of the brightest transmission specialists in the British motor industry. Almost at once he suggested that he could provide a lowered third gear, which would also give a lowered overdrive third, by asking his craftsmen in the experimental departments to machine some new gears. When I thanked him for solving a difficult problem without fuss, he merely growled, 'Any bloody fool could have worked that out!' Any fool, perhaps, but I certainly had not thought of it…

Without overdrive, George's lowered third gear would have made the gearbox almost unusable, but when the drivers

'played tunes' with the overdrive switch they had a totally practical seven-speed transmission. The much wider gap between overdrive third and direct top gear was immediately noticeable, and the use of overdrive second filled in a mighty gap between second and third. We leaned heavily on Laycock's overdrive specialists to make sure that their uprated, but complex, box of tricks never let us down in the heavy 2000. It rarely did.

Although I knew that the cars needed more ground clearance, I was not willing to jack up the suspension to get the whole car higher off the ground – the rear suspension geometry would have been ruined if we had done that. Instead, we specified special 15in TR4-type steel disc wheels along with larger front-wheel disc brakes and special calipers. All this had the effect of raising the overall gearing, so we countered this by using the lowest rear axle ratio that Jones's engineers could machine – 4.55:1. At the same time Harry Webster persuaded Salisbury Transmissions of Birmingham to provide American-type Powr-Lok limited-slip differentials, similar to those used on the works TR4s of 1963. Salisbury, no doubt, hoped that Triumph would eventually adopt these for production cars, but this was never done.

The finalised transmission was an excellent compromise – good ratios combined with standard casings and basic hardware, all very carefully assembled by the experimental transmissions department. Even so, there was always as much torque as this assembly could handle, and there were several breakages in the early years.

The result was a totally specialised and very low-geared rally car, which in spite of its great bulk accelerated like a moon rocket – steady at first, then ever faster. In 1965 *Motor* tested a 150bhp works car – EHP 78C – and the figures achieved by the magazine are given in the accompanying table, together with those of a standard car for comparison.

When three cars started the Spa-Sofia-Liège marathon in August 1964, the works team had already carried out a lot of pre-event testing, mainly using AHP 424B. Everyone was confident, especially the drivers. After 1962 and 1963, when the low-slung TR4s had battered themselves almost to destruction on the rocks of Yugoslavia, the use of the 2000 saloons seemed to be an ideal solution. Naturally there was shielding under the engine and gearbox, but deflector shields were also fitted ahead of the rear semi-trailing suspension arms. Everything we knew about the Liège, and every bitter experience of the previous two years, had gone into the preparation of these machines.

This was to be the last of all the Belgian-organised marathons – if only we had known that in advance – because public opposition, brought about by the event's effect in disrupting the flow of increasingly heavy holiday traffic, was about to kill it off. It was also to be the fastest and toughest of the marathons, for there would only be a single one-hour halt for the entire 96 hours, at the turn-round time control in Sofia, capital of Bulgaria, and only 21 of the 106 starters would reach the finish. In 1964, as ever, the conditions would be hot and dusty throughout, with the route using rough, unsurfaced tracks. In its report, *Autosport* described the event as a 'Legendary Marathon'.

For the moment, though, the works team faced up to the 96-hour event with great confidence. My personal ambitions were to see at least two of the cars finish, with at least one of them in the top five. The Austin-Healey 3000s were expected to set the pace, which the 2000s could not match, but there were high hopes of matching the works Rover 2000s and 3-litres, the Ford Cortina GTs, and the Citroën DS19s.

Everything started well except that our Dunlop radial-ply SP3 tyres, which we were contracted to use, seemed puncture-prone in Yugoslavian conditions. Whereas most of the Rovers dropped out before Sofia, the Triumphs were still going strongly by the time the route wound down the mountains into Titograd, on the Adriatic coast. But suddenly, between the Stolac and Split controls, with only a few hours of rough stuff remaining, all three cars broke down with the same problem – the rear suspension cross-beam mountings broke away from the floorpan pressings and deranged the suspension.

The cars could go no further, and it was no consolation to any of us when inspection showed this to have been caused by metal fatigue. It took days to patch up the cars and get them back to Coventry, where Triumph's engineers were aghast when they saw what had happened. Nothing like that had turned up in pavé testing at the prototype stage, so we were at least providing them with knowledge to make the cars better in the future. The solution was to reinforce the floorpans in that area – not a problem regulations-wise – and the result was a complete and lasting success. Never again was a Triumph saloon car, not even any of the World Cup 2.5 PIs, forced out of a rally with such problems, and in two

TRIUMPH 2000 PERFORMANCE FIGURES *Motor* magazine, 1965	Works car	Standard car
0–30mph	3.4sec	4.1sec
0–60mph	10.4sec	13.6sec
0–80mph	18.8sec	26.8sec
0–100mph	33.9sec	–
Standing quarter-mile	17.8sec	19.4sec
Top speed (overdrive top)	111mph	98mph
Top speed (direct top)	105mph	94.5mph
Third gear (overdrive)	91mph	89mph
Third gear	75mph	75mph
Second gear (overdrive)	61mph	–
Second gear	50mph	50mph
First gear	32mph	31mph

Maximum engine speeds were 6,500rpm (works car) and 5,000rpm (standard car)

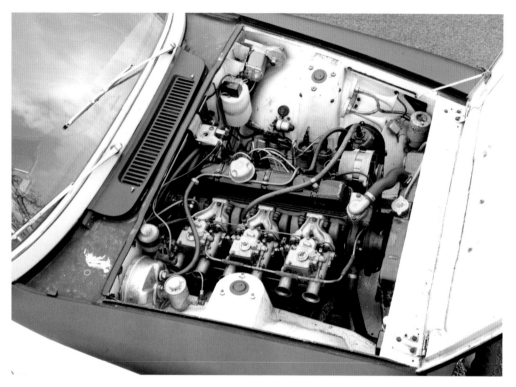

The engine bay of a Group 3 works 2000 of 1964–65. The main feature, of course, is the triple dual-choke Weber carburettors, although standard cast-iron exhaust manifolds were retained. Peak power was approximately 150bhp – and fuel consumption was horrendous.

years not a single bodyshell had to be replaced due to age and decrepitude.

We had no excuses, and we made none. The fact that all the Rovers and Fords had failed as well was little consolation, especially as three works Citroën DS19s – ultra-modern cars with nine years of rally experience behind them – did make it back to Belgium.

For the next few weeks the 2000s had to be ignored as the entire team then concentrated on the Spitfires, which produced fine performances in the Tour de France and the Geneva rally. For the RAC rally of November, however, all four works cars were prepared, for AHP 424B was loaned, at Harry Webster's request, to Peter Bolton. This time, too, there was an important innovation: for the very first time Dunlop produced radial-ply tyres with an off-road tread – SP44 Weathermasters – and this gave Terry Hunter and I the excuse to go and test them against regular SP3s on the loose-surface test track at Bagshot.

The traction advantages of these SP44 Weathermaster tyres on gravel were considerable, although tarmac handling suffered. Since almost all of the 60-odd stages on the RAC had loose surfaces, we decided to use them, with excellent results. Our stage times were impressive and the six-cylinder engines sounded magnificent – and the publicity gained by the cars was immense. The fact that only one other Group 3 machine – one of the formidable works Austin-Healey 3000s – beat Roy Fidler's car gives a measure of how far the project had come in a matter of months. Unfortunately Dunlop could only promise limited supplies of SP44 Weathermasters

– BMC were trying to hog all they could for use on the works Austin-Healey 3000s – so in the end some difficult decisions had to be made.

At this point I left Standard-Triumph for a different career, initially with *Autocar* magazine, but I kept my links with the team by arranging to become Roy Fidler's co-driver in an ambitious British rally programme. Although Fidler was as fast as usual, and the cars were mainly robust and easy to fettle, they continued to suffer from a number of mechanical frailties, mostly connected with the rear axles. Lack of funds also meant that some components had to be used for longer periods than was ideal. By mid-1965 this programme was in disarray, and was eventually abandoned.

One brand-new car, the left-hand-drive EHP 78C, was built up for 1965 and was originally intended for new recruit Simo Lampinen's exclusive use, but in the end the young Finn did not get his hands on it until the very end of 1965, when he so nearly won the Welsh International rally.

I hope that my next observation will not sound too much like sour grapes, but the fact is that the cars were not used as intensively in 1965 as they might have been had I still been running the programme. With Lampinen joining the team as a paid professional, his loose-surface skills could have been used more frequently with the 2000s and I believe that the cars could have been successful if they had tackled the Safari or the Acropolis, but it was not to be. Of course, it did not help that the rough-and-ready Spa-Sofia-Liège event had had to be abandoned.

With the emphasis in 1965 more firmly in favour of the still-developing Spitfire rally cars and racing cars, the works 2000s only appeared four times on events outside the British Isles. Although some extra, inventive homologation was made to the FIA documents for 1965, this was never co-ordinated into a major entry of Group 3 2000s.

Triumph was hit very hard by a change in regulations for 1966. The FIA's new Appendix J regulations included severe restrictions on the specification and use of saloon cars in Group 3, and also abolished the right to homologate certain options. The works 2000s and Spitfires were both affected, and life became very difficult for Ray Henderson in planning Triumph's motorsport future. In international events saloons would simply no longer be able to compete as much-modified Group 3 cars.

Nevertheless, Board approval was given to a competition programme for 1966 but with a much lower budget – £55,000 – than in the previous two seasons. Sir Donald Stokes was not at all happy about the limited success so far achieved, for as far as he was concerned motorsport was a waste of money unless a car was winning outright. He once stated that the results achieved in the USA by 'Kas' Kastner's TR4s and TR4As warranted the expenditure, but he doubted whether anything else was worth it.

The expectation for 1966 was that works 2000s would

only compete in the Monte Carlo, Safari and RAC rallies, but the idea of sending works cars to the Safari was soon abandoned. However, £4,000 was made available to Leyland East Africa to back their own Safari entries of four locally prepared 2000s, but that did not help as none of them finished.

Because Group 1 and Group 2 regulations obliged the 2000s to run with the standard Zenith-Stromberg carburettors and standard manifolds in 1966, they were rendered uncompetitive against the Lotus-Cortinas and other 'homologation specials'. Harry Webster briefly considered putting into production a limited-run 2000 'hot rod' with three SU carburettors, but the company's Product Planning function was unimpressed and this never came to anything.

In any case, the works team's first event of 1966 – the Monte Carlo rally – ran to its own very constricting rules, which required all entries to be in Group 1 form and therefore virtually standard. Accordingly, Ray Henderson's mechanics had to build up a set of brand-new 2000s that had little more than 90bhp (instead of the 150bhp of the 1964–65 examples), standard gear ratios, 13in wheels and standard differentials.

Because teams with 'homologation specials', such as BMC with the Mini-Cooper S and Ford with the Lotus-Cortina, were much better placed on the Monte, it was always realised that Triumph would struggle in 1966. It might be possible to beat the deadly rivals at Rover, but there were no illusions about Triumph's chances against the big Citroën DS21s and the Lotus-Cortinas.

The Monte, therefore, was not a happy event for the team. Although Roy Fidler finished 14th overall, and his 2000 was the fourth car home among the 'front engine/rear drive' runners, the two other works cars retired, one with a broken gearbox, the other with a smashed differential. Even this result flattered Roy a little, for this was the year of the disqualification fiasco, when a number of leading cars, including the works Minis, were disqualified after the event on very flimsy grounds.

Even though the 2000s had not been involved in the scurrilous events, Sir Donald Stokes was not amused. As in later years, he saw little point in spending money for 'his' cars to finish out of the running, nor was he interested in sponsoring the sale of special cars to rectify that situation. Within weeks, therefore, the works effort was run right down. Cars were sold off, drivers were released from contracts, and the department effectively went into suspended hibernation.

Two very limited programmes, however, survived – one for racing and one for rallying. Firstly, Roy Fidler arranged to buy one of the 2000s for use in British rallies; this was FHP 993C, his Monte Carlo car, in rather hybrid form, updated with a Group 3 Weber-carburettor engine but on 13in wheels and the associated suspension. Secondly, Bill Bradley, who had raced a Spitfire in 1965, started a British Saloon Car

Viscount Kim Mandeville drove this works-prepared 2000 in the 1967 East African Safari rally and is seen manoeuvring the car ready for loading on to the aeroplane to Africa. On this event cars had to run in near-standard Group 1 or Group 2 form, rather than as more competitive Group 3 machines.

Kim Mandeville (check shirt) and Stuart Allison finished a very creditable third overall in their works-prepared but privately financed Group 2 2000 in the 1968 East African Safari.

Championship Group 5 racing project with a fuel-injected 2000! Both efforts enjoyed a measure of factory backing and both cars were prepared in Coventry, although in neither case were these entries accompanied on events by a posse of works mechanics. The racing car lived in Coventry between events, while Fidler kept the rally car at home near Stockport unless major rebuilds were required.

Both of these cars had a most positive effect on what would follow in what we may call the 'Abingdon Years'. Fidler's car continued to provide experience and data of what was needed of a rally car, while Bradley's car, which was technically troublesome throughout the year, showed that there was, indeed, potential in the Lucas fuel injection system being developed by Triumph for the road cars that would surely follow. Fidler, in particular, laboured under all the usual problems of a semi-privateer – finance, time, and the difficulty in developing his car much further than the condition in which he acquired it – yet managed to win the RAC British Rally Championship of 1966 with victories and strong placings in the second half of the season.

Even so, the outcome of the RAC British Rally Championship hinged on the result of the very last event of the year, the International Welsh, which was settled on well-known special stages. Even though FHP 993C was getting tired after a very busy season, including the very demanding RAC rally where it just failed to finish, the car hung together well enough for Roy to stage a close fight with Tony Chappell's Lotus-Cortina and finish in second place, which was enough to win the championship by a tiny margin.

Faced with a quite appalling lack of PR skills at the RAC, where for some reason they were reluctant to publicise their own rally championship, Standard-Triumph decided to mount its own celebration. Fidler told me that technical chief Harry Webster asked him to visit the Fletchamstead North factory.

'As I walked into his office,' Roy recalled, 'he had organised a press conference where he presented me with a silver cigarette box, which had engraved on it: "Presented to Roy Fidler by the directors of Standard-Triumph International Ltd in recognition of his brilliant achievement in winning the 1966 RAC British Rally Championship in a Triumph 2000." And there was a cheque for £100 in it!'

Prior to the conclusion of the RAC British Rally Championship, there had been no luck at all on the RAC rally, where yet again Fidler's works-loaned 2000 suffered from a whole range of problems – punctures, a noisy rear axle and finally a broken engine fan blade that punctured the radiator – that all contributed to his enforced retirement.

For 1967 Fidler continued with a very restricted programme, but funds were restricted and there was little chance of improving FHP 993C any further. Although it was well prepared and generally reliable, it could not record any more outright victories. Its value to the company, however, came at the very end of its works career when it was converted into the first of the 2.5 PI saloon prototypes.

2680 KV

Colour Sergeant John Rhodes ploughing through impossible going in 2680 KV in the London Motor Club's TV Autopoint in December 1963.

FIRST REGISTERED	19 SEPTEMBER 1963
ENGINE SIZE	1,998cc
MODEL TYPE	2000

This car, and the single event that it tackled, is only included as something of a curiosity, for it was not a seriously developed car and it took part in an unusual event. It was, in fact, one of the earliest cars to come down the production line at Canley, for it carried the chassis number MB 5DL and the engine number was MB 8HE. In modern motor-industry parlance we would probably call it a 'pilot-build' model.

As far as Standard-Triumph was concerned, however, this outing was important because the event – officially called the London Motor Club Autopoint – was broadcast live on TV on a Saturday afternoon in December. The competition took place on unmade tracks over demanding terrain and involved an amazing variety of vehicles, some with four-wheel drive. Held at the Hungry Hill Army testing area near Aldershot, it was in effect a point-to-point, but for machinery rather than horses.

Whatever happened, this was a 'win-win' situation. If the car won any of the 'races', that would be a real honour, but if it did not... well, this was only a bit of fun after all. The driver of the 2000 was Colour Sergeant John Rhodes, not the soon-to-be-famous Mini racer but a club-standard rally driver who was also a regular soldier. In fact the car performed with honour, showed impressive traction in appallingly muddy conditions, and made the company's publicists very happy.

COMPETITION RECORD	
1963 TV Autopoint	
Colour Sergeant John Rhodes	Two wins, one second place

AHP 424B

FIRST REGISTERED	1 JULY 1964
ENGINE SIZE	1,998cc
MODEL TYPE	2000

The RAC rally of 1964 was the first event for AHP 424B, driven by Peter Bolton on this occasion.

Months after it had been built and prepared, and following some testing, this car was finally given a start on a rally, driven on the 1964 RAC by Peter Bolton, who had crashed so ignominiously on his previous drive in a works Triumph (see page 102). As on that occasion, the team was reluctant to provide one of its precious cars to a driver who was not up to it, but once again Bolton, a motor trader, pulled every possible string with top management and got his way.

As a result of the bitter experiences with structural failures on the recent Spa-Sofia-Liège, all four of the works 2000s had had considerable reinforcement added to their bodyshells in the area close to the rear suspension cross-beam mounts, but they were otherwise unchanged; it should also be noted that there were spells on this event when Dunlop SP44 cross-country treaded tyres were available. Predictably enough, at least to the team if not to higher management, Bolton never matched the pace of the professionals in the other three cars, but he did manage to keep the car going and eventually finished, well down the field.

Things looked up when the team decided to support Roy Fidler in a serious British rally programme in one or other of the Group 3 cars, and I was his co-driver whenever I had the time at weekends, although I was about to leave my role as team manager for a new career in journalism. First time out for our new pairing, in AHP 424B, was the Welsh International, which started from Cardiff and included 300 miles of Forestry Commission special stages. Our 2000 started first on the early stages and soon took the lead in the event, although there were early problems with the brake servo that could not be solved quickly, causing Roy Fidler to have to use much more braking pressure than he would have liked.

Unhappily, a persistent engine misfire worsened through the second half of the event and a solution could not immediately be found by the non-factory mechanics who were tending the car, so we were forced to retire after running out of time near the Llandovery control. Later the problem was traced to a faulty distributor, which could have been substituted so easily if it had been discovered in time.

Next time out, with the engine problem solved, Roy and I took the car to an encouraging fifth place on the Shunpiker rally in North Wales, a round of the *Motoring News* championship where navigation was almost as important as the performance of the car. A week later the same high-class field attacked the Welsh Marches rally in south Wales, where our 2000 won outright. Soon after this, with hopes now high, our hard-working car suffered a blown cylinder-head gasket on the *Express & Star* rally, which took place in north Wales.

In our next event, the Wales-based Nutcracker rally, we had another setback when Roy put the car off the road over a blind brow while leading, and we had to retire. As his co-driver, I went back up the road to flag down other cars that might have joined the big Triumph, but unfortunately one of them did

COMPETITION RECORD	
1964 RAC	
Peter Bolton	Finished
1965 Welsh	
Roy Fidler	Did not finish
1965 Shunpiker	
Roy Fidler	5th overall
1965 Welsh Marches	
Roy Fidler	1st overall
1965 *Express & Star* National	
Roy Fidler	Did not finish
1965 Nutcracker	
Roy Fidler	Did not finish
1965 Gulf London	
Roy Fidler	Did not finish
1965 RAC	
Jean-Jacques Thuner	2nd in class

precisely that, sweeping me off the road and causing some injury to my ankles and hips. The result was a night in hospital followed by two weeks off work waiting for the damage to start to heal – and I missed the Circuit of Ireland that followed.

The following month the car did not even make the start of the Showers rally, for its rear axle broke while we were driving to the start in mid-Wales, with me at the wheel, and we were stranded for many hours – no mobile phones in those days! In June, much to my embarrassment, exactly the same thing happened on the way to the Scottish rally.

There were high hopes, even so, of a good performance at the end of June on the Gulf London rally, which incorporated a start and finish in London, along with good-quality forestry stages all round the country. AHP 424B started well in a star-studded field and was soon running at the top of the lists. Then in the 30-mile Dovey stage, near Machynlleth in Wales, a half shaft broke, stranding the car miles from support, and yet again there was huge disappointment.

Then came the last event of 1965 for which the Group 3 works Triumph 2000s would be eligible – the RAC rally. AHP 424B was one of four 2000s entered and it was earmarked for Jean-Jacques Thuner, who was determined to match and preferably beat Roy Fidler and Simo Lampinen in other works 2000s. With much snow all over the British Isles, however, Thuner could not match his colleagues for pace but he did put in a steady performance to finish second in class to Timo Mäkinen in a works Austin-Healey 3000.

After the RAC rally AHP 424B was not used again in a major event.

AHP 425B

Jean-Jacques Thuner liked his rally cars to have a '5' in their registration number, which explains why he usually drove AHP 425B when a team of 2000s were entered. Here he is on the 1964 RAC rally, on an early special stage before the highly tuned 2000's rear axle failed.

FIRST REGISTERED	1 JULY 1964
ENGINE SIZE	1,998cc
MODEL TYPE	2000

This car was the second of four brand-new 2000s introduced in mid-1964. On reflection it was extremely brave of the company to commit three of the quartet to take part in the toughest rally of all in those days – the Spa-Sofia-Liège.

Although we did not know it at the time, this would be the last 'Liège' of all. Jean-Jacques Thuner was allocated AHP 425B and he looked forward to a boulevard ride compared with his bone-shattering experiences on two previous Liège marathons with the low-slung works TR4s.

Although Thuner never challenged for the lead, he looked destined for a solid finishing position until well after the route turned back from the one-hour halt in Sofia. AHP 425B first suffered several punctures, and then suddenly faltered between the Stolac and Split time controls in the mountains close to the Adriatic coast. The mountings of the rear suspension crossbeam had begun to tear away from the floorpan of the car, rendering it undriveable, and no further progress was possible.

Amazingly, the other two team cars (AHP 426B and AHP 427B) suffered near-identical failures so close by that all three of them were parked nose to tail at the side of a Yugoslavian road! Forever afterwards, incidentally, the team was grateful to the BMC team mechanics who took a lot of time to help patch up these rival cars so that all could be driven back to Belgium.

Suitably refurbished, and reinforced around the rear suspension mounting beam areas, ADU 425B was then driven by Thuner on the RAC. After completing the West Country and Welsh special stages, he was most cruelly eliminated on the Whinlatter stage in the Lake District when the differential broke up. This failure was a new one at the time but would become depressingly common in the following year, as it happened to several more team cars on later events.

For the Monte Carlo rally of January 1965, when the wintry conditions were severe, Peter Bolton once again talked his way into the use of a works 2000, once again he was allocated a car – AHP 425B – against the department's wishes, and once again he achieved nothing. In terms of possible positive publicity, this time Bolton had persuaded the BBC TV programmme *Sportsview* to become involved in his entry, but it was all a damp squib. Having started from London, alongside the four-headlamp Spitfires, Bolton's car blew its engine in northern France and that was that; post-rally examination revealed a stripped camshaft skew gear, something the engineers had not seen before.

In what was, ultimately, an unsuccessful and short career, AHP 425B then tackled its fourth rally in a nine-month period when Rob Slotemaker, who had not previously driven a Group 3 2000, was invited to tackle his home event, the Tulip rally, alongside team-mate Jean-Jacques Thuner. Starting well and leading Thuner in his category and class, Slotemaker then encountered blizzard-like conditions around the Ballon d'Alsace speed hill-climb and the Col de Faucille near Geneva – and this was in May! At one point he was reduced to removing the car's floor mats to put them under the spinning rear wheels

to try to provide some traction – an emergency tactic that got him out of trouble but by then the engine was damaged through over-revving. AHP 425B finally arrived at the next control with steam pouring from every possible joint and the car had to retire. It was not rallied again by the factory.

COMPETITION RECORD	
1964 Spa-Sofia-Liège	
Jean-Jacques Thuner	Did not finish
1964 RAC	
Jean-Jacques Thuner	Did not finish
1965 Monte	
Peter Bolton	Did not finish
1965 Tulip	
Rob Slotemaker	Did not finish

AHP 426B

FIRST REGISTERED	1 JULY 1964
ENGINE SIZE	1,998cc
MODEL TYPE	2000

The third of the new team cars was allocated to Roy Fidler and Don Grimshaw for the Spa-Sofia-Liège in 1964. Like AHP 425B, it suffered punctures at an early stage – Dunlop was not proud of its record on this event – before succumbing to the same rear-end suspension/structural failure and coming to a halt very close to its sister car.

After it had been recovered and repaired, the car was used to great effect three months later by Roy Fidler on the RAC rally, which was as long, rough and arduous as ever. Surrounded by a phalanx of works Ford Cortina GTs, Volvos, Mini-Coopers and the usual Austin-Healey 3000s, Roy could do no more than hope for a place in the top ten and, true to form, he therefore set out to last the distance. He did so, and never lost touch with his peers.

By the time the event reached the second breakfast halt, at Turnberry in Scotland, Fidler was hovering just outside the top ten, slightly behind Terry Hunter in a sister 2000. Then Hunter made a schoolboy error in over-sleeping at that halt and received a big time penalty for leaving late, so Roy was now unchallenged as team leader. By the time the event came back to the Home Counties, he had risen to sixth place overall and the only Group 3 car ahead of him was Timo Mäkinen's Austin-Healey 3000, which, by the time it staggered to the finish in London, was close to collapse with a cracked gearbox casing that had necessitated regular and copious replenishment

Looking very smart, AHP 426B about to start the 1964 RAC rally from London, with Roy Fidler at the wheel; this combination would finish sixth overall.

of precious oil. Roy had come so very close to winning the Group 3 category...

AHP 426B then sat around, unused and seemingly neglected, until mid-1965, when ex-team member John Sprinzel acquired sponsorship – and guaranteed exposure – from the *Weekend Telegraph* magazine and persuaded Triumph's public relations team that it would be a good idea to tackle the French Alpine rally. This meant that the team turned up at the start in Marseilles with four 'prototype' 1.3-litre Spitfires and this single Group 3 2000, still complete with its triple-Weber engine and 15in wheels. From the point of view of planning service and support arrangements, it was far from ideal that the Spitfires were all due to run at the head of

The works team loaned a 2000, registered AHP 426B, to John Sprinzel and Daily Express *journalist David Benson for the French Alpine rally of 1965. Unhappily the gearbox failed, high in the French Alps. '*

the field whereas the 2000's position was near the back of a 93-car convoy.

Sprinzel started strongly, although he found the latest Alpine rally schedules for Group 3 cars quite impossibly fast. After 24 hours, though, with all the classic hill-climb tests already tackled once, he found himself second in the class, thanks to the faster Porsches dropping like flies. Then, unfortunately, the gearbox stripped third gear and time could not be found to change that, and within hours a further gear also became faulty. Two loops of the Allos sections were now called for, and here Sprinzel's two-geared Triumph gave up once and for all; after using 12 gallons of oil in the gearbox in as many hours, the crew were reduced to top gear, which just would not manage the steep slopes of the Allos.

For the RAC rally, which followed in November 1965, the car was carefully rebuilt to Group 2 rather than Group 3 specification, so that Roy Fidler could attack a different category from his team-mates. This meant that the car had to run with twin SU carburettors, smaller wheels and smaller brakes. However, the non-standard wide-ratio gearbox was retained, on the assumption that no British scrutineer would know about this or wish to have the gearbox casing opened so that the teeth could be counted!

Thus detuned, the car was considerably slower than it otherwise would have been, but Fidler set out in considerable good humour to deliver a strong result. By half distance he was not only leading the car's 2-litre capacity class but was also in a superb seventh place overall, with every car ahead of him of the engine-over-driving-wheels variety and therefore having the benefit of inherently better traction. After a most impressive display of skill, stamina and sheer bloody-mindedness, Fidler finished fifth overall. Not only that, but he also won the 2-litre capacity class and was the top-placed Brit in an event dominated by Scandinavians.

This was such an excellent result that technical chief Harry Webster immediately authorised an ultra-speedy preparation

Roy Fidler's prize for winning his class in the 1965 RAC rally with AHP 426B was a free entry in the 1966 Swedish. Here he is in February 1966 during pre-event preparations – in what constituted full daylight in a Swedish winter.

turn-round of AHP 426B so that Roy could compete in the Welsh International rally, which was to take place within just a few days. This was one of those events that has been recalled with much enthusiasm by many Triumph enthusiasts in recent years. Not only was it the first-ever Welsh International but it also attracted two works 2000s to do battle with Roger Clark in a works Lotus-Cortina and several other factory-backed entries. Although Fidler could not quite keep up with Simo Lampinen's sister car, he kept going quickly and steadily through two nights and 38 special stages, finally taking third place overall behind Lampinen and Clark's victorious Lotus-Cortina. It was an excellent way for the hard-working team to end the season.

Early in 1966 this now-venerable car got another chance to stretch its legs. By finishing fifth in the RAC rally, Fidler won himself a sponsored entry in the 1966 Swedish rally, and he took it up with great relish. Neither he nor his co-driver, Alan Taylor, had ever before entered the Swedish, which was run entirely on snow-covered special stages, so there was little hope of success. In fact he went off the road on several occasions in AHP 426B and finally ran out of time, which resulted in reporter Graham Gauld commenting, 'Roy Fidler had long since retired with a backache through digging the Triumph 2000 out of the snow banks, but he continued for a while, practising his snow-driving techniques...'

Back in the UK Roy began juggling a two-car programme, so he did not drive AHP 426B again until Easter, when, running in the Group 2 category, he tackled the four-day Circuit of Ireland. This was a long-distance, multi-stage marathon around the Emerald Isle containing no fewer than 50 special stages, many of them on tarmac surfaces. Against strong competition from other works teams and drivers, Roy drove the big Triumph as hard as it would go and ended up in Larne for the finish in fourth place overall and winner of his capacity class.

COMPETITION RECORD	
1964 Spa-Sofia-Liège	
Roy Fidler	Did not finish
1964 RAC	
Roy Fidler	6th overall
1965 French Alpine	
John Sprinzel	Did not finish
1965 RAC	
Roy Fidler	5th overall, 1st in class
1965 Welsh	
Roy Fidler	3rd overall
1966 Swedish	
Roy Fidler	Did not finish
1966 Circuit of Ireland	
Roy Fidler	4th overall, 1st in class

AHP 427B

FIRST REGISTERED	1 JULY 1964
ENGINE SIZE	1,998cc
MODEL TYPE	2000

This was the third of the new 2000s to start the 1964 Spa-Sofia-Liège, and although Terry Hunter seemed to have the measure of the event straight away – he was leading the other team cars by the time they reached mid-Yugoslavia – his car also suffered the same structural/rear suspension failure as its team-mates and had to retire at virtually the same place. If ever there was a classic case of fatigue failure, this was certainly it.

The story of Terry Hunter and the 1964 RAC rally has been told several times, usually with bias, and at times with real rancour and misquotation in the air. The car itself, like team-mate Roy Fidler's AHP 426B, performed magnificently throughout, and was actually slightly faster on individual special stage times, but it was dragged back by several incidents and eventually finished 13th overall and third in class. There was a minor roll in an early stage – but with virtually no damage to the bodyshell – and then a more serious accident when a collision with a bridge parapet resulted in a crumpled front wing on the driver's side. Those difficulties were then compounded by the crew's failure to clock out of the breakfast halt at Turnberry in Scotland, resulting in a 30-minute penalty.

To put it bluntly, Hunter overslept. He blamed team management for not waking him and team management blamed co-driver Patrick Lier for not standing guard. The consequence was that the car did not leave the control for some time after its schedule demanded. Many years later Hunter blamed me, suggesting that I had promised to wake him but that I too had been asleep – quite untrue! Within the team itself Hunter's reputation never recovered, and after just one further event, the 1965 Monte Carlo rally (see page 159), he was fired.

AHP 427B was thoroughly refreshed during the winter of 1964/65, eventually being made ready for Roy Fidler and Don Barrow to drive in the Circuit of Ireland, which started from Bangor and finished at Larne, by way of a 1,370-mile route that penetrated as far as Killarney and involved three days' motoring, including two nights on the road. The car was still in full Group 3 tune, which included the triple-Weber carburettor installation, all of which it most certainly needed as it had to compete against other works cars, including those from the BMC Mini-Cooper S and Ford Cortina GT teams. Because this was an event run mainly over tarmac special stages, and without pace notes, the 2000 had

Terry Hunter in AHP 427B, about to take the start from Spa, Belgium, in the 1964 Spa-Sofia-Liège rally. In that event, competing cars started three abreast!

Terry Hunter and Geoff Mabbs in the 1964 Spa-Sofia-Liège marathon – the rear suspension mountings of AHP 427B broke in deepest Yugoslavia.

to struggle hard against other quick machinery and rarely figured in the top five or six stage times. In the end the crew finished a valiant second in their Group 3 (Grand Touring) class, behind Roger Clark's modified Ford Cortina GT.

This was not an event without incident! Even before the start AHP 427B developed a cylinder head problem, which was only solved by taking the car to a Triumph dealer in Belfast to seek the 'loan' of a standard head. Then at one point Fidler was temporarily, and wrongly, disqualified from the event for having a non-standard car, the official concerned having found it impossible to keep up with the 2000 on the open road! This gentleman had not read the regulations carefully and failed to realise that the 2000 was

John Sprinzel and David Benson in AHP 427B took third place in their capacity class in the 1965 RAC rally, this car's last event as a works entry.

EHP 78C

FIRST REGISTERED	5 MARCH 1965
ENGINE SIZE	1,998cc
MODEL TYPE	2000

Originally prepared during the winter of 1964/65, EHP 78C – the only left-hand-drive car among the Group 3 2000s – was originally intended for Simo Lampinen's use. Other than its left-hand-drive layout, this car had the same specification as the other Group 3 cars – triple Weber carburettors and 15in road wheels – and naturally included the bodyshell reinforcements that had been applied to the existing cars in the fleet.

For its first event, the snow-infested Tulip rally of 1965, EHP 78C was allocated to Jean-Jacques Thuner as Lampinen on this occasion drove 'his' new Spitfire instead. Steady and reliable as usual, the Geneva-based tarmac specialist kept the car on the road, blizzards and all, and was one of very few drivers to remain unpenalised on the road sections, his reward being third place overall in the GT category and a class win too. It was a measure of the Tulip's odd handicapping system, which took account of a car's engine size, that the GT category was won by a 998cc Hillman Imp and that the Morley twins' Austin-Healey 3000, the fastest car on scratch times, finished behind Thuner's Triumph 2000!

Six months later, for the RAC rally, Lampinen finally got his hands on the left-hand-drive car that had been prepared for him in the first place. This RAC was all set to be a marathon event, starting and finishing in London by way of a night halt at Perth, Scotland, taking in 57 special stages in the

running in the Grand Touring category – all the same he needed some persuading that works Group 3 2000s really were as rapid as that! In addition there were persistent problems with the headlamp wiring, and drama at a roadside petrol halt when the attendant managed to fill the boot, not the tank, with high-octane fuel. Not realising that the filler cap was in a non-standard position, he prised off the rubber bung that closed off the redundant filler neck and embarked on his task…

Months later the car was loaned to John Sprinzel for the RAC rally but not as a full works entry. This outing was sponsored by the *Daily Express*, which provided a co-driver, David Benson, the newspaper's motoring correspondent. This was certainly good for publicity, if not for a top result. Sprinzel admitted that his own best days as a driver were over but felt that his ability to generate column inches was not, and on that basis he set out to drive steadily in the Group 3 category. He did absolutely everything that could be expected of him by finishing third in his Group 3 2-litre class behind Austin-Healey 3000 driver Timo Mäkinen and Triumph team-mate Jean-Jacques Thuner.

The car then went into honourable retirement.

COMPETITION RECORD

1964 Spa-Sofia-Liège	
Terry Hunter	Did not finish
1964 RAC	
Terry Hunter	3rd in class
1965 Circuit of Ireland	
Roy Fidler	2nd in class
1965 RAC	
John Sprinzel	3rd in class

EHP 78C after winning its class in the 1965 Tulip rally. From left, John Gretener, competitions staffer Gordon Birtwistle and Jean-Jacques Thuner.

West Country, Wales, the Yorkshire moors, Kielder Forest and the Lake District. In his column in *Autosport*, BMC's Paddy Hopkirk suggested that Lampinen would struggle in his 'underpowered' 2000, but Simo clearly did not believe this. He set off at a great pace and was soon established well up the leader board, even though a rear shock absorber had to be replaced after only a handful of stages. After successfully tackling the first half of the rally and getting as high as fourth or fifth place, the big car blew a cylinder head gasket on one of the Kielder stages and was forced to retire.

Nothing daunted, the team then repaired and refreshed EHP 78C for Lampinen to use on the Welsh International rally, which took place only a few days later. This event was notable for the presence of other significant works machines, including Roy Fidler in AHP 426B, Tony Fall in an Abingdon-prepared MGB and Roger Clark first time out in a Lotus-Cortina – with me as his co-driver. Starting and finishing in Cardiff, with 38 special stages and covering most of Wales, this was a rally where the outcome was in doubt almost to the end.

Throughout the event Lampinen and Clark fought it out, stage by stage, and fastest time after fastest time. At breakfast after the first overnight scramble, Lampinen trailed Clark by just nine seconds, and soon took the overall lead, although both cars needed attention – steering on the Lotus-Cortina, front suspension on the Triumph 2000 – as the second day progressed. Then five stages from the end, on the Llanbed stage, Lampinen put the big Triumph off the road in thick fog and lost more than ten minutes in getting it retrieved. What had looked like an outright win turned into a valiant second place by the finish.

With its worth as a Group 3 car now at an end, the works career of EHP 78C ceased at this point.

Simo Lampinen in full flow in EHP 78C at Oulton Park in the 1965 RAC rally, in which he was challenging for the lead when the engine expired on the second night.

Simo Lampinen tiptoes over very icy roads on a Welsh forestry stage in EHP 78C during the 1965 RAC rally.

COMPETITION RECORD

1965 Tulip	
Jean-Jacques Thuner	3rd in GT category
1965 RAC	
Simo Lampinen	Did not finish
1965 Welsh	
Simo Lampinen	2nd overall

FHP 991C

FIRST REGISTERED	30 NOVEMBER 1965
ENGINE SIZE	1,998cc
MODEL TYPE	2000

During the winter of 1965/66 the factory built up four near-identical new Group 1 cars, of which three were entered for the Monte Carlo rally. FHP 991C was one of the quartet but did not compete, having been used, as planned, for testing and some reconnaissance before the event. As a consequence of the team being progressively run down after the Monte, it left the rally fleet virtually unused.

COMPETITION RECORD
None in rallying: used only for testing and pre-event practice

FHP 992C

FIRST REGISTERED	30 NOVEMBER 1965
ENGINE SIZE	1,998cc
MODEL TYPE	2000

The second car of the four new Group 1 2000s built up was originally intended for use throughout the 1966 season and allocated to Jean-Jacques Thuner, but it only took part in one event – the Monte Carlo rally.

The Group 1 restrictions were so severe that few performance-improving features could be used and even the standard front seats had to be retained. Apart from attention to damper settings and the use of Ferodo-specification brake pads and linings, the most significant change was to fit a 4.1:1 rear axle ratio. Although not revealed at the time, the actuation of the Laycock overdrive was also altered so that an overdrive second gear was available – something that was not done on road cars and was permissible under Group 1 regulations...

Along with the Fidler and Lampinen entries, FHP 992C started the event from London, making its way to Monte Carlo by way of Dover, Liège, The Hague, Rennes, Limoges and Avignon, after which there were two long loops to be tackled with a total of 12 special stages. Although the experienced Thuner was looking forward to grappling with icy and snowy conditions in the big but agile Triumph, he was forced out during the first long classification loop when the gearbox gave trouble, and then the differential failed – an on-going problem with these cars that was never completely solved. *Autocar*'s rally reporter commented: 'The 2000 arrived on the end of a tow rope, its very deranged final drive making a noise like a rock crusher...'

That was the end of this car's motorsport career and it was sold off soon after its return to Coventry. It was also the end of Thuner's career with the works team, although he continued to compete, and win, with privately owned Triumphs in his native Switzerland.

COMPETITION RECORD	
1966 Monte	
Jean-Jacques Thuner	Did not finish

FHP 993C

FIRST REGISTERED	30 NOVEMBER 1965
ENGINE SIZE	1,998cc
MODEL TYPE	2000

Technically identical to the other three new 2000s built for the 1966 season, FHP 993C was allocated to Roy Fidler for the Monte Carlo rally and was the only one of these cars to finish the event.

Fidler endured an eventful Monte but in his usual exuberant manner he kept going to the end. A failed alternator had to be changed during the first long loop and later he went off the road, but he still finished 14th overall. He also came fourth in the unofficial 'front-engine/rear-drive' category, for the vast majority of the top finishers had engine-over-driving-wheels layouts, which were more competitive on snow and ice.

This car might then have been sold off into obscurity but for Roy arranging to take it over for use in British events, and it enjoyed a very active career over the next two years. First time out, in a concentrated assault on the British Rally Championship, he tackled the *Express & Star* rally in Wales and finished second overall in this mainly navigational event.

With FHP 993C, Roy Fidler – in high spirits – and Alan Taylor ready to start the 1966 Monte Carlo rally, in which they finished 14th overall.

Roy then decided to miss the Scottish rally in June on the grounds that it was too long and too hard on the car – he was paying some of his own repair bills by this time!

Nonetheless, later in June he elected to enter another massively demanding event, the Gulf London rally, which started and finished in London, visited most parts of England and Wales, plus the Scottish borders, and included 34 special stages. There was no overnight halt in the demanding schedule, but Gulf provided free fuel and there was the tantalising prospect of a £1,000 prize for the winner – that was the cost of a new Lotus-Cortina.

Fidler started off in FHP 993C with high hopes, and was up into third place overall ahead of several other works Ford, BMC and Saab cars after the stages in Yorkshire and the Kielder forests. Sadly, there was then a long delay to replace a badly bent front suspension strut followed by terminal engine failure during the dash back down the M6 motorway.

Things then suddenly became brighter during the second half of this UK-only season. Once repaired after the Gulf London disappointment, FHP 993C tackled the Bolton National rally, which featured a very lengthy stage on the MoD-owned Eppynt ranges, covering several laps of the most demanding tarmac roads in that area. Fidler was delighted to record his first outright victory in the car!

Shortly after this Fidler and FHP 993C also won the Cavendish rally, a navigational event in the Derbyshire Peak District, although a visit to Wales for the Rally of the Vales yielded nothing when Roy put the car off the road only an hour after the start. Victory on the Bournemouth rally, a one-night British event with a number of special stages, was another great boost, but Roy's bigger aim was to put up another good performance on the RAC rally.

Unhappily, everything conspired to frustrate Roy's hopes on the RAC. At one point he was leading the 2-litre class, but then he had to contend with punctures, a time-consuming off-track excursion and a rear axle that got progressively noisier. Finally he reached the dreaded Kielder complex, where a fan blade broke off and punctured the water radiator. No water, a red hot engine – that was that!

Only two weeks after the RAC rally, FHP 993C, suitably rebuilt with a fresh engine and yet another new rear axle, turned up at the start of the Welsh International rally, an event on which the fate of the 11-event RAC British Rally Championship hinged. Faced with competition from Ford, BMC and Rootes works cars, Fidler knew that he would have to extract every ounce of power from the ageing 2000, and drove it harder than ever. There were 29 stages, most of them on Forestry Commission territory, crammed into just 36 hours of rallying. Fidler set seven fastest times and was always on the leader board, but in the end he was pipped by just 38 seconds by local hero Tony Chappell in a privately owned but works-specification Lotus-Cortina. It was an enthralling end to a busy season.

COMPETITION RECORD	
1966 Monte[1]	
Roy Fidler	14th overall
1966 *Express & Star*	
Roy Fidler	2nd overall
1966 Gulf London	
Roy Fidler	Did not finish
1966 Bolton	
Roy Fidler	1st overall
1966 Cavendish	
Roy Fidler	1st overall
1966 Rally of the Vales	
Roy Fidler	Did not finish
1966 Bournemouth	
Roy Fidler	1st overall
1966 RAC	
Roy Fidler	Did not finish
1966 Welsh	
Roy Fidler	2nd overall
1967 Circuit of Ireland	
Roy Fidler	5th overall
1967 *Express & Star*	
Roy Fidler	2nd overall
1967 Scottish	
Roy Fidler	Did not finish
1967 Gulf London	
Roy Fidler	6th overall
1967 Rally of the Vales[2]	
Roy Fidler	5th overall
1967 RAC	
Roy Fidler	Event cancelled

[1] After this rally FHP 993C was loaned to Roy Fidler for all subsequent events, but it continued to be partly maintained and supported by the factory.
[2] After this rally FHP 993C was converted to 2.5 PI prototype specification (see Chapter 7).

The final fling for Group 2 2000 saloons followed in 1967, when Roy Fidler undertook a limited programme in FHP 993C, which did not receive any further mechanical development. The car's first outing came in the five-day Circuit of Ireland, which started from Lisnafillan (near Ballymena), trekked all the way down to Killarney and then returned to Larne, embracing many special stages, almost all of them on tarmac. Held over the Easter weekend, this rally attracted several other works cars, including a Mini-Cooper S for Paddy Hopkirk – the eventual winner. On this occasion Roy's co-driver was a *Motoring News* journalist called Attis Krauklis, a rallying specialist who could best be described as large and ebullient in both stature and character! On an event like this the 2000 was always going to struggle to be competitive, but Roy gave it everything and usually set times in the top six. Sheer perseverence was finally rewarded by fifth place overall and class victory behind two Mini-Cooper Ss and two Lotus-Cortina 'homologation specials'.

Six weeks later the car was entered in the one-day *Express & Star* rally, where all the special stages were located in Wales, all of them in daylight. In many ways this event was the 1966 Welsh rally all over again, for it became a day-long battle between the big Triumph – with Alan Taylor back in the co-driver's seat for this occasion – and Tony Chappell's ex-works Lotus-Cortina, and yet again the Ford beat the Triumph by a matter of seconds.

Then came the Scottish International rally, another multi-stage marathon on fast, dusty special stages all over Scotland. Starting from Glasgow and centred on Grantown-on-Spey, this event occupied five days and more than 60 special stages. The Triumph faced other works cars from BMC, Ford, Rootes and Saab, who sent their latest 96 V4s. This was the sort of endurance event where the rugged 2000 was always competitive, although it could not match the pace of Roger Clark's new Lotus-Cortina Mk2. Fidler pressed on well, although the Triumph needed a change of front suspension struts before the first arrival at Grantown-on-Spey, where it was in sixth place. Still going strong on the fourth day, the car then went off the road in the Fetteresso stage, and could not be retrieved – there was little damage to the car but a lot to the driver's demeanour.

Fortunately, the big saloon was then prepared anew in three weeks so that Roy could contest the Gulf London rally, which, as described, offered significant financial inducements as well as being very prestigious. Starting and finishing at Manchester Airport, the event had a complex, arduous route taking in Wales, southern Scotland and the Yorkshire forests, with 58 special stages in three days and virtually no time for rest let alone sleep. Faced with competition from works cars from Ford, Saab, BMC, Volvo and Porsche-Sweden, this was going to be quite a task by any contemporary rallying standards.

Although outpaced by sheer horsepower, Roy Fidler and co-driver Barry Hughes were determined to make up for that by sheer strength, experience and bloody-mindedness. Early in the event, however, Roy put the long-suffering 2000 off the road in a Welsh forest, where it rolled, quite gently, and suffered roof damage and a broken windscreen. Nothing daunted, the crew donned goggles and overcoats, and drove on for some hours until they could get the screen replaced. Two days later, with a car that had otherwise behaved well, they brought it home in sixth place overall, beaten only by full works cars – a Lotus-Cortina, two Saab V4s and two Porsche 911s!

This gallant old car's final fling as a 2000 came in September 1967, when Roy started the Rally of the Vales, a Welsh event based on Llandrindod Wells. This 19-hour event had a concentrated layout of 11 special stages, most of them on loose surfaces, which suited the big car very well. Second overall at half distance, the car dropped back slightly towards the end when the engine suffered a bout of misfiring, but it still managed fifth overall.

And that, as far as works Group 2 motoring was concerned, was that. FHP 993C then disappeared back into the works team workshops to become a prototype 2.5 PI – a transformation that is described in Chapter 7.

FHP 994C

FIRST REGISTERED	30 NOVEMBER 1965
ENGINE SIZE	1,998cc
MODEL TYPE	2000

Brand new for 1966, FHP 994C was mechanically the same as the three other Group 1 cars built for the Monte Carlo rally, although this one had left-hand drive as it was built for Simo Lampinen to drive. After a relatively uneventful run to Monte Carlo, and in the mountains behind Monte Carlo, this car's run came to an end at the St Sauveur control, where it had to be parked with a broken gearbox. That was the end of its very short works career as a rally car.

FHP 994C, with a grinning Simo Lampinen alongside, ready to start the 1966 Monte Carlo rally.

COMPETITION RECORD
1966 Monte
Simo Lampinen   Did not finish

UNREGISTERED

ENGINE SIZE	1,998cc
MODEL TYPE	2000

Bill Bradley, who lived in Warwickshire, quite close to the Triumph factory, enjoyed such a successful Spitfire racing car season in 1965 (see pages 146-147) that a proposal he put to Triumph for 1966 – to race a much-modified 2000 – was taken seriously by Harry Webster. The result was that an unregistered 2000 took part in British Saloon Car Championship events throughout the year – but with very little success.

Because this car raced throughout 1966 without a registration number, there has been some uncertainty about its provenance. However, there is absolutely no doubt that it was converted from one of the Group 1 2000 saloons that the team had prepared for use in the 1966 Monte Carlo rally. As no records from this period have been kept, it is not possible to establish this car's precise identity with certainty, but it is probable that it was FHP 991C, the car that was used only for testing and reconnaissance.

Until 1966 a 2000 would not have been competitive in the British Saloon Car Championship, for this series had catered for Group 2 cars – what we now describe as 'homologation specials'. In particular, the Ford Lotus-Cortina had been specifically developed with motorsport in mind and little else could keep up. For 1966 the RAC completely changed the regulations, allowing what were called Group 5 cars to compete – meaning that many non-specialised cars could be made competitive.

Effectively a Group 5 car was a Group 2 car to which a mass of extra tuning equipment could be added and major changes made to the chassis. The standard car's bodyshell, engine block and gearbox casings had to be retained, but virtually everything else was now authorised, including major modifications to engines (new cylinder heads were allowed), transmissions, brakes and suspension layouts (but standard pick-up points had to be retained), along with features such as ultra-wide wheels and extensive body lightening. Even with all these 'freedoms', however, the 2000 was significantly heavier than many of its contemporaries.

Bradley put in some of his own finance, but the preparation of the car was always done in Ray Henderson's competitions department. Some chassis development was carried out, and the car ran on wide-rim Minilite magnesium-alloy wheels and Dunlop racing tyres. The real innovation, however, was that the 1,998cc engine ran on a Lucas fuel injection system that was really the forerunner of what would be launched in production form on the TR5 of 1967 and the 2.5 PI of 1968.

This engine was reputed to develop at least 160bhp.

Thus equipped, the car seemed to be a credible prospect early in the season, if not a race-winning one, and tester Gordon Birtwistle recalls getting down to the previous 2-litre Group 2 lap time at Brands Hatch. The new Group 5 cars of 1966, however, were in general a good deal faster than this. As Patrick McNally wrote in his end-of-season review in *Autosport*: 'The domination of the two-litre category by the "works" Lotus-Cortinas was complete. The flexibility of the rules gave Colin Chapman all the encouragement he needed, and his cars, which not only won their class but also won outright on some occasions, were highly sophisticated pieces of machinery…'

This became startlingly obvious at the first race of 1966 – Snetterton in April – when F1 star Jim Clark's Lotus-Cortina finished third overall behind two colossally powerful Ford-USA models, and when Jim went on to record three outright victories later in the season it really was 'game over'. And so it was for the Triumph too. Well before the end of the championship the programme was terminated and no further 2000 saloon racing was ever contemplated.

In 1966 the company prepared and supported Bill Bradley in a fuel-injected 2000 in the British Saloon Car Championship. Although it never carried registration plates during the season, this was thought to be FHP 991C.

COMPETITION RECORD	
1966 British Saloon Car Championship	
Bill Bradley	Took part in eight races

CHAPTER 6:
SPITFIRE AND GT6R (1964–66)

It's a miracle that the Spitfires performed so well at Le Mans and in rallying during 1964 and 1965. At the time there was virtually no previous competition experience with the running gear – the use of the engine in 803cc and 948cc form in Standard Eights, Tens and Pennants was barely relevant – and there was no conclusive evidence that it could be made to perform to the necessary level, at least not for 24 hours flat out on a race track or for up to four days on a tough rally. Looking back, there was every reason for the 1964 campaign to have been a fiasco and for the 1965 programme to have been cancelled months in advance. But it worked – and it worked well. Credit for that must be given to Harry Webster's team, particularly his engine specialists.

The analysis that follows concentrates initially on the evolution of the Le Mans Spitfires, for almost everything developed for the rally cars – in different workshops – was produced in parallel, and not always in the same glare of publicity. Although Triumph had been to Le Mans during the 1950s, there were no significant technical links with that period by 1964. Ken Richardson had always held together the programme at Le Mans and he left the company after the 1961 race, so all such continuity was lost – although we should note that ace mechanics like Ray Henderson had been involved with the TRS models.

But there was hope – and ambition. Although Standard-Triumph's new owners, Leyland, had closed down the old competitions department in 1961, technical chief Harry Webster was determined to see it reborn, in his own image. With small budgets wheedled out of his new bosses – first Stanley Markland, then Sir Donald Stokes, both originally from Leyland Motors – Webster reopened a department at the engineering centre at Fletchamstead North. For two years the motorsport effort was limited to using TR4s and Vitesses, but for 1964 Harry was determined to expand and to make a return to Le Mans. How could Triumph perform with honour at Le Mans? Not in the 2-litre class, for sure, where Porsche's latest 904s had 180bhp and weighed only 1,450lb. And certainly not in the even larger-engined, high-tech category populated by Ferraris and the soon-to-appear Ford GT40. Triumph looked at the small-engined classes, therefore, and saw that the fastest special-bodied 1.1-litre Alpine-Renaults had lapped at 94mph – and without a trace

This early example of the Spitfire's 1,147cc 70X engine, as developed for use on works Spitfire race and rally cars in 1964, shows the two twin-choke Weber carburettors and the tubular exhaust manifold, mated to the new-type eight-port cylinder head, of cast iron in this instance.

of hubris wondered if highly modified Spitfires could match or even exceed that. After all, if BMC could enter Sprites and Midgets to perform with honour in the same categories, why not do the same with Spitfires? Using slide rules, intuition and a bit of historic insight, the company's technical experts concluded that the cars, which would run in the Group 3 category, would need to reach a top speed of at least 130mph in order to be competitive at Le Mans.

Some years later, incidentally, I learned that BMC's motor-sport bosses, when first faced with competition from Spitfires, thought it a bit of a joke, but it took precisely two outings in 1964 – the Le Mans 24 Hours and the Tour de France – for them to change their opinion. Thereafter they took the cars very seriously, as did the rest of the motor sport establishment.

Triumph's decision to go ahead was not made until the autumn of 1963, after which progress was rapid, for the target was always Le Mans in June 1964, and – if possible – the test weekends there in April. In fact in less than six months, between November 1963 and April 1964, the engineers turned the Spitfire from a 63bhp/92mph road car into a 100bhp/130mph racing car. Because the decision had been taken to run them as Prototypes, the racing cars would use all-aluminium bodies, special engines with new cylinder

RAY HENDERSON

In 1964 Ray Henderson had too much to do. Not only did his team of mechanics have to prepare six new Spitfires for rallying, but he also had to link up with the building of four new racing Spitfires for the Le Mans 24 Hours. Yet he still found time to co-operate, enthusiastically, in the evolution of the Group 3 2000 saloons. But he had done it all before – and he would do it again.

Henderson's career started at Standard's Canley factory in 1943 as office boy in the drawing office and ended with him running the development workshops at Fletchamstead North in 1986. He was closely involved with every Triumph project throughout that period: he worked on the original TR2 Mille Miglia car of 1954, he was a stalwart of the 'Cape Town/Tangier/Coventry' Herald expedition of 1958, and he was at Le Mans with the TRS 'Sabrinas' in the early 1960s.

He was, quite literally, invaluable. Without Ray, reopening the competitions department in 1962 would have been a nightmare. From 1965 he managed that competitions department, his responsibilities including the 1966 Group 1 2000s, the still-born GT6R Le Mans contender, the original prototype 2.5 PI rally cars of 1967 and the one-off four-wheel-drive 1300 rallycross machine.

When the British Leyland competitions department got the job of preparing the 2.5 PIs for the London-Mexico World Cup, Ray was the indispensible link between the two operations in Coventry and Abingdon.

When race-ready for Le Mans in June 1964, the engine bay of the Spitfires looked like this. The three racing cars ran with cast-iron cylinder heads on that occasion and the engine produced 98bhp. Note that there was still only a single-circuit braking system at this stage of the car's development.

heads, and all-synchromesh TR4 gearboxes. To reach – and sustain – the required 130mph maximum speed, two things were needed: a lot of horsepower and a good aerodynamic shape. The development of the fastback shape came almost by chance, but finding the extra power took time.

At about this time a new one-off styling exercise, a Spitfire GT fastback, by Italian designer Giovanni Michelotti had just arrived in Coventry, and that car's shapely roof was adopted for the works racing cars. The same style would eventually be used on the GT6 road car, in pressed steel with a smart lift-up tailgate. For the racing cars, a series of simple glass-fibre 'layovers' were taken from this original prototype, but without provision for a tailgate. The body style provided space for a very large fuel tank, which was homologated under one of the 'freedoms' granted to Group 3 machines.

A panel was also inserted into the front grille aperture to cut down the rush of air through the radiator. The bitter lessons learned with the TR3S cars in 1959, when normal grille openings had been retained, together with cooling fans on the engines, were not repeated. Nowhere at Le Mans was slow, so there was no likelihood of overheating. Apart from the glass-fibre roof panels, the bodyshells were made entirely of aluminium, assembled from a limited set of aluminium panels produced as 'end-of-run' items after the manufacture of large production batches in pressed steel.

The racing cars were universally regarded as strikingly pretty little machines, but was the shape a good one aerodynamically? As far as I am aware, no-one ever knew the answer to that. No-one ever used mathematics to prove or disprove Michelotti's eye for a line and no-one ever bothered to evaluate a car in a wind tunnel to find out – but the shape certainly worked!

To get the horsepower, Triumph decided it needed a new eight-port cylinder head for better breathing. In earlier years a prototype head had already been made but not, it seems, fitted to a car, and certainly not to a Herald or a Spitfire – although a more mundane version of it was scheduled for use in the still-secret front-wheel-drive 1300 then under development. So this existing design was thoroughly reworked, mainly in the engine development department by Dennis Barbet and Graham Sykes. Two closely related types of eight-port cylinder head – one in cast iron, one in aluminium – were developed in parallel, both with a newly profiled camshaft, huge valves and tiny (10mm) sparking plugs, and they were matched to twin-choke Weber carburettors. Within months the cast-iron head had been chosen for the 1,147cc engine of the racing cars, with a '24-hour' rating of 98bhp at 6,750rpm.

A pit-lane scene at the Le Mans test weekend on a rather bleak day in April 1964. The paint used for the competition numbers on the cars washed away in the rain!

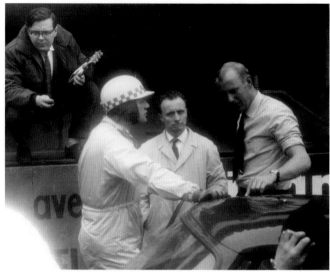

Peter Bolton (in helmet) and Rob Slotemaker (shirt sleeves) discuss the new Spitfire Le Mans car during the April 1964 test weekend, with John Lloyd (in raincoat) listening carefully.

The first day of testing at Le Mans, in April 1964, saw two brand-new racing Spitfires out on the track, at this time still with normal-shape front ends.

From personal experience I can confirm that these engines were pigs to start from cold, mainly because of the use of the tiny plugs, but in all other respects the effort had been worthwhile. There would be several serious engine failures, but the alternative – running less highly tuned engines and therefore rendering the Spitfires less competitive – was never seriously considered.

Other features included wide-rim cast-aluminium wheels, larger brakes, a limited-slip differential, a 3.89:1 final drive ratio and modified suspension. The entire package was painstakingly developed, with a lot of input from chief test driver Fred Nicklin, who not only did considerable assessment work at the MIRA proving ground near Nuneaton but also shared the test driving at Oulton Park and Silverstone. Like Norman Dewis at Jaguar, Nicklin was sometimes under-appreciated by the company's management.

The first car ran at Oulton Park early in April 1964, and two cars then appeared at the Le Mans practice weekend later in the month. It was at these Le Mans trials that the decision was made to adopt faired-in headlamps. Just as Sunbeam had done with its own works Le Mans Alpines of the early 1960s, Triumph decided to copy the shape of the very effective Jaguar E-type on the basis that if it worked for Jaguar it ought to work for them too. It did! Once again, and without recourse to wind-tunnel testing, the attractive new shape was produced with an eye to style by the body department's specialists – not by Michelotti. They were delighted with the reception their cars received.

Then followed another very important decision. With the TRS programme, Harry Webster had always been unhappy that the cars were often stabled a long way from the engineering department. To keep close control on the Spitfire programme, therefore, he had the four new Le Mans cars entirely built at and run from Fletchamstead North, with his Experimental Manager John Lloyd in charge of the whole programme and Sales Manager Lyndon Mills appointed team manager for events. All four racing cars took shape in the workshops very close to Lloyd's office, and this operation was always kept completely separate from the nearly works rally team's workshops – only about 50 paces away – where the rally Spitfires and later the 2000 saloons were to be based, the two operations having their own staff of mechanics.

NEW KID ON THE BLOCK: 1964

Although time was always desperately short, one of the cars (ADU 4B) was taken to Silverstone in May 1964 for a pre-Le Mans test and flogged round and round the full Grand Prix circuit for two days, as fast and as hard as possible. The purpose was not to try to set any records but to see if the car, and particularly its highly stressed engine, would stay in one piece – and it did. As a dry-sump installation was not used, the main considerations were to assess the need or otherwise for an engine oil cooler, and to see that repeated hard cornering did not starve the engine bearings of oil at the critical moments. Chief test driver Nicklin preserved an internal factory report and it showed that well over 12 hours were completed at Silverstone and the engine survived. This was a great relief, as the original test engines – and that fitted to Roy Fidler's 412 VC rally test car – had both suffered lubrication problems.

For the 1964 Le Mans 24 Hours Triumph took all four racing cars to France, although only three of them – ADU 1B, ADU 2B and ADU 3B – started the race. The objective, first and foremost, was to achieve an honourable finish, but the real bonus would be to win the up-to-1,150cc category. That, incidentally, was going to be tough, for there would be no fewer than 11 rivals – four Alpines, four Bonnets (built by René Bonnet), two CDs (built by Charles Deutsch) and a single Austin-Healey Sebring Sprite.

There was another problem that all the Triumph drivers would have to face – on the long Mulsanne Straight their 130mph Spitfires would be around 60mph slower than the fastest Ford GT40s and Ferrari 275 Ps. Not only would the Spitfire drivers have to keep their eyes glued to their rear-view mirrors, but they would also have to worry about being blown sideways every time a massive 400bhp monster came scything past them – which would happen frequently.

Pre-event scrutineering went well and practice was uneventful. In the race itself the small-engined cars settled down to lap regularly, and unobtrusively, behind the fireworks up front, where the Ford GT40s initially challenged the Ferraris only to drop out quickly. Right away it was clear that the 1.1-litre Spitfires were almost as fast as the 2-litre Sabrina-engined TRSs had ever been, for they were lapping in less than five minutes and had a 134mph top speed – with the engines turning over at around 7,000rpm.

But it did not last. Only two hours into the race, ADU 1B crashed on the long right-hand curve after the pits, under the Dunlop bridge. Was the Spitfire pushed off line by a faster car, or did driver Mike Rothschild just overcook it? We

never found out.

Worse followed, for at 04.30, after just over 12 hours, Jean-Louis Marnat also crashed ADU 3B. Marnat was actually going quite slowly at the time, and later it was conclusively shown that he had been suffering from exhaust gas poisoning, for the car had earlier been damaged by an earlier 'off' at Tertre Rouge and fumes were persistently entering the cabin.

ADU 2B, however, went on, and on, finally completing the gruelling 24 hours at an average speed of 94.7mph. A year earlier that would have been enough to secure the class win, but there had been advances and two 1.1-litre special-bodied Alpine-Renaults finished ahead of the gallant Spitfire. The good news, though, was that the Triumph comprehensively beat the works Austin-Healey Sprite, which was 124 miles behind it.

LIGHTER, FASTER, VICTORIOUS: 1965

A year later Triumph was back at Le Mans with four further-developed Spitfires, all of which started the race. ADU 1B and ADU 3B had been rebuilt with completely new coupé shells, and three of the cars – ADU 1B, ADU 2B and ADU 4B – had been raced in the Sebring 12 Hours, after which ADU 1B needed a second rebuild because Peter Bolton had rolled it.

Even though the works rally Spitfires had beaten all the Alpine-Renaults in the 1964 Tour de France, to the great

Three 'as-new' Spitfires ready to start the Le Mans 24 Hours in June 1964. ADU 1B was driven by Mike Rothschild and Bob Tullius, ADU 2B by David Hobbs and Rob Slotemaker, and ADU 3B by Jean-Louis Marnat and Jean-François Piot. ADU 2B would finish third in its capacity class.

cylinder heads, as previously used on the works rally cars but deemed too risky to run at Le Mans in 1964. According to reports from Le Mans, top speed rose to more than 135mph – phenomenal for a Spitfire – although this was still not a match for the ultra-low French machines or the special-bodied 1.3-litre works Austin-Healey Sprite that turned up.

The Spitfires were now homologated as GT cars, rather than prototypes, something that Triumph had somehow managed to persuade the authorities to accept for the Sebring 12 Hours earlier in the 1965 season.

All four works racing Spitfires started at Le Mans, and after a long and demanding 24 hours Harry Webster and his board colleagues at Leyland-Triumph could not have been more pleased. In only their third racing appearance, the smart British Racing Green Spitfires put in a gritty performance, two of the four cars finishing 13th (ADU 4B) and 14th (ADU 3B) overall, and a resounding first and second in their capacity class. Driven by Jean-Jacques Thuner and Simo Lampinen, better known as members of the works rally team, the class-winning car averaged 95.1mph, which was faster than the singleton Spitfire finisher of 1964.

The best news of all was that the fleet of theoretically faster Alpine-Renaults had been comprehensively defeated once again, for all six of them retired – all with stress-related engine or transmission failures. After the previous year's Tour

All four updated Spitfire racing cars were taken out to Florida to contest the 1965 Sebring 12 Hours race, although ADU 3B did not actually compete. Here they are seen being 'unpacked' after the long journey from the UK in February/March 1965.

distress of the French manufacturer, Triumph was still shocked by the sheer pace of the rear-engined French cars and made big efforts to improve. The cars were lightened considerably, their weight down from 1,625lb to 1,520lb according to official Le Mans figures, through the use of thinner-gauge steel for their chassis frames and a prototype GT6 transmission instead of the heavy TR4 assembly. The engines now produced 109bhp at 7,300rpm thanks mainly to light-alloy

---

SPITFIRE AND TRS COMPARED

For Triumph at the Le Mans 24 Hours, astonishing advances were made between 1961, when the highest-placed Sabrina-engined TRS finished ninth, and 1965, when the Spitfire won its capacity class. After an interval of only four years, Triumph had produced a 1.1-litre Le Mans prototype that was almost as fast as the 2-litre TRS had ever been. Not only that, the 1.1-litre engine was production-based, whereas the 2-litre engine was entirely special. Here is a summary of how the cars compared in Le Mans specification.

	Spitfire (1965)	TRS (1961)
Engine size	1,147cc	1,985cc
Power output	109bhp	155bhp
Unladen weight	1,510lb	2,127lb
Power/weight ratio	161bhp/ton	163bhp/ton
Top speed at Le Mans	c135–140mph	c130mph
Distance covered in 24 hours	2,283 miles	2,373 miles

A rare period colour shot of a works Spitfire racing car shows the livery of Bill Bradley's ERW 412C. Individual cars had different front-end colouring, purely for recognition purposes. By this time this car ran with outsize rear wheels of 5.5in rim width.

The works Spitfire rally cars at the factory in September 1964, ready for the Tour de France. In that event they would be driven by, from left, Jean-Jacques Thuner/John Gretener, Bill Bradley/Roy Fidler and Rob Slotemaker/Terry Hunter. Newly converted to a permanent fastback style, complete with glass-fibre roof panels, they had also 'borrowed' the long-nose bonnets from the Le Mans cars – note the blanking panels in the front grilles.

de France, that made it two routs in nine months and Triumph's French importers were delighted!

Of the two cars that retired, one was crashed at Maison Blanche when Rob Slotemaker tried to get out of the way of a faster car, while the other suffered a split oil cooler – a one-in-a-million failure. As a consequence the two surviving Spitfires received attention to their oil coolers, losing a lot of time in the pits.

Nothing more could surely have been expected of these fleet little coupés. If the surviving cars had not needed lengthy pit stops they might just have beaten the 1.3-litre Sprite, but that was the only might-have-been in a splendid weekend.

This works team did not appear in any other major events. Performance levels at Le Mans were increasing rapidly and the tiny Spitfires were gracefully retired in the belief that they could not be as competitive in 1966. That was a wise decision, for the fastest of the 1.3-litre cars in 1966, an Alpine-Renault, averaged no less than 108.35mph, which was way out of the Spitfire's reach. But honour was satisfied: the Spitfires had made their name and Triumph's Le Mans adventures were now at an end.

SPITFIRE RALLY CARS

There was a fundamental difference between the works Spitfire racing cars and the works rally Spitfires. Whereas the racing cars were built entirely from scratch in the experimental workshops, the rally cars – five of them at first, all painted powder blue – were built on the regular assembly lines at Canley before being stripped out and comprehensively modified for rallying. The basic reason for this was that the racing cars had all-aluminium bodies (apart from

their glass-fibre roofs) while the rally cars started life with normal steel body structures to which aluminium outer panels were later added. A further difference between them was that the TR4 transmission used on the original racing cars could not be adopted for the rally cars because of homologation restrictions.

A significant time schedule was involved here and must be related. As described in Chapter 4, the last event for the

Giant-killing. Two works Spitfires – ADU 7B on the front row, ADU 5B on the second – ready to start the one-hour street race at Pau in the 1964 Tour de France. Two of the works Alpine-Renaults, which were soundly defeated by the Spitfires, and the works long-nose MGB are also in shot. Note the Le Mans-type cast alloy road wheels.

works rally TR4s was the Shell 4000 rally in Canada in 1964, and in February these three cars were driven to Immingham to board a trans-Atlantic merchant ship. As soon as they had left the competition department's workshops, the five new Spitfire road cars – all fitted with removable steel hardtops and 3.5in steel disc wheels – were delivered, hot from the assembly lines just a mile or so away. Preparation began almost immediately.

The first event for the new rally Spitfires was the French Alpine rally. Testing and route surveying were scheduled for May and the rally itself started on 23 June, literally the day after the completion of the Le Mans 24 Hours race. There seemed to be little time to spare. Even so, there had been talk in some quarters – from Roy Fidler in particular – of tackling an earlier event, the Tulip rally, before the cars were really ready, but this was firmly resisted. Terry Hunter, who had joined the team, even offered to enter the Tulip at his own expense, but this request was turned down.

Mechanically, the rally cars were originally rather different from the racing cars, for they used the aluminium-head version of the 1,147cc engine, which produced just over 100bhp. These were much the most highly tuned engines used by Triumph in motorsport up to that time and there were gloomy forecasts about their longevity, but they did a great job. For the first event the gearboxes were the Vitesse type, which had much closer ratios than the Spitfire's gearbox, was more robust, and had already been homologated as the alternative allowed by the regulations; this gearbox was matched to the still-secret GT6-specification

rear axle complete with limited-slip differential. As with the racing cars, at no time was the use of overdrive ever considered. Herald Courier 4.5in pressed steel road wheels were used as supplies of the expensive light-alloy racing Spitfire wheels were very restricted.

The second event in the programme was a very big one – the Tour de France. This was a ten-day race/rally involving long races at most of France's principal race circuits as well as a lot of hard road rallying. For Triumph, the significance of the Tour de France was that there was a lot of long-distance circuit racing, where marks were awarded for the distances covered within a time limit, allied to the fact that a complex handicapping factor split the event into Grand Touring and Touring categories, and into capacity classes. Although the objective was to win the appropriate capacity class if that could be achieved – and in particular to defeat the works Alpine-Renaults on their home ground – back-of-the-envelope estimates indicated that the Spitfires might also perform well in the lucrative Handicap capacities. Could they beat the Porsche 904s on the track? Certainly not. But on Handicap, maybe they could.

However, there were two issues to be overcome and team personnel put them to technical chief Harry Webster at a crucial meeting. First, the team stated that it was necessary to rebuild the rally cars so that they would be as fast as the racing cars in a straight line. Second, driver complaints about the Vitesse-type gearbox, which did not have synchromesh on first gear, had to be addressed, especially as the use of tall Le Mans gearing for the circuit work meant that first gear would be used a lot on the road sections.

The three 'regular' Spitfires – ADU 5B, ADU 6B and ADU 7B – were therefore sent back into the specialist body workshops to have their lift-off bubble-top hardtops replaced by modified versions of the racing cars' fastback glass-fibre hardtops grafted on to the existing bodyshells. There was one significant difference, however, in that the rally cars had a removable 'letterbox' panel higher up in the tail, in the glass-fibre part, to allow a spare wheel to be loaded and unloaded more quickly and comfortably by the crew. A big 18-gallon light-alloy fuel tank, as used in the Le Mans cars, was also installed: of inverted L-section, this tank, which was already homologated, occupied almost all of the space immediately behind the two seats, where the standard tank had been fitted. The snap-open filler cap was positioned high up on the right-hand side of the glass-fibre roof section.

For this event only, these three cars used the lift-up bonnet assemblies originally fitted to the Le Mans cars, complete with the faired-in headlamps. These were borrowed from the race team and repainted blue: two of them were from the undamaged Le Mans cars that finished the race and the third was a spare that was already in stock. After use on the rally cars, they were returned to the racing department with grateful thanks, and repainted British Racing Green.

Two of the works Spitfires with team manager Ray Henderson (red shirt) at a French Alpine rally service point. The cars are ADU 5B of Jean-Jacques Thuner/John Gretener and AVC 654B of Simo Lampinen/Jyrki Ahava – and that is a Porsche 904 behind them.

Out of the blue at that important meeting, Harry Webster suggested that the rally cars should be fitted for the Tour de France with prototype GT6 gearboxes, which looked visually like the Vitesse type and had similar internal ratios, but, crucially, had synchromesh on first gear. This was amazing because the GT6 was still two years away from launch and these gearboxes really could be likened to gold dust – but it was typical of transmission specialist George Jones that his specialist engineers were able to produce a handful of these 'boxes for the team's use in a matter of two months.

For the 1965 season the first important technical change was the adoption of a unique new bonnet style with a pair of dipping headlamps let into pods mounted on top of the bonnet immediately inboard of the main headlamps. This was not done merely to ape the works Austin-Healey 3000s, which adopted a similar restyle at this time, but because Lucas had finally made the first prototype quartz-iodine headlamp bulbs available. These were much more powerful than conventional bulbs, but only had single filaments, which meant that they had to be fitted to the outer headlamps.

When full-beam was in use the Spitfires had four headlamps showing, but when the dipswitch was operated the main headlamps were extinguished.

Two other significant changes were seen during 1965, although by this time there was little point in developing these exceptional little rally cars much further as it had become known that FIA regulations would outlaw alternative cylinder heads and lightweight bodywork in 1966. First, as explained in the section on ADU 5B (pages 150-152) a temporary change from the all-synchromesh gearbox to one with an unsynchronised first gear was enforced for the cars that started the Geneva rally, but swiftly reversed afterwards. Second, the cars that contested the French Alpine rally were entered as 'prototypes' and ran with larger 1,296cc engines, using cylinder blocks that were about to be launched in the front-wheel-drive 1300 saloon.

After Simo Lampinen's 'prototype' car won the entire Prototype category in the French Alpine rally, the programme came to a close and the cars were all sold off – several survive to this day.

TESTED BY *AUTOCAR*

After the end of the Spitfire works rally programme, Standard-Triumph loaned ADU 7B to *Autocar* magazine – where I had become a staff member a few months earlier. Along with the all-synchromesh transmission and a 4.55:1 rear axle ratio, it was fitted with the latest aluminium-head 1,147cc engine, for which 105bhp at 7,250rpm was claimed.

The test was written by the magazine's technical editor, Geoffrey Howard, who could truthfully be described as a self-confessed 'philistine' when it came to motorsport. This explains why he was quite amazingly rude about the car's lack of refinement and why he made no comment at all – not one word – about the little car's handling.

Its performance, however, was measured in *Autocar*'s usual meticulous way, and it is worth comparing some of the figures with those of the original 1962 road car:

	Rally car ADU 7B	Road car 1962 model
Max speed	105mph	92mph
Max speed in third gear	90mph	69mph
0–30mph	4.1sec	5.0sec
0–60mph	10.3sec	17.3sec
0–80mph	18.0sec	36.9sec
0–100mph	33.9sec	–
Standing quarter mile	17.8sec	20.9sec
Overall fuel consumption	15.3mpg	31.2mpg

412 VC

FIRST REGISTERED	1 JUNE 1962
ENGINE SIZE	1,147cc
MODEL TYPE	SPITFIRE

Before it even turned a wheel as a development car for the 1964 Spitfire rally programme, 412 VC had already enjoyed an active, intense, colourful career as a 'Bomb' prototype. Originally constructed in the engineering workshops in the first weeks of 1962 although not registered until June, it was used for everything from handling development to performance testing. The second Spitfire ever built and the first to be completed in Coventry, it carried the experimental Commission Number of X692.

Equipped with left-hand drive and right-hand drive during 1962, it led an eventful life immediately before the Spitfire launch. In the autumn of 1963, when the decision was made to concentrate motorsport activity on Spitfires and 2000 saloons in 1964, 412 VC had already been upgraded to include an overdrive transmission and a steel hardtop, and was immediately handed over to the works team as a development hack. It became the first Spitfire, therefore, to run with an eight-port engine with Weber carburettors and was used to develop the handling, Fred Nicklin and Gordon Birtwistle doing the high-speed driving and soon turning the original tail-happy chassis into a very manageable little beast.

The car was then allocated to Roy Fidler and John

light-alloy panels had not yet been delivered and the engine was nowhere near complete readiness. Thereafter the car's early career is best described as chequered, for all the faults that might otherwise have appeared on the real works cars manifested themselves on 412 VC – but that, after all, was its purpose.

The next few events were successful as development exercises but not always in terms of results. In February the car got off to a very strong start on the Shunpiker rally in Wales, but its engine lost all oil pressure after only ten timed controls. After an engine rebuild, which apparently gave the engineers a lot of development guidance, 412 VC took part in the very snowy Welsh Marches rally two weeks later. Fidler was fastest for much of the event and would undoubtedly have won except for a broken throttle linkage, which caused a lengthy delay before makeshift repairs could be made – nevertheless the car finished fourth overall.

The next weekend, however, the Spitfire retired again, suffering engine problems on the Targa Rusticana. By this time it was clear that much work was needed before the car could be competitive on international events. It seemed that 412 VC attracted incident, for on the *Express & Star* rally in March it not only hit a tree but also bent a wheel and eventually shed its exhaust silencer!

After all that, the hard-working 'test' car deserved a rest, and got it. With Roy Fidler off to Canada to compete in the Shell 4000 rally in a works TR4 (see page 107) and with the entire competitions department building nine new race and rally Spitfires, there simply was not time to devote to 412 VC. Although this marked the end of the car's works career, it still had much high-speed mileage to complete as its subsequent owner used it regularly and successfully in British club racing.

Yes – the very first of the works Spitfires. First it was a prototype in 1962, then a press launch car, then the original works rally car. It led a hard life!

Hopwood to use in a variety of British events in the early months of 1964. It finished an astonishing second overall on its very first outing, the international Welsh rally in January, beaten only by Barrie Williams' 1,071cc Mini-Cooper S and setting several fastest times along the way. For this event the Spitfire was far from fully developed, for

COMPETITION RECORD	
1964 Welsh	
Roy Fidler	2nd overall
1964 Shunpiker	
Roy Fidler	Did not finish
1964 Welsh Marches	
Roy Fidler	4th overall
1964 Targa Rusticana	
Roy Fidler	Did not finish
1964 *Express & Star*	
Roy Fidler	Finished

412 VC had already been a hard-working prototype before it was entrusted to Roy Fidler to drive on the Welsh rally of 1964 – the first-ever works Spitfire to start an event. Along with co-driver John Hopwood, he urged the little car to take second overall.

ADU 1B

FIRST REGISTERED	1 JUNE 1964
ENGINE SIZE	1,147cc
MODEL TYPE	SPITFIRE (racing car)

The mechanical specification, overall style and equipment of this car was identical to that of the other three original Le Mans cars: ADU 2B, ADU 3B and ADU 4B. Although ADU 1B carried the first registration number in the sequence of four, it was not the first to be completed and made ready to race – instead ADU 4B was the car that was completed first and undertook early testing.

This car was affectionately known as 'the American car', for both of its drivers for Le Mans were from the USA: Bob Tullius was the 'hot-shot' of the time in TR4s in SCCA racing while Mike Rothschild had driven factory TR3S and TRS cars at Le Mans in previous years. The team's plan for ADU 1B was for it to lap consistently at just under five minutes for the next 24 hours, a tactic that, if successful, would allow it to qualify as a finisher at the end of the race.

Right from the start the car established itself as the second fastest of the three Spitfires, and after the first hour it was already up to 40th place, with 14 other cars behind it. Everything seemed to be settling in well until, after no more than two hours, Rothschild spun at high speed under the Dunlop Bridge on the long right-hander after the pits. The car was severely damaged but Mike, thank goodness, was unhurt.

Following this setback it took months for ADU 1B to be reconstructed around a completely rebuilt bodyshell, using a considerably lighter version of the chassis frame and the all-synchromesh gearbox of the still-secret GT6 type as already débuted successfully on the rally cars for the Tour de France and Geneva rallies in the autumn of 1964. Once complete, ADU 1B was one of three cars of this improved specification entered for the Sebring 12 Hours of 1965, held in the balmy climate of Florida in March.

All four Spitfire racing cars made the trip to Florida and this time ADU 3B took its turn to be the spare, for it was seen at the track but not actually raced. The cars went by sea, not air, and Gordon Birtwistle recalls that they probably travelled on a ship laden with new Triumph sports cars destined for sale in the USA. Peter Bolton and Rothschild shared ADU 1B at Sebring but Bolton unfortunately managed to roll it and its race ended there. Although the chassis was still straight, another major bodyshell rebuild was required before the Le Mans 24 Hours in June.

At Le Mans ADU 1B was allocated to David Hobbs and Rob Slotemaker in the hope that they would repeat their achievement of 1964, when they brought a Spitfire to the

finish. Right from the start, the crew settled down to enjoy themselves, lapping at close to 100mph in company with the lone works MGB – a 1.1-litre Triumph keeping up with a 1.8-litre MG! Their steady progress continued throughout the night until, with dawn approaching, Slotemaker lined up the car once again to drift through Maison Blanche flat out, dipped his lights to let a faster car go through at the same moment, and went off the road…

After this, the Le Mans Spitfires were not used again in anger by the factory. ADU 1B eventually became the basis of the GT6R racing car, which was never completed (see page 166) and was eventually dismantled. In recent years, however, a car carrying the ADU 1B identity has been lovingly and painstakingly recreated, like a jigsaw, with the use of some works parts, and reputedly goes even quicker and handles even better than any Spitfire did in the mid-1960s!

ADU 1B looking rather sorry for itself after Peter Bolton crashed it at Sebring in March 1965. Happily the chassis was not damaged and the car ran in the 1965 Le Mans 24 Hours, although it again failed to finish after Rob Slotemaker put it off the road.

COMPETITION RECORD
1964 Le Mans 24 Hours
Mike Rothschild/Bob Tullius — Did not finish
1965 Sebring 12 Hours
Peter Bolton/Mike Rothschild — Did not finish
1965 Le Mans 24 Hours
David Hobbs/Rob Slotemaker — Did not finish

Complete with fastback roof style and 'E-type' faired-headlamp nose, the works Spitfire racing cars were as different from standard as regulations allowed. In 1964 four of these cars were built – ADU 1B, ADU 2B, ADU 3B and ADU 4B.

These neat little lamps were built into the doors, so that race officials and factory 'spotters' could see the competition numbers during darkness.

Every front-end detail of the Spitfire racing cars was carefully conceived, although there was no time for wind-tunnel testing.

All the works Spitfire racing cars ran in this form, with front and rear bumpers removed, hot air exit vents in the sides of the front wings, the 'E-type' nose, and smaller cold air intakes at the front.

The rear of the works Spitfire racing cars incorporated chassis brackets for quick-lift jacks and a removable panel that allowed easy access to the spare wheel.

The two round fairings mounted low on the front shielded the standard hinge arrangement for the bonnet.

Full harness safety belts have been fitted to ADU 1B in later life, but these were not available to the drivers, nor wanted by them, in 1964–65.

The large clip-over fuel cap required pierced lugs to allow it to be sealed by race officials during the Le Mans 24 Hours.

A massive 80-litre/18-gallon fuel tank was homologated for the racing Spitfires and mounted between the rear wheel arches; it was replenished through the right-hand side of the coupé bodyshell.

Brutally simple in layout and equipment, this is the fascia and instrument panel layout of the works racing Spitfires. The rev counter is ahead of the driver's eyes, but the speedometer remains in its standard position in the middle.

Aerodynamic fairings behind the rear wheels of the works racing Spitfires did not originally figure in the specification, but were added in the weeks leading up to the first racing appearance at Le Mans in 1964.

To save precious seconds at pit stops, the racing Spitfires were fitted with mounting points for quick-lift jacks to be applied. Why white? So that they could readily be seen at night!

ADU 2B

FIRST REGISTERED	1 JUNE 1964
ENGINE SIZE	1,147cc
MODEL TYPE	SPITFIRE (racing car)

This is ADU 2B in the 1964 Le Mans 24 Hours, where David Hobbs and Rob Slotemaker finished third in class.

The second of the Le Mans cars was allocated to David Hobbs and Rob Slotemaker. Hobbs was a young British racing driver and ex-Jaguar apprentice who lived close to the Coventry factory and carried out a good deal of the Spitfires' pre-event testing, while Slotemaker was already well known

ADU 2B, the Spitfire that finished third in class at Le Mans in 1964, makes a routine refuelling stop before David Hobbs takes over for a long stint. Extra protection for the headlamp covers was applied for daytime running in the early hours of the race, to protect against stone damage, and hastily torn away as darkness approached, as evidenced by the remnants of sticky tape on the surrounding bodywork.

as a Triumph works driver and would also drive for the rally team later in the year. Many years later Hobbs – by then a much-respected commentator and analyst covering Formula 1 on US television – recalled the pleasure he got in driving the little Spitfire even though he had tackled the 24 Hours the year before in a big V8-engined Lola GT! The difference, though, was that in 1964 he would finish the race...

Having lapped in practice at 4m 59.8s, ADU 2B set out on the long race as the fastest of the three Spitfires. Reliable throughout, it had moved up to 26th place after 12 hours and finally came home in 21st place. By averaging 94.7mph, it took fourth place in the 3-litre 'Prototype' capacity class, behind a Porsche and two of the very special Alpine-Renaults. This was an excellent showing on the Spitfires' very first event and it proved that the engine development work so carefully, but hurriedly, carried out by Ray Bates's design team during the previous winter had been extremely resourceful. The rally team, which was due to start the French Alpine rally the following day, was most encouraged.

ADU 2B was then rebuilt, modified and updated for 1965. Like the other racing cars, it received a lighter chassis frame, a GT6-type gearbox and a more powerful engine. For the Sebring 12 Hours it was allocated to two American drivers, Bob Tullius and Charlie Gates, who were doing great things with Triumphs in SCCA racing.

Somehow these brave young men kept the car afloat – literally – during the time when the race was afflicted by a massive cloud burst which lasted for a full hour, completely submerging the pit lane and much of the mechanics' equipment. There was something to be said, it seemed, for light weight and mechanical simplicity, as *Autosport*'s editor Gregor Grant reported: 'With the big cars reduced to a crawl, or stationary at their pits, the smaller GT machines came into their own... Also impressive were the MGBs and the Spitfires, which were continually passing the big bangers...'

Once the rain had stopped and the track had dried out, the field settled down again and ADU 2B eventually finished third in its class, close behind a works MG Midget – one with special bodywork that looked nothing like a normal Midget – and the other Spitfire (ADU 4B).

Back in the UK, the car was prepared for Peter Bolton and Bill Bradley to drive at Le Mans where, in lightweight form, it was expected to be capable of 140mph. The car started well, but at a very early stage the engine oil cooler sprang a leak, allowing all the engine oil to drip away – with terminal consequences.

Although ADU 2B did not reappear as a works racing car, it was retained in Coventry and loaned to Bill Bradley for an intensive Spitfire racing car programme of his own for 1966. The car was prepared – and sometimes repaired – at the factory, but no factory personnel went to the races and Bradley paid all running expenses. This car benefited from the various chassis and development advances that the

Triumph factory had already planned for the '1966' works cars, and would certainly have appeared on the GT6R (see page 166).

As Bradley later told me: 'During the latter part of 1965 a lot of testing was done. A lengthy list of modifications was agreed by Harry Webster. This resulted in easily the fastest and best-handling Triumph Spitfire that was ever produced...' The most significant modification was to abandon the original swing-axle rear suspension in favour of a coil spring/strut type of independent rear end (together with a modified chassis frame), which produced a big improvement in handling and rear-end grip.

At first this car was quite unbeatable in its capacity class, in Britain and in Europe, but its end came abruptly in June 1966 when it crashed at the Nürburgring and was effectively destroyed. Bradley and his co-driver Steve Neal were leading their class when the race-leading Chaparral of Phil Hill/Jo Bonnier clipped their car and punted it off the track. It was soon replaced by a new car, ERW 412C, which was also very competitive.

Celebrations at the finish of the 1964 Le Mans race, with drivers David Hobbs (left) and Rob Slotemaker sharing champagne with George Turnbull, Triumph's general manager.

COMPETITION RECORD
1964 Le Mans 24 Hours
David Hobbs/Rob Slotemaker   3rd in class
1965 Sebring 12 Hours
Bob Tullius/Charlie Gates   3rd in class
1965 Le Mans 24 Hours
Bill Bradley/Peter Bolton   Did not finish
Loaned to Bill Bradley in 1966 for sports car racing
but written off in June at the Nürburgring.

ADU 3B

FIRST REGISTERED	1 JUNE 1964
ENGINE SIZE	1,147cc
MODEL TYPE	SPITFIRE (racing car)

When entries closed for the Le Mans 24 Hours in 1964, Standard-Triumph was allocated two starting places for its Spitfires, and decided to submit ADU 1B and ADU 2B for those places. In the run-up to the event, however, the company was also allocated a reserve entry, which could become available if other confirmed entries dropped out in practice or at the last minute. ADU 3B was made race-ready, therefore, and taken to the circuit on the same transporter as its sister cars, and everyone in the team was delighted when the car was eventually granted a start – one of just two reserves to be promoted that year.

With advice and assistance from the French Standard-Triumph importers, two French drivers – Jean-François Piot and Jean-Louis Marnat – were taken on and, with the very minimum of experience of the new car, duly qualified. Right from the start their Spitfire soon proved to be the fastest of the trio: after three hours they were two places ahead of the Hobbs/Slotemaker car, and after eleven hours they were three places ahead of it. But soon after half distance, at 4.30am, the car suddenly crashed and was almost totally destroyed. Marnat was driving at the time and came weaving past the

ADU 3B at speed at Le Mans in the early stages of the 1964 Le Mans race, with its makeshift padded headlamp covers still stuck firmly in place.

Driven by Jean-François Piot and Claude Dubois, ADU 3B finished second in its class in the 1965 Le Mans 24 Hours. The small light on the roof above the driver's door was for recognition purposes from the pits.

pits, going quite slowly and clearly about to pass out. Factory test driver Gordon Birtwistle, who was working with the team at the race, remembers what happened.

'He had been hit up the back by another car [at Tertre Rouge] and the rear panel that gave access to the spare wheel had fallen out. He was getting exhaust fumes into the car, which were affecting him, but he didn't know that. The car passed us in the pits weaving down the straight, not going very fast, and it just glanced off the end of the pit counter close to the Alpine-Renault team, then went over and buried itself into the foot of the Dunlop bridge on the outside of the corner.'

Although the car was demolished, Marnat, mercifully, was only slightly injured and recovered soon enough to drive another Spitfire (ADU 5B) in a race at Montlhéry in October. ADU 3B was effectively recreated over the next six months to the same enhanced specification as the other team cars and made the journey to Sebring in March 1965. It did not race there, however, taking its turn to be the team 'spare', avail-

Seen towards the end of the gruelling Le Mans 24 Hours in 1965, ADU 3B displays the slightly different grille insert panel that the cars used in that race alone – mainly to ensure sufficient cooling for the 109bhp/1,147cc engines.

able for use if any of the other three cars gave trouble in practice – which they did not.

Accordingly ADU 3B was still fresh for Le Mans in 1965. There it was allocated once more to Jean-François Piot, this time partnered by another of the team's seasoned rally drivers, Claude Dubois, who had not previously raced a Spitfire but had been in the Triumph team of TR3S cars in 1959. The pair kept going steadily, making sure the oil cooler problem that seemed endemic on the Spitfires that year was kept under control, and eventually finished 14th overall, having averaged more than 91mph.

ADU 3B was last seen in France, undergoing active restoration, but at the time of writing had not yet resurfaced.

COMPETITION RECORD
1964 Le Mans 24 Hours
Jean-Louis Marnat/Jean-François Piot   Did not finish
1965 Le Mans 24 Hours
Claude Dubois/Jean-François Piot   2nd in class

ADU 4B

FIRST REGISTERED	1 JUNE 1964
ENGINE SIZE	1,147cc
MODEL TYPE	SPITFIRE (racing car)

Although ADU 4B was the fourth of the original quartet of Spitfire Le Mans cars and shared the specification of the other cars, it enjoyed two distinctions. First, it was completed before any of the other cars, and therefore selected for endurance testing at Oulton Park and Silverstone in April/May 1964. Second, it did not race at all in 1964. Its racing career, therefore, was confined to two events in 1965.

The car's first outing was at Sebring, where it ran to the same enhanced chassis specification as the other Spitfires. It was entered for two experienced American drivers, Ed Barker and Duane Feuerhelm, who were recommended by Kas Kastner, and in the race Mike Rothschild also drove the car. Like the other American-crewed Spitfire (ADU 2B), it survived the mid-race monsoon-like conditions remarkably well, keeping going when many other cars simply drowned out, and ended up second in its capacity class, close behind the very special works MG Midget – this was the only time in two years that a Spitfire was beaten by a Midget or a Sprite in a race or on a rally.

Back in Europe, ADU 4B then became the reserve entry for Le Mans, where the three other team racing Spitfires were guaranteed starting positions, but at a late stage the organisers granted Triumph a fourth starting slot too. Behind the scenes in Coventry there was pandemonium, for it was then

Late on in the 1965 Sebring 12 Hours, which started in daylight and finished in darkness, ADU 4B makes a pit stop on its way to second place in its capacity class.

far too late to engage experienced racing drivers for this entry. In a move that smacked of desperation, Ray Henderson drafted in Simo Lampinen and Jean-Jacques Thuner from the rally team, and even nominated Roy Fidler as reserve driver for the entire squad. None of them had ever tackled Le Mans before, although Thuner had at least raced on the circuit in his Spitfire in the 1964 Tour de France.

The result was an unexpected and splendid triumph. The seasoned rally drivers qualified without fuss, settled down to do whatever they were asked to do on the track, and listened

When ADU 4B went to the Le Mans test day in April 1964, the racing car project was still very new and every completed lap proved something – this car, however, initially served as a spare and did not take part in the 1964 Le Mans 24 Hours.

At a late stage Triumph was granted a fourth Spitfire entry at Le Mans in 1965, so the 'spare' car, ADU 4B, was pressed into service and rally drivers Jean-Jacques Thuner and Simo Lampinen speedily drafted in to drive it. To their great joy, they not only finished the race but also won their capacity class.

ADU 4B hard at work in the 1965 Le Mans 24 Hours, where it won its capacity class.

carefully to Rob Slotemaker, who they knew well from his works rally connections and who gave them good advice after his Le Mans experiences the previous year. They came home 13th overall, winning their capacity class, beating the other surviving Spitfire (ADU 3B) and averaging 95mph throughout the 24 hours. Of equal importance to the French Triumph importer was that, yet again, not a single Alpine-Renault made it to the finish, really rubbing in the quality of the Spitfire to the French public. Furthermore, Lampinen and Thuner almost matched the 1.3-litre works Austin-Healey Sprite, which finished just one place ahead of them.

After a period of ownership by two American enthusiasts, ADU 4B returned to the UK early in the 2000s and remains in excellent condition.

COMPETITION RECORD
1965 Sebring 12 Hours
Ed Barker/Duane Feuerhelm   2nd in class
1965 Le Mans 24 Hours
Jean-Jacques Thuner/Simo Lampinen   1st in class

ADU 5B

FIRST REGISTERED	1 JUNE 1964
ENGINE SIZE	1,147cc
MODEL TYPE	SPITFIRE (rally car)

For its first event, the French Alpine rally of 1964, ADU 5B was still only in what proved to be a partially developed specification, like its sister cars on this event (ADU 6B and ADU 7B). Although the aluminium head, eight-port, 102bhp engine, Vitesse gearbox and running gear were as up-to-the-minute as the team could make them, these cars were still running with conventional body styles, including a lift-off metal 'bubble-top' hard top.

Although the smallest type of Laycock overdrive was already available on Spitfire production cars (my own road car had an overdrive 'box in 1964) and homologated with the FIA, overdrive was never used on the high-revving competition cars. The truth is that none of the factory's transmission design/development specialists were ready to trust the durability of the small overdrive in transmitting 100bhp. Instead the team juggled with different rear axle ratios and yet another type of gearbox, which was not homologated, would soon be used.

The latest FIA Group 3 regulations, as applied by the organisers of the French Alpine rally, did not authorise the

removal of front and rear bumpers, so these had to be retained. Accordingly, the three Alpine entries looked very normal except for their engine-cooling vents – on the front wings above and behind the wheel arches – and the addition of three extra driving lamps, with the usual 'Cyclops' lamp in the centre flanked by a pair of lamps immediately outboard of the line of the front overriders. Perspex for the side windows and hard-top rear window helped to reduce weight.

Although Jean-Jacques Thuner already had a Spitfire of his own at home in Switzerland and had sampled ADU 8B (the spare/practice car) a few days earlier, he was only introduced to ADU 5B at the start in Marseilles. The time schedules on this event were as fiercely fast as ever, and although the Spitfires made it through the first night without mishap, this situation soon changed. Clean from Quatre Chemins to Sigale to Entrevaux, ADU 5B performed well on the Allos and Cayolle speed tests, until Thuner encountered a non-competing car driven by a Belgian tourist and collided with it. Damage to the Spitfire was not extensive, but it was enough to put the car out of its first event as the oil cooler, which was mounted behind the front grille, was ruined.

Once back in Coventry, ADU 5B was converted into one of three race-car 'lookalikes' for the Tour de France. Thuner aimed to do all the driving on the circuits, and on most special stages, but because the event regulations required that the co-driver also drive in two tests along the way, co-driver John Gretener was told that he would have to tackle hillclimb speed tests in the French Alps. For him that was a real novelty…

The 10-day event had only just got under way from the start in Lille, northern France, when two of the four Spitfire entries – ADU 6B and ADU 467B – blew up during the first circuit test, at Reims. This meant that for the next week and more there would only be two remaining Spitfires, and with no team orders being applied it would be fascinating to see whether Thuner or Rob Slotemaker (in ADU 7B) could beat the works Alpine-Renaults in their class.

For those of us who watched events unfold, this was a week to remember. The two Spitfires were never far apart, both were reliable, and both had the measure of the Alpine-Renaults – for a time it looked as if they would gloriously take first and second in their capacity class. Thuner, the rally driver who occasionally raced, and Slotemaker, the can-do racer who rallied well on tarmac surfaces, were very evenly matched. On the very last day of the event, though, ADU 5B was on its way from the overnight halt in Grenoble to the finish in Nice, with only three hillclimb tests to complete, when a piston suddenly melted and immobilised the car. Thuner was distraught, as well he might have been, and the team was both shattered and puzzled, for this was an engine that had already completed nearly 4,000 miles over the previous days.

Even so, there was little spare time for wailing, gnashing of teeth or navel-gazing, for immediately after the Tour de France ADU 5B was trailered to Paris, where it was provided with a new race engine and hastily refurbished for the Paris 1,000km race at Montlhéry, crewed by the French pairing of Jean-François Piot and Jean-Louis Marnat. This was a major sports car race, dominated by 4-litre Ferrari prototypes, so the Spitfire could do no more than put up what one might call a 'gallant performance'. Which indeed it did, never putting a wheel wrong, circulating like clockwork, averaging 77.05mph, and winning its capacity class.

Thereafter ADU 5B enjoyed a winter's rest, for it was not to appear again until mid-1965, when Jean-Jacques Thuner drove it in the Geneva rally. It was before the start of this rally – the one on which two works Spitfires had shone so very brightly in 1964 – that real controversy hit the team. At pre-event scrutineering the two cars were suddenly pulled over and threatened with exclusion on the grounds that they were not being presented in homologated condition. Gordon Birtwistle was running the cars in the absence of Ray Henderson, who was at Le Mans, and explained to me the circumstances many years later.

'Someone had talked. The scrutineer wanted to know how many gears were synchronised, and I told him the vehicle was in accordance with homologation papers. That was a porky pie. He insisted on driving the car. I told him that no one but my drivers and I would drive the cars. But we were in a tricky situation, especially as the Le Mans cars had the same gearbox fitted. I went off to have a word with Jean-Jacques and, suddenly, I heard the Spitfire started up in the scruti-

neering hall. The scrutineer reversed it at high speed, then rammed it into first gear and accelerated forward – the change was as smooth as silk.

'The scrutineer then gave us an ultimatum. We could only start the event if we rebuilt the gearboxes to standard specification and, if we won anything, we would have to have them stripped afterwards. There was no choice. We took the cars to Blanc & Paiche [the Triumph importers in Geneva], borrowed two standard cars from the showroom and worked through the night to install non-synchromesh first gears in our Spitfires...'

All this, of course, came about because the works cars were running with prototype GT6-style gearboxes in which first gear was synchronised, whereas the gearbox fitted to standard road cars did not have synchromesh on first. The fact that the alternative gearbox ratios had been listed for more than a year, and were the same whether or not first-gear synchromesh was fitted, did not impress this particular scrutineer. Fortunately, no word of this mini-scandal reached Le Mans, where the same all-synchromesh gearboxes were fitted for the 1965 race in which the cars triumphed. It was altogether fitting that the drivers of the class-winning Spitfire at Le Mans (ADU 4B) should be the two patient individuals who had suffered so much in Geneva!

Despite the rumpus that disrupted their preparations, the two Spitfires, driven by Jean-Jacques Thuner and Simo Lampinen, proved to be impressively fast and reliable throughout the Geneva rally. Thuner, a tarmac specialist who knew some of the speed hillclimbs just that bit better than

This 1964 Tour de France roadside maintenance for ADU 5B is routine – hence everyone's relaxed body language. From left, Rob Slotemaker, Jean-Jacques Thuner, John Gretener, team boss Graham Robson and mechanic Mick Moore.

Lampinen, a loose-surface special stage expert, finished fifth overall and won his capacity class. Honour was satisfied and the errant scrutineer was not in evidence at the finish.

On its return to Coventry ADU 5B was thoroughly rebuilt and modified for the French Alpine, which took place towards the end of July 1965. This was an event that included an FIA Group 6 prototype category for the first time – which meant that non-homologated machines could run. As a consequence the works team decided that all four of the 'front-line' Spitfires – ADU 5B, ADU 6B, ADU 7B and AVC 654B – should be significantly modified, not only to make them even faster than before but also to get them out of Group 3, and therefore out of the reach of the works Mini-Cooper S models that were increasingly being used in the 1.3-litre class.

Although the cars looked visually familiar, they were all equipped with what were familiarly known in the factory as 79X engines rather than the usual 70X type. These were 1,296cc engines (with bore/stroke of 73.7/76mm) that Ray

Bates' enthusiastic team had speedily developed to produce 117bhp, the new engine size being available because series production of the Triumph 1300 saloon was about to start. The four cars ran in powder blue livery, with smart white steel disc wheels, a four-headlamp nose and a swivelling Lucas spotlight in the centre of the roof panel. The all-synchromesh gearbox that had caused controversy in Geneva was also reinstalled.

The French Alpine rally took place in high summer in the French Alps between Marseilles, Geneva and Monte Carlo, on roads that were almost all open to the public, and run at insanely high target average speeds. Looking back, it is extraordinary that such an event could have survived for so long, and that it remained so popular with drivers and teams. Along with his team-mates in the other 'prototype' Spitfires, Thuner battled hard against other prototypes, mainly Porsches, including a formidably fast six-cylinder 904 driven by Eugen Böhringer. The Porsches may have been faster but they were not as reliable and none of them finished, at least one of them crashing out. To the joy of the Triumph team, both Thuner in ADU 5B and Lampinen in AVC 654B completed this hot marathon to win the entire Prototype category.

COMPETITION RECORD

1964 French Alpine		
Jean-Jacques Thuner		Did not finish
1964 Tour de France		
Jean-Jacques Thuner		Did not finish
1964 Paris 1,000km		
Jean-François Piot/Jean-Louis Marnat		1st in class
1965 Geneva		
Jean-Jacques Thuner		1st in class
1965 French Alpine		
Jean-Jacques Thuner	2nd in Prototype category	

ADU 6B

FIRST REGISTERED	1 JUNE 1964
ENGINE SIZE	1,147cc
MODEL TYPE	SPITFIRE (rally car)

Technically identical to ADU 5B, Jean-Jacques Thuner's car, ADU 6B was allocated to Roy Fidler and Don Grimshaw for its first event, the French Alpine rally. The car started very healthily but on the second day it suddenly faltered and eventually had to retire when the engine threw a

connecting rod through the side of the cylinder block.

Roy was eventually called to a meeting at the factory and firmly expected to be fired for breaking the engine. Instead he found that Harry Webster's team had carried out a forensic examination of the engine and discovered an inherent fault in the machining of the connecting rods on the production line, so there was considerable appreciation that the problem had come to their attention!

For the Tour de France, which followed in September 1964, ADU 6B received all the updates applied to the other works cars for this event, along with the loan of a stream-lined nose from one of the Le Mans cars. Bill Bradley of the Midland Racing Partnership was brought in as Roy's partner and scheduled to drive in the circuit races, while Roy would drive for the road sections. Things looked very promising but unhappily the engine melted a piston on the warming-up lap of the first race, at Reims; Shell, the sponsor of the race, had apparently supplied some sub-standard fuel.

Refreshed at the factory, stripped of its Le Mans-style bonnet and given a lower-ratio back axle to make it more suitable for a speed hillclimb type of rally, ADU 6B was then allocated to Jean-Jacques Thuner to compete in his national event, the 2,000km Geneva rally, four weeks later along with Terry Hunter in ADU 7B. This event, which started and finished in Geneva, included in its itinerary most of the hills that had become famous, and familiar, through their use on the French Alpine rally.

Thanks to a performance handicap formula that seemed to favour smaller-engined sports cars, Thuner and Hunter were both highly competitive throughout, helped by the absence of several works teams. Fastest outright on more than one occasion, and always very close behind Hunter's class-winning car, Thuner ended up second in class and fifth overall. It was a gratifying end to the Spitfire's first year, especially for Jean-Jacques, who was still bitterly disappointed by his other car's engine failure on the Tour de France.

For 1965 ADU 6B gained the new four-headlamp bonnet style, as fitted to the other works Spitfires, and started the Monte Carlo rally from London along with its team-mates. On this occasion it was allocated to Rob Slotemaker – its third new driver in six months – and British co-driver Alan Taylor. The weather on this Monte was awful, equally as wintry as in the white-out year experienced by the works Vitesses in 1963, but Slotemaker coped manfully throughout. Although his stage times were no match for those of Simo Lampinen, who drove on snow a lot in his native Finland, Rob lost very little time in the blizzard conditions that were encountered even before the stages began.

On the final night, with six further stages to be tackled, Slotemaker maintained his position, overhauled Lampinen's sister can when it hit engine trouble, and took a creditable second in class. Creditable? Well, yes, extremely creditable, for the winner of that class was Timo Mäkinen's works Mini-Cooper S, which also won the event outright in what has often been called the 'drive of the century'!

Amazingly, this Spitfire then took a holiday for the next six months, tucked away in a corner of the workshops while Rob did other things, including driving works 2000 saloons in rallies and a racing Spitfire at Le Mans. Then for the French Alpine rally it was allocated to Roy Fidler and treated to a major update, like the three other fastback Spitfires, including the fitment of the non-homologated 1,296cc engine. Because I was Roy's co-driver on this event, I hope it will be in order to recall the light comedy that accompanied the car's retirement.

After the completion of several speed tests on which Fidler was equally as rapid as his team-mates, there had been time

Halfway to Monte Carlo in January 1965, Rob Slotemaker's ADU 6B is seen in company with Val Pirie's SMART entry, which retired when it ran out of time.

Near the end of the Monte Carlo rally of 1965 – amazingly without snow – at the Pont Charles Albert time control, just north of Nice and close to sea level. ADU 6B was driven by Rob Slotemaker and finished second in its capacity class.

for major service attention at Entrevaux before resuming. Roy picks up the story: 'After about 12 hours we were hurtling along. I think we'd just had the wheels changed, and there was a drop on the left side, and a big mountain on the right. All of a sudden I saw a rear wheel passing us, it bounced once, then disappeared, never to be seen again by a human being. After that, I couldn't steer the car, it slithered along, and went straight across a slight-right-slight-left before I managed to stop it...'

All this happened on the north side of the famous Allos stage, as the car was descending in the valley towards Barcelonnette, and had been caused by rear wheel studs breaking and allowing the wheel to detach itself. By the time we had extracted the spare wheel through the 'letterbox' slot in the glass-fibre tail and concluded that it was not possible to cobble it up to continue, one of Ray Henderson's support cars finally arrived to make repairs. At this point the rally was on its way to the overnight halt in Grenoble and it was not a great detour for the support car to take ADU 6B to Geneva, along with Roy and me. We were deposited with the crippled car at Blanc & Paiche, got a lift to the airport and returned to London in no time by British European Airways, still in racing overalls and carrying crash helmets!

Back in the UK, the car had a 1,147cc engine put back in and was loaned to a scratch team from Coventry's Godiva Car Club for the Six-Hour Relay at Silverstone, after which it was finally sold off.

COMPETITION RECORD	
1964 French Alpine	
Roy Fidler	Did not finish
1964 Tour de France	
Bill Bradley	Did not finish
1964 Geneva	
Jean-Jacques Thuner	5th overall
1965 Monte Carlo	
Rob Slotemaker	2nd in class
1965 French Alpine	
Roy Fidler	Did not finish

ADU 7B

FIRST REGISTERED	1 JUNE 1964
ENGINE SIZE	1,147cc
MODEL TYPE	SPITFIRE (rally car)

Only once did the works Spitfires appear wearing the same type of 'bubble' hardtop as thousands of other road cars – thereafter they took on the stylish fastback shape. This is Terry Hunter in ADU 7B on the 1964 French Alpine, where he missed winning a Coupe des Alpes by just one minute.

The third car in the new team of Spitfires, ADU 7B, was technically the same as the other cars, and was almost new when it reached the start of the French Alpine rally in Marseilles. Its driver, Terry Hunter, was also new to the team, although he had already carried out the bulk of the pre-event practice and recce activity in ADU 8B.

For the first 24 hours of the event, ADU 7B did very well and it was still unpenalised on the road when a management mistake caused the car to be held too long at a service halt. Young Hunter and co-driver Patrick Lier then found themselves running behind a punishing schedule on one section and lost one minute – and that one minute stopped them from winning a Coupe des Alpes. The schedule of that particular section had been unashamedly 'pruned' and several other cars were also unfairly penalised, but subsequent protests proved to be in vain. The stewards, one of whom was British, were later described as 'spineless', but the damage was done. In the end that delay cost Hunter his Coupe, but no more, as Rauno Aaltonen's Mini-Cooper 1275S, winner of the Spitfires' capacity class, had been just a little faster on the speed tests. Not that this made the team management any happier about the unsatisfactory outcome.

For the ten-day Tour de France, ADU 7B received all the changes and updates already described for its sisters, this time the crew being Rob Slotemaker and Terry Hunter. Slotemaker would drive all the circuit races – lengthy time trials at Reims, Rouen, Le Mans, Cognac, Pau, Albi, Clermont-Ferrand and Monza – while Hunter would tackle the majority of the nine speed hillclimbs.

As already noted, this was the event where this Spitfire not only fought a week-long battle with team-mate Thuner's ADU 5B – there were no team orders – but also against the works Alpine Renaults. The gaps between them were always small and nothing was resolved until the final day, when ADU 5B blew its engine. ADU 7B started steadily, then took third place in the Handicap category in the two-hour Le Mans race, second on Handicap at Cognac, first on Handicap at Clermont-Ferrand – and was

Fred Nicklin and Gordon Birtwistle did a great job in trimming the Spitfire's handling for motorsport use, but these cars still picked up an inside rear wheel on occasion – but they were fitted with special limited-slip differentials and this was not a major problem. This is Rob Slotemaker in ADU 7B on the 1964 Tour de France. Note that the front grille blanking panel has been removed.

never outpaced thereafter as this arduous event unfolded.

All looked good for a grandstand finish until, on the last two days, the Spitfire's big fuel tank developed a leak, some-thing that became obvious when the car ran out of fuel on a road section. Although the fumes were nauseating for the crew, the leak was fortunately towards the top of the tank

ADU 7B was the most successful of all the works Spitfires in 1964 and 1965. Here it is in 1.3-litre 'prototype' form, proudly carrying number 1, for Rob Slotemaker (at the wheel) to drive in the 1965 French Alpine rally.

Rob Slotemaker and Alan Taylor passing through a French provincial town and going strong in the 1965 French Alpine rally, but ADU 7B's 1.3-litre prototype engine later blew and caused them to retire.

Although similar to the Le Mans cars, the works Spitfire rally cars were subtly different in many details, including the use of standard bonnets (with modification) and different window and stowage arrangements.

Special light-alloy road wheels were fitted to works Spitfire rally cars; rim width was initially 4.5in, later 5.5in.

This rear view of ADU 7B could have been taken at any point from September 1964, when the fastback roof was first fitted.

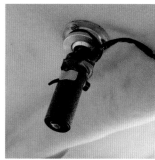

Those were the days when swivelling roof spotlights were still road-legal in motorsport and very popular with crews; Lucas provided the hardware.

The first quartz-halogen headlamp bulbs, which became available in 1964, were only single-filament types, so extra lamps had to be mounted inboard for dipping purposes and were first seen on the works Spitfires early in 1965.

Rear details include a reversing lamp and the 'letterbox' slot in the tail panel where the spare wheel is accommodated.

ADU 7B, along with its several team-mates, was rallied in this form throughout 1965.

Not the tidiest of passenger compartments: the aviation-type clock is authentic for the period, but the Halda Tripmaster did not exist when this car was originally built in 1964.

Lovingly rebuilt and prepared for use in classic rallying, ADU 7B now has full harness safety belts; conventional three-point belts would have been used in 1964–65.

and so it was possible to plug the split with various get-you-home methods and run the car with the tank only part-filled, supported by a service car following wherever possible on the road sections with cans of fuel!

The effort was all worthwhile. The gallant little car was rewarded with a capacity class win, fifth overall in the GT Handicap category, and tenth overall on scratch – beaten only by four Ferrari 250 GTOs, four Porsche 904s and a 1.6-litre Alfa Romeo! The French Triumph importer was positively ecstatic, especially as the French Alpine-Renault team effort had been humiliated.

There was little time for ADU 7B to bask in glory. Four weeks later it was back on the start line of the 2,000km Geneva rally, which was run to a performance handicap formula that favoured small-capacity sports cars. Fitted with a light-alloy bonnet of conventional Spitfire shape and a low axle ratio to suit the various hillclimb tests, the car was driven by Terry Hunter and ran very close throughout to Thuner's sister car, both of them setting fastest times overall on various speed hillclimbs. By the end, the team's feverish calculations showed that Hunter had won the GT category overall, and finished second overall in the entire event to Henri Greder's 1964 Ford Falcon. Following this same car's

The bonnet/front wing assembly on a works Spitfire rally car was made entirely of aluminium; side vents were always included, but the extra headlamps were introduced for 1965.

superb performance in the Tour de France, this was a remarkable result.

Three months later, and now with the new four-headlamp nose, it was allocated to Terry Hunter and Patrick Lier for the Monte Carlo rally, starting from London. After a much-observed fracas with his team management the night before the start, Hunter was in no mood to tackle a long event like this, yet still managed to reach the Chambéry control as one of only nine crews to make it through the blizzards from London. Soon after this, however, he went off the road on the Col de Granier and was eliminated.

What happened after that is equally well recorded. On the last night he somehow managed to get his Spitfire, still carrying its competition numbers, on to some of the stages, claiming that he was trying to help his team-mates. He was stopped by officials and, when found to have been drinking, arrested by the gendarmerie and put in jail for the night.

This detail of the roof and window arrangement shows the massive fuel filler cap and the slot in the Perspex side window through which cabin air was encouraged to exit.

This overhead shot of ADU 7B on the 1965 French Alpine rally shows off the sleek lines of the works fastback Spitfires. The vast fuel tank behind the seats is visible, with filler cap adjacent in the roof panel.

After his return to the UK he was dismissed from the team.

ADU 7B was not used again for six months but finally reappeared in Rob Slotemaker's hands for the French Alpine rally. Like its team-mates, it ran in highly-developed 1.3-litre 'Prototype' form and was going great guns until it blew its engine mid-stage. There was nothing rare about this failure, for by the 1960s Triumph was taking the pragmatic view that it was better to be competitive and suffer such failures from time to time, rather than build cars like the works TR3As that might be relied upon to finish but might also be relied upon to get beaten…

COMPETITION RECORD
1964 French Alpine
Terry Hunter   3rd in class
1964 Tour de France
Rob Slotemaker   1st in class
1964 Geneva
Terry Hunter   1st in GT category, 2nd overall
1965 Monte Carlo
Terry Hunter   Did not finish
1965 French Alpine
Rob Slotemaker   Did not finish

ADU 8B

FIRST REGISTERED	1 JUNE 1964
ENGINE SIZE	1,147cc
MODEL TYPE	SPITFIRE (rally car)

Although five new Spitfire rally cars were completed in the first months of 1964, one of them – ADU 8B – was never actually used on a rally, not even as a 'clone' for any other car. As was usual for a Standard-Triumph works team of the period, there were to be three regular team entries but a fourth car would be built, not only for use in practice and testing but also as a reserve in case of a serious accident to any other car.

So it was that ADU 8B was used exclusively for test and development work, probably completing more miles than any other car on the fleet. Because of this role it always operated with the normal series-production removable hard top, never receiving the fastback style that graced the three other regular cars in works use. It was worked very hard in the weeks leading up to the start of the French Alpine rally, Terry Hunter doing much of the driving on this expedition, but was somewhat damaged in a road accident in northern France when returning to the factory after the event. Similarly, it again provided valuable service in the weeks leading up to the Tour de France.

COMPETITION RECORD
None, but used extensively for testing, development and practice assignments in 1964–65.

As an 'add-on' to the official works rally team of Spitfires, Triumph's public relations department financed Stirling Moss's secretary, Val Pirie, to drive ADU 467B for 12 months from June 1964. Taken outside Stirling's home in London's Mayfair, this posed shot shows a Spitfire from the press fleet – a car that did not appear in any competition guise.

ADU 467B

FIRST REGISTERED	9 JUNE 1964
ENGINE SIZE	1,147cc
MODEL TYPE	SPITFIRE (rally car)

Val Pirie's green-painted SMART Spitfire, which never had the fastback body conversion, was maintained alongside the other works cars. Here mechanic Mick Moore adds the rally plates for the 1965 Monte. Note the new-for-1965 headlamp layout, which included single-filament quartz halogen bulbs in the main headlamps and the central spotlight.

Soon after work began on developing new Spitfires, a fifth 'semi-detached' car was added to fleet, reserved solely and exclusively for Val Pirie, who was then Stirling Moss's secretary and personal assistant. She had already started rallying in other makes of car, but her link with Triumph came because BP, the contracted fuel supplier to Triumph, was Stirling Moss's fuel sponsor – the marketing links between all parties were obvious.

Officially the car was entered by SMART (Stirling Moss Automobile Racing Team) but it was based in Coventry. Signed in the spring of 1964, the deal was for one year, with an option to extend it should it prove to be successful. This explains why the car ran in events between June 1964 and May 1965. Pirie was clearly not as comfortable with the car as she had originally hoped and was certainly not as quick as the men by whose standards her test and stage times were inevitably measured, and she also complained bitterly that she had 'second-class treatment' from the works mechanics during events. She was probably relieved when her and the factory's obligations came to an end, and dropped out of rallying soon afterwards.

Technically this car had the same chassis and running gear as the other works Spitfires, except that it was never treated to the glass-fibre fastback hard top seen on ADU 5B, ADU 6B and ADU 7B from their second event onwards. It was always painted in Stirling's favourite colour, Renault Borneo Green, which was close to what most of us called 'BP green'.

ADU 467B was brand new for use in the 1964 French Alpine rally. As Pirie had very little rally experience, she asked to have a co-driver allocated to her and the task went to Yvonne Hilton, who was very well known in British rallying but lacked overseas experience. Val, in fact, put the car so far off the road during the event that a sturdy breakdown truck was needed to retrieve it.

There was no more luck on the Tour de France, where Anita Taylor was Pirie's partner, the strategy being that Anita, a rising star in British saloon car racing, would drive all the circuit races. On the first test of the event, a race at Reims, the car threw a connecting rod, wrecked the engine, and went no further.

For the 1964 RAC rally, where ADU 467B was to be the only works-backed Spitfire to tackle the special stages, Val had yet another co-driver in Susan Reeves, who was rally driver David Seigle-Morris's girlfriend and later his wife.

This did not have much effect on her fortunes, for Pirie was always a long way off the pace, ran a long way behind the works 2000 saloons on the road, and sometimes arrived at service points after the crews had been obliged to leave for their next appointment. Val complained that if she had always had the promised service support she would have performed better – but the special stage times told a different story.

For the car's two outings in 1965 the new four-headlamp nose was grafted into place but the original bubble top was retained. Despite full and unstinting help from the factory on the Monte Carlo rally, including use of the latest in studded tyres, she gradually lost time and was finally eliminated. Val's last appearance in this car was on the Tulip rally but she was well down the listings throughout. With the year-long contract then at an end, the programme was terminated as there seemed to be no prospect of success.

The car was eventually sold off by the works and became very successful in British club racing.

COMPETITION RECORD	
1964 French Alpine	
Val Pirie	Did not finish
1964 Tour de France	
Val Pirie	Did not finish
1964 RAC	
Val Pirie	Did not finish
1965 Monte Carlo	
Val Pirie	Did not finish
1965 Tulip	
Val Pirie	Did not finish

AVC 654B

FIRST REGISTERED	22 DECEMBER 1964
ENGINE SIZE	1,147cc
MODEL TYPE	SPITFIRE (rally car)

As already detailed in Chapter 5, when the young Finnish star Simo Lampinen was signed up for the 1965 season it was agreed that dedicated left-hand-drive cars – a 2000 saloon and a Spitfire – would be built for him. This new Spitfire, therefore, had left-hand drive and was ready for Simo to drive on his first event for the team – the Monte Carlo rally of 1965.

Like the other mainstream team cars, AVC 654B featured the long glass-fibre roof, the instantly recognisable four-head-lamp bonnet style, the 18-gallon fuel tank and the GT6-style transmission. Along with Rob Slotemaker in ADU 6B and Terry Hunter in ADU 7B, it started from London, the three cars looking very smart as they lined up for the ceremonial flag-waving of the start.

Simo settled in straight away, showed off his mastery of snowy conditions, and proved to be easily the fastest of the Spitfire drivers. After six long special stages, he had taken 125m 16s compared with Slotemaker's 135m 15s – and was significantly faster than any other true sports car in the event. If he had not had to run for a time on the road with the very minimum of lighting – due to a battery that rather mysteriously flattened itself – and lost a total of 18 minutes on tight road sections, he would surely have been much higher than tenth when the last night's dash over six more stages began. On stage times, in fact, he was ahead of both Eugen Böhringer's Porsche 904 and Peter Harper's Sunbeam Tiger, which would eventually finish second and fourth respectively.

The last night, however, was a grave disappointment, for in the depths of a blizzard Lampinen's Spitfire developed engine problems that could not be solved at the side of the road, and the car only just dragged itself to the finish. Reported as retired in more than one press outlet, the car was in fact classified as a finisher, 24th overall and third in class.

Four months later it was ready to take part in the Tulip rally, where a typically complex handicap formula was once again in place. It was thought that the handicapping might favour a Spitfire if Lampinen was as rapid in the little coupé as expected, although the factory hedged bets by also entering two Group 3 2000 saloons. But it was not to be. Lampinen was indeed fastest in his class at the Nürburgring, and on other early special stages and short hillclimb tests, but the clutch suddenly failed when he set off up the classic Trois Epis hillclimb test in the French mountains close to Strasbourg. He was left stranded, and out of the event.

The left-hand-drive car was then speedily rebuilt in time for Lampinen to take part in the Geneva rally alongside Jean-Jacques Thuner in ADU 5B. Like its sister Spitfire, the car

Simo Lampinen in AVC 654B, the only left-hand-drive version of the works Spitfire fleet, on a surprisingly snow-free section of the Monte Carlo rally, in the foothills just behind Nice.

Simo Lampinen in AVC 654B high in the Alps during the 1965 Geneva rally, where he finished second in class to Jean-Jacques Thuner's sister car.

Outright victory with AVC 654B in the Prototype category of the 1965 French Alpine rally was Simo Lampinen's finest hour with the works team – his Spitfire's 1.3-litre engine survived four days and nights while the works Porsche 904s all hit trouble. This bare outcrop is near the summit of the famous Mont Ventoux hillclimb.

A rare colour shot of a works rally Spitfire: Simo Lampinen in AVC 654B leads one of its sister cars through a French town on the 1965 Geneva rally.

suffered severely at pre-event scrutineering (see page 151) and had to run with a substitute gearbox, a standard one without synchromesh on first gear. All the same Simo managed to finish, second in class, very close behind Thuner.

The highlight of this car's short works career – four events in seven months – came in July 1965 when Lampinen drove it in the prestigious French Alpine rally as a 1.3-litre 'Proto-type'. Along with team-mate Thuner's ADU 5B, it survived the horrifically fast, demanding, hot conditions and ended up winning the entire Prototype category.

After this, the car was not used again as a full works machine, and was eventually sold off to Scandinavia. Apparently it survives to this day.

In this shot of Simo Lampinen's AVC 654B on the 1965 French Alpine rally, the 'letterbox' panel for access to the spare wheel is clearly visible below the rear window.

COMPETITION RECORD	
1965 Monte Carlo	
Simo Lampinen	3rd in class
1965 Tulip	
Simo Lampinen	Did not finish
1965 Geneva	
Simo Lampinen	2nd in class
1965 French Alpine	
Simo Lampinen	1st in Prototype category

ERW 412C

FIRST REGISTERED	6 APRIL 1965
ENGINE SIZE	1,147cc
MODEL TYPE	SPITFIRE (racing car)

This car, registered in 1965 but not raced until mid-1966, was the replacement for ADU 2B, which Bill Bradley had been driving on loan from the Triumph factory since the beginning of the year, but had unhappily been destroyed at the Nürburgring in June 1966. In every way ERW 412C looked identical to the factory racing cars of the period, with the smooth nose style, fastback coupé roof, cast alloy wheels and big fuel tank. As with ADU 2B, it was very successful.

I have not been able to uncover details of this car's competition history. Some years ago, however, Bill Bradley told me that in 1966 alone the two cars – ADU 2B and ERW 412C – won their capacity class 14 times out of 18 starts, and that at the time they held class lap records at Brands Hatch, Crystal Palace, Goodwood, Mallory Park, Oulton Park and Snetterton.

The remains of ERW 412C are still owned by Bradley, who plans to restore it one day.

ERW 412C was the fifth works Spitfire race car, built up in 1965 for Bill Bradley to use in British and European sports car events. The car was always maintained at the factory but Bradley paid all his operating expenses for this programme.

COMPETITION RECORD
Loaned to Bill Bradley for UK and European events in 1966, without direct factory involvement.

UNREGISTERED

ENGINE SIZE	1,147cc
MODEL TYPE	SPITFIRE (racing car)

Soon after the works team had competed in the Le Mans 24 Hours and the French Alpine rally in the summer of 1965, John Lloyd and Ray Henderson started work on a special order. Their brief was to build a new, unique and special lightweight version of the Spitfire racing car for Walter Sulke, who ran ZF Garages, the Standard-Triumph distributorship in Hong Kong. Sulke's intention was to race this car in that region, starting with the Macau Grand Prix in November 1965. Still controlled by the Dutch at that time, Macau, like Hong Kong, was attached to the Chinese mainland, and would eventually revert to Chinese sovereignty. It had a demanding little street circuit that would attract many of the top single-seater teams and drivers in later years.

It is important to stress that this car was unique and newly constructed – it was not a conversion of one of the existing racing cars. Because the budget for the project was so tight,

construction and design did not start until a survey had been made of the spare parts that remained available at the culmination of the Le Mans programme. Fortunately this was found to include vital items such as chassis frames, an incomplete all-aluminium bodyshell and an up-to-date race engine!

Accordingly work started on what became known as the 'Macau car'. It was powered by the latest 109bhp 1,147cc race engine, and matched to a close-ratio GT6-type gearbox and a 4.11:1 rear axle ratio. The rest of the chassis was also closely based on that of the the racing cars and featured 5.5in alloy road wheels.

Visually there was a touch of Jaguar D-type and E-type about the style of this right-hand-drive car. The shape of the nose was almost exactly like that of the Le Mans cars, with moulded bumper/overrider areas and a sleek aluminium/glass-fibre bonnet/wing assembly that also included headlamps behind moulded covers. Instead of the standard windscreen there was a screen of curved Perspex, and carefully shaped Perspex panes replaced the standard wind-up windows in the doors. No passenger seat was fitted and a detachable panel was made to cover that side of the car. A rigid central strut linked the body above the unique instrument panel with the rear deck, which was moulded from glass-fibre. This deck was Spitfire-like in profile but behind the driver's seat there was a moulded glass-fibre

Details of the Macau car, as originally built with a 1,147cc engine, show that the tub was made almost entirely from aluminium panelling; a simple fascia/instrument panel was used.

Built up in the autumn of 1965 from an unused works bodyshell, along with any other spare parts that Ray Henderson's team could lay its hands on, this Spitfire was sent out to Hong Kong for Walter Sulke to race in the Macau Grand Prix – which is why it became known as the 'Macau car'.

The front end of the 'Macau car' was the same as that of a Le Mans Spitfire, but the rear end used standard-shaped body panels in light alloy. The hump behind the driver's seat paid homage to cars like the Jaguar D-type and housed the large fuel filler cap.

headrest that also included the fuel filler cap and neck. As originally built, the enormous Le Mans-type racing car fuel tank was fitted.

Before the car left for Hong Kong at the end of October 1965, test driver Fred Nicklin drove it on the high-speed test facilities at MIRA, where it lapped the high-speed banked track at 122mph and showed a 130mph top speed.

In the Macau race on 28 November Sulke managed third place in a 30-lap race against a variety of other sports cars and even some Formula Junior single-seaters. Later in the same race weekend, Albert Poon took second place with the car in the Portuguese Trophy race.

Although the Macau car was never raced under direct control by the works competitions department, it was not entirely set loose on its own. In the first weeks of 1966 it was apparently returned to Coventry and then, after refurbishment, shipped to Kas Kastner in California in April 1966. As it was no longer under the control of the British works department, it now leaves this story.

COMPETITION RECORD
None directly in works hands – exported for Walter Sulke to race in Macau when completed.

UNREGISTERED

ENGINE SIZE	1,998cc
MODEL TYPE	GT6R (racing car)

After the 1965 Le Mans 24 Hours, technical chief Harry Webster realised that the works racing Spitfires had nothing else to prove. Race speeds had rocketed so far in just two years that it was unlikely that homologated Spitfires would even be fast enough to qualify to start the 1966 race. If they were to be raced again, the existing layout would need to be further improved by spending heavily on a larger, more powerful engine, different rear suspension and perhaps a unique body style.

For a time, therefore, some thought was given to entering cars as GT6 prototypes, with the 2-litre six-cylinder engine that the production GT6 was soon to inherit. Rally experience with the Group 3 2000 saloons (see Chapter 5) had already shown that this engine was basically very tough, and that the latest cylinder head intended for the TR5 – and eventually all other versions of this engine – showed promise of being a deep breather too.

Ray Henderson's small team started by stripping out ADU 1B and beginning to evolve the prototype of what became known as the 'GT6R' model. The original car would have run with Weber carburettors, but thoughts were already turning to the potential power output of at least 170bhp that was forecast with the use of fuel injection on this engine – such an engine would be raced in a works Triumph 2000 in 1966. It was also intended to adopt the strut-type independent rear suspension that was in use, very effectively, in Bill Bradley's 'loan' Spitfire racing car (ERW 512C).

This was always going to be 'Mission Impossible', for the GT6R, as a prototype, would have had to compete at Le Mans in 1966 in the 2-litre class, which was already well populated with Porsche 906s, Matra-BRMs and Dino Ferraris. As it transpired, that class was to be won by the Jo Siffert/Colin Davis Porsche 906, which finished fourth overall and averaged 118mph for the 24 hours, a pace that would have been beyond the capability of the prototype Triumph, no matter how much development work was done.

Not that we were ever to find out. Following the industry-wide shambles that afflicted production motorsport for a time after the 1966 Monte Carlo rally, when the dominant British Mini-Coopers and Lotus-Cortinas were disqualified after the event on a spurious 'illegal headlamp' technicality, Triumph chairman Sir Donald Stokes decided to cease all works motorsport activity. The GT6R project was an immediate casualty and the car was broken up. No trace of it remained.

But if it had raced with 170bhp, its top speed would surely have been over 150mph, maybe even 160mph. Perhaps it could have been competitive at Le Mans…

Only two photographs of the stillborn GT6R project seem to have survived, these showing the stage at which the project was abandoned in the early weeks of 1966. Based on the refurbished ADU 1B, the GT6R used a six-cylinder 1,998cc engine. At this early stage the manifolding was as used in the Group 3 works 2000 rally cars (note the cast-iron exhaust manifold), but a tubular inlet manifold – probably with Lucas fuel injection – would have featured on the completed car.

This was the half-finished state of the GT6R when the project was abandoned in early 1966 (the archive negative is dated '30-12-1965'). The dual-circuit braking system, which was never used on the works Spitfires because the regulations did not allow it, is clear from the bulkhead details. Power output was expected to be 170bhp from 2-litres – but would the car ever have been competitive against the standard-setting Porsche 904s in the class? We will never know because the GT6R was broken up shortly afterwards.

CHAPTER 7:
THE 2.5 PI
(1967–72)

Much-modified plumbing under the bonnet of the 1970 World Cup 2.5 PIs, with provision being made for fresh air to enter the inlet manifold by way of the grille ahead of the windscreen. This was done to make sure that the engine did not drown when fording streams.

As already mentioned in Chapter 5, the story of fuel-injected Triumphs in British motorsport began well before such a system was put on sale in a road car, and nearly four years before the first fuel-injected Triumph saloons reached their customers. It was not until 1970 that their potential was finally realised, when the beautifully prepared 2.5 PI cars from Abingdon so nearly won the *Daily Mirror* London-Mexico World Cup rally.

Even so, in five short years, the 2.5 PI programme would go from farcical to competent, and from there to a heroic endeavour, ending in commendable if underrated success. Except for the year of the World Cup rally, the programme was under-funded and sometimes misunderstood by management. As far as most knowledgeable observers – drivers, team managers, journalists – were concerned, it could have been so much more memorable.

The first fuel-injected 2000 racing car of 1966 was not successful (see page 131), but there were high hopes that fuel-injected saloons with larger engines might do better in rallying. For a time, however, these had to remain hopes, as nothing could advance on this front until a fuel-injected car was in production, and homologated, or if events could be found where prototype cars were eligible. In the meantime, as already described in Chapter 5, Roy Fidler bought one of the redundant 2000 team cars in 1966 and drove it to magnificent success, and often excess, becoming British Rally Champion that year..

Three things then made a great impact on what was to follow. First, in 1967 Triumph introduced the TR5, which had a 2,498cc version of the established six-cylinder engine fitted as standard with the latest Lucas fuel injection system. Second, the factory also proposed to insert the same engine, modified in certain minor ways, into a top-of-the-range derivative of the 2000. Third, at the end of that summer the RAC's motorsport body let it be known that it would introduce a 'prototype' category for the RAC rally.

Suddenly, the sun came out at Fletchamstead North. For an enterprising character like Ray Henderson, it was the work of but a few days for his technicians to pre-empt the mainstream engineering workshops by building his own 'PI' (Petrol Injection) prototype. By using every ounce of knowledge already gained with the works 2000s, and by pushing the interpretation of the Group 6 category to its limits, it was suddenly possible for a really red-blooded rally contender to be built. Although this was not the very first 2000-based road car to run with a 2,498cc engine, it was certainly the first to break cover, in November 1967.

Originally, the master plan was that only one car would be rebuilt to this specification – Roy Fidler's own well-used 2000, FHP 993C, which had originally been a works 2000 MkI prepared for the 1966 Monte Carlo rally. But soon a sponsor in the shape of *The Sun* newspaper, which was also to sponsor the RAC rally, waved money at the newly crowned F1 World Champion, New Zealander Denny Hulme, and to a works team that would take him on board to compete in the rally. *The Sun* would, no doubt, have preferred to place Hulme in a more 'fashionable' team such as Ford or BMC, but Triumph became the obvious choice after those two companies turned down the newspaper's offer. Ford had already signed up Graham Hill, while BMC had a contractual obstacle as it was firmly tied to using Dunlop tyres whereas Hulme's F1 obligations meant that he would have had to run on Goodyears.

Thus prompted by Standard-Triumph's Public Relations chief, Keith Hopkins, Henderson had the chance to beg for another car to be made available to him, this duly coming from the company's press fleet. GVC 689D, already one year old and having done the rounds as a demonstration vehicle, then became the second of the prototype fuel-injected works cars for the 1967 RAC rally. As it turned out the RAC rally was cancelled less than 24 hours before its scheduled start from London Airport because the rapidly spreading outbreak of bovine foot and mouth disease had made an increasing number of roads and special stages completely out of bounds. Both cars were disposed of, and that, unhappily, seemed to be that.

The following year, 1968, was pivotal for Standard-Triumph in motorsport, and indeed for the cars under consideration here. Leyland got together with BMC in January 1968 to form British Leyland, and one consequence was the decision to give BMC's competitions department at Abingdon responsibility for the motorsport activity of every brand in the new British Leyland empire. As British Leyland's competitions manager, Peter Browning, who had been in his BMC post since January 1967 and had no previous links with Triumph, was briefed to make the rounds of all the individual companies involved – Austin-Morris, Jaguar, Rover and Triumph – to see which of the many existing and planned models might be useful in motorsport. As related in Chapter 8, he soon concluded that a forthcoming small Triumph saloon with a still-secret 16-valve 2-litre engine – a model that would eventually appear as the Dolomite Sprint – was the most promising of all, but that as an interim strategy he would like to see the new 2.5 PI saloon car, which was introduced in October 1968, developed for use in long, tough, demanding rallies.

Thus it was that several MkI 2.5 PIs were prepared for rallying in 1969 before being replaced by the more modern MkII variety in 1970. Although the motorsport career of the MkIs was short, the experience gained of their chassis and drivetrain behaviour was invaluable to what would follow.

A huge amount of testing was done before the World Cup rally started: this is the hard-working WRX 902H on the rough-road tracks at Bagshot.

WORLD CUP 1970:
THE BIGGEST CHALLENGE OF ALL

From the very moment it was conceived in 1969, the World Cup rally of 1970 promised to be an amazing event. Between 19 April and 27 May, the world's best rally cars and crews fought their way from London to Mexico City, through snow, floods and searing heat, sometimes at incredibly high altitudes, to complete the World Cup rally.

Only 23 of the 96 starters made it to the finish – but two of those were works Triumph 2.5 PIs. Not only that, but Brian Culcheth's car took a stirring second place, with Paddy Hopkirk backing him up in fourth place.

I was lucky enough to be part of the organising team and, like everyone else involved, whether competitors, organisers or officials, I will never forget the sheer drama of the world's longest and toughest rally. Well over 40 years later the 'World Cup' legend is intact – for no other rally has ever surpassed it and probably never will.

At least a year before the *Daily Mirror*-sponsored event started from London's Wembley stadium, teams had started to plan their assaults. In 1968 the London-Sydney Marathon had opened everyone's eyes, but this was to be a much bigger and tougher challenge. London to Mexico City, by way of Eastern Europe and most of South America, was going to last for six weeks and measure 16,244 miles.

Not only would it be longer, harder and more demanding than any previous rally, but there would be some enormously long special stages, called 'primes'. In Argentina, Bolivia and Peru, too, there would be entire days when the cars would be rallying – racing, even – at more than 10,000ft. The highest pass would be above 16,000ft.

It would be an adventure even to start, an achievement to make it to the finish, and an incredible feat to win it outright. Peter Browning, British Leyland's competitions manager, thought that Abingdon-prepared cars could win this one, and soon concluded that the Triumph 2.5 PI was one of the most suitable cars for that job.

Although the world of rallying knew early in 1969 all about schemes to run such an event, it was not officially launched until mid-year. This allowed Browning to use his patient negotiating skills to gain approval, beg for backing and to be allowed to choose the right cars and crews for the British Leyland assault.

Because British Leyland had gained such enormous publicity from the London-Sydney Marathon of 1968, management was always keen to go one better in 1970. Although a Hillman Hunter had won that event, Paddy Hopkirk's BMC 1800 had finished second and Rauno Aaltonen's sister car had come sixth.

Amazingly, not only did Browning get approval to enter four Triumphs, but his mechanics went on to build two Austin Maxis and one Mini 1275GT as well. No one expected the 1275GT to finish, but Browning's hope was that it might lead the event for a few days, and make early head-lines. Special Tuning, next door to the famous works department at Abingdon, would also prepare no fewer than six non-Triumph cars of one type or another for private owners who were paying their own way.

At one time British Leyland management also considered using a team of Range Rovers alongside the Triumphs. That possibility, however, faltered when the launch date of the still-secret 4x4 slipped back, not helped by a disastrous test session where Geoff Mabbs crashed a prototype Range Rover in full view of Rover management!

As already related, in 1967 Ray Henderson's tiny depart-ment in Coventry had prepared the very first prototype 2.5 PI rally cars for use in that year's RAC rally, which was cancelled, and the 2.5 PI production car that followed was revealed in October 1968. Accordingly, when Abingdon decided to start developing its own 2.5 PIs in 1969, it imme-diately turned to Henderson for basic advice. Abingdon's expertise, and its much larger budget, would soon allow the cars to get better and better, but Ray's huge experience would certainly give them a flying start. Not only did Ray know all about the extra stiffening that would benefit the bodyshells, but he could also advise on installation details in the engine bay and numerous quirks of suspension set-up.

According to Abingdon authority Bill Price, the specifica-tion of the very first 2.5 PI rally car from the department, UJB 643G, was supplied mainly by Henderson. After Paddy Hopkirk drove the car in the Austrian Alpine rally, where it retired with clutch failure, it was rebuilt for Brian Culcheth to drive in the Scottish rally, where the 4.55:1 rear axle failed. This was not unexpected, as Roy Fidler's cars had suffered from repeated axle failures in previous years.

With the World Cup Rally project officially announced in mid-1969, Abingdon intensified its development efforts with the 2.5 PI, which was about to become the longer, smarter MkII derivative. The driving crews were also settled. First of all Andrew Cowan, winner of the London–Sydney Marathon in a Hillman Hunter, was signed to drive a big Triumph, and then the man who finished second in that event in a BMC 1800, Mini rallying hero Paddy Hopkirk, joined the team. Evan Green and 'Gelignite' Jack Murray from Australia were also invited aboard to repeat their efforts of the London–Sydney Marathon, where they had heroically reached fifth place in their BMC 1800 before being stranded for hours in the Australian desert.

Abingdon then set about preparing three new 2.5 PI MkIs, which rallied only once, in the 1969 RAC rally, and then became test and recce cars for the World Cup rally. When built in 1969 these three cars – VBL 195H, VBL 196H and VBL 197H – had to comply with homologation regulations, which meant that they were not nearly as special as the World Cup cars that would follow. Even so, the steady build-up of experience ensured that these 2.5 PI MkIs, equipped

As part of the works team's meticulous planning for the World Cup rally, the ex-RAC rally MkIs were used as route-survey cars in South America. Here Brian Culcheth and Paddy Hopkirk discuss a development point with two of Abingdon's motorsport mechanics.

with Minilite wheels, were good, solid, well-prepared machines. Although they were outpaced on the RAC rally by specialised competition cars such as the works Escorts, Lancias and Porsches, they took first, second and third places in their class, with Andrew Cowan's car, VBL 197H, finishing 11th overall.

Immediately after the RAC rally, two of the cars – VBL 195H and VBL 196H – were shipped out to Argentina while the third car stayed at home and got involved in testing. In the meantime, Abingdon settled on the crews and, eventually, the specification of the cars they would drive.

Before the event began, there was alarm about the demands of the route. With many instances of two or three days of hard driving between official rest halts, crew fatigue was forecast to be a big factor. Not only that, but driver endurance at high altitudes would also be a factor because sections of the route through the South American Andes were so high and so long.

Two-up or three-up? Peter Browning gave his drivers a choice, forecasting that there might be a 50/50 split of opinion. In the end, only Brian Culcheth chose to go two-up, he, significantly, having carried out a more comprehensive pre-event survey in South America than the other drivers. Cowan, Hopkirk and Green chose to take a third crew member with them.

A great deal of unsung and largely unpublicised test and development work was carried out in MkI and MkII cars during the winter of 1969/70, both in the UK and in South America. In the UK, not only did an ex-RAC rally MkI and

VBL 197H in use as a recce/route-survey car in the snows of Europe before the 1970 World Cup rally.

the two early cars – UJB 642G and UJB 643G – work hard for their living at this time, but another brand new MkII, WRX 902H, also did its share. Development engineer Eddie Burnell, a formidably capable driver known at Abingdon as 'Fast Eddie', did a great deal of high-speed testing, especially on the rough-road circuits at Bagshot and on tarmac at Silverstone, with team drivers adding their efforts when they were not away in Europe or South America on route-survey and recce duties.

Starting in the winter of 1969/70, Abingdon prepared four brand-new 2.5 PI MkIIs to take part in the World Cup rally. Although they looked superficially like attractively reliveried road cars, they were very different under the skin. As well as Abingdon personnel, Ray Henderson in Coventry and Pressed Steel at Swindon had input into the final specification of the rally cars themselves.

Specially prepared for this event by Pressed Steel, the bodyshells were much stiffer than normal, for they had a great deal of reinforcement, including double skinning of certain panels and the use of foam-filled sills. To keep the weight down, all opening panels – doors, bonnet and boot lid – were pressed in aluminium. The wheel arches were flared to give clearance for oversize 15in x 5.5in Minilite wheels and rough-treaded Dunlop tyres, and the bumpers were removed at front and rear. A reprofiled boot lid allowed twin spare wheels to be carried, while the addition of two extra fuel tanks increased total fuel capacity to 32 Imperial gallons. Other features included an aluminium roll cage, Perspex side and rear windows, and a roof-mounted air intake for the cabin, taken from a BL commercial vehicle.

The engines developed approximately 150bhp. They featured stronger blocks and crankshafts, TR6 camshaft profiles, Janspeed exhaust manifolds and larger alternators. To take account of potentially sub-standard fuel supplies in South America, the engines were retuned with a lower 8.5:1 compression ratio. One ingenious feature, developed on location in South America with advice from Lucas technicians, was that the settings of the petrol injection metering unit could be adjusted by a hand-controlled quadrant on the fascia panel, allowing crews to compensate for reduced air densities at extreme altitude. Intake air for the engine was taken from the grille ahead of the windscreen rather than from the front of the car, to avoid water ingress to the engine when crossing deep fords or encountering floodwater.

The transmission comprised a Stag-type four-speed gearbox with overdrive, a 3.7:1 final drive ratio and a Salisbury Powr-Lok limited-slip differential. Braking was by Stag-type front discs and rear drums, while shock absorbers were by Koni. Suspension reinforcement included strengthened front stub axles, a strut brace over the top of the engine (linking the MacPherson strut towers) and comprehensive underbody skid shielding, all of this adding up to an exceptionally solid structure. Spare structures were also purchased from Pressed Steel – this was to be an important factor behind the rebirth of Andrew Cowan's shattered car.

Assistant competitions manager Bill Price got the job of co-ordinating the massive service and support effort, which was organised in two ways and involved every available mechanic from Abingdon. In Europe mechanics were ferried round what Price himself whimsically described as the 'easier European sections' in a twin-engined Cessna Skymaster chartered from Southend Air Taxis. For the much longer and more demanding South and Central American sectors, mechanics usually flew from base to base by commercial airlines, while a massive four-turbo-prop Bristol Britannia 'Whispering Giant' chartered from British Caledonian Airways was used to position mechanics and massive supplies of spare parts in various locations. Price himself spent a lot of time travelling in and even living in this vast machine, which became known as 'Browning's Bomber'!

The build-up to the World Cup completely dominated all activity at Abingdon. Apart from the Triumphs, Abingdon personnel also had to prepare the two Austin Maxis (for Rosemary Smith and for a former Red Arrows crew) and the Mini 1275GT 'sprint' car (for John Handley). There was virtually no time to prepare cars for any other events in 1969/70 except for a TV Rallycross at Lydden Hill and an Austin Maxi entry for Rosemary Smith on the Circuit of Ireland. Both of these outings, in any case, were meant to provide experience of cars intended for the World Cup rally itself.

The starting order was determined in February 1970 at a ceremony at the Café Royal in London's Regent Street, England football captain Bobby Moore drawing the numbers

All four works 2.5 PIs posed before the start of the 1970 World Cup rally. From left: Brian Culcheth, Neville Johnston, Johnstone Syer, Paddy Hopkirk, Tony Nash, Andrew Cowan, Uldarico Ossio, Brian Coyle, Evan Green, Hamish Cardno and 'Gelignite' Jack Murray.

from a bag. A 2.5 PI MkII was drawn first, but it was the privately entered example of Bobby Buchanan-Michaelson. All of the works cars were well down the field and, unfortunately for Abingdon's planners, three of the Triumphs were scheduled to start within ten minutes of each other, at numbers 88, 92 and 98. Later in the event, when lateness would be measured in hours rather than minutes, this was no longer found to be detrimental.

Most of the last-minute panics seemed to concern late delivery of spare parts, the arranging of publicity photo-calls and the settling of final details to do with creature comfort in the cars, especially in the PIs that would be carrying three people. These included special seat covers in sheepskin and the facility for the co-driver's seat to be folded flat to form a bed. But it was not all bad news comfort-wise, as Hamish Cardno, due to ride as a third crew member with Evan Green and Jack Murray, wrote in *Motor* magazine before the event began: 'I was also surprised to see how much room there was in the back. At one time I feared I'd be curled up in a little bundle with my knees scraping my chin, but from the look of the car it should be quite a comfortable trip...'

The day of the start, 19 April, was bedlam. Everyone seemed to have forgotten something, and no one among the 96 nervous crews admitted to having had a good night's sleep before the 'off'. The big adventure started from Wembley stadium, where British Leyland's chairman, Lord Stokes, greeted the Abingdon crews and made it clear that nothing less that outright victory would be acceptable. Then England football manager Sir Alf Ramsey flagged off the first starters. Although British Leyland hoped that the PIs could win, there was no doubt that works competition from Ford (seven Escorts) and Citroën (four DS21s) was a major threat.

Over the next seven days 4,500 miles would be covered between London and Lisbon, with only one overnight rest halt, at Monza in northern Italy. With flat-out primes to be

tackled in Yugoslavia, Italy, France and Spain, this was going to be a real test – although the British Leyland crews who had already surveyed the South American sections thought it looked positively easy!

The first flat-out prime, in Yugoslavia, was an old Spa-Sofia-Liège car-breaker, linking Titograd to Kotor, and here the route suddenly got more demanding and the competition more serious. Evan Green put his PI briefly off the road on this prime, then on the second prime two of the Triumphs were held up by a broken-down truck, and then one of the cars broke its rear dampers – and this was only in the first four days.

After the Monza halt things got worse. Green's PI suffered a broken valve guide, and then broke a wheel on the Quatre Chemins prime, a favourite stretch of mountain road in

Time for service and repairs: this is the service park at the Monza control/night halt of the World Cup rally, with XJB 305H (Brian Culcheth) and XJB 302H (Paddy Hopkirk) both receiving routine attention.

France originally made famous on the French Alpine rally during the 1960s. The wheel breakage threw the car off the road into a tree and nearly three hours passed before a breakdown truck was able to drag it back on to the serpentine road. The car staggered on, by this time well bent, and running with one fuel injector pipe exhausting raw fuel to the outside world through a vent.

For the others, the first week was less eventful. After five primes Brian Culcheth's car was sixth, the other PIs being eighth and eleventh. It was an encouraging start.

Seventy-one rally cars were then loaded on to the SS *Derwent*, which shipped them sedately across the South Atlantic to Rio de Janeiro in Brazil. On Friday 8 May all four works PIs, including the sick Green/Murray/Cardno machine, took the restart in boiling hot conditions. Now it got fast, furious and very primitive.

For the next three weeks, none of the roads – not even the flat-out primes – would be closed to other traffic, so there would always be the danger of meeting massive trucks and other cars – and wild animals too. Most of the roads would have loose surfaces, and some of the bridges would be decidedly rickety. Between Rio de Janeiro and Buenaventura in Colombia, the route would go through eight other countries and include ten primes, the longest of which, in Peru, measured 560 miles! There would be extremes of weather, from intense heat to extreme cold at the high altitudes. Rivers in full spate might have to be crossed, enormously high passes would have to be scaled, and fatigue would become the real enemy. Then there would be the dust…

The first three days in South America, to Montevideo in Uruguay, saw the big Triumphs move rapidly up the field. During this phase René Trautmann's leading Citroën DS21

Brian Culcheth finished in a magnificent second place on the World Cup rally in XJB 305H. Somewhere in southern Europe he enjoys a sprint during a prime on tarmac roads.

crashed, Roger Clark's Escort hit a non-competing car (when Roger's co-driver was at the wheel) and the other big Citroëns fell back, outpaced, leaving two Ford Escorts leading the event and Culcheth's PI in fourth place. Only 52 cars were still running and for all the crews a night's sleep was welcome.

After the scenic ferry crossing of the River Plate to Buenos Aires, the flat-out motoring resumed. By the time the route reached Santiago, Chile's capital, on 13 May, only 43 cars remained – one of the retirements being the Green/Murray/Cardno Triumph.

Now the time had come for the crews to tackle mountain roads and tracks at incredibly high altitudes. All the works cars carried oxygen bottles, for at more than 15,000ft the air would be very thin and any exertion quite exhausting. Ford, incidentally, later spun a good yarn that Roger Clark, on his recce, was asked to find a girl at 14,000ft, make love to her and report back on the effort required. Roger, they insisted, cabled back: 'Unable to find girl at 14,000ft – but found 14 girls at 1,000ft. No problems!'

Then came the monstrously difficult 480-mile Gran Premio prime in the Andes, in northern Argentina, which Brian Culcheth described as being like 'driving from Edinburgh to Dover, mainly in fog, on unmade roads strewn with rocks and animals, at an impossible schedule.' And it was all at high altitude too.

This was where the men were firmly separated from the boys, where Culcheth and Hopkirk both surged up the leaderboard – but where Andrew Cowan's PI crashed. Andrew was following in the dust of Jean Denton's Austin 1800 and, blinded by the morning sun, plunged off the road. The PI rolled and ended up on its roof. All three crew members, who were not wearing crash helmets, suffered broken bones and ended up in hospital at Salta, northern Argentina, but miraculously all made complete recoveries.

This left the Triumph team down to just two runners. Although they were going strong, suspension, wheel and windscreen breakages all caused delays. On the run into El Alto de la Paz, where the 13,000ft height caused much altitude sickness among crews, officials and press men, Hopkirk's rally very nearly ended when the quill shaft to the rear differential failed. To reach him, mechanics had to be rushed back up the road against the flow of traffic, and then change the entire axle assembly quickly enough to get him to La Paz in time.

By now only 39 cars were running, and time penalties were enormous, but Culcheth was up to third and challenging Rauno Aaltonen's Escort for second place. The next prime was the Route of the Incas, a 560-mile monster through the Andes, almost all of it above 15,000ft, with the highest point of all, the Ticlio pass, at 15,870ft. The target time of 11 hours was devastating and matching it was quite out of the question for everyone.

The two surviving big Triumphs were thrust to their very limits. Predictably, Hannu Mikkola's fleet little Escort was fastest of all, 81 minutes behind schedule, but Culcheth's heavier PI lost only 18 more minutes and got closer to Aaltonen's Escort. Hopkirk took 32 minutes longer than Culcheth – the extra weight of a three-man crew made a difference, especially at this height – but he gained two places. Now only 30 cars were still running and two more of the much-fancied Citroëns had dropped out.

The fight to the finish would be between the big Triumphs and the fleet of Fords. Durability, not performance, was now going to pay off. Although British Leyland's mechanics kept on repairing and rejuvenating the PIs as best they could, both cars were suffering from the relentless battering of so many miles of rough roads.

Although the run from Lima to Buenaventura, in Colombia, was regarded as an easy wind-down after the horrors of the Andes, it almost put paid to Hopkirk's PI. Having completed the final prime in a very fast time, Paddy put the PI off the road soon afterwards, badly bending the front end. Had co-driver Neville Johnstone not been savvy enough to by-pass the plumbing of the broken oil cooler, and had the BL mechanics not later been able to straighten out the front suspension, Paddy might have been forced out. Instead he struggled on, still in fourth place, his car still with severe damage at the front.

The rally organisers had been unable to find any route by road or track from Colombia to the Panamanian Isthmus, so a ferry trip was the only way to get to Panama. After two restful nights on board the Italian liner SS *Verdi*, 26 crews were ready for the final leg of this magnificent marathon, a 51hr 30min dash up through Central America to Mexico City. With Culcheth still in third place and Hopkirk fourth, there were still two primes to be tackled, and Culcheth went flat out to make up the gap on Aaltonen.

After pushing hard in the Costa Rica section, he pressured Aaltonen so much that the Finn put his Escort off the road, kinking a fuel-supply pipe in the process and losing nearly an hour. At long last the Triumph was up into second place, but with absolutely no hope of catching Mikkola's Ford. As if to celebrate, Culcheth then recorded the fastest time of all on the last speed section, the Aztec prime in Mexico.

Only 23 cars eventually straggled into the final holding control at Fortin, in the south of Mexico, for an overnight stop where there was much to celebrate for Triumph, and, of course, for Ford. Celebrations went on far into the night, the hotel swimming pool received a number of fully clothed visitors, and no one seemed to need a lot of sleep.

Then came the final 200-mile run into the Aztec Stadium in Mexico City, where the football World Cup competition was soon to begin. This was a light-hearted convoy of rally cars, stragglers and service crews, behind Mexican police and rally officials. With no pressure remaining, high jinks were the

order of the day: cars often drove three and four abreast on the dual-carriageway sections, while Timo Mäkinen let off a fire extinguisher and popped it through the window of team-mate Aaltonen's Escort.

Once in Mexico City, the drive to the stadium was hair-raising, with police outriders on Harley Davidsons ruthless in clearing the way. When the cars eventually reached the stadium, Formula 1 driver Graham Hill, the FA's Sir Stanley Rous and Edward Pickering of IPC (owners of the *Daily Mirror*) were there to greet them.

The champagne flowed, the photographers had a bean-feast, and almost everyone was happy. Almost everyone... As Hamish Cardno later wrote in *Motor* magazine:

'British Leyland were too cautious. Their most likely potential winner, the Triumph 2.5 PI, was less nimble than the Escorts because of its size, but on those primes where sheer straight-line performance was an advantage, its higher top speed paid off. However, excessive caution on the part of two of their best three crews cost them dearly... Brian Culcheth stuck his neck out and reckoned it was worth trying two-up, a decision which must make the second place even more satisfying.

'Basically the Triumph has emerged from the event as a very good car. Apart from fairly frequent replacement of front struts and shock absorbers – components put under great stress by the weight of the cars and their crews – they gave no trouble...'

Lord Stokes, though, did not ever seem to have understood this, or the great achievement of the works Triumphs. Only weeks after the event he announced the closure of Abingdon, and by the end of the year the glory of this monumental event seemed to have been forgotten within British Leyland.

Conditions on the 16,000-mile World Cup rally varied from rough tracks to fast tarmac – the works 2.5 PI was developed to cope with all of them. This is Paddy Hopkirk, who finished fourth, on the stony San Remo stage in Italy.

WORLD CUP RALLY RESULTS

Interim results at Lisbon (with penalties)

1	Citroën DS21	(R. Trautmann/J-P. Hanrioud)	5min
2	Ford Escort 1850	(H. Mikkola/G. Palm)	7min
3	Citroën DS21	(G. Verrier/F. Murac)	9min
4	Ford Escort 1850	(T. Mäkinen/G. Staepelaere)	21min
5	Citroën DS21	(P. Vanson/O. Turcat/A. Leprince)	31min
6	**Triumph 2.5 PI**	**(B. Culcheth/J. Syer)**	**32min**

71 cars still running, including four works Triumphs

Interim results at La Paz (with penalties)

1	Ford Escort 1850	(H. Mikkola/G. Palm)	3hr 52min
2	Ford Escort 1850	(R. Aaltonen/H. Liddon)	4hr 54min
3	**Triumph 2.5 PI**	**(B. Culcheth/J. Syer)**	**4hr 57min**
4	Citroën DS21	(G. Verrier/F. Murac)	5hr 12min
5	Ford Escort 1850	(S. Zasada/M. Wachowski)	5hr 40min
6	**Triumph 2.5 PI**	**(P. Hopkirk/A. Nash/N. Johnston)**	**5hr 44min**

39 cars still running, including two works Triumphs

Final results at Mexico City (with penalties)

1.	Ford Escort 1850	(H. Mikkola/G. Palm)	9hr 7min
2	**Triumph 2.5 PI**	**(B. Culcheth/J. Syer)**	**10hr 25min**
3	Ford Escort 1850	(R. Aaltonen/H. Liddon)	10hr 46min
4	**Triumph 2.5 PI**	**(P. Hopkirk/A. Nash/N. Johnston)**	**12hr 26min**
5	Ford Escort 1850	(T. Mäkinen/G. Staepelaere)	14hr 31min
6	Ford Escort 1850	(J. Greaves/T. Fall)	19hr 31min

23 cars finishers, including two works Triumphs

From left, Johnstone Syer, Brian Culcheth, team manager Peter Browning and Lord Stokes at Wembley stadium just before the start of the 1970 World Cup rally.

FHP 993C

FIRST REGISTERED	30 NOVEMBER 1965
ENGINE SIZE	2,498cc
MODEL TYPE	2.5 PI (prototype)

FHP 993C spent much of 1966 and '67 in Roy Fidler's hands, effectively as an 'arm's length' works 2000, and he worked it so hard in British Championship rallies that it started no fewer than 13 events, winning three of them (see pages 128-130). The car was then returned to the works team's workshops in Coventry in the autumn of 1967 for conversion to prototype 2.5 PI specification, complete with a 150bhp 2.5-litre fuel-injected TR5 engine, and with all the suspension and chassis components that had been developed for the 2000 in recent years. Its first event would be the RAC rally.

This car and its sister, GVX 689D, ran with a special gas-flowed cylinder head, a free-flow exhaust system and a 4.55:1 rear axle ratio complete with Salisbury limited-slip differential. In testing the car was tried with both 5.5in and 4.5in Minilite alloy road wheels of 13in diameter, and the plan was to carry two spare wheels mounted in a pair of neat cocoons behind the front seats. Although the 2.5 PI might not have been as fast in a straight line as some of the opposition from Ford and BMC, it was hoped that it would be as rugged and reliable as the 2000 saloons had been in their latter events, and it was certainly the highest-performance version of the big saloon yet to have been prepared.

Testing prior to the RAC rally was satisfactory, and the Goodyear tyres made necessary by the second car's driver contract – World Champion Denny Hulme used Goodyears in F1 – presented no problems. Both cars scrutineered without dramas – and then the bombshell fell. During the run-up to the RAC, which covered 2,500 miles and included no fewer than 69 special stages, an outbreak of bovine foot and mouth disease had spread rapidly across the country, making it ever more impractical for the rally to take place, as no cars could enter the increasing number of prohibited areas. On the evening before the start of the event, the unhappy decision was taken to cancel it.

The expensively prepared original 2.5 PI prototypes could not be used, especially as all rallying was subsequently cancelled by the RAC for many weeks. Triumph disposed of FHP 993C at a very knock-down price to Roy Fidler, who soon sold it on.

COMPETITION RECORD
1967 RAC
Roy Fidler   Event cancelled

GVC 689D

FIRST REGISTERED	4 OCTOBER 1966
ENGINE SIZE	2,498cc
MODEL TYPE	2.5 PI (prototype)

This car started life at Motor Show time in 1966 as a factory-owned and factory-based 2000 demonstrator, but it was donated to Ray Henderson's department after the decision was taken to prepare a 'clone' to FHP 993C for the 1967 RAC rally. Within weeks it was transformed into the second of the 2.5 PI prototypes.

The master plan was that *The Sun* newspaper would part-sponsor the deal and that the newly crowned F1 World Champion, New Zealander Denny Hulme, would drive the car on the RAC rally. At this stage in his career, Hulme was usually to be seen behind the wheel of a Repco-engined Brabham F1 car, and was about to move on to the McLaren-Ford team for 1968. As this would be Hulme's first-ever British rally, all manner of administrative strings had to be pulled with the RAC to provide him with a suitable licence. Apart from all the established rally stars, he would have to compete against another past F1 World Champion as Graham Hill was scheduled to drive a works Ford Lotus-Cortina. Because Hill's start number was 9 and Hulme's was 12, the two could hope to see a lot of each other during the course of the event!

I was proud to be asked to co-drive for Hulme on the RAC. By now working for *Autocar* magazine, I met him for the first time at a hastily arranged test session at the MoD's Bagshot rough-road test track in Surrey. Pictures exist of Denny driving a hack 2000 on the open road, and at Bagshot, but this was not a serious occasion, and this car, GKV 305D, has no place in the competition story. For the record, GKV 305D had a very standard carburettor engine and was not prepared in any way for rallying, other than a sump guard being fitted.

Hulme's new rally car, GVC 689D, had exactly the same specification as Roy Fidler's FHP 993C, but the cancellation of the RAC rally meant that it had no chance to prove itself. Shortly afterwards, *Autocar* magazine was loaned the car and the magazine's test of it appeared in its issue of 25 January 1968. The performance figures are summarised below.

PERFORMANCE		
	GVX 689D	Standard car
Top speed	117mph	93mph
0–60mph	9.2sec	14.1sec
0–80mph	15.1sec	29.9sec
0–100mph	24.5sec	–
Standing quarter mile	16.7sec	19.4sec
Overall fuel consumption	17.9mpg	24.5mpg

After this, there was no further use for the car in motorsport, so it was decommissioned.

COMPETITION RECORD	
1967 RAC	
Denis Hulme	Event cancelled

UJB 642G

FIRST REGISTERED	MAY 1969
ENGINE SIZE	2,498cc
MODEL TYPE	2.5 PI MkI

This was one of the first 2.5 PIs to be prepared by the British Leyland competitions department at Abingdon, UJB 643G being the other. Both were used for testing, development and endurance running during the second half of 1969. The basic specification had originally been supplied to Abingdon by Ray Henderson in Coventry, but the cars progressively became more and more specialised, and also became 'Abingdonised'.

Unlike UJB 643G, this car never appeared in public, or in

Although UJB 642G was a fully prepared 2.5 PI rally car, it was only used for testing and development. Here it seen, hard at work, at Bagshot on pre-World Cup testing duties.

any major sporting event, although it was loaned to John Sprinzel as a route-survey car for the European section of the forthcoming World Cup rally. Later it was used for intensive test and rough-road endurance running at the well-known Bagshot test track.

COMPETITION RECORD
1969–70
Used solely as test/development /endurance proving car.

UJB 643G

FIRST REGISTERED	MAY 1969
ENGINE SIZE	2,498cc
MODEL TYPE	2.5 PI MkI

Once Peter Browning's strategy of developing the 2.5 PI – especially with the World Cup rally of 1970 in prospect – had taken shape, the Abingdon organisation set about building cars. UJB 642G, as already noted, became the team's original test car, while UJB 643G was made ready to go rallying as soon as possible.

Initially the new car was relatively under-developed. Although it had an updated chassis, complete with the well-developed undershield system, it had a virtually standard engine. Its first event was the 1969 Austrian Alpine rally and driver Paddy Hopkirk, more used to nimble Minis and brutally fast Austin-Healey 3000s, found the car difficult to master at first. He was only 15th fastest on the first special stage but kept plugging away and began setting top six times

Paddy Hopkirk and Tony Nash in UJB 643G, the first 2.5 PI to start an international rally – the Austrian Alpine of 1969.

until, towards the end of the event, the clutch failed completely and immobilised him. The car had to be returned to the UK by train.

Amazingly, within two weeks the car was then made ready to take part in the long, dusty and very demanding Scottish rally, where Brian Culcheth got his chance to have a go, partnered by Johnstone Syer. The car was running in the Group 6 'prototype' category, with Minilite cast-alloy road wheels and a 4.55:1 rear axle ratio, and without front and rear bumpers. Brian clearly enjoyed a car like this as he soon settled into the upper end of the leader board, although a cracked exhaust manifold – caused by a distorted undershield pushing the pipe upwards – hampered his progress. At half distance he was in third place, behind Simo Lampinen's works Saab V4 and Andrew Cowan's works Hillman Rallye Imp.

A major delay followed when the car then broke its back axle – a failure that was not unknown on these cars. Rally reporter John Davenport noted in *Autosport*: 'When the BLMC mechanics came to drop in the new unit, they found that its front brackets had been welded to the trailing arm carriers, and stubbornly refused to become unwelded, despite much coaxing from Den Green and his men. The whole job ran for two hours, which meant that Culcheth and Syer had to miss two stages...'

Although Culcheth eventually managed to get going again, he eventually finished well down, in 24th place – but the car still took second place in its capacity class. This marked the end of this car's short but eventful rally career, although it proved very useful in subsequent months, both as a test and practice car for the RAC rally and in preparation for the 1970 World Cup Rally too.

When this role ceased, it was sold off to up-and-coming rally driver Chris Sclater.

COMPETITION RECORD	
1969 Austrian Alpine	
Paddy Hopkirk	Did not finish
1969 Scottish	
Brian Culcheth	2nd in class

VBL 195H

FIRST REGISTERED	OCTOBER 1969
ENGINE SIZE	2,498cc
MODEL TYPE	2.5 PI MkI

At the end of the summer of 1969, British Leyland decided to enter a team of 2.5 PI MkIIs in the 1970 World Cup rally, but as an interim exercise, and to learn what could be experienced with the earlier cars, it was decided to enter a full team of three 2.5 MkIs for the 1969 RAC rally. The chassis platform of the MkI and MkII types was the same, the basic difference being that the MkIIs, which were not announced until October 1969, had lengthened nose and tail sections.

Three brand-new right-hand-drive MkI cars – later to be registered VBL 195H, VBL 196H and VBL 197H – were therefore purchased before production of that body style ran out in September, and were prepared at Abingdon. Except for tiny details to suit the drivers' individual preferences, each shared the same mechanical specification.

After the work already carried out on UJB 642G and UJB 643G, Abingdon had got the measure of what had to be improved, and how it needed to be done. Bill Price's summary of the work done is extremely helpful:

'Apart from raising the compression ratio to 10.4:1 and a special side exhaust, the rally car engines were fairly standard. The transmission was fitted with overdrive (which operated on all forward gears), Koni shock absorbers fitted front and rear, a 4.55:1 limited-slip final drive, and the inevitable Ferodo DS11 pads/VG95 linings were included in the spec. Additional jacking points were added to the body on each side, designed for use with a hydraulic pillar jack.'

By this time the works had settled on the use of 7 x 13in Minilite alloy wheels fitted with Dunlop SP44 Weathermaster tyres. As it happened, when a deluge of snow descended on the Welsh stages of the RAC, the 7in Minilites were found to be unsuitable, so narrow standard steel wheels were sometimes used instead!

On an event that became increasingly blanketed by snow as it went on, works cars with their engines over the driving wheels – including Lancia Fulvias and Saabs – dominated and the 2.5 PIs struggled to remain competitive. Even the driver of VBL 195H, Paddy Hopkirk, who gained much of the pre-event publicity because of his Monte-winning fame, had already stated privately that he thought the Triumph was too big and bulky to succeed.

Paddy's fears were soon confirmed, but a running battle between the Triumphs and the works Datsun 1600SSS cars kept up the interest to the very end. Towards the end the gearbox on Hopkirk's car began to give trouble and had to be changed at Machynlleth. Together with delays caused by a

faulty clutch, this relegated him to 15th overall and he could only finish second in the capacity class. It was not until the last quartet of stages, in the West Country, that the works Datsuns clinched the Manufacturers' team contest, but this had been a very promising start for the Abingdon-based Triumph team.

Although VBL 195H was no longer to figure as a front-line car, it was soon shipped out to South America, where it proved to be valuable for surveying the route for the World Cup rally.

Paddy Hopkirk in action in VBL 195H on the 1969 RAC rally, on his way to second in class.

COMPETITION RECORD	
1969 RAC	
Paddy Hopkirk	2nd in class

VBL 196H

FIRST REGISTERED	OCTOBER 1969
ENGINE SIZE	2,498cc
MODEL TYPE	2.5 PI MkI

This car was mechanically identical to VBL 195H and VBL 197H, the 'difference' being that it was to be driven by Brian Culcheth. Brian had already spent some months surveying the route of the 1970 World Cup rally and also practising parts of it in mainland Europe. He was really fired

Brian Culcheth drove VBL 196H to third in class on the 1969 RAC rally.

Somewhere in South America with their ex-RAC rally MkIs, Brian Culcheth, Brian Coyle and Andrew Cowan pause during their recce for the 1970 World Cup rally, with VBL 196H to the fore.

up about this event and, knowing that 2.5 PIs would be used for it, was determined to treat the 1969 RAC rally as an opportunity to get to know the car better still.

As with the other works Triumph drivers on this RAC rally, Culcheth's fortunes suffered from the weather, the weight of his car and problems in getting grip on snowy surfaces. Finishing third in class, there was little he could do about the enormous competition from the horde of Scandinavian drivers in their front-wheel-drive cars.

After the RAC rally this car was sent off to South America to join VBL 195H for route-surveying and practice duties for the forthcoming World Cup rally.

COMPETITION RECORD	
1969 RAC	
Brian Culcheth	3rd in class

Full team line-up before the 1969 RAC rally, with VBL 197H to the fore. From left: Brian Coyle, Andrew Cowan, Paddy Hopkirk, Tony Nash, Johnstone Syer and Brian Culcheth.

On the 1969 RAC rally, Andrew Cowan's 2.5 PI MkI, VBL 197H, carried number 1 in honour of his great success in the London-Sydney Marathon, which he had won outright.

VBL 197H

FIRST REGISTERED	OCTOBER 1969
ENGINE SIZE	2,498cc
MODEL TYPE	2.5 PI MkI

The third of the new 2.5 PI MkIs prepared at Abingdon, VBL 197H was mechanically the same as its sisters and was to be driven by Andrew Cowan on the 1969 RAC rally. One interesting quirk of its specification was that although it had been seen to look identical to its sisters in a pre-rally photograph, with extra driving lamps at grille level, on the event itself Andrew chose to have the driving lamps moved to a position above the level of the headlamps.

With no more than minor problems reported along the way, Cowan found himself in 11th place at the halfway point in Blackpool. After struggling along for hours, in increasingly deep snow, he confirmed that 11th place, and won his capacity class.

Later this car, like its two sisters, was used as part of the recce and route-survey team for the 1970 World Cup rally.

COMPETITION RECORD	
1969 RAC	
Andrew Cowan	1st in class

WJB 189H

FIRST REGISTERED	NOVEMBER 1969
ENGINE SIZE	2,498cc
MODEL TYPE	2.5 PI MkII

COMPETITION RECORD
First used as a management service/'chase' car, then converted for endurance testing.

This is believed to have been the very first MkII delivered to Abingdon and it was originally used as a management car in the service team for the 1969 RAC rally. During the winter of 1969/70, however, it was fitted out with Stag front springs, estate-car rear springs and Koni shock absorbers, along with some 15 x 5.5in Minilite wheels, and was used for a considerable amount of suspension testing and development in connection with the World Cup rally. It never competed in an event.

WRX 902H

FIRST REGISTERED	1 FEBRUARY 1970
ENGINE SIZE	2,498cc
MODEL TYPE	2.5 PI MkII

This car was an early-build, right-hand-drive 2.5 PI MkII that Abingdon took over at the end of 1969, turning it into a 'Bagshot' test car for pre-World Cup rally trials. A variety of drivers, notably 'Fast Eddie' Burnell of the competitions department, put in many miles to prove out the quality of the basic design, and determine the changes needed for the World Cup cars.

Once the team had departed for the World Cup rally in April 1970, WRX 902H was temporarily stored at Abingdon. Immediately after the World Cup rally, the car was refurbished and further modified to make it suitable for Brian Culcheth to drive in the Scottish rally. As in 1969, when Brian had driven UJB 643G on the same event, WRX 902H was entered in the Group 6 category, which meant that numerous modifications were allowed. The car was lightened as much as possible (saving an estimated 400lb), front and rear bumpers were removed, and the engine was equipped with three twin-choke Weber carburettors instead of the still-troublesome Lucas fuel injection. This made a big difference: according to Abingdon's records the 'Scottish' engine produced 153bhp compared with the 127bhp of the World Cup rally engines. Small wonder, therefore, that Brian Culcheth has always insisted that this 2.5 PI was the one he liked best.

From start to finish there was a big battle for victory, with Culcheth up against Roger Clark's Ford Escort RS1600 and Harry Kallstrom's works Lancia Fulvia HF, with Paddy Hopkirk's Mini Clubman 1275GT always close behind.

Towards the end of the hot and dusty event, Clark's Escort engine gave trouble and finally expired, while Kallstrom was excluded for taking too long at a service halt, and eventually running more than 30 minutes behind his road schedule. As Kallstrom thought he had won, protests and counter-protests ensued, the rally stewards took ages to make up their minds, and Culcheth's provisional victory was not finally confirmed until some weeks later.

'Fast Eddie' – Eddie Burnell of the Abingdon development team – presses on in WRX 902H during testing at Bagshot before the 1970 World Cup rally.

WRX 902H *was not only an invaluable test car before the 1970 World Cup rally but it was also driven to victory in the 1970 Scottish rally by Brian Culcheth, who judged it the best 2.5 PI he ever drove.*

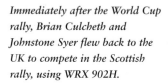

Immediately after the World Cup rally, Brian Culcheth and Johnstone Syer flew back to the UK to compete in the Scottish rally, using WRX 902H.

Brian was ecstatic and the British Leyland team was ecstatic – but top management did not seem to be impressed. Within weeks Lord Stokes directed that the entire competitions operation at Abingdon should be closed down, which meant that no more totally 'official' 2.5 PIs were to be seen in future. The successful car was set aside at Abingdon and eventually sold off.

COMPETITION RECORD	
1970 Scottish	
Brian Culcheth	1st overall

XJB 302H

FIRST REGISTERED	1 APRIL 1970
ENGINE SIZE	2,498cc
MODEL TYPE	2.5 PI MkII

This car was crewed on the World Cup rally by Paddy Hopkirk, Tony Nash (Hopkirk's regular co-driver) and Neville Johnston. Originally Paddy's race mechanic in the 1950s and later his business partner in the motor trade in Northern Ireland, Johnston was an accomplished amateur race driver and would also prove to be a resourceful 'bush mechanic' on the event.

As a long-established BMC/British Leyland driver, Paddy was one of the big stars of the ceremonial send-off at Wembley stadium, although he had to wait for ages before he was able to roll off the ramp and start the long journey

halfway round the world, owing to having been drawn to run at a lowly number 98. The bookmakers had made him the pre-rally favourite with odds of 10/1, but he was closely followed by four Ford Escort drivers; his teammates, Andrew Cowan and Brian Culcheth, were rated at 14/1 and 16/1 respectively.

Paddy, of all people, realised that he could not win in the first few days, but he could certainly lose, so he ran himself in carefully. He dropped his first minute on the first prime, in Yugoslavia, then suffered more than 20 minutes' delay on the second prime, where there was a damaged/blocked bridge to be circumvented. He then 'cleaned' the Italian prime, was only four minutes late on the Quatre Chemins prime in France, and another eight minutes late on the high-speed section in Portugal. The car still looked immaculate when it was loaded on to the boat in Lisbon, but Paddy was down in eighth place.

As Culcheth had forecast, the really tough stuff then began in South America, where the primes were very long and mostly loose-surfaced, although the big Triumphs could often attack much of that mileage at more than 100mph. It was here that sheer reliability, rather than brave driving, was the real asset, so Paddy made up a place, to seventh, by the time the event rested at Montevideo, in Uruguay.

Up into the Andes for what seemed like days on end, the Triumphs – and the rival works Fords – forged further and further ahead of the other survivors. Through Chile, Argentina and Bolivia the pace was relentless until suddenly, after the end of the Bolivian prime and on what passed for a main road in that under-developed country, the 2.5 PI suddenly expired, just 50 miles from the overnight rest halt at La Paz. The transmission had failed, owing to a broken input quill shaft to the rear differential.

Not even the resourceful Johnston could repair such a catastrophic failure at the side of the road. Fortunately, the *Daily Mirror*-sponsored BMC 1800 driven by Peter Jopp, Willy Cave and Mark Kahn soon appeared, its crew sized up the situation and decided to attempt a tow, even though this was strictly against rally rules.

'We towed the Triumph for about 60km,' Jopp later admitted, 'stopping several times to conceal the tow rope whenever a helicopter buzzed around. We were constantly watching in the mirror, worried that we would be seen by another competitor giving an illegal tow…'

Team co-ordinator Bill Price now takes up the story: 'We were sitting at La Paz and the local radio was broadcasting a commentary… the British BL importers, whose Spanish was good, of course, suddenly said: "The local radio has just told us that Paddy Hopkirk has broken down, with a broken diff".'

The outcome of all this was that team boss Peter Browning commandeered a Jeep and a local driver to take a BL mechanic, complete with a replacement rear axle, to drive against the flow of rally traffic to reach the stricken Triumph. Soon after, he also sent mechanic Den Green on the same quest, this time with a new quill shaft – and hoped that this would retrieve the situation. Amazingly this 'Thunderbirds International Rescue' operation worked, for the mechanics were soon able to repair the car and, because quite a bit of 'recovery time' had been built into the rally schedule at this point, Paddy still made it the La Paz control with minutes to spare.

Hopkirk was now sixth overall, 47 minutes behind teammate Culcheth in XJB 305H. He then put in an absolutely storming performance on the next prime, which was all at high altitude and had a target time of 11 hours! Although he finished 2 hours 11 minutes late, he was still fourth fastest overall on that prime. Then, when second fastest overall in the Ecuadorian prime followed, he found himself

fourth overall in the rally – but many minutes behind overall rally leader Hannu Mikkola's Ford Escort.

In theory it was an easy run from there to the ferry at Cali in Colombia, where the cars were to be shipped to Panama – yet Paddy put the car off the road: 'I was stupid.

The cactus is real, this being in Argentina on the 1970 World Cup rally. At this point XJB 302H was still in perfect, if somewhat care-worn, condition.

In the darkness, in the depths of South America, Paddy Hopkirk and XJB 302H press on during the World Cup rally. By the end of the event, the car looked somewhat battered, but Paddy still took fourth place.

I just lost it. I locked up the front end and went straight off into a ditch... I felt a complete idiot. In fact the radiator and oil cooler were both damaged, but my co-driver Neville Johnston did a wonderful job and managed to get us going.'

Much attention from BL mechanics was needed to make the car truly roadworthy again, and during this work partial rear brake failure, owing to a split pipe, was diagnosed. After a significant rebuild that included front suspension strut changes and fitment of a new water radiator, the battle-scarred 2.5 PI was ready to face the last leg from Panama City to Fortin in Mexico. Two primes remained – and Paddy was fastest outright on the first of them and third fastest on the other.

'When we got back to England,' Paddy told me, 'I was entertained to lunch at the Costa Rican Embassy. They presented me with a certificate recording my win on their prime, and the fastest time ever across Costa Rica...'

As a result XJB 302H consolidated its position as fourth overall, supporting Brian Culcheth's sister car in a fine team result on the world's toughest and most famous rally.

Once back in the UK, this car did its share of appearances on the 'show circuit', but was not rallied again and was soon sold off into private ownership.

COMPETITION RECORD	
1970 World Cup	
Paddy Hopkirk	4th overall

XJB 303H

FIRST REGISTERED	1 APRIL 1970
ENGINE SIZE	2,498cc
MODEL TYPE	2.5 PI MkII

This was always known as the 'Australian' entry, for its lead driver was Australian star Evan Green and his partner 'Gelignite' Jack Murray. 'Gelignite'? Murray was well known for his love of practical jokes and for his expertise in the use of explosives for what would now be described as 'recreational use'. Because this team also picked up sponsorship from Britain's *Motor* magazine, they chose to take as their third crew member the magazine's rallies editor, Hamish Cardno, who aimed to send back regular despatches as the event unfolded.

In every way XJB 303H was mechanically identical to the other three works 2.5 PI cars. Although all three crew members were seasoned rally competitors – Cardno was a British co-driver of some note – they were not expected to match the times of the other leading BL stars – at least not at first. And nor did they, especially after suffering the same blockages as the other team cars experienced in Yugoslavia on the second prime.

Their car was the first of the Triumphs to encounter mechanical problems. Even before they reached the first overnight halt, at Monza in northern Italy, XJB 303H had suffered from a brake problem (on the first prime), failing rear suspension dampers, a grumbling bearing in the rear axle and – worst of all – an engine that persistently dropped to five cylinders, thought to be caused by a failing piston. The engine misfire seemed to be incurable at the side of the road,

but everything else was speedily repaired.

Although the car was still healthy enough to be one of 23 that 'cleaned' the San Remo prime in Italy, it suffered a calamitous delay on the French Quatre Chemins prime when Green put it off the road. As Cardno later wrote in *Motor* magazine: 'About 10km (6.2 miles) from the start of the prime... there was a bang like a pistol shot, we veered to the left slightly, then shot off the road and into the trees... and dropped down to come to rest at a crazy angle about 15ft (4.6m) down from the road.'

The reason, it transpired, was that the left front wheel had broken away from the hub, and the car could not be retrieved by breakdown truck until every other rally car had gone through. The crippled car was eventually able to limp out of the prime, where BL service awaited it, but it was knocked about and had to carry on with the fuel-injection supply to the damaged cylinder disconnected, by way of a pipe spraying raw fuel to the outside world.

By Lisbon the car was 69th out of the 71 survivors that were loaded on to the boat for Rio de Janiero. The team was praying that somehow XJB 303H could keep going in South America, and somehow or other it did until the cars reached Argentina, although it remained at the back of the fast-contracting field. On the second of the incredibly long and dusty Argentine primes, however, the 'death rattle' was finally heard, the damaged piston let go, it put a hole in the side of the block, and that was that.

Like Hopkirk's car, it was speedily sold off after its return in the UK.

COMPETITION RECORD	
1970 World Cup	
Evan Green	Did not finish

XJB 304H

FIRST REGISTERED	1 APRIL 1970
ENGINE SIZE	2,498cc
MODEL TYPE	2.5 PI MkII

There were high hopes for this entry because it was crewed by Andrew Cowan and Brian Coyle, who had driven the winning Hillman Hunter in the original marathon rally – the 1968 London-Sydney Marathon. For their third crew member they wisely elected to take along Uldartico (Lacco) Ossio, a cheerful and enthusiastic young Peruvian who had some rallying experience and, crucially, was a Spanish speaker – this would be useful to every member of the British Leyland team in so many ways during their time in South and Central America.

This crew's World Cup rally started gently, for they motored steadily down to Sofia in Bulgaria, turned south, and then 'cleaned' the first prime from Titograd to Kotor – the only works 2.5 PI to do so. They then got heavily snarled up in the 'broken-down truck' and damaged bridge incidents on the second prime, and because they were running at number 43 – almost an hour ahead of Hopkirk's and Culcheth's sister cars – the delays were more serious. Although they then 'cleaned' the San Remo prime and dropped only four minutes on the Quatre Chemins section, they were well outside the top ten in Lisbon when they were loaded on to the Brazil-bound boat.

Thereafter it was a struggle to get back on terms but, aided by setting the best time on the prime in Uruguay, they had risen to tenth place at the Montevideo overnight halt, just nine minutes behind Paddy Hopkirk. More fast times on the Argentinian and Chilean primes all helped – until near-tragedy struck in northern Argentina.

Cowan had elected to wait for hours before starting the eight-hour prime from Rodeo to La Vina so that it could be tackled mostly in daylight, but this meant that he would set off near the end of the field. Bill Price picks up the story.

'Andrew Cowan went off the road near Salta, just before the end of the prime, when following in the dust of the BMC 1800 [of Jean Denton]. They had been preparing to overtake and in the dust and the rising sun, mistook the direction that the road was bending. The car landed on its roof about 20ft (6.1m) below the road, completely wrecking it...'

Although all the crew were hurt and had to be taken to hospital in Salta, they all fully recovered. The car, on the other hand, was a complete write-off, but what was left of it eventually had to be brought back to Abingdon for ritual elimination in order to satisfy customs requirements.

Amazingly, a complete ready-prepared spare 'World Cup'

With Andrew Cowan at the wheel, XJB 904H is ready for the start of the 1970 World Cup rally. Lord Stokes stands alongside to see how his company's money is being spent.

Andrew Cowan and XJB 304H picking their way carefully through a big crowd at a time control in Montevideo, Uruguay, on the South American section of the World Cup rally.

Still looking purposeful, well over 40 years after the 1970 World Cup rally, this is the only one of the works 2.5 PIs that survives in good condition.

Built for one purpose, to win the 1970 World Cup Rally, the works 2.5 PIs rode high and were fitted with this unique layout of forward-facing lights.

The odd-looking appendage between the driving lamps of this World Cup rally 2.5 PI is the socket for the quick-lift jack.

This is how the quick-lift jack is fitted to the rear of the car.

This car, which received a new shell after its horrendous accident on the World Cup rally, carried a crew of three people. The purpose of the vent below the flag was to encourage hot air out of the crowded engine bay.

Please sir, where is the wiring diagram? This complex layout controlled the electrics of a World Cup rally 2.5 PI.

All four works 2.5 PIs built for the World Cup rally ran without bumpers and had flared wheel arches to accommodate wide-rim 15in wheels.

This intake in the roof provides fresh air to the cabin.

The World Cup rally cars carried very prominent competition numbers; the 'coffee' decal was one of the organisers' sponsorship deals.

The interior of the World Cup rally 2.5 PI was full of essential kit.

Actuation of overdrive on the World Cup rally 2.5 PI is by this switch fixed to the gear lever.

To keep the co-driver comfortable, a sheepskin cover was provided for the passenger seat.

This mysterious-looking quadrant could be used to alter the settings of the ignition system and Lucas fuel injection to suit the huge altitude differences encountered on the event – from sea level to 16,000ft.

Everything has a purpose on this World Cup rally 2.5 PI, including the bulged boot lid, the fixings for the quick-lift jack, the flared wheel arches and the towing eyes.

Twin spare wheels and tyres could be carried in the boot, thanks to its modified lid.

For the World Cup 2.5 PIs, the complex rear light clusters of the standard car were replaced with three simple Lucas lamps on each side.

Andrew Cowan in XJB 304H on the serpentine World Cup rally prime held in France. Later in the event, this car unfortunately crashed, with significant injury to the crew – all thankfully made complete recoveries – and severe damage to the car, which was later rebuilt around a spare works bodyshell.

bodyshell already existed at Abingdon, so towards the end of 1970 this shell and the wreckage of the original car were sold off in a package deal. In 1971 what was effectively a reshelled XJB 304H, complete with all the original components that could be transferred, reappeared in all its glory and was used in club motorsport. It is this car – the only running survivor of the four 'XJB' works 2.5 PI MkIIs – that now appears at events all round the UK.

COMPETITION RECORD
1970 World Cup
Andrew Cowan   Did not finish

XJB 305H

Two of the works 2.5 PIs at rest, ready to check in at a time control in eastern Europe during the World Cup rally. This gives a chance to point out preparation details: the sturdy mounting for the front fog lamps, the use of Minilite road wheels, the extra air vents in the front wings (from the engine bay) and the addition of an extra fresh air inlet at the front of the roof.

FIRST REGISTERED	26 MARCH 1970
ENGINE SIZE	2,498cc
MODEL TYPE	2.5 PI MkII

After doing more testing, practising and pre-event surveying in South and Central America than any other member of the team, Brian Culcheth concluded that he would tackle the entire event two-up, accompanied only by his regular co-driver/navigator Johnstone Syer. Not only that, but he also concluded that there was little need to get

Judging by the village signboard in the background, this shot of XJB 305H is almost certainly in Yugoslavia, in the early stages of the World Cup rally. Brian Culcheth drives while Johnstone Syer sleeps.

involved in the hurly-burly of setting fastest stage times in the European section, where minutes separated the top placings, when he knew that lateness penalties in South America would probably be measured in hours.

This explains why he rarely figured in the fight for prime wins during the first week, although he got involved in the delays caused by a stranded truck on the second prime, in Yugoslavia: 'Ford and Citroën had recced one way and we had recced another – and on the event there was a bridge down on our way. We had to go back and rejoin the other route. That cost us 15–20 minutes…'

This explains why Brian was 'only' sixth – 27 minutes off the pace – when the cars reached Lisbon, but the hard work was just about to begin.

For the next three weeks in South and Central America Culcheth and XJB 305H fought a valiant battle against the

fleet of Ford Escort 1850s, which were perhaps not as fast in a straight line but were more nimble on the twisty primes. On some primes the big Triumph could reach, and maintain, 120mph, and on more than one 'cleaned' prime Culcheth averaged more than 100mph. Despite sustaining various punctures, he began to move up the leader board and by the time he reached Montevideo in Uruguay he was up to fourth place, and on arrival in La Paz he was third.

The event, though, was proving to be enormously gruelling. On the incredibly long prime in northern Argentina, 510 miles with a target time of eight hours, Culcheth and Syer elected to sleep for a time before the start and to tackle the entire prime in daylight. This was wise, for they stormed through the dusty mountains to take fourth fastest behind three Escorts.

'After that prime,' Brian recalls, 'we were so tired that I had to be carried out of the car to a caravan that British Leyland had hired and collapse into a bed for two hours – I was completely exhausted.'

Then came the incident that could have been terminal.

'Our windscreen was now so badly cracked from the previous peppering received in Uruguay that we decided to have it changed in La Paz. When the mechanics got the old screen out in many pieces they found that the replacement screens sent from England were the wrong size, and fell hopelessly through the large 2.5 PI screen area.

'Stuart Turner, Ford's competitions manager, very generously came to our rescue and loaned us an Escort screen, which fitted height-wise, but was about two and a half inches short on each side, so the gap was made up with cardboard and bits of sticky tape, making us a bit short of vision…'

No matter how bodged the repair looked, it was in this

condition that the car survived for another ten days! Culcheth's experience and sheer endurance then saw the car claw its way up to second overall by the time the competitive elements of the World Cup rally ended at Fortin, south-east of Mexico City. In the end he was 78 minutes behind the winning Escort of Hannu Mikkola, but well ahead of any other surviving car. Only 23 cars made it to the end of this phenomenal event.

After the event, and after this magnificent performance, XJB 305H was returned to Abingdon, where several buffoons from British Leyland top management, in their blinkered wisdom, had concluded that the effort had been an expensive failure. For a time it looked as if this car would be sold off, but Culcheth – as a fully professional rally driver – needed something to do and had other ideas.

Night-time, and a flat-out prime in South America, with Brian Culcheth and Johnstone Syer hard at work in XJB 305H; all the European primes were tackled in daylight.

After the car's exploits in the World Cup rally of 1970, Brian Culcheth used XJB 305H in European events during 1971. Much later, after years of disuse, it was scrapped.

One more enterprise would delay the 2.5 PI's demise from European competition by a further year. This was a 'semi-works' operation run by Brian Culcheth with Castrol sponsorship and using his ex-World Cup rally 2.5 PI. Brian relates how the project began.

'Bill Davis, who was Triumph's top director, called me to a meeting, where I found that he was particularly keen to continue Triumph's association with sport. But there wasn't any money…'

Brian then cast around and found funds from Castrol (the international oil company) and from British Leyland International (for promotional work), the result being the setting up of Brian Culcheth Team Castrol. Although other BL cars would eventually be involved, in 1971 the team's one and only mechanical asset was his ex-World Cup rally 2.5 PI, which had been sitting, neglected, in a corner at Abingdon since its return from Mexico City in the summer of 1970.

Costs were high, of course, and in the end this new team managed just three starts in international events. The first was the Welsh International rally, where the scrutineers initially saw fit to reject the stout-hearted ex-World Cup rally car because they considered that it had an 'inadequate roll cage' – yet Andrew Cowan probably owed his life to the rugged construction of the World Cup rally 2.5 PIs. This was very much a sprint event in which the big Triumph was always going to be at a disadvantage, but in spite of suffering some fuel-feed problems Culcheth managed to finish 14th.

Then came the Scottish, an event dear to Brian's heart that he badly wanted to win again. This 2.5 PI was neither as light

nor as powerful as WRX 902H, the car that he had used to win in 1970, but it was still competitive on the long and often rocky stages. Fourth at one point, the car eventually finished tenth after Brian put it off the track on two occasions on different special stages.

Finally there came the hot, rough Cyprus rally in September – the only overseas event the team started and a very creditable one. The 2.5 PI was ideally suited to the surfaces of this event but not for the twisty nature of its stages, so second place overall was an excellent result.

And that really was the end of a concentrated two-season international career for XJB 305H, which went back into neglected storage at Abingdon. In later years it was displayed at the newly founded British Leyland collection of historic vehicles, but by the 1980s it had become a rusty relic and, unbelievably, was scrapped by the order of top BL management.

COMPETITION RECORD

1970 World Cup
Brian Culcheth .... 2nd overall
1971 Welsh
Brian Culcheth .... 14th overall
1971 Scottish
Brian Culcheth .... 10th overall
1971 Cyprus
Brian Culcheth .... 2nd overall

KNW 798

FIRST REGISTERED	1972 (DATE UNKNOWN)
ENGINE SIZE	2,498cc
MODEL TYPE	2.5 PI MkII

Although the unique demands of the East African Safari might have been a stimulating challenge, the factory wisely decided not to spend shedloads of money on an event that the big Triumphs might not finish at all. Accordingly, until 1972 there was no question of providing works assistance to any 2000 or 2.5 PI entry.

Even so, in 1968 the redoubtable Viscount Kim Mandeville finished third overall in his own 2000 (see page 119), following this up with sixth overall in his 2.5 PI MkII in 1970. Perhaps this explains why the Kenyan Triumph importers, Benbros, eventually found enough financial support to commission a works-built 2.5 PI MkII to tackle the 1972 event in Group 2 form.

This event has now gone down in history as the year of the 'myth-breakers', in which a Europe-based driver, Hannu Mikkola, won the event outright in a Ford Escort RS1600. This was an amazing performance, but because the feat generated mountains of publicity few remember that Brian Culcheth and local-co-driver 'Lofty' Drews took a very creditable class victory too.

Their brand-new car was prepared by the Special Tuning department, the customer-orientated operation at Abingdon that Lord Stokes had not closed down because it was very profitable. KNW 798 had many recognisable features shared with the World Cup rally entries, but, as ever, there did not seem to be enough time to give the new car a proper pre-event shakedown, so a lot of detail work remained to be done after it had been flown out to Nairobi. Brian recalls just how much trouble they had.

'One thing I had discussed with Bill Davis was the potential of the 2.5 PI in the Safari, but we had a rally of considerable mechanical problems. It started only 100 miles after the start when an antelope went into the front of the car, and the horns went straight through the radiator. There was water gushing out everywhere. I was with 'Lofty' Drews, a local co-driver, so we got some mud and tried to cake it up, but that didn't work properly. Then we saw a privately owned Triumph 2000 sitting in a driveway, and you can guess the rest! We begged the radiator from the owner, and changed it.'

But that was not the half of it. Later in the event the gearbox stripped most of its gears – nothing new there when one recalls the mid-1960s 2000 saloons – and after the halfway halt the rear window dropped out, just as had occurred several times in pre-World Cup rally testing. Finally,

because of the incessant battering of this amazing event, the whole of the rear end of the body began to break away from the cabin. This was strapped up as much as possible with stout rope, but by the finish the boot looked as if it was ready to fall off there and then.

Even so, Culcheth and Drews were able to finish, way down in 13th place overall but first in their capacity class. Amazingly, the car somehow survived the years of neglect that followed and was painstakingly restored, becoming a significant part of the classic rallying scene in the UK.

Brian Culcheth and 'Lofty' Drew drove this 2.5 PI, locally registered KNW 798, to a class win in the 1972 East African Safari.

COMPETITION RECORD	
1972 East African Safari	
Brian Culcheth	1st in class

CHAPTER 8:
DOLOMITE SPRINT, RACE AND RALLY (1972–78)

Although the Dolomite Sprint was not originally intended to be a competition car, in the 1970s it became one of British Leyland's most successful saloons in racing and rallying. Not only that, but it was initially available to wave the company flag at a time when there was only one other car from the sprawling British Leyland empire in use competitively in motorsport – the Richard Longman Mini 1275GT.

Three principal factors made it possible to turn the Dolomite Sprint into a motorsport success. First, the 16-valve engine proved to be exceptionally tuneable and durable. Second, the independent Broadspeed racing car team, funded by the factory, was amazingly effective, to an unexpected degree. Third, by this time the British Leyland works competitions department was as experienced as any other such organisation in the business.

And yet the fact is that the Dolomite Sprint did not come along until eight years after the announcement of the model on which it was originally based. In those eight years all manner of changes were made to the basic design, not least a change from front-wheel drive to rear-wheel drive, but by the mid-1970s, when the Dolomite Sprint's motorsport reputation was its height, this lengthy heritage meant that it did show up looking a little too narrow in the track and high in

The Dolomite Sprint engine, unveiled in 1973, was the very first British unit to combine a 16-valve cylinder with opposed valves, all actuated from a single camshaft. In 2-litre form, more than 220bhp was ultimately available in racing car guise.

the cabin. This aspect did nothing for the handling, although heroes like Andy Rouse and Tony Dron soon learned to cope with it.

This story started way back in 1965 with the launch of the Triumph 1300. This was Triumph's first – and, it transpired, only – front-wheel-drive design. As the 1.3-litre engine, a detuned Spitfire unit, was situated longitudinally above the transmission rather than transversely alongside it, the bonnet line was rather high and this in turn affected the design of the whole of the four-door bodyshell.

The 1300 and its later derivatives, the 1300TC and the 1500, were all commercially successful front-wheel-drive cars, but the company then set out on a series of outwardly perverse and unrelated modifications. First of all, it produced a two-door version of the bodyshell and completely rejigged the driveline and floorpan to make the car rear-wheel drive. This was the Toledo, after which came the 1500TC, effectively a glossy 1.5-litre Toledo derivative with four doors and lengthened front and rear sections.

The most ambitious move, however, had already been determined, with the decision to create an all-new four-cylinder 1.7-litre engine – the 'slant four' – for a whole variety of applications. Fitted with single-overhead-camshaft valve gear, this engine got its name because it was installed at a 45-degree angle in the engine bay, leaning over to the left side of the car. This angled configuration was conceived because a 90-degree V8 engine could easily be spun off, with certain machining facilities shared, and used in 3-litre form for the Stag. The first versions of the four-cylinder engine were sold to Saab, and then a 1.85-litre version powered the new Dolomite – a famous Triumph name from the 1930s.

Soon after this, top management at British Leyland concluded that the marketing profile of the Triumph brand should be gradually eased upmarket, an ambition that some described as the 'BMW solution' – which was ambitious to say the least. One consequence was that a 2-litre 16-valve version of the new 'slant four' was developed during 1969–70. As British Leyland's empire included Jaguar and Coventry Climax, it was logical to use existing cylinder-head design expertise from those quarters – and it was logistically convenient because all the engineers involved were based in Coventry.

Meanwhile, in 1968–69 Peter Browning, newly elevated by British Leyland to the post of competitions manager for the entire group, had carried out his corporate survey of the company's existing and planned products to assess what might be suitable for use in motorsport. Knowing that the relatively lightweight Toledo was about to go on sale and that there were plans to produce a 16-valve version of the 'slant four' engine, Browning suggested that a limited-production Toledo with the new 16-valve engine could be a very promising 'homologation special' – Triumph's equivalent of the Ford Escort Twin-Cam. A single prototype, coded 'Toledo Rallyman', was built in Coventry in 1970–71 with an 1,850cc version of the 16-valve engine, carrying the experimental commission number X807 and registered TKV 35J – but nothing became of the project.

RALLY CARS

After the absorption of Standard-Triumph within British Leyland in 1968, Ray Henderson's scaled-down department in Coventry found itself with nothing significant to do, the four-wheel-drive 1300 (see Appendix 1) having been written off and the 2.5 PI programme completely taken over by Abingdon. He and Gordon Birtwistle turned their attention, therefore, to what would become the Dolomite Sprint. It might not have been as light a car as Browning's proposal for a 16-valve Toledo would have been, but it looked very promising indeed.

Thus it was that the original Dolomite Sprint competition car was born in the spring of 1972 and eventually made its début on that year's Scottish rally, a full year before the production car was announced. Registered CKV 2K and carrying commission number X826, this was the only Dolomite Sprint, as it transpired, to be built and prepared in Coventry. Henderson was in charge of the project and Birtwistle carried out much of the development driving.

Once CKV 2K had been handed over to Abingdon, all future Triumph rallying was run from there. This particular Dolomite Sprint played a big part in solving numerous development problems, including shock absorber durability, a rear differential problem and persistent failures in the original layout of rear suspension, where trailing and semi-trailing links were a feature.

By 1973 the once-dormant works competition department at Abingdon was gradually coming back to life under the Special Tuning banner, first of all with such outwardly unpromising cars as the Austin Allegro and Morris Marina, but then, towards the end of that year, with the Dolomite Sprint. A more determined – and better financed – approach to motorsport then followed, which included the arrival of PR man Richard Seth-Smith as manager of Special Tuning (to succeed Basil Wales) and the reappointment of Bill Price as workshop supervisor (after three years away from the company).

Through the period 1974–75 the development emphasis was very much on the Dolomite Sprint, but over the winter of 1975/76 the Sprint then had to take second place to the new TR7, whose career is described in Chapter 9. Although Seth-Smith later moved back into the PR department of British Leyland, he kept hold of the managerial reins until January 1976, when Bill Price became manager of British Leyland ST (as the operation had now become).

With the Dolomite Sprint coming towards the peak of its development, for 1977 BL appointed John Davenport as its new director of motorsport, which meant that Price automatically became his deputy. When Davenport arrived, as the team was moving into a modern new building in the Abingdon complex, he found that his homologation team, led by Ron Elkins, had managed to get twin dual-choke Weber carburettors approved for use in Group 1 – incredible though it seemed. The regulations required 5,000 cars to have been built in 1976 with that specification…

The works rallying career of the Dolomite Sprint rally cars, however, came to an end less than a year later, in September 1977, because the team wanted to concentrate on the development of the TR7 and TR7 V8 models. This meant that the latest batch of homologation items would be much more valuable to the Broadspeed-run racing cars.

From 1969 to 1977, Brian Culcheth (above) and Johnstone Syer were the stalwart drivers in the works Triumph rally cars of the period.

Brian Culcheth (behind the wheel) and Ray Hutton during the 1975 Avon Tour of Britain, in which they took second overall in this Group 1 Dolomite Sprint.

CKV 2K

FIRST REGISTERED	19 MAY 1972
ENGINE SIZE	1,998cc
MODEL TYPE	DOLOMITE SPRINT

Brian Culcheth hustling CKV 2K along on the Scottish rally, the Dolomite Sprint's début event in June 1972 – a whole year ahead of the model's public launch.

CKV 2K, the original prototype works Dolomite Sprint, competing in the Portuguese TAP rally in September 1972.

This Coventry-registered car was originally built at the Triumph experimental department in 1972 as a prototype Dolomite Sprint ('Swift' was the factory code name for the model) and was the machine Ray Henderson used for initial motorsport development, with Gordon Birtwistle doing the test driving.

CKV 2K was first seen in June 1972 at the Scottish rally, where such non-homologated cars were allowed to compete on that occasion. This was a full year before the Dolomite Sprint road car was ready to go on sale, which explains why fellow competitors and media people were not allowed to look under the bonnet of the new car. Like the forthcoming road car, it was equipped with the 1,998cc 16-valve engine backed by a TR4/2.5 PI-type four-speed gearbox with overdrive. Flared wheel arches allowed wider-than-standard wheels and tyres to be fitted.

It was a promising but inauspicious beginning. Although Brian Culcheth set some surprisingly competitive special-stage times on the hot, dusty Forestry Commission stages, the car suffered from weak shock absorbers and these had to be changed several times. With much crashing of the suspension and grounding of the sump shield on rocky stages, CKV 2K finally finished second in its class.

In general, however, the car was thought to have potential, Culcheth being quoted as saying in mid-event that it 'had the makings'. It was prepared, therefore, for use in the Portuguese TAP rally in September. This was not a full-blooded effort, as exemplified by the fact that PR man Simon Pearson drove the car down from Coventry to Southampton at the last moment in order to put it on the ferry to Spain! Service was provided by Gordon Birtwistle, who was ostensibly 'on holiday' for the week, from a well-loaded Range Rover with Special Tuning's Ron Elkins alongside him.

The miracle was that the car started the event well, even running among the leaders for a time, but then the engine lost power and finally one of the rear axle locating links broke off, causing the car to be stranded well away from the service support. It was only after the car's return to Coventry that it was discovered by the mechanics that the engine had broken one of the rocker arms in the valve gear, effectively making it a three-cylinder unit!

Shortly afterwards the car was handed over to the BL competitions department at Abingdon and from that moment the Coventry competitions department effectively closed down. Ray Henderson went on to higher responsibilities in the general engineering operation, where the very first TR7 prototypes were then taking shape, while Gordon Birtwistle eventually left the company.

Although CVK 2K had no more front-line competition activity, it carried out many test and development duties, including many gruelling hours at rough-road test facilities such as the military tracks at Bagshot. Work included testing of Don Moore engines, different Minilite wheels, Bilstein shock absorbers (preferred to the standard Girlings) and a modified rear suspension linkage that included parallel trailing arms and a Panhard rod for transverse location.

Brian Culcheth discusses the Dolomite Sprint project with Abingdon's Ron Elkins during the 1972 TAP rally of Portugal. At this time the car's 16-valve engine was still very secret...

COMPETITION RECORD	
1972 Scottish	
Brian Culcheth	2nd in class
1972 TAP (Portugal)	
Brian Culcheth	Did not finish

FRW 812L

FIRST REGISTERED	7 FEBRUARY 1973
ENGINE SIZE	1,998cc
MODEL TYPE	DOLOMITE SPRINT

The very first of the true works Dolomite Sprint rally cars began to take shape at Abingdon in the spring of 1973, some months before the road car went on sale in mid-summer. Because the official competitions department was still in suspended animation – it had been closed at Lord Stokes' behest in the autumn of 1970 – this car was originally in the care of Basil Wales' Special Tuning operation, which was run from the same factory. Along with RDU 983M, it became one of the most intensively used works cars – or perhaps I should say 'works identities' – that Abingdon possessed in the 1970s.

One of the first batch of production cars built at Standard-Triumph in the spring of 1973, FRW 812L was developed into a rally car to FIA Group 2 specification and made its début in March 1974 on the TAP rally of Portugal, crewed by Brian Culcheth and Johnstone Syer. Because of the way in which the department's rally effort was being administered and financed through London-based British Leyland Interna-

tional (BLI), the car was entered by British Leyland Portugal and run in the Portuguese distributor's colour scheme.

The new car had a rather inauspicious start, although it went on to have a long and distinguished works career. On a very early special stage, the Sintra stage north of Lisbon, it suffered a bent steering rack and the mechanics were not able to fit a replacement before the car ran out of time. The rack proved to be a continuing concern on these cars, as did the location and detailing of the trailing and semi-trailing arms in the rear suspension linkage, although at least a limited-slip differential gave hope for the future.

BLI again financed the entry of Culcheth and Syer on the Antibes-Grasse rally, which was based on tarmac stages in the south of France. After carrying out a good practice session, the crew hoped for a good result, but those hopes were dashed on the start line of the very first stage. An electric wiring fire developed, filling the cabin with smoke and wiping out some of the forward illumination. There was more drama to follow, for a few stages later the alternator came loose, threw its belt, and in all the damage that followed the cooling radiator was holed!

The car was repaired and made ready for the same crew to contest the 24 Hours of Ypres rally in Belgium. After a very encouraging start – press reports spoke of lying second overall against a massed entry of 2-litre Escorts, Porsche 911s and 1.8-litre Alpine-Renaults – the car suddenly faltered when its self-adjusting rear brakes overheated and caught

Brian Culcheth and Johnstone Syer used FRW 812L to finish fifth overall in the Snowman rally of 1976.

followed by an outright victory.

According to British Leyland's PR machine at the time, the Group 2 Dolomite Sprint engine was now producing up to 200bhp – a welcome advance on the 1974 outputs usually quoted. A new enterprise called Team Unipart/Castrol was also set up, and initially planned to compete in a very ambitious programme of ten British events, although one more, the Tour of Dean in January, was added at very short notice. FRW 812L, which had been so badly damaged on the 1974 RAC rally, received a smart new colour scheme for its new bodyshell.

The first event, the Tour of Dean, brought an early exit: Culcheth went off the track on the very first stage and damaged the rear axle and rear suspension, while on the very next stage the engine somehow moved on its mountings and allowed the fan to puncture the water radiator, bringing almost instant retirement. Things finally looked up, however, on the Yorkshire-based Mintex Dales rally, which used fearsome stages close to Pickering and Scarborough. Culcheth picked his way carefully over the ice, frost, mud and gravel – and even a touch or two of tarmac – to finish a very creditable seventh overall.

Eventually, in March 1975, there was joy for the works Dolomite Sprint team when FRW 812C won its first rally outright. The team had taken the gamble of entering it in the Hackle rally, a Scottish Championship event based at Kirkcaldy, and although the entry did not include many other top-grade runners, all concerned were delighted when the car won by the narrow margin of 21 seconds from Bill Taylor's Ford Escort RS1600.

Three weeks later the same crew returned to Scotland, this time to tackle the Aberdeen-based Granite City rally against much stronger competition, including both Roger Clark and Billy Coleman in new-shape Ford Escort RS1800s. Culcheth brought the car home in a cultured fourth place overall, behind those RS1800s and one other fast Ford. Now he was setting the pattern that would persist for the next two seasons of rallying.

Although the team and the driving crew were getting more and more confident with the performance of this Group 2 Dolomite Sprint, all their hopes were dashed on the Welsh rally in May. Culcheth already knew that the Triumph would struggle against the modern generation of 16-valve Escorts, which were considerably lighter, but he was dismayed to find just how far off the pace the car was on the dry, dusty Welsh stages. At one point he was trying so hard that he went off the road, and on a later section the front suspension broke a tie bar. In the end he was relieved to take 11th overall.

FRW 812C then had a two-month lay-off while Culcheth used SOE 8M instead, re-emerging to tackle the Jim Clark rally, which provided a mixture of special stages, some on tarmac and some in the Kielder forestry complex, some in daylight and some at night. Brian, who found the 'old' car

fire, setting light to the brake fluid too.

The team had to put these problems in the first three events down to experience, and it would take more testing and more rally outings to expose every failing. Much of that testing was carried out by CVK 2K at Bagshot and this certainly helped FRW 812L to look and feel more purposeful on the Scottish-based Burmah rally, which ended in Dunoon, within sight of the awesome US Navy nuclear submarine base at Holy Loch. By this time Abingdon was claiming 205bhp from the Dolomite Sprint's 2-litre engine, and the car was certainly very fast until its retirement. On the Glen Shellish stage Culcheth spun the car and it blocked the stage, immobile because a front suspension ball joint had failed.

The last event of 1974, the RAC rally, brought yet another retirement, the fifth in a row, although it could not be blamed on either the car or its unfortunate driver. On the first night, Culcheth was catching Amilcare Ballestrieri's Lancia Beta Coupé, which was laying a thick cloud of smoke from its blown engine, and suddenly encountered a tree that had been displaced into the track by another competitor. The tree tore away the Triumph's front suspension and entered the passenger compartment. To quote co-driver Syer, 'another six inches and we would have been competing for the ladies' prize'.

The 1975 season began in a more upbeat manner than 1974 had ended, which was a great relief to everyone in the works team. The improvement that was needed soon arrived, for the first creditable finish came within two months, closely much more to his liking than SOE 8M, came out fighting from the start and finished a storming third overall, beaten only by two Ford Escorts.

Culcheth hoped for another good result in the Dunoon-based Burmah rally one month later, but was disappointed. When rushing downhill on the Rest And Be Thankful stage – a famous venue that was usually tackled uphill – he encountered a big rock in the road and had to tweak the Sprint to one side to avoid it, only to fall into a large pothole that damaged the steering arm, which ultimately came away from the rest of the suspension.

The following month, on the Isle of Man, FRW 812C suffered yet another accident when it encountered three sheep on a special stage. Aside from the consequences for the poor animals, the incident bent the front suspension, and two stages later the Sprint went out for good when the differential broke.

When the car reappeared for use in the Tyneside-based Lindisfarne rally in October, the team suggested that this might be its final appearance, for the intention on the forthcoming RAC rally was to contest Group 1 with a different Sprint. So Culcheth set out to get among the all-conquering Ford Escort RS1800s if he could. Mainly concentrated in the Kielder forests, the Lindisfarne was held in terrible autumnal weather that year. Try as he might, Culcheth could not quite match Roger Clark's pace in the winning Escort, and it did not help that at one point the underside of his car hit a destructive part of Northumberland, causing a lot of damage to the sump guard but fortunately not to the sump itself. Third overall, several minutes off the pace, was no less than the car deserved.

However, that was not its final appearance. After a winter's rest the gallant old car was brought out of storage, given a new corporate colour scheme and readied for three events early in 1976, starting with the Inverness-based Snowman rally. Over 22 special stages, some in snow and ice, Culcheth showed that he and his car were still competitive, even though, as ever, he had to face a fleet of 16-valve Escorts, one of which was now driven by Ari Vatanen! Although Brian eventually took fifth place, it was an eventful day for him. He went off the road at one juncture, then suffered a delay with a stalled engine, and finally, towards the end, the throttle linkage came adrift, costing him more than two minutes before he could jury-rig a quick fix.

Culcheth then enjoyed another reliable run in the Mintex, finishing a sparkling seventh overall on this 36-stage event. Finally, in March, FRW 812C set out on its last rally as a works car, the Aberdeen-based Granite City, where it was vital to make the correct choice of tyres for stages that were often hampered by snow and ice. Unhappily, Culcheth's car suffered many problems, including a bent steering rack and a broken front brake calliper, and eventually he ran out of time – a downbeat way for this car to come to the end of its very busy career.

COMPETITION RECORD	
1974 TAP	
Brian Culcheth	Did not finish
1974 Antibes-Grasse	
Brian Culcheth	Did not finish
1974 24 Hours of Ypres	
Brian Culcheth	Did not finish
1974 Burmah	
Brian Culcheth	Did not finish
1974 RAC	
Brian Culcheth	Did not finish
1975 Tour of Dean	
Brian Culcheth	Did not finish
1975 Mintex	
Brian Culcheth	7th overall
1975 Hackle	
Brian Culcheth	1st overall
1975 Granite City	
Brian Culcheth	4th overall
1975 Welsh	
Brian Culcheth	11th overall
1975 Jim Clark	
Brian Culcheth	3rd overall
1975 Burmah	
Brian Culcheth	Did not finish
1975 Manx Trophy	
Brian Culcheth	Did not finish
1975 Lindisfarne	
Brian Culcheth	3rd overall
1976 Snowman	
Brian Culcheth	5th overall
1976 Mintex	
Brian Culcheth	7th overall
1976 Granite City	
Brian Culcheth	Did not finish

RDU 983M

FIRST REGISTERED	14 MARCH 1974
ENGINE SIZE	1,998cc
MODEL TYPE	DOLOMITE SPRINT

Built specifically to comply with FIA Group 1 regulations, RDU 983M made its début in that form on the BRSCC-promoted, Avon-sponsored Tour of Britain race-cum-rally of

Eppynt: this was one of the tarmac stages of the 1975 Tour of Britain in which Brian Culcheth's Dolomite Sprint excelled.

Service for the Dolomite Sprint before one of the races on the 1975 Tour of Britain – the men with their backs to the camera are Ray Hutton (left) and Brian Culcheth.

July 1974. The car – or at least its identity – was eventually used on no fewer than 20 British Championship events, including three appearances in successive Tours of Britain. It won the Group 1 category on such events no fewer than seven times – an outstanding success record.

The 1974 Tour of Britain was bigger, better, more competitive and of much higher profile than the first such event of 1973. Starting and finishing from a hotel north of Birmingham, this three-day event included long races at BRSCC-associated circuits together with special stages located as far apart as East Anglia and Wales. By happy chance, the British Leyland competitions department at Abingdon had officially been reactivated just a few weeks earlier, allowing just enough time for a competitive new Group 1 car to be completed.

As there was little testing time available, the car was much more standard than it would eventually become, and drew heavily on experience so far gained on the works-backed Sprints that Broadspeed was already running in the British Saloon Car Championship. Brian Culcheth was asked to drive the car, his partner on this occasion being Ray Hutton, editor of *Autocar* magazine. Although Ray had little previous co-driving experience, he did a great job, especially in keeping his driver happy and afterwards telling the whole world about his experiences.

Most of the rally headlines in the Dolomite Sprint's 2-litre class were created by the ding-dong battle that developed between two works Ford Escort RS2000s driven by Roger

Brian Culcheth and Ray Hutton in the Group 1-specification works Dolomite Sprint on the Tour of Britain of 1975 – the car finished a splendid second overall.

Clark and Gerry Marshall. But the new Triumph was always competitive and set fastest stage times on the Norwich Show-ground and Ingestre Hall special stages before trouble struck. First the engine's distributor cracked, then a leaking carburettor helped to start a small fire, which was soon extinguished. Hours later, in the race at Oulton Park, the Sprint's engine developed a serious misfire owing to further leakage from the carburettor installation and this time there was a bigger fire. Marshals out on the circuit quickly extinguished the flames, but the car could not be retrieved in time for it to continue. Later, after testing, a simple alteration to the float chamber installation cured this recurrent problem.

Amazingly, this Group 1 Sprint was not used again until the following year's Tour of Britain. A waste of resources? Not when one considers what a compact operation this competitions department actually was, with most of the team engrossed in the Dolomite Sprint Group 2 programme and already at work on the TR7 rally cars that would soon arrive on the scene.

As in the previous year, the 1975 Tour of Britain was limited to FIA Group 1 cars and centred on a hotel near Birmingham. It included five races and 16 rally stages in a 1,000-mile road section, and practice and pre-event reconnaissance were banned – and strictly policed. The latest Dolomite Sprint, its engine benefiting from newly homologated 2in SU carburettors and a modified camshaft profile, looked to be extremely competitive – and indeed it was. Brian Culcheth and co-driver Ray Hutton looked forward to another intense battle against the best of the Escort RS2000s, which on this occasion meant Tony Pond in a MkI RS2000 run with some works assistance.

Fancied contenders fell away throughout the event. Neither Tony Lanfranchi's Chrysler Barracuda nor a Stuart Graham-prepared Chevrolet Camaro lasted the distance – but the Dolomite Sprint was extremely reliable. Between them Culcheth and Pond won most of the individual stages and races, and by the last morning Pond was ahead by more than 80 seconds. Even though Culcheth then took 38 seconds back in two Eppynt stages and the Mallory Park race, it was not enough and he had to settle for second place, just 47 seconds behind at the end of a superb three-day performance.

Once again British Leyland put the car back in store for some months, for it did not reappear until the RAC rally in November. The result on this important event, where the world's best Group 2 cars from 15 factory teams dominated the headlines, was all that could be hoped for. Starting from York and returning there by way of 72 of the UK's toughest forestry special stages, the Group 1 Sprint kept going despite some minor suspension problems caused by the pounding inflicted on the stages – and it won the category outright. It was just reward for the team on one of the world's most prestigious rallies.

Retained as the newly revitalised team's Group 1 car for

1976, RDU 983M was allocated to new recruit Tony Pond, partnered by David Richards. First time out, on the Shellsport Tour of Dean, most media headlines were being made by the meteoric progress of the youthful Ari Vatanen in his works Escort RS1800, but Pond motored rapidly and safely to win the Group 1 category in this opening round of the British Championship.

Second time out, the car had to travel all the way to Inverness to contest the Snowman rally, where there were 22 stages on decidedly mixed surfaces, including snow and ice.

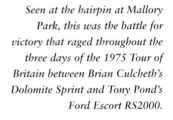

Seen at the hairpin at Mallory Park, this was the battle for victory that raged throughout the three days of the 1975 Tour of Britain between Brian Culcheth's Dolomite Sprint and Tony Pond's Ford Escort RS2000.

By the time its development was complete, the Group 1 Dolomite Sprint was a formidable little rally car and Brian Culcheth proved it by taking RDU 983M to outright victory in the Group 1 category of the RAC rally of 1975. Two more hard seasons of rallying would follow for this valiant car.

Tony Pond (left) and Brian Culcheth became British Leyland team-mates in 1976, both of them driving Dolomite Sprints and, later, TR7s.

Unhappily, the car blew its engine after a main-bearing failure and loss of oil pressure. On the Mintex that followed, however, Pond had a trouble-free run in Group 1, winning the category by nearly four minutes and finishing tenth overall, which encouraged British Leyland to celebrate with massive adverts in the specialist press. Only weeks later, the same crew tackled the snow-affected Granite City, where Tony Pond astonished the rally establishment by staying on the tracks for 19 stages and regularly putting himself among the top times, including outright fastest on one stage and second fastest on three others.

Pond now turned his attention to the new TR7 rally programme, so RDU 983M was entrusted to Jersey driver Pat Ryan. This was a real promotion, for Ryan had previously been struggling unsuccessfully with the job of getting any results out of the Abingdon team's Austin Allegro.

First time out, on the Welsh, Ryan struggled to come to terms with his car, which suffered all manner of minor problems, including a persistent misfire that left him with a distinct lack of power at times. Third in the Group 1 category was scant reward for a determined effort to reach the finish. Nor was there any better luck on the Scottish, where Ryan struggled with all sorts of problems and finished well off the

pace. He went off the road at a very early stage (requiring a bent steering rack to be speedily changed) and then the overdrive stopped working, while on the final day there were breakages to a petrol-feed pipe and a locating arm in the rear suspension.

Then came the Tour of Britain, now backed by Texaco. Once again this event was for Group 1 cars only and the Dolomite Sprint, with a claimed 180bhp, was expected to show well, especially as its driver, Tony Pond, had won the previous year. Wrongly described in the *Autosport* rally report as 'new', RDU 983M set out to tackle this three-day event that now comprised more special stages, 27 of them, but only four circuit races.

Unhappily, Leyland and Broadspeed had not solved all of the 16-valve engine's shortcomings. Although Pond set fastest times on two early stages, during the Cadwell Park race at the end of the first afternoon his engine lost all its oil pressure, which damaged the crankshaft main bearings and brought about his immediate retirement. To quote BL's Bill Price, 'Poor Tony was becoming disenchanted with Broadspeed engines'. And so was the team. Although Broadspeed was continuing to produce phenomenal race engines for the Dolomite Sprint, Abingdon now turned instead to Don Moore for preparation of engines for rallying.

RDU 983M then reverted to Pat Ryan for more rallies and he really got to grips with it on the next event, the Dunoon-based Burmah rally, which included 17 forestry stages. Even though the sump guard fixings came partially adrift at one point, Ryan managed to win Group 1 and took seventh place overall, beaten only by three works Ford Escort RS1800s, two privateer RS1800s and Andy Dawson's very powerful Datsun Violet.

For the Manx Trophy rally Ryan's co-driver was Fred Gallagher, who would go on to great things with Tony Pond in later years. Ryan had a virtually trouble-free run for three days, not only ending up ninth overall behind a mass of much more powerful cars – including the two works TR7s – but also winning Group 1 outright once again. It was the same story on the forestry stage-based Lindisfarne rally that followed, Ryan unobtrusively winning the entire Group 1 category and finishing tenth overall behind, among others, seven Escort RS1800s!

Ryan then put in a rather undistinguished performance on the Castrol 1976 rally, a non-championship event often used for what we might call 'pre-RAC rally testing'. After shooting off down a badly marked 'wrong slot' on one stage and going off again on a Dovey stage, he was beaten in the Group 1 category by a works Chrysler Avenger.

This hard-working car's season ended in a most unsatisfactory way on the prestigious RAC rally. Encountering a very rough section on one of the Kielder stages, Ryan was unable to avoid over-revving the engine when the rear wheels lifted, bending one of the 16 valves and having to retire.

In 1977 the valiant RDU 983M embarked on a fourth gruelling season. Pat Ryan was again its driver and the objective was to win the Group 1 category of the British Open Rally Championship. As it transpired the car would start five events before being retired mid-season in favour of the much newer MYX 175P.

First time out, in January, on the Newport-based Shellsport Dean, the newly refurbished saloon suffered a time-consuming 'off' in one stage, losing any chance of Group 1 victory. Although disappointed, Ryan could at least look forward to using the latest homologation package, including a pair of twin-choke Weber 48DCOE carburettors – which played a big part in taking claimed peak power beyond 200bhp! This was the latest of a series of homologation coups for which British Leyland was becoming notable at this time: although the regulations stated that 5,000 cars had to be manufactured with such kit, this was not remotely the case with the Dolomite Sprint!

The new engine, however, was of little help on the Yorkshire-based Mintex, where lack of grip and evil handling on copious ice and snow presented considerable difficulty. The misery of this outing was compounded by fuel pump failure in the middle of the first stage where mechanics could not reach the car.

Next came the Circuit of Ireland. That the car was now very fast in the right conditions was never in doubt and it was easily leading Group 1 and lying seventh overall at the end of the first day, but at the end of the second day, as the rally was approaching Killarney, Ryan had a huge accident. *Autosport* described what happened: 'After a long series of flat-out kinks, the road ahead turned into a deceptive tightening left-hander. Pat Ryan misread the bend and came in some 40mph too fast. When he realised his mistake, he slung the car sideways, but the car got away from him on some conveniently placed mud and the Triumph hit the bank very hard on the offside front wing, coming to rest among some willow trees way off the road.'

In a matter of weeks a miraculously reborn car appeared at the start of the Welsh International rally – the same car, that is, if we go by the registration number! Pat Ryan, who in the meantime had had a good run in the Granite City rally in another Dolomite Sprint, took to his 'new' car with great determination, although several 'moments' lost precious time – an off-the-road incident in Penmachno, a high-speed spin on a forestry stage and another error on Eppynt that resulted in a bent steering rack. But he drove back up through the field to record ninth place overall and second in Group 1, a category that he had really deserved to win.

The very final rally for RDU 983M was the long, fast, dry, gruelling Scottish rally, where Group 1 competition was fierce and there were no fewer than 60 special stages. Components of the old car were beginning to show their age, which might explain why Ryan had to drive eight stages

without the use of front brakes! Later he suffered a bent steering rack after the car's front wheel clouted a large rock, and it took ages for him to find enough 'service time' to have the rack changed. It did not help either that the rear axle casing was later found to be distorted. In the end Ryan finished third overall in Group 1, behind a Ford Escort RS2000 and a Chrysler Avenger GT, both of which were works-assisted.

COMPETITION RECORD

1974 Tour of Britain	
Brian Culcheth	Did not finish
1975 Tour of Britain	
Brian Culcheth	2nd overall
1975 RAC	
Brian Culcheth	1st overall and Group 1
1976 Tour of Dean	
Tony Pond	1st overall and Group 1
1976 Snowman	
Tony Pond	Did not finish
1976 Mintex	
Tony Pond	1st overall and Group 1
1976 Granite City	
Tony Pond	1st in Group 1
1976 Welsh	
Pat Ryan	3rd in Group 1
1976 Scottish	
Pat Ryan	5th in class
1976 Tour of Britain	
Tony Pond	Did not finish
1976 Burmah	
Pat Ryan	1st in Group 1
1976 Manx Trophy	
Pat Ryan	1st in Group 1
1976 Lindisfarne	
Pat Ryan	1st in Group 1
1976 Castrol 76	
Pat Ryan	2nd in Group 1
1976 RAC	
Pat Ryan	Did not finish
1977 Tour of Dean	
Pat Ryan	Did not finish
1977 Mintex	
Pat Ryan	35th overall
1977 Circuit of Ireland	
Pat Ryan	Did not finish
1977 Welsh	
Pat Ryan	2nd in Group 1
1977 Scottish	
Pat Ryan	3rd in class, 12th overall

SOE 8M

FIRST REGISTERED	9 MAY 1974
ENGINE SIZE	1,998cc
MODEL TYPE	DOLOMITE SPRINT

Although this was a new car as far as the team was concerned, in fact it was already a year old. Registered in Birmingham in May 1974, SOE 8M was originally used by John Bloxham with support from Abingdon, but by no means was it a full-blown works car.

Now, in the complex way in which such things can sometimes pan out in motorsport, the year-old machine found its way back to Abingdon, where it was thoroughly refurbished, very possibly with a new bodyshell. In this way it became a new Group 2 works Dolomite Sprint, which, in the Master Plan, might have taken over from the hard-working FRW

When homologated and prepared for Group 2 motorsport, the body shell of a Dolomite Sprint had prominent wheel arch extensions to cover the wide wheels and rally tyres.

812L – but things did not work out like that.

In the early hours of the 44-stage Scottish International rally, Brian Culcheth found that SOE 8M was not as fast or as predictable as his old car. Early on he lost time when he collected two punctures in one stage and suffered a broken suspension Panhard rod soon afterwards. Halfway through the event, when in the Grampians and back up to eighth place, Brian then put the car off the road on the 30th stage in Kindrogan forest, seriously damaging the shell when the car landed upside-down on a tree stump and then rolled several times before coming to rest.

This, in fact, was the beginning and the end of this car's works career. Although it was eventually repaired, it never again appeared on an event – but the identity of the car survives to this day.

COMPETITION RECORD
1975 Scottish
Brian Culcheth   Did not finish

SOE 8M was used only once as a front-line works Dolomite Sprint – Brian Culcheth drove it in the 1975 Scottish rally but it was written off in an accident during the event.

By the mid-1970s, the specification of the works Dolomite Sprints had settled down, with major sponsorship from Unipart on display.

The works Group 2 Dolomite Sprints had flared wheel arches and the usual Minilite magnesium wheels with Dunlop tyres.

The 'office' of the Group 2 Dolomite Sprint in mid-1970s form.

This Group 2 works Dolomite Sprint features extra Lucas driving lamps, which were fitted with padded covers to provide protection from flying stones during daylight.

The boot is occupied by a larger-than-standard fuel tank, repositioned battery, and a fat spare wheel; note that the filler cap is tucked in the corner of the opening.

The co-driver of the works Dolomite Sprint was faced with a Halda Twinmaster, lots of switches and controls, and an extra 'panic' horn button.

Typical Abingdon detail on this Dolomite Sprint includes extra 'Land Rover-type' holding-down straps for the boot lid and reinforcement for the towing eye.

MYX 175P

FIRST REGISTERED	1 MAY 1976
ENGINE SIZE	1,998cc
MODEL TYPE	DOLOMITE SPRINT

MYX 175P took second place overall in the 1976 Tour of Britain, crewed by Brian Culcheth and Ray Hutton.

Although the works team had been planning for some time to retire FRW 812L, it was not until it had finally been paid off that the next new works Dolomite Sprint, the Group 1 MYX 175P, was ready for use.

The original plan was for the car to début on the Texaco-sponsored Tour of Britain in July 1976, but British Leyland International put up extra finance in advance and this persuaded the team to enter it in the Lucien Bianchi rally in Belgium, where Brian Culcheth was asked to drive. In fact this was a waste of time, for the new car suffered a cylinder head gasket failure and had to retire.

Then came the Tour of Britain, for which the Dolomite Sprint was ideally suited, and Brian's partner once again was *Autocar* editor Ray Hutton. This time the big battle was expected to be between the two works Dolomite Sprints of Culcheth and Tony Pond – no team orders! – and a fleet of works Ford Escort RS2000s. Two of the RS2000s disappeared at a very early stage, both with damaged transmissions, and Pond's RDU 983M soon blew its engine, leaving Culcheth to settle into a rally-long battle with Ari

Vatanen's RS2000. The Dolomite Sprint proved faster than Vatanen's RS2000 on many of the stages, but was slightly outpaced in the four circuit races – and Culcheth had minor setbacks along the way.

His car suffered from a jammed throttle linkage in the Silverstone race and he had to keep switching off the ignition when he needed to slow down! Soon afterwards he went off on a stage, bending the steering rack, which really required replacement but there was never enough time to achieve that. And in the final race, at Mallory Park, the engine began to overheat. In the end Vatanen emerged as the winner, but Brian was a mere 52 seconds behind in second place.

After a long rest, the refurbished and updated MYX 175P was in scintillating form for the Granite City rally in April

1977. Not only did Pat Ryan win Group 1 but he was also eighth overall, behind a selection of Ford Escort RS1800s and Vauxhall Chevette HSs – this was a very heartening comeback after the big accident he had suffered a little earlier in the Circuit of Ireland (see page 201). Two months later, however, the car retired after being pressed into service on the Jim Clark Rally to replace the aged RDU 983M. Although MYX 175P shone on the first tarmac stages of the event, it expired on the first forest stage when the engine lost its oil pressure and had to be switched off to avoid total mechanical annihilation.

Soon after, the works team at Abingdon announced that the Dolomite rally programme was coming to the end and that there would be no presence in 1978, so this left just two international events – the Manx and the RAC – on the calendar for the rest of 1977. Pat Ryan used MYX 175P for one of these events, the Manx, which was run entirely on tarmac special stages, with pace notes. He was tasked with winning Group 1 – and not to crash the car under any circumstances!

In a copybook performance, Ryan settled down and performed sensationally well, taking the Group 1 award yet again and finishing a stirring seventh overall too. But most of the headlines after this event were made by Brian Culcheth's performance in the works TR7 (see page 230) and his increasingly stormy relationship with team boss John Davenport.

Driving MYX 175P, Pat Ryan and Mike Nicholson won the Group 1 category of the Manx Trophy rally in 1977.

Brian Culcheth (top) and Ray Hutton (below) crewed the Group 1 Dolomite Sprints that tackled the Tour of Britain from 1974 to 1976.

COMPETITION RECORD	
1976 Lucien Bianchi	
Brian Culcheth	Did not finish
1976 Tour of Britain	
Brian Culcheth	2nd overall
1977 Granite City	
Pat Ryan	1st in Group 1
1977 Jim Clark	
Pat Ryan	Did not finish
1977 Manx Trophy	
Pat Ryan	1st in Group 1

DOLOMITE SPRINT: WHEN IS 'STANDARD' NOT STANDARD?

For many reasons – company policy and the car's weight in particular – the 16-valve Dolomite Sprint was not likely to become an outright rally winner, but eventually it became a formidable Group 1 rally car.

Even though, in theory, Group 1 in the 1970s meant 'standard', if a manufacturer could convince the authorities that 5,000 of a particular item of optional equipment had been manufactured, then this could also be homologated. This explains why the Dolomite Sprint had become so competitive by 1976, and why it became even more so from 1978 onwards.

The most convincing proof of this came when *Autosport* magazine arranged to borrow three cars that had so electrified the crowds on the 1976 Texaco Tour of Britain, one of them being MYX 175P, the Dolomite Sprint with which Brian Culcheth had taken a rousing second place overall. Tony Pond drove each of the cars – the other two were the winning Ford Escort RS2000 and a Vauxhall Magnum coupé – and provided his comments for the fascinating pictorial feature that followed in the issue of 22 July 1976.

Although it was evident that the Dolomite Sprint was faster in a straight line than the Ford Escort RS2000 that just shaded it on the event, Pond's main gripe about the Triumph was its lack of a 'quick' steering rack: 'The low gearing on the steering makes it hard work to hold, and pick-up accurately… it's the steering that really hinders your progress.'

Each works team also provided details, with prices, of the extra equipment that had been fitted to their cars to make them so fast. Triumph quoted the cost of 'blueprinting' an engine by Don Moore as £350, to which was added £110.25 for a homologated Group 1 engine kit with 2in SU carburettors and their associated manifolds, and £45 for an STR0139 camshaft 'to suit the induction kit'. In addition there was an exhaust system at £60, a close-ratio gearbox kit at £75 and a limited-slip differential at £147.50.

'Standard'? Don't be facetious…

RACING CARS

Except for entries of works rally cars in the race-cum-rally Tour of Britain between 1974 and 1976, most works – or 'works-supported' – racing Dolomite Sprints were prepared by Broadspeed, operating from their modern workshops on the Banbury Road, south of Southam. The two operations were kept entirely separate apart from the fact that Broadspeed cooperated closely with Abingdon on the subject of homologation and supplied engines and engine parts to Abingdon for the four-cylinder TR7 rally programme. Besides Broadspeed, three lesser teams – John Handley's RCD car, Rob Mason's Arden car and John Hine's Bill Shaw Racing – were also supported.

Andy Rouse, Broadspeed workshop manager and highly successful racing driver, recalls clearly that there was virtually no contact between the two operations – Southam and Abingdon – and that he and Ralph Broad did almost all the work on the racing cars in the 1970s. It must have been a frenetic time for them, as they also had to oversee the design, development and construction of the big Jaguar XJ5.3C racing cars during the same period.

Work at Broadspeed began in the late autumn of 1973 and the Dolomite Sprint was duly homologated on 1 January 1974. Plans were immediately laid, jointly by Leyland ST and Broadspeed, for two cars to contest the British Saloon Car Championship, which was to be limited to Group 1 cars for the first time. This was a major upheaval for the teams already involved, including Broadspeed, as the championship had been run for Group 2 cars from 1970 to 1973 and this compulsory 'detuning' meant that a great deal of new thinking was needed.

Frenetic workshop activity followed under Rouse's watchful eye. The Sprint might have had a most promising 16-valve engine, but it was handicapped by using small brakes and having an inherently high roll centre to the rear suspension, and neither shortcoming could be eliminated by inventive homologation until changes were approved for 1978. As well as managing the whole exercise, Rouse would also drive the lead car; the identity of the second driver, Tony Dron, was revealed only days before the first event, at Mallory Park in March 1974.

Thereafter, Broadspeed concentrated almost entirely on the British Saloon Car Championship, building new cars for the start of a season and generally selling them on at the end of a season, usually to overseas clients. Since Broadspeed had no spare cars in its fleet, a season without crashes was always desirable – and the company was very fortunate that this hope was usually delivered.

What follows is a year-by-year record of what the various Broadspeed cars achieved, not by individual car identities but by championship campaigns. Unlike all other aspects of the works Triumph story, it has not been possible to identify the individual cars involved. Not only did Broadspeed's records for these programmes get destroyed at some point (the business was dissolved at the end of the 1970s), but the racing cars themselves also never carried registration numbers or any other obvious distinguishing features.

What we do know, however, is that the racing cars were always disposed of by Broadspeed after a single season, and usually they were sold on to well-financed privateer teams or owners. For example, after the end of the 1974 racing season there were adverts in the specialist press offering both works Dolomite Sprints for sale at an asking price of £4,000 each. In view of the fact that the cars had been so successful, there was a rush to buy...

1974

When, in March 1974, British motor racing stuttered back into life following a winter-long ban imposed by the sporting authorities as a consequence of the energy crisis that had erupted in the autumn of 1973, Broadspeed was ready with two brand-new cars prepared for that season's British Saloon Car Championship. They were in quite a mild state of tune – the imposition of Group 1 regulations had seen to that – and it would be a couple of years before some aggressive homologation from Abingdon would be able to add further equipment and make the racing Dolomite Sprints into formidably fast little four-door saloons. Nevertheless, these two cars were well developed and it was claimed that Broadspeed's Andy Rouse had already completed 2,800 miles of testing before the start of a season in which Rouse and Tony Dron would be the team's drivers.

In a profile published in *Autosport* magazine, Ralph Broad's work on the Dolomites was carefully analysed. Among the detail improvements explained, Broad asserted that, 'with very, very careful blueprinting and making everything to absolute perfection, we managed to get 174bhp'. The rest of the enhancement came from persistent and dedicated work on the handling, which resulted in different

Two important personalities in the Dolomite Sprint racing team at Silverstone in 1974 – Ralph Broad (right) and Andy Rouse.

A very familiar sight in the 1970s: Andy Rouse, complete with garland, ready to take a lap of honour after winning his category yet again in the Dolomite Sprint during the 1974 British Saloon Car Championship.

Andy Rouse (left) and Tony Dron flank team boss Ralph Broad at the 1974 Spa 24 Hours, where their works Dolomite Sprint finished fifth overall.

rubber bushes being specified all round, and on the evolution of suitable tyres with Dunlop.

There were two basic problems with the Dolomite Sprint as a racing car. The first was that the brakes – front discs, rear drums – were not up to the job because they were not large enough, as Rouse recalls: 'We just had to drive round the problem by trying to scrub off speed going into a corner without setting the brakes on fire. We spent a lot of time working on brake materials, and I think we ended up using a pad material that had been used in military tanks!' The second problem was that the layout of the rear suspension gave a high roll centre that made the cars oversteer very readily – although this was a trait that Rouse and Dron seemed to quite enjoy.

The first meeting, at Mallory Park on a wet weekend early in March, featured two touring car races, the one involving the Dolomite Sprints being for cars under 2,500cc. Broadspeed was delighted to see both of its cars on the front row of the grid, Rouse's car having lapped in 1m 4.6s. In the 30-lap race Rouse took a lead that he never relinquished, while Dron held second for much of the distance despite a faulty overdrive switch that kept allowing the transmission to revert to direct drive. As a consequence, on the very last lap the engine blew up most emphatically, producing a smokescreen and strewing bits of itself all over the track.

Only a week later the championship moved to Brands Hatch for a 20-lap support race to the Formula 1 Race of Champions. This time there was one race for all capacities, from 1.3 litres to 5.7, and Rouse and Dron qualified fifth and sixth. In another wet race they were competitive but both hit problems: Rouse's problem was on the track, as his car started misfiring due to an alternator problem and he finished a lap down on the leaders; Dron, who experienced

RACING CAR OR RALLY CAR?

In mid-1974 Broadspeed prepared one new Dolomite Sprint for Tony Dron and Henry Liddon to use in the Tour of Britain (in compulsory Group 1 specification) and then converted it for Andy Rouse and Dron to drive in the Spa 24 Hours race (in 'Group 1¾' specification). A choice has had to be made! Was this originally a rally car turned racer, or a racer that masqueraded as a rally car on its first event?

For the sake of tidiness, and because Broadspeed did not build any other Dolomite Sprints for rallying, I have chosen to include this car in this 1974 racing section. When used in the Tour of Britain it carried the Coventry registration number OVC 304M and was sponsored by Henly's, the British Leyland dealership. As already noted in the section concerning Brian Culcheth's fortunes in the Tour of Britain with RDU 983M (see pages 198-199), this three-day event was an intriguing mixture of races and rally stages.

'I was stuffed on the Tour of Britain,' recalls Dron. 'All the other front-runners had trick Dunlops – but I could not obtain them. Our car was completed just 48 hours before the event and I tested it on Avon Wide Safety GT tyres, which were great on Escorts. The Sprint was astonishingly undriveable on them, so I was forced to run on Avon radials, which fell apart in the races. That's why I only finished fifth overall. If you looked at the stage results on their own, I was first overall!'

The use of 'road' tyres was compulsory, but some teams flirted with sporting illegality. Dron used the best tyres that the event sponsors, Avon, could provide and ended up as the highest-placed Avon-shod competitor, his fifth place being a mere 55 seconds behind Roger Clark's winning works Escort RS2000.

more overdrive problems, finished the race in seventh place, but his car was then disqualified after its ride height was found to be lower than the regulations allowed.

It was at least dry for the next race, at Silverstone in early April. The two works Dolomite Sprints won their 2-litre capacity class, but on this fast track they could not stay with the large-engined cars. Then came the busy Easter, with races at Oulton Park on Good Friday and Thruxton on Easter Monday.

Rouse qualified third on a drying track at Oulton Park and would have been well placed in the race if the car's overdrive had not refused to play, and the cylinder head gasket finally blew. Even with a new engine installed over the weekend, he could only qualify fifth at Thruxton and finish fourth in the

25-lap race, with yet another engine problem resulting in overheating. Dron's weekend was less adventurous, except in qualifying at Thruxton when he flew off the track after a front suspension ball joint snapped, causing an extensive rebuild of the front suspension to be done in time for him to start the race.

At Silverstone in May Rouse qualified eighth fastest but was beaten in the race by Barrie Williams' rotary-engined 2.3-litre Mazda RX3. A disappointing weekend was then compounded, weeks later, by the car's disqualification from the results on a technicality of engine homologation, but it was later reinstated.

Apart from skirmishes over the regulations, the Group 1 pattern of racing seemed to have settled down by the time the cars appeared at Thruxton on Whit Monday and at Brands Hatch in July for the British GP meeting. Rouse did really well in both 20-lap races, finishing third overall at Thruxton and fourth overall at Brands Hatch, and winning his class both times.

A week later Broadspeed sent two different works-supported cars to Belgium to contest the Spa 24 Hours race. This was run to what the media whimsically called 'Group 1¼' regulations, which allowed the Dolomite Sprints to race with twin dual-choke Weber carburettors. The 'official' Broadspeed entry, crewed by Rouse/Dron, was the car with which Brian Culcheth had just tackled the Tour of Britain (as explained in the panel on the previous page), while John Hine/Freddie Grainal were in the second entry.

In the race the cars fought a losing battle against the Alfa Romeo 2000 Coupés, which were virtually of Group 2 specification. The Triumphs, which could reach 146mph on the long Masta straight, soon began to suffer the familiar weakness of inadequate front disc brakes, but it did not become a huge problem because Spa, a super-fast circuit, had only one truly hard braking application per lap, for the La Source hairpin. Amazingly, both cars soldiered on throughout the 24 hours, their highly stressed engines running reliably, and the reward for Rouse/Dron was fifth place overall, despite their car suffering from a badly secured steering rack. Their 280 laps of the picturesque 8.76-mile course equated to an average speed of 102mph.

The next round of the championship, at Ingliston in Scotland, saw the field split into two 25-lap races because this tiny Scottish circuit could only accept 16 starters per event, so the works Dolomite Sprints competed in the race for cars up to 2,500cc. Rouse was on pole but suffered a tardy getaway and then had more of the familiar brake problems, in the end finishing third, well down on Tom Walkinshaw's winning Ford Escort RS2000.

It was a similar story at Brands Hatch at the end of August, but the big surprise was that John Hine, in another 'supported' works Dolomite Sprint run by Bill Shaw Racing, rushed off into the lead and won the 20-lap race outright.

Although the two Broadspeed cars qualified at Oulton Park with exactly the same lap time, they were sharing only tenth place – race-by-race performance varied quite widely during this championship although on this occasion a factor was the presence of four 5.7-litre Chevrolet Camaros. Rouse's race was irretrievably ruined when the throttle linkage became deranged at the very start, while Dron finished third in the 2.5-litre class.

Next came the RAC Tourist Trophy race at Silverstone, where the competing cars were faced with a 313-mile slog lasting well over three hours. With the big 5.7-litre Camaros setting the pace, Broadspeed's usual pair of Dolomite Sprints qualified in midfield, but the experience of their drivers was expected to be a big factor in this race.

It was not to be Andy Rouse's day. His car soon faltered with a split fuel tank, a long-range item that had been installed specially for this race in mind. The pit stop for it to

---

COMPETITION RECORD 1974

Mallory Park (2½-litre race)	Andy Rouse	1st overall
	Tony Dron	Did not finish
Brands Hatch	Andy Rouse	3rd in class
	Tony Dron	Disqualified
Silverstone	Andy Rouse	1st in class
	Tony Dron	2nd in class
Oulton Park	Andy Rouse	1st in class, 6th overall
	Tony Dron	2nd in class
Thruxton	Andy Rouse	1st in class, 4th overall
	Tony Dron	2nd in class, 6th overall
Silverstone	Andy Rouse	2nd in class
	Tony Dron	4th in class
Thruxton	Andy Rouse	1st in class, 3rd overall
	Tony Dron	3rd in class, 5th overall
Brands Hatch	Andy Rouse	1st in class, 4th overall
	Tony Dron	3rd in class
Spa, Belgium (24 Hours)	Andy Rouse/Tony Dron	5th overall
	John Hine/Freddie Grainal	9th overall
Ingliston (2½-litre race)	Andy Rouse	3rd overall
	Tony Dron	5th overall
Brands Hatch	Andy Rouse	3rd overalle
	Tony Dron	6th overall
Oulton Park	Tony Dron	3rd in class
	Andy Rouse	6th in class
Silverstone (Tourist Trophy)	Tony Dron	3rd overall, 1st in class
	Andy Rouse	Did not finish
Snetterton (2½-litre race)	Andy Rouse	1st overall
	Tony Dron	Did not finish
Brands Hatch	Tony Dron	5th overall
	Andy Rouse	15th overall

Castrol Anniversary British Saloon Car Championship: Rouse second overall (67 points to winner Bernard Unett's 69) and first in class.

be rectified took more than 30 minutes, putting Andy out of contention, but he rejoined the race. It was all to no avail, however, for a front disc brake had to be replaced and then the rear wheel studs broke too.

Dron, on the other hand, was driving like a man possessed, and was already up to sixth overall at one-fifth distance. Making just one routine pit stop to refuel the car, he carried on relentlessly, easing his Dolomite Sprint up to second place overall. It looked likely to stay that way, but five laps from the end one of the surviving Camaros passed the Triumph. Nevertheless, third place behind two Camaros was a superb result – no one could ask for more than that.

In October the two cars appeared at Snetterton, where the weather was foul and the track streamed with water. After the overdrive in Rouse's car stopped working on the warm-up lap owing to failure of the electrically actuated solenoid, the two drivers gained the stewards' approval to swap cars on the grid so that Rouse, with his championship advantage, had the better car. Andy led for all 20 laps of the 2.5-litre race, while Dron eventually fell out after his car picked up a slow puncture in one of the rear tyres.

The last race of the season, in wet weather at Brands Hatch in mid-October, developed into what was later called a 'demolition derby', for Rouse, who had been running with the leaders on the wet track, never recovered his pace after going off at Druids when trying to overtake Tom Walkinshaw's works Ford Capri, badly damaging the Dolomite Sprint's front suspension. Dron, on the other hand, kept out of trouble and finished fifth overall, beaten very narrowly in the 2.5-litre class by Barrie Williams' Wankel-engined Mazda RX3.

Although Broadspeed had usually been at the centre of any spirited discussion – and dissension – about the regulations in 1974, there was no doubt that the two team cars had performed remarkably well in a series dominated by massive Chevrolet Camaros. After the end of the year the cars were speedily sold off, so that new, better replacements could be prepared for 1975. And there really were only two cars: when I discussed this with Andy Rouse he grinned and suggested that he and Dron took good care not to damage either car severely!

1975

Nothing much seemed to change for the 1975 British Saloon Car Championship other than the sponsor's identity, Southern Organs taking over from Castrol. Incidentally, the owner of Southern Organs, Sydney Miller, disappeared in controversial circumstances towards the end of the year, owing much money to the RAC for undelivered sponsorship payments! As in 1974, the series visited all the established British circuits and big-engined Chevrolet Camaros dominated in terms of outright victories. The class structure, as before, provided a 2.5-litre category into which the Broad-

Andy Rouse won the British Saloon Car Championship of 1975 in this Broadspeed-prepared Dolomite Sprint. Sir Ronald Edwards, who was Chairman of British Leyland at the time, is seen posing proudly by it when it later went on exhibition.

speed Dolomite Sprints fitted neatly.

Broadspeed built two new cars and Andy Rouse continued to lead the programme as well as drive for the team, while Roger Bell, editor of *Motor* magazine, now drove the second car. The cars were supported by Piranha ignition and carried new sponsorship livery. Much testing work was done before the season started and it was claimed that the handling was much improved.

The first race of the year was held at a teeming wet Mallory Park in March, where the up-to-2,500cc cars had their own race. Broadspeed started as it hoped to continue throughout the year, with Rouse winning the race and team-mate Bell second. Rouse also dominated his class in the second race of the season, at the Race of Champions meeting at Brands Hatch, although Bell's car retired with an overdrive failure.

The next two races, back to back over the Easter weekend, saw Rouse dominate his class yet again, and at Thruxton he was actually second overall, behind Richard Lloyd's 7.4-litre Chevrolet Camaro; Bell delivered two more excellent back-up performances at these races. At Silverstone in the support race to the Formula 1 International Trophy, Rouse took sixth place behind five Camaros with Bell just a few seconds back in eighth place.

At the next race, at Brands Hatch, the field was again divided into two races for cars above and below 2.5 litres, and this time Rouse did not win, finishing a very close second to Barrie Williams' 2.3-litre Wankel-engined Mazda RX3. Onwards to the high-speed curves of Thruxton, and there

Rouse was fourth overall, beaten only by three Camaros. At Silverstone on Whit Monday the two works Dolomite Sprints totally dominated the 2.5-litre race, Rouse winning yet again and setting a new lap record for the short circuit, and three weeks later at Mallory Park he repeated the dose.

By this point in the season Andy was well ahead in the championship. It was against all the trends, therefore, that at Snetterton in June his Triumph lost all its oil pressure and had to be retired – but team-mate Roger kept going to win the class instead.

The big event of the year was the 20-lap support race at

THE TROPHÉE DE L'AVENIR CAR

In addition to its concentrated British Saloon Car Championship programme, towards the end of the summer Broadspeed also revealed its dedicated Trophée de l'Avenir Dolomite Sprint, which was all set to compete in the RAC Tourist Trophy race at Silverstone on 5 October. This 107-lap race was run to what were called Trophée de l'Avenir regulations, which were based on Group 1 but with further specific modifications allowed. Much of the engine could be modified or enhanced, brake freedoms included the use of ventilated discs and cooling air scoops, wider tyres along with wheel arch extensions were permitted, and aerodynamic spoilers could be fitted at front and rear.

By begging and pleading at British Leyland, Broadspeed gained approval to produce one such special car. Its 2-litre engine produced 235bhp at 7,750rpm, fuelled by two twin-choke 48 DCOE carburettors and fitted with a four-branch exhaust system. There was a close-ratio five-speed gearbox, the rear suspension included Panhard rod location, the front brakes had 10.3in discs, and 9.0J x 13in alloy wheels were used.

In the TT it was usual, but not obligatory, to have two drivers, but Andy Rouse – a very determined character – elected to do the whole race himself. He qualified the new car on the front row of the 36-car grid and once the race started he soon occupied fourth place, behind much more powerful cars. A clash with Vince Woodman's Camaro, however, saw him have to dive into the pits for repairs and a wheel change. His race was effectively over from that point and he finally retired.

Although the intention to develop this car for 1976 was sound at the time, it did not happen. And although Broadspeed developed a very competitive specification, this was never again used on works Dolomite Sprints.

Silverstone for the British GP and all the usual suspects were present, which meant that the works Dolomite Sprints really had no chance of beating the Camaros that started ahead of them. Rouse qualified on only the fourth row of the grid but soon settled into sixth place as the race progressed. Two of the larger cars later retired and Rouse ended up third overall, which was a remarkable performance. Bell struggled with a defective gearbox in the sister car but managed to finish second in class.

Rouse and Bell then took second and third places overall on the tight little circuit at Ingliston, beaten by just a single 5.7-litre Camaro. Then Andy went one place better at Brands Hatch on August Bank Holiday Monday – and was the championship leader again.

At Oulton Park in September, amazingly, only one Camaro finished ahead of Rouse in the 20-lap race, but so did Brian Muir in the Shellsport/Bill Shaw Dolomite – a car that had

---

COMPETITION RECORD 1975

Mallory Park (2½-litre race)	Andy Rouse	1st overall
	Roger Bell	2nd overall
Brands Hatch	Andy Rouse	1st in class, 3rd overall
	Roger Bell	Did not finish
Oulton Park (2½-litre race)	Andy Rouse	1st overall
	Roger Bell	Did not finish
Thruxton	Andy Rouse	1st in class, 2nd overall
	Roger Bell	3rd in class, 6th overall
Silverstone	Andy Rouse	1st in class, 6th overall
	Roger Bell	3rd in class
Brands Hatch (2½-litre race)	Andy Rouse	2nd in class, 2nd overall
	Roger Bell	4th in class, 4th overall
Thruxton	Andy Rouse	1st in class, 4th overall
	Roger Bell	Did not finish
Silverstone (2½-litre race)	Andy Rouse	1st overall
	Roger Bell	2nd overall
Mallory Park (2½-litre race)	Andy Rouse	1st overall
	Roger Bell	Did not finish
Snetterton	Roger Bell	1st in class, 8th overall
	Andy Rouse	Did not finish
Silverstone	Andy Rouse	1st in class, 3rd overall
	Roger Bell	2nd in class, 6th overall
Ingliston	Andy Rouse	1st in class, 2nd overall
	Roger Bell	2nd in class, 3rd overall
Brands Hatch (2½-litre race)	Andy Rouse	1st overall
	Roger Bell	3rd in class, 3rd overall
Oulton Park	Andy Rouse	2nd in class, 3rd overall
	Roger Bell	10th overall
Silverstone (Tourist Trophy)	Roger Bell/Jenny Birrell	4th in 2-litre class
Brands Hatch	Andy Rouse	1st in class, 4th overall
	Roger Bell	Did not finish

Southern Organs British Saloon Car Championship: Rouse first overall

looked very promising early in the season. Bell's car suffered brake problems, the Dolomite Sprint's familiar weakness, and flames actually emanated from the front brakes on the cooling-down lap after the finish!

For the 107-lap RAC Tourist Trophy race at Silverstone in October Roger Bell teamed up with Jenny Birrell in his usual BTCC machine, while Rouse drove the special new car described in the panel on the previous page. Bell and Birrell circulated bravely and strongly, but their car was less competitive in a race that allowed more technical freedoms – which their regular Group 1 Dolomite Sprint could not exploit. They were well inside the top ten before the refuelling stops began, but in the end they slipped back to fourth in class after the car's engine started to misfire horribly.

The last race of the season was held at Brands Hatch over 20 laps of the full grand prix circuit. Both Rouse and Bell qualified for the second row of the grid, but were matched for pace by Brian Muir in Bill Shaw's Shellsport Dolomite Sprint. As usual several Camaros contested the race lead while Rouse and Muir scrapped for fourth place and victory in their class until the very end. It was only through an audacious move on the final lap that Rouse passed Muir to win the class, giving him enough points to secure the drivers' championship outright.

In September 1975, even before the motor racing was all over, Broadspeed offered its entire 1975 équipe for sale, '...comprising of both Andy Rouse and Roger Bell's cars,

complete with all spares, including wheels, tyres, engines, gearboxes, axles, brakes, etc, etc. We invite reasonable offers...'. At the time it seemed surprising that the company should have a complete clear-out, but at this time Broadspeed had started work for Jaguar on the hugely complex XJ5.3C racing programme.

1976

After making public in September 1975 the intention to stop racing the Dolomite Sprint, within a matter of a few weeks Broadspeed was told by its British Leyland masters to reverse that policy and prepare brand-new cars for the 1976 British Saloon Car Championship, which was now sponsored by Keith Prowse. Andy Rouse, who still worked at Broadspeed in a car-preparation role, would be the team leader once again, with Steve Thompson now his team-mate.

The change of policy came about because the RAC, in its wisdom, decided for 1976 to limit the series to 3-litre engines, thus getting rid of all the Camaros, and also tweaked the class structure so that the Dolomite Sprints were now competing in the 2.3-litre capacity class. The Triumphs would now become genuine contenders for outright victories – and so it transpired. The Dolomite Sprints were so fast that there were rumours suggesting that they had well over 200bhp in 'Group 1½' form. But the cars were always likely to suffer from braking deficiencies as the front disc brakes were simply not large enough for the task.

At the opening round, a support race for the Formula 1 Race of Champions at Brands Hatch in March, Rouse duly put his car on pole and was in the leading group of Ford Capris from the start of the race. After 16 laps, however, his car suddenly left the road at Hawthorn's bend due to the throttle pedal breaking and becoming jammed under the brake pedal, but he managed to finish, fifth in class and ninth overall.

The two Dolomite Sprints then had no luck at all at Silverstone. Both cars destroyed their gearboxes during practice, and Rouse's also blew a head gasket. During the race Rouse spent the entire 20 laps scrapping for outright victory only for his car to run out of fuel on the last lap. Thompson's car also retired after its engine threw a connecting rod.

Things went better at Oulton Park on Good Friday when Rouse fought hard among the fleet of 3-litre Ford Capris to take fifth place overall and win his class, while Thompson backed him strongly to finish third in class. Three days later, at Thruxton on Easter Monday, Rouse started from the front row of the grid, led the race for eight laps, then retired with a broken camshaft follower, while Thompson took eighth overall and was second in the 2.3-litre class.

The next race took the series to Thruxton again, and again the Dolomite Sprints were very competitive. Rouse put his car on pole but Tom Walkinshaw's 3-litre Ford Capri got the better of him in the 22-lap race, beating him to the line by

COMPETITION RECORD 1976			
Brands Hatch		Andy Rouse	5th in class, 9th overall
		Steve Thompson	Did not finish
Silverstone		Andy Rouse	Did not finish
		Steve Thompson	Did not finish
Oulton Park		Andy Rouse	1st in class, 5th overall
		Steve Thompson	3rd in class, 7th overall
Thruxton		Andy Rouse	Did not finish
		Steve Thompson	2nd in class, 8th overall
Thruxton		Andy Rouse	1st in class, 2nd overall
		Steve Thompson	Did not finish
Silverstone		Andy Rouse	2nd in class, 4th overall
Brands Hatch		Andy Rouse	Did not finish
		Derek Bell	1st in class, 2nd overall
Mallory Park		Andy Rouse	2nd in class, 7th overall
		Geoff Lees	4th in class, 9th overall
Silverstone (Tourist Trophy)	Andy Rouse/Chris Craft/Derek Bell		6th in class, 14th overall
	Andy Rouse/Brian Muir/David Hobbs		Did not finish
Snetterton		Andy Rouse	1st in class, 2nd overall
Brands Hatch		Andy Rouse	2nd in class, 3rd overall

Keith Prowse British Saloon Car Championship: Rouse seventh overall (47 points to winner Bernard Unett's 90) and second in class

just one second. Thompson, on the other hand, crashed out – and at this point in the season decided not to continue.

At Silverstone on Whit Monday there was just a singleton works entry. Despite having complained pre-race of lack of power and brakes, Rouse scrapped throughout with Dave Brodie's Mazda RX3 over third place, the rotary-engined rival eventually taking the place by a whisker and winning the 2.3-litre class.

Broadspeed brought Derek Bell on board as Thompson's replacement and at the 20-lap race that supported the British GP at Brands Hatch this immediately paid off. Rouse and Bell both started the race up front, battling with the Capris and Gerry Marshall's Vauxhall Magnum coupé. While lying second overall, Rouse's car suddenly faltered with transmission problems and dropped out, leaving Bell to take over second place and win the capacity class.

At this point in the season the Dolomite Sprints were beginning to slip in the horsepower race against massed ranks of Capris as well as increasingly competitive class rivals in the form of a works Vauxhall Magnum (entered by Dealer Team Vauxhall) and Mazda RX3 (entered by Mazda Dealer Team). At Mallory Park, where Geoff Lees was recruited as the second works Triumph driver, Rouse could only take seventh overall with Lees ninth, respectively second and fourth in their class. Neither could quite match Gerry Marshall, who drove his Vauxhall so aggressively that a variety of misdemeanours – including nudging Rouse's car into a spin at the hairpin – earned him a reprimand from the stewards.

As in previous years, BL wanted to enter two Dolomite Sprints for the 500km RAC Tourist Trophy race, a round of the European Touring Car Championship for Group 2 cars. Taking advantage of Group 2 freedoms for this race, Broadspeed fitted the engines with twin dual-choke Weber carburettors, as on the works TR7 rally cars of the day, and power output was about 220bhp. Each car could have three drivers, and the entry list was most confusing in this respect. Broadspeed's principal interest at this race was the début of the works Jaguar XJ5.3C, with Derek Bell, David Hobbs and Andy Rouse the Broadspeed-prepared car's nominated drivers. That was all well and good, but Rouse's name was also down for both Dolomite Sprint entries, while Bell and Hobbs were each nominated in one of the Triumphs!

This all turned out to be a waste of time and resources as the Dolomite Sprints were unable to keep up with Group 2 Alfa Romeo and BMW class rivals in this long race, which lasted nearly four hours. The car driven by Rouse and Chris Craft car needed lengthy pit stops for brake pads to be changed and a broken gear lever to be repaired, but otherwise circulated steadily and finally ended up sixth in class and 14th overall, 13 laps behind the winning BMW 3.0CSL. The second Dolomite Sprint did not figure at all and dropped out with head-gasket failure.

One of the TT entries was then restored to its usual 'Group

1½' specification to compete at Snetterton. Rouse, who qualified seventh fastest, raced well in soaking wet conditions and finished second overall, behind Gordon Spice's 3-litre Capri.

The end-of-season Brands Hatch race in October was a 15-lapper run in damp conditions on the full-length grand prix circuit. Rouse started from the front row and grappled for the overall lead with three or four other cars until his car's overdrive began to slip in and out of engagement, but he still managed to finish third, not far adrift of Colin Vandervell's winning 3-litre Ford Capri and Gerry Marshall's class-winning Vauxhall in second place.

At the conclusion of the championship, therefore, Rouse ended up second in the 2.3-litre capacity class to Marshall and seventh overall. This was the end of Andy's superb three-year spell as a works Dolomite Sprint driver, but he remained with Broadspeed for another two years as the company's chief development engineer.

1977

For 1977 Broadspeed supported just a single Dolomite Sprint entry in the Tricentrol-sponsored British Saloon Car Championship and Tony Dron returned to the team to drive it. As before, the series required the car to be run in Group 1 form, although the RAC Motor Sport Association continued to allow various extra 'freedoms' in what was affectionately called 'Group 1½'. There were very useful improvements to the car, including the use of newly homologated twin dual-

Tony Dron in the 1977 Dolomite Sprint on his way to winning the 20-lap race at Oulton Park on Good Friday. By this time the 2-litre engine produced 210bhp.

This study is so typical of the works Dolomite Sprint, which tended to oversteer when pushed to the absolute limit, largely because of the high roll centre of the standard suspension.

choke Weber carburettors, helping the engine to deliver a claimed 210bhp. The Dolomite Sprint also acquired ventilated disc brakes – a desperately needed advance – and a special close-ratio version of the four-speed gearbox, without overdrive.

Broadspeed often brought two identical-looking cars to race meetings, and Dron would practise and qualify with either or both of them, then make his choice for the race at a

late stage. Since the cars did not carry registration numbers, it is now impossible to identify which was which. Even Dron recalls that the cars were, 'admirably similar, so much so that even I couldn't tell them apart'.

Dron's mission was not only to win in the 2.3-litre category, which it was confidently assumed he would be able to achieve, but also to aim for occasional outright wins over the 250bhp 3-litre Ford Capris that made up the main opposition.

In the first round at Silverstone Dron finished third overall. Then at Brands Hatch he took a stirring second place overall, just 4.5 seconds behind Colin Vandervell's Capri. And at Oulton Park on Good Friday he went one better to win outright, by just 0.2sec from Gordon Spice's Capri.

This was a very encouraging start to the season, especially as Broadspeed was heavily committed to running the Jaguar XJ 5.3C cars in the European Touring Car Championship and could not always spare a lot of time to support the Dolomite Sprint. But there was disappointment on Easter Monday at Thruxton, where Dron disputed the lead throughout, only to make a mistake when he saw the chequered flag prematurely. Instead of crossing the line at full speed on the final lap, he thought the race was already over and pulled into the pits, dropping to seventh place by the time he had re-emerged and completed one more lap.

At Silverstone at the end of May Gordon Spice took pole position with his BMW 530i in very wet conditions and Dron then equalled his time! For the race, which started on a damp track, team management insisted that an old set of intermediate tyres be used, but these proved to be the wrong choice. Although Tony managed to hold a slender lead for four laps, his slick-shod rivals then eased away as the racing line dried and eventually, with his tyres completely finished, he pulled into the pits to retire.

Three weeks later at Thruxton Dron not only put his Dolomite Sprint on pole but in the 20-lap race he also held off all but one of the Capris, ending up just 1.6 seconds behind Chris Craft's winning car.

This 'oh-so-near' season continued in July at newly opened Donington. In a rough, bumping-and-boring race, it was really no consolation for Tony that he once again totally dominated the 2.3-litre category and set fastest lap, for it was outright victories he was after. He finished second overall to Stuart Graham's 3-litre Capri, just 1.2 seconds behind.

The next outright victory, however, followed immediately, and to the joy of all concerned it came in front of huge crowds at Silverstone for the British GP. Still able to choose between two Dolomite Sprints, Dron achieved the most unusual feat of qualifying both of his cars in pole position, seeing off the closely matched 3-litre Capri fleet. In the 20-lap race he was never headed, although several Capris tried to attack his lead before their tyres overheated. After 36 minutes' racing he secured his second outright win of the season, finishing a comfortable 12 seconds ahead of Chris

COMPETITION RECORD 1977		
Silverstone	Tony Dron	1st in class, 3rd overall
Brands Hatch	Tony Dron	1st in class, 2nd overall
Oulton Park	Tony Dron	1st overall
Thruxton	Tony Dron	1st in class, 7th overall
Silverstone	Tony Dron	Did not finish
Thruxton	Tony Dron	1st in class, 2nd overall
Donington Park	Tony Dron	1st in class, 2nd overall
Silverstone	Tony Dron	1st overall
Donington Park	Tony Dron	1st overall
Brands Hatch	Tony Dron	1st overall
Thruxton	Tony Dron	1st overall
Brands Hatch	Tony Dron	2nd in class, 5th overall

Tricentrol British Saloon Car Championship: Dron second overall (48 points to winner Bernard Unett's 49) and first in class

Craft's Capri. It was an absolutely brilliant display.

Three weeks later the series returned to Donington and Dron delivered an astonishing repeat performance. Pre-race, Broadspeed did a mid-week test session during which Tony crashed one of the Dolomite Sprints so heavily that the car was destroyed and his right foot badly bruised. The cause was total brake failure because of a burst hydraulic seal. After much attention from the physiotherapist of nearby Nottingham Forest football club, he was able to make the race, despite finding it difficult to walk, and beat Craft's Capri by 2.6 seconds, setting a new saloon car lap record in the process!

Dron was now truly on a roll, although the injury troubled him for a good six weeks. At Brands Hatch at the end of August he once again put the Dolomite Sprint on pole, once again outpaced his rivals to the first corner, and once again won outright. He finished the 20-lap race 10.8 seconds ahead of Vandervell's 3-litre Capri and set fastest lap in the 2.3-litre category. None of his class competitors were even close.

It was the same story, but only by a whisker, at Thruxton. Dron qualified fastest, scrapped with several Capris throughout the 20-lap race, and hit the front on the last corner of the last lap. That made it four wins in a row, and no one, not even the cynical bosses at British Leyland, could possibly have asked for more.

The end of this scintillating season came in October at Brand Hatch, where Dron put the Dolomite Sprint on pole and battled with the Capris for much of the 20-lap race, although progressively hampered by team boss Ralph Broad's decision to over-rule him on tyre choice. He led the class convincingly at first but his car's handling deteriorated as the race progressed and he lost the class lead to Jeff Allam's Vauxhall Magnum at the last moment, ending up only fifth overall at the finish.

Although Dron was never in the hunt for the drivers' title – Bernard Unett in a 1.3-litre Chrysler Avenger won that for the third time in four years – he ended the season with the fantastic record of five outright victories and ten class wins.

1978

Once again British Leyland officially supported a single Broadspeed-prepared Dolomite Sprint for Tony Dron, who continued to have the use of two cars at most meetings. As before, the British Saloon Car Championship, again sponsored by Tricentrol, was run to 'Group 1½' regulations.

A surprise for this new season, however, was that there was an additional Hermetite-sponsored Dolomite Sprint entry for John Fitzpatrick. This car was also prepared by Broadspeed and, stated Hermetite, 'run in conjunction with Leyland Motorsport'. So it was that the Dron and Fitzpatrick cars were prepared alongside each other at Southam, by the same technician, and were identical to each other, their specifications being essentially unchanged from the previous season.

The progress of the second car was somewhat hampered by the fact that Fitzpatrick was sometimes absent at clashing European events, so it was also driven by Win Percy (twice) and Derek Bell (once), both of whom had impeccable racing credentials but limited Dolomite Sprint experience.

As ever, the competition had moved forward for this new season and in particular Ford had progressed from the Capri II to the four-headlamp Capri III, with homologated improvements that seemed to add a little pace – and there were so many Capris too! Even so, things started very well at Silverstone in March when Dron put his Dolomite Sprint on pole and led the race from start to finish on a streaming wet track, winning by a very comfortable 23 seconds. Fitzpatrick's car was not ready and did not appear.

Dron, however, was convinced that the Sprint had been 'out-homologated' by the Ford Capris, and that he would not win any more races unless conditions were abnormally wet. The fortunes of the Dolomite Sprints did indeed take a dip over Easter. On Good Friday at Oulton Park Dron again put his car on pole but was beaten in the race by no fewer than four Capris, while Fitzpatrick trailed him with second in the class and seventh overall. Three days later, at Thruxton, Dron again finished fifth behind four Capris, while Fitzpatrick retired after only two laps with smoke billowing from his car.

Five weeks later, on Whit Monday at Brands Hatch, the two Dolomite Sprints had to tackle appallingly wet conditions. Fitzpatrick in the Hermetite car led for some distance before being overhauled by Gordon Spice's Capri, but then the Dolomite Sprint slid off the road and out of the race.

The headline of this issue of Autosport *tells a story. Before the second Donington race of 1977 Tony Dron had a big crash at the track during a mid-week test, sustaining a badly bruised right foot. He took part in the race even though he could barely walk – and won it!*

The first round of the 1978 British Saloon Car Championship – Tony Dron led from start to finish in streaming wet conditions.

'I might have been leading at this point,' Tony Dron recalls, 'but this was the very first corner at Oulton Park in 1978 – after which the 3-litre Capris picked me off, one by one.'

That left Dron in second place and there he finished, 12 seconds adrift of Spice.

Dron was finding it increasingly difficult to keep up with the Capris, which not only had larger and more powerful engines but also seemed to be getting the better of the tyre battle. Although he qualified on the front row at Silverstone, he could not stay with the Capris in the race and then was further handicapped when the throttle stuck open at Woodcote. After throwing the Dolomite Sprint sideways to help slow it down, Dron had to drive 'on the ignition key' for the rest of the race, but managed to retain his class lead to the flag.

At Donington Park in June, Dron qualified fifth, 0.5sec slower than the leading Capri, and finished sixth, while the Hermetite car was unable to start the race after an engine problem in practice. Things were no more encouraging at Mallory Park, where Dron finished seventh, a second a lap slower that Gordon Spice's winning Capri, with the sister Dolomite Sprint eighth in the hands of Win Percy.

It was a similar story at Brands Hatch, in the British GP supporting race, where Dron could only qualify 11th, although he took sixth in the 20-lap race itself and, as ever, won the capacity class. Weeks later, the same scenario unfolded at Donington Park, where no fewer than six Capris led Dron across the line, although once again he won his class.

Things then went from bad to worse when the series returned to Brands Hatch, with Dron's car suffering a puncture and a broken throttle linkage, while the Hermetite car holed its water radiator after nudging another car. At Thruxton the two works Triumphs started the 20-lap race behind no fewer than eight Capris and both were involved in a panel-bending mêlée before the first corner, Fitzpatrick's Hermetite car getting so mangled that a pit stop was needed to secure the bodywork with gaffer tape.

Although the season had started quite well, the Broadspeed team could not wait for it to end by the time they arrived at Oulton Park for the last round. Driving the Hermetite car, Win Percy out-qualified Dron, but neither Dolomite Sprint shone in the race, Dron's car breaking a half-shaft and Percy's shedding a wheel-balance weight, which caused so much vibration that a pit stop was necessary.

Despite the numerous problems that hit his cars towards the end of the year, Dron still managed to win the Dolomite Sprint's category of the British Saloon Car Championship by a huge margin. It was a fitting way to bring the car's front-line racing career to a close as there was no further works Dolomite Sprint programme planned by the factory. The two 1978 Broadspeed cars were sold off to a team founded by Gerry Marshall, and supported by Triplex and Esso for use as private entries in 1979.

COMPETITION RECORD 1978

Silverstone	Tony Dron	1st overall
Oulton Park	Tony Dron	1st in class, 5th overall
	John Fitzpatrick	2nd in class, 9th overall
Thruxton	Tony Dron	1st in class, 5th overall
	John Fitzpatrick	Did not finish
Brands Hatch	Tony Dron	1st in class, 2nd overall
	John Fitzpatrick	Did not finish
Silverstone	Tony Dron	1st in class, 5th overall
	John Fitzpatrick	2nd in class, 6th overall
Donington Park	Tony Dron	1st in class, 6th overall
Mallory Park	Tony Dron	1st in class, 7th overall
	Win Percy	2nd in class, 8th overall
Brands Hatch	Tony Dron	1st in class, 6th overall
	Derek Bell	2nd in class, 7th overall
Donington Park	Tony Dron	1st in class, 7th overall
	John Fitzpatrick	2nd in class, 8th overall
Brands Hatch	Tony Dron	4th in class, 11th overall
	John Fitzpatrick	Did not finish
Thruxton	Tony Dron	3rd in class, 10th overall
	John Fitzpatrick	2nd in class, 9th overall
Oulton Park	Tony Dron	Did not finish
	Win Percy	4th in class, 10th overall

Tricentrol British Saloon Car Championship: Dron third overall (83 points to winner Richard Longman's 100) and first in class

CHAPTER 9:
TR7 AND TR7 V8 (1976–80)

The modest but successful rebirth of the Abingdon works team in 1973–74 finally persuaded British Leyland to commit to a more ambitious programme. Starting up again at Abingdon, initially under the control of ex-BL PR man Richard Seth-Smith and with the experienced Bill Price securely back on board, money was invested in a larger programme of rallying that was to centre around the still-secret TR7.

The often tortured birth, development and evolution of the TR7 – known as 'Bullet' by Triumph in its formative years – has often been told, so at this point it is only necessary to present the bare bones of what it was, why it was engineered in a particular way, and why it was originally intended to be built in a new factory at Speke, on Merseyside. As every Triumph enthusiast knows, there was absolutely no technical connection between the new 'Bullet' and the long-running TR6 that it would replace.

Back at the start of the decade, the ambitious plans of British Leyland centred on two major projects that were to be connected in many ways: one was the car that became the TR7; the other was a hatchback/saloon family of small-to-medium size coded 'SD2' (Specialist Division 2), which was intended to replace the Dolomite range. Central to this plan was that the cars would share much of the latest Triumph 'corporate' running gear, including derivatives of the Dolomite's overhead-camshaft 'slant four' engine along with a modernised range of MacPherson strut independent front suspensions, four- and five-speed gearboxes, and new rigid rear axles of 'light' or 'medium' duty depending on the engine to which they would be matched.

Both of these planned new models were to have their own individual pressed-steel unit-construction bodyshells, and that of the TR7 would be capable of evolving from a compact two-seater sports car into a longer-wheelbase 2+2 coupé derivative. The TR7 was originally engineered solely as a steel-roofed coupé because it seemed likely at that time that forthcoming legislation in the USA – the main market for the TR7 – would outlaw convertibles. In fact there was a protracted legal challenge to this intention and it finally succeeded, so the proposed legislation was never enacted. But by the time the decision was finally handed down it was too late for Triumph to change course: the coupé bodyshell was

already tooled up for production and it was judged to be too expensive to rush through a convertible alongside it.

After extensive research, including visits to the US by technical chief Spen King to meet various managers, opinion-formers and personalities, it was decided to use a well-located beam-axle rear suspension rather than the flawed semi-trailing-link independent system that had been found under the 2000s, 2.5 PIs and TR6s of earlier years.

There was one other important decision. Inspired by the way Ford of Europe was evolving its new Capri range, British Leyland wanted the fully developed TR7 to become progressively available with various engine options. All early production TR7s would have the eight-valve 2-litre 'slant four' engine, the 16-valve derivative – as used in the Dolomite Sprint – would be added later for the 'TR7 Sprint', and a 'TR8' version with Rover's 3.5-litre V8 would follow. The 'performance' engines would be matched to a sturdy new type of five-speed all-synchromesh gearbox.

Abingdon's favoured few within motorsport first saw the TR7 before it went into production in 1974/75 and began

The first famous victory for Tony Pond and the TR7 V8 came in June 1978 when SJW 540S, on its very first outing, won the 24 Hours of Ypres against the might of European competition, including well developed Lancia Stratos and Porsche 911 models.

This was 'the office' of the original four-cylinder works TR7s of 1976 and 1977 – these cars had right-hand drive.

testing an old development hack soon after that. As the new sports car was not scheduled to go on sale in Europe until 1976, however, there was no immediate rush to commit it to a rally programme.

Knowing that the team would only be allowed to work on the four-cylinder cars at first, Bill Price and Ron Elkins, the much-respected and resourceful 'homologation kings' at Abingdon, settled down to work out which was the best combination of TR7 permutations for the works team to use and somehow or other to get homologated. One needed to be expert – some would say inventive – at reading and interpreting FIA homologation regulations in order to produce an extremely good works TR7 rally specification from such unpromising beginnings, and rally enthusiasts should congratulate Price and Elkins for that.

Although the homologation papers were originally prepared in February 1975, when British Leyland planned to place the car in the FIA's Group 3 category and claim that the necessary 1,000 cars had been produced, homologation was not formalised until 1 October 1975, when the only TR7 road car on sale to the public – and at that time only in the USA – used the eight-valve 2-litre engine and a four-speed gearbox without overdrive. In the papers two sets of internal gearbox ratios were listed (the standard set and another with slightly different ratios and more robust internals) along with Borg Warner Type 65 automatic transmission, and two rear axle ratios (3.63 and 4.11) along with a 'heavy-duty' alternative that would shortly appear on some versions of the Rover SD1.

Besides all that, the first amendment sheet (numbered 1/1V) was appended on 1 October 1975 and listed a most audacious range of additional modifications and alternative equipment. Cleverly, British Leyland managed to get

approval in Group 4, for motorsport-intended TR7 derivatives, by listing a 16-valve Dolomite Sprint type of engine, a Dolomite Sprint type of gearbox (which had definite technical links with TR4 and 2.5 PI gearboxes) and a J-type overdrive. Also approved was a further alternative gearbox (the five-speed about to be used on several versions of the TR7), rear disc brakes and four additional rear axle ratios (3.08, 3.45, 3.89 and 4.55); three months later three more axle ratios (4.89, 5.14 and 5.29) were also approved. Other items were listed as optional equipment: the 'medium-duty' rear axle already in use on the Rover SD1, the SD1's five-speed gearbox (slated for early adoption in the TR7), and four-wheel disc brakes.

Everyone involved in rallying, including rivals in other teams, was impressed with what had been achieved in the homologation process. Every major homologated component, after all, already existed in the appropriate quantity in other models in the British Leyland range. Incidentally, there was a basic mistake in these papers that was not picked up by the authorities: although the 16-valve layout was accurately laid out – 'Inlet direct through bucket tappets, Exhaust indirect via rockers' – the number of valves per cylinder was given as '2' rather than '4'!

Although BL Motorsport was very serious about making a good rally car out of the unpromising TR7, the initial publicity hype surrounding the programme was ludicrous, with everyone expected to believe that the car would hit the ground running and immediately start beating the all-conquering 16-valve MkII Ford Escorts.

The reality was very different. Bill Price wrote the following recollections of sampling a pre-production prototype: 'The car seemed far from ideal in many areas, with similar rear axle location to the [Dolomite] Sprint, a short wheelbase, a single OHC engine, and it was rather heavy. The wedge shape, with the possibility of homologating the right parts, plus the knowledge that a vee-8 engine was coming, made this model about the only one which had a chance of being developed for rallying...'

As almost every aspect of the TR7 was new to motorsport, help had to be drawn from every possible quarter. The original Group 4 16-valve engine and overdrive transmission, for example, benefited from expertise already gained by Broadspeed's Dolomite Sprint racing cars (see Chapter 8) and Don Moore's rallying engines. Much of the lightening work, however, had to come from Abingdon's own experience and memory banks, together with the engineering and installation of the safety roll cage.

Inevitably there were delays and significant hold-ups came from the Triumph factory itself, with supplies of the close-ratio gears for the five-speed gearbox and the promised heavier-duty rear axle taking ages to arrive. Two brand-new 16-valve cars – KDU 497N and KDU 498N – were prepared just as soon as components could be acquired, but early-season entries in British events had to be cancelled and in the end the first public appearance of the works TR7s was on the International Welsh rally, where the drivers were Brian Culcheth and Tony Pond – but neither managed to get to the finish of the event.

The first car, in fact, did not run until March 1976, and at the time was still running with the standard road-car type of rear suspension, which featured trailing and semi-trailing radius arms, but no Panhard rod of any type. A Panhard rod layout was tested by mid-summer and standardised later in the year: it is significant that the first consistently successful performances followed this change, which improved traction and made the TR7's handling more predictable.

The first finish was achieved on the Burmah rally in August, and the first podium finishes quickly followed in September and October, with Pond third in both the all-tarmac Manx and the gravel-stage Castrol 76 rally in mid-Wales a few weeks later. Then came the first victory, in a relatively minor event, the Raylor, which used the fast forestry stages of Yorkshire.

As the school reports might have said, the team and the cars 'could do better'. And, indeed, they did do better in 1977. They also found themselves coping with a much-expanded and more ambitious operation after the arrival of John Davenport as director of motorsport. A former rally co-driver with much international experience, Davenport was a forceful character who rapidly introduced a more functional, less happy-go-lucky atmosphere into the rally programme. One of his main aims in 1977 was to steer the existing four-cylinder TR7s towards participation in European rallies as well as British ones, with Brian Culcheth and Tony Pond the team's drivers on all occasions. In the end the 1977 programme included six European events, where the TR7's pace on tarmac stages promised to make up for some of the problems it had faced in British forests in 1976.

To quote Peter Newton, writing in his 'Special Stage' column in *Autosport*: 'Foreign events such as these have obviously been chosen for a number of logical reasons. First one must presume that a large proportion of the competition budget is coming from Leyland International this year: thus rallies have been chosen not necessarily because of their Championship status but with their promotability and marketing possibilities in mind. Secondly, the above events allow a "breathing space" to develop the great potential of their new rally car out of the public spotlight [a clear reference to the secret TR7 V8]. Thirdly, these continental events nearly all involve pace notes and practising, a preamble which few British teams ever master. It must be clear to observers that Leyland's plans involve logical progression in the years to come, and such a progression eventually means World Championship rounds.'

Although now at the zenith of their development, the four-cylinder TR7s had finally gained useful supplies of the robust

five-speed gearbox and the stronger rear axle, and they were using all-round disc brakes and engines with strengthened cylinder blocks, with engine tuning mainly by Don Moore. Yet the cars were still not as fast as the Ford Escort RS1800s and Vauxhall Chevette HSs with which they had to compete on a regular basis.

There was one very welcome outright victory during 1977 when Tony Pond's ageing car, KDU 497N, won the Belgian Boucles de Spa in February, and various second and third places were also achieved. But the team became increasingly focused on the V8-engined TR7, which would take over completely in 1978. During the year David Wood joined the team as engineering manager and he would concentrate on engine work, especially with V8s.

This was also the season in which the team's relations with the British motoring media reached a new low: British Leyland habitually reacted badly to criticism, even though it was mainly justified, and Davenport made a number of lasting enemies in the media. Furthermore, the team's drivers did not get on well with their own management, and this played a significant part in the departures of Culcheth at the end of 1977 and Pond at the end of 1978.

Meanwhile, testing of the first V8-engined car finally began in August 1977, when the hard-working but reclusive KDU

Tony Pond was the first team driver who really mastered the handling and character of the TR7 rally car.

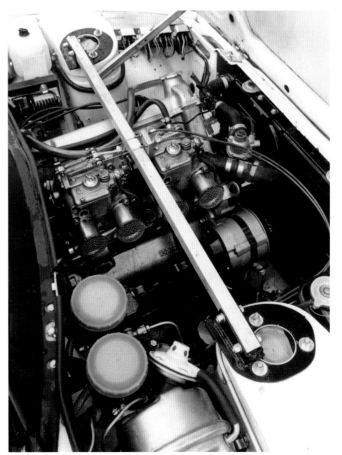

Fred Gallagher was the most successful of the co-drivers to guide TR7s and TR7 V8s in the 1976–80 period.

The four-cylinder TR7 used a much-tuned version of the 2-litre 16-valve Dolomite Sprint power unit, fed by twin dual-choke Weber carburettors. Peak power was approximately 220bhp. A structural brace ran above the engine, connecting the front suspension towers.

496N was re-engined and then put through its first shake-down testing at Cadwell Park. The car would be homologated as a 'TR7 V8' because the TR8 production car had yet to go on sale. To minimise engine development delays, the first engine installation in KDU 496N featured Offenhauser/Warneford inlet manifolds, twin-choke Weber carburettors and Janspeed-made exhaust manifolds and downpipe systems. Much work concentrated on developing what was called the 'mid-range axle', as used on the Rover 3500 road car, and in gaining reliability.

Work continued during the winter of 1977/78 and more progress was made when a second new V8-engined car joined the programme – although KDU 496N later suffered serious damage when it was rolled in testing. All development work on the four-cylinder cars had ceased by this time, with the team becoming impatient for the V8-engined car to be homologated.

TR7 V8: HOMOLOGATION AT LAST

After two full years of rumours, counter-rumours and denials, the works team finally unveiled its TR7 V8, and had it homologated in Group 4 on 1 April 1978. Before beginning to outline the developments that followed over the next three years, it is worth analysing that homologation in some depth, as the details were complex. Or might 'confusing' be a better word? On purpose or by accident? Let us just say that technical manager Ron Elkins skilfully massaged every allowance and assumption that FIA and RAC motorsport officials

Early works rally versions of the TR7 V8 used engines fuelled by two dual-choke Weber carburettors.

would allow...

Right from the start, there was the marketing department's insistence that the rally car should always be called a TR7 V8, for the TR8 had not yet been launched. One Group 4 requirement – that 400 cars should have been built – had demonstrably not been met and this was glossed over, BL pointing out, rightly, that the first production run of the new car, called the TR8 (not the TR7 V8), had been held up by a winter-long strike at the Halewood factory. Additional confusion was caused because Group 4 homologation came under FIA Recognition number 654, and that form described the cars as 'TR8'...

Then there was the question of the engine size. As fitted to all Rover SD1 saloons and all Range Rovers up to this point, the size of the V8 was universally quoted as 3,528cc. But for the TR7 V8 the engine size was stated to be 3,492cc by the simple means of under-quoting the cylinder bore as 88.4mm rather than its actual 88.9mm. The same stratagem, incidentally, was carried out on the Rover SD1s that competed in the British Saloon Car Championship and the European Touring Car Championship.

The choice of transmissions, too, was a masterpiece of options, at least on paper. There were two sets of Rover-Triumph SD1-type five-speed ratios (conventional and close-ratio), provision for overdrive 'on third and fourth' gears, a Borg Warner automatic gearbox, and another four-speed close-ratio gearbox that has now been identified as that of the MGB GT V8, although no surviving member of the team recalls that it was ever used in a works car. No fewer than 18 different final drive ratios were listed, ranging from 2.99:1 to 6.17:1, although only three – 5.3:1, 4.8:1 or 4.5:1 – eventually came to be used for real, the choice depending on the event, the nature of the stages and sometimes driver preference.

There was continual work on engine development: the immediate target for the V8 engine was a torquey 300bhp, and when a fuel-injection installation was eventually finalised there were hopes of more. Why was so much power needed? At the time the two main targets were the Ford Escort RS1800, whose engine produced 240–250bhp in a significantly lighter and more driver-friendly car, and the Ferrari-engined Lancia Stratos with a claimed 290bhp.

In 1978 and 1979, however, the problems were more personal than technical. It was evident that John Davenport's management was sometimes abrasive and that he often ignored, or subverted, information fed to him by his workforce. As the 1978 season progressed it was clear that the team's star driver, Tony Pond, was becoming increasingly disillusioned with the cars, the team and the management. His contract with BL allowed him to drive other makes of car and by mid-summer he was doing just that, notably with the Chrysler Sunbeam-Lotus development project, and his defection, confirmed in October, came after the RAC rally.

Davenport's problems were manifold for the 1979 season.

Not only did he have to oversee the further development of the TR7 V8 so that it became much more reliable and driver-friendly, but he also had to recruit new drivers and restore the morale within the ranks that had slumped so much since his arrival. To his great credit, Davenport picked his new drivers very carefully.

His choice of a British rising star was Graham Elsmore, the 27-year-old from the Forest of Dean who had harboured ambitions to get an offer from Ford but had been disappointed because that company's cupboard of drivers was already overfull. Davenport then got the approval of his paymasters to enter the TR7 V8s in a number of European events, which explained why he then signed up Per Eklund of Sweden and Simo Lampinen of Finland, with Frenchman Jean-Luc Thérier also driving on occasion – all of these drivers had winning records with other teams.

Elsmore took longer to settle in with the TR7 V8 than he had hoped, so from mid-season the works team took the brave decision to loan one of its works cars, OOM 514R, for him to drive on lesser events, mostly rounds of the Castrol-*Autosport* National Championship – a series that was a rung below the RAC series and did not admit overseas drivers.

This new line-up was always going to be a controversial choice, and when event followed event without any more success than in 1978, criticism grew: there was a dispiriting number of retirements caused by engine failures and the season brought no victories at international level. It did not help that the general reputation of BL, as British Leyland's combative little chairman Sir Michael Edwardes insisted that it should now be called, was declining in this period.

During 1979 the TR7 V8s suffered a variety of reliability problems, not least to the engines, which were still by no means as dependable as rival units, such as Ford's ubiquitous BDA, and encountered lubrication problems with the scavenge pump circuitry. Even so, development work continued, not least in the intention to use fuel injection instead of twin-choke Weber carburettors. Following consultations with Lucas and Pierburg, the German concern, which was already supplying injection equipment to several manufacturers in its home market, started development work at its own premises.

By mid-summer Pierburg was ready for a fuel-injected TR7 V8 to be given its rallying début, with the power output said to be 320bhp, allied to more mid-range torque and better fuel economy. One such car, Eklund's, was so equipped for the 1000 Lakes in August, but the outing was not a success and the injected car would only be seen once more that year, on the RAC rally. Development continued into 1980 but unsolved problems persisted through the year, and even at the end of the programme these had not all been eliminated.

At the end of a 1979 season that was best described as 'troubled', there was an almost total clear-out of drivers and a realignment of the programme for 1980. Although Eklund remained on board, Lampinen retired completely from

The second version of the works TR7 V8 engine included the use of Pierburg fuel injection, which was troublesome at first but finally delivered a reliable 320bhp. This view shows an early test installation.

Towards the end of its life the TR7 V8 rally car sometimes used four Weber carburettors; Janspeed did much of the original engineering work on this very neat and effective kit.

John Buffum was the most successful TR7/TR8 driver in North America in cars that he prepared himself.

Per Eklund was already a renowned rally driver when he was signed by the works team to grapple with TR7 V8s in 1979 and 1980.

David Richards rose to rallying fame in the 1970s, notably with Tony Pond in TR7 V8s, before going on to found Prodrive and other businesses.

Roger Clark drove a works TR7 V8 throughout the 1980 British rally season. As Roger's business had just acquired a British Leyland dealership, his signing was all the more logical.

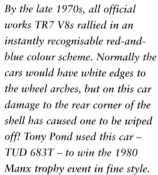

By the late 1970s, all official works TR7 V8s rallied in an instantly recognisable red-and-blue colour scheme. Normally the cars would have white edges to the wheel arches, but on this car damage to the rear corner of the shell has caused one to be wiped off! Tony Pond used this car – TUD 683T – to win the 1980 Manx trophy event in fine style.

competitive driving and Elsmore was released, while no place could be found for Terry Kaby.

There were, however, two sensational signings. Tony Pond returned to the team only one season after he had left to join the Talbot Sunbeam-Lotus works team, while Roger Clark, released by Ford after its temporary cessation of motorsport, joined British Leyland for an ambitious programme of British events. Roger's signing was not made public until late in January 1980, when it was made clear that his business had just acquired a British Leyland dealership in Leicester – so he was happy to have all the publicity connected with a change of motorsport allegiance.

Technically, the TR7 V8 was only gradually improved during 1980, which would prove to be its final works season in rallying. With development work on the Pierburg fuel injection system proving troublesome, Bill Price somehow gained approval to persuade Salisbury-based Janspeed to develop yet another version of the big V8 engine, this having

no fewer than four horizontally mounted Weber twin-choke carburettors. This was an installation that seemed to work well almost from the start of development, and it was soon applied to works cars.

Nevertheless, it was the engines that gave the most trouble in this final season for the works TR7 V8s. In the first half of the season, for instance, no fewer than eight retirements were forced by engine or engine-related maladies. The fact that the TR7 V8 was probably the fastest British rally car in a straight line was no consolation.

One interesting development, however, was the team's gradual realisation that Dunlop tyres were not the most suitable for all events and all conditions. After a great deal of testing of other makes, including Pirelli, the team concluded that Michelin tyres were better for some surfaces, so Dunlop or Michelin were used as judged appropriate to the event concerned. By the end of 1980, in fact, Michelin had become the favoured brand, and some estimates put the advantage provided by the French company's tyres at three seconds a mile on loose surfaces.

By the autumn of 1980 the team's future in motorsport was increasingly in doubt, with the TR7 V8 programme looking more and more vulnerable. Production of MGBs at Abingdon came to a halt in October and corporate preparations were immediately made to sell off the entire factory site – within weeks the existing competitions department was the only building still active.

Finally, after yet another frustrating outing for the TR7 V8s on the RAC rally of 1980, the parent company put out a statement. The TR7 V8 programme was abruptly cancelled, in favour, it was suggested, of new Mini Metros and Rover 3500s. Triumph's participation in works motorsport finally came to an end.

KDU 496N

FIRST REGISTERED	UNKNOWN
ENGINE SIZE	1,998cc/3,528cc
MODEL TYPE	TR7, THEN TR7 V8

Although Abingdon built up three rally-prepared four-cylinder TR7s in 1975/76, one of them – KDU 496N – did not appear in public or compete in any events. Instead it had a very valuable career in testing and development. In particular, it became the very first of the V8-engined rally test cars at Abingdon, carrying out these duties in 1977 and 1978, at one point suffering a badly damaged bodyshell after a roll.

This car's specification at first paralleled that of the other sister cars – KDU 497N and KDU 498N – before it became the true predecessor of all the TR7 V8s that followed from 1978 onwards.

COMPETITION RECORD
None: this car was used only for testing and development.

KDU 497N

FIRST REGISTERED	UNKNOWN
ENGINE SIZE	1,998cc/3,528cc
MODEL TYPE	TR7, THEN TR7 V8

Well before the works Triumph TR7s were unveiled, Richard Seth-Smith and Bill Price at Abingdon had thought long and hard about how to wring the most out of the four-cylinder cars for what they hoped would be a limited period of rallying before the V8 version came along. As already described in the preamble to this chapter, this did not happen as quickly as was originally expected, which may explain why the specification of the four-cylinder cars did not advance as far and as fast as some had originally envisaged.

Pushing the bounds of homologation regulations to their very limit, Seth-Smith and Price specified a works rally car that bore only a passing relationship to the production TR7s of the time. The words 'chalk' and 'cheese' spring to mind: the production car's key features were an eight-valve engine of 105bhp with a four-speed gearbox; the works rally car had

It was not until the 1960s that competition cars came to have notable registration numbers, but during the 1970s many such identities were rendered meaningless by constant 'cloning' through renewal of bodyshells and interchanging of other major assemblies.

Ford was particularly adept at this process, but British Leyland was by no means blameless. This is how BL's director of motorsport John Davenport, when asked about the works fleet, muddied the waters in an *Autosport* interview during the early weeks of 1979.

'I think the thing to realise is that, like Ford or Chrysler or any other team, we don't really look upon them as complete cars. For instance, the axles are checked back into the stores when they are taken out of the car, and then it's the stores that deal with the servicing of the axle: currently, that's done by Salisbury.

'Therefore, if you ask me how many complete cars we have got, I will have to go out into the workshop and count. To us a shell or a body is just one component that goes to make up a rally car. It just so happens that, because of the way cars are registered in this country, a particular body may have a particular number on it at the time...'

Make of that what you will...

a 16-valve engine of 220bhp with an overdrive version of the four-speed gearbox.

Because of the unsatisfactory state of evolution at nationalised British Leyland, it took much longer to get TR7s ready to go rallying than had been hoped. Originally planned to happen at the start of 1976, the launch date was put back and this first car, KDU 497N, did not run until 4 March 1976. As originally built, the 2-litre engines of this first batch of cars featured two twin-choke Weber 45 DCOE carburettors and produced 220bhp.

Although it was always intended that the works TR7s

The first of the official works TR7s started testing in March 1976. Along with KDU 498N, this was one of the hardest-working TR7s that year.

would use five-speed SD1-type gearboxes, these were not ready in time and instead the Dolomite Sprint package – a four-speed gearbox with overdrive – was adopted. Similarly, front disc/rear drum braking was used in the beginning, although the plan had been to fit discs all round. Excessive weight looked to be a potential shortcoming, but the team was pleasantly surprised by the strength of the standard coupé bodyshell.

There was PR bombast at the press preview for the two new works rally cars, KDU 497N and KDU 498N, and they made their début on the Welsh rally with great optimism. The team's performance on the Welsh, however, was a fiasco. Brian Culcheth completed only one special stage in KDU 497N before its engine's cylinder head gasket failed, putting him into instant retirement; this unit had been prepared by Don Moore, whose previous engine-preparation record had been excellent.

It was a similar story on the Scottish rally, where the car nearly expired on the first day, with the car's engine misfiring and issuing plumes of oil smoke on the Forest of Stages. This malaise should have been terminal but the team decided to use the rest of the rally as a testing session. After the restart of the rally following its first overnight halt at Ayr, the team, contrary to all the rules, fitted a new engine that had been whistled up from Abingdon by van and accomplished the task in only one hour and 20 minutes. Not that this helped. After completing the Rest And Be Thankful stage, the TR7

was flat out over the 'yumps' of the next stage, at Glenkinglas, when the newly installed engine blew up in the biggest possible way, bits of it exploding out under the bottom of the car! The team was totally humiliated by this episode and press reaction was extremely negative.

Much development work was carried out during July on the two works TR7s. The rear suspension geometry was completely revised, now having a five-link set-up of two parallel radius arms and a transversely positioned Panhard rod to locate the axle – as on a Group 2 Escort! As supplies of the close-ratio five-speed gearbox had finally become available, the four-speed-plus-overdrive installation was abandoned on this car. Engine-wise, the contract for preparation passed from Broadspeed to Don Moore, whose engines would prove to be more reliable and durable.

Under strict instructions to finish the Burmah rally at almost any cost, and never mind the pace, Culcheth drove steadily by his high standards and finally managed to record 15th place overall; he even found time to stop on the first stage to see if he could drag team-mate Tony Pond back on to the track! Six months after it first turned a wheel, this was the first time a works TR7 finished a rally.

The team's luck, surely, would have to change soon, and on the Isle of Man, in the Manx Trophy rally, it duly did. All the hard work that had been put in to making the TR7 an excellent tarmac rally car finally paid off as the cars took third and fifth places – although various observers pointed out that they were still too heavy and not as powerful as the benchmark Ford Escort RS1800s.

Driving KDU 497N, Culcheth, who had practised assiduously, matched team-mate Tony Pond's times throughout the event and bought his TR7 home in fifth place. On one stage the car suffered a broken engine mounting that also deranged the throttle linkage, so he had to complete the stage by driving 'on the ignition switch'! In the end Culcheth finished only 31 seconds behind Pond's sister car and missed out on fourth place by just a single second from Brian Nelson's Porsche 911 Carrera.

There was no such luck, however, on the Lindisfarne rally that followed. The TR7's engine suffered persistent cutting out, and at one point this distracted Culcheth so much that he put the car off down a firebreak, well and truly putting him out of contention.

Both works TR7s were then thoroughly revised for the 'pre-RAC-rally test' otherwise known as the Castrol 76 rally, held in mid-Wales. For this event the engines were fitted with 'Don Moore' camshafts as opposed to 'Broadspeed' ones, the result being a lot more mid-range torque but 4bhp less at peak. But the wait for a 'quick' steering rack and rear disc brakes continued. In the end Culcheth managed eighth overall even though he suffered a puncture on one stage and an off-course diversion on another.

As with KDU 498N, there now came a winter's rest, as

Big crowds watch Brian Culcheth in KDU 497N on his way to eighth overall in the Castrol 76 rally.

brand-new cars were used on the RAC rally, which ended the 1976 season.

For its first appearance of 1977, the Tour of Elba, KDU 497N received a new bodyshell and a four-wheel disc-brake installation, but the engine was still pegged at 220bhp. This was not a happy event for the car, its troubles including broken rear wheel studs and the loss of first gear in the five-speed gearbox, which was eventually changed. With rear axle dramas also sorted out, Culcheth achieved some good stage times – including a second fastest and two third fastest – that put him on course to finish among the top five or six, but then a minor component in the Weber carburettor throttle linkage snapped, causing him to run out of time.

This ageing car then had a torrid week on the Scottish rally, with all manner of problems that included no fewer than 11 punctures in the Dunlop tyres. Culcheth could not record more than an occasional fast time on the leader board and ended up ninth overall, 13 minutes 30 seconds behind Pond's sister car. It was probably around now that Culcheth concluded that his long association with the British Leyland team was coming towards an unhappy end...

That impression must have been reinforced when this dear old car, now creaking at the seams, was sent to contest the Mille Pistes rally in the south of France. Although the stages were notoriously rough and not at all suitable for low-slung sports cars, Culcheth, the seasoned 'pro', kept the four-cylinder TR7 away from the worst of the rocks but it still ended up with substantial underbody and suspension damage, the worst problem being a rear shock absorber that broke and flailed about, rupturing the fuel tank. Fourth overall was Brian's reward for sheer gritty determination while troubled, he said, by 'a bad back'.

To Culcheth's amazement and disgust, this now very tired and tatty car put in an appearance on the all-tarmac Tour de Corse. Throughout the 13-stage event the car suffered severe clutch problems, but somehow the mechanically sympathetic Culcheth kept it going and managed to finish in a remarkable 11th place. By this time Brian knew that his contract with the works team would not be renewed and he sensed that the team did not seem to be totally behind him any more...

That was the end of KDU 497N as a four-cylinder TR7, but it was then reincarnated as a TR7 V8, complete with a new bodyshell, for the following season; budget restrictions precluded the build of new cars in big numbers at that time. The car resurfaced in September 1978 on the Ulster rally in the hands of Derek Boyd and co-driver Fred Gallagher. Looking and sounding in great shape throughout the event, it led from the start and remained quite unassailable until stage 26, only a handful of stages from the finish, when the engine suddenly snapped a rocker shaft, which deranged the valve gear and brought the car to a halt.

That was the first of four occasions in 1978 that KDU 497N would start but not finish, and second time out, on the

Brian Culcheth struggled to get KDU 497N to the finish of the 1977 Tour de Corse and finally came in 11th overall. This was the final appearance of this car in four-cylinder form: in 1978 it would be reborn as a TR7 V8.

COMPETITION RECORD	
1976 Welsh	
Brian Culcheth	Did not finish
1976 Scottish	
Brian Culcheth	Did not finish
1976 Burmah	
Brian Culcheth	15th overall
1976 Manx Trophy	
Brian Culcheth	5th overall
1976 Lindisfarne	
Brian Culcheth	Did not finish
1976 Castrol 76	
Brian Culcheth	8th overall
1977 Tour of Elba	
Brian Culcheth	Did not finish
1977 Scottish	
Brian Culcheth	9th overall
1977 Mille Pistes	
Brian Culcheth	4th overall
1977 Tour de Corse	
Brian Culcheth	11th overall
1978 Ulster[1]	
Derek Boyd	Did not finish
1978 Manx Trophy	
Derek Boyd	Did not finish
1978 Cork	
Derek Boyd	Did not finish
1978 Hitachi Rallysprint	
Derek Boyd	Not classified

[1] *First event as a newly shelled TR7 V8.*

Manx, was no luckier. With his car set up to handle just like Pond's sister TR7 V8, which would go on to win the Isle of Man event, Boyd started well but on only the second special stage, Brandywell, the engine's oil pump drive belt jumped off, all engine oil pressure was lost and early retirement was inevitable.

Nor did Boyd fare any better in September on the Cork 20

rally, where his car's gearbox seized while he was lying second. The very last event, in November, was the Hitachi Rallysprint in Northern Ireland. Again Boyd failed to finish because of various breakdowns, including a defective battery master switch and the failure of an HT lead.

In many ways the works team was glad to see the back of a car that had not been a successful one.

KDU 498N

FIRST REGISTERED	UNKNOWN
ENGINE SIZE	1,998cc/3,528cc
MODEL TYPE	TR7, THEN TR7 V8

Finished only two days before the start of its first event, the Welsh International of 1976, this car was barely ready for Tony Pond to drive, and certainly not rally-proven. In the end it lasted only eight special stages before the engine lost all its oil pressure, ruining the main bearings. The blame for this was placed with Broadspeed, who had built the engine in the first place.

It was a similar story on the Scottish rally, which followed only a month later, when the car lasted only ten special stages on the first day before the engine suffered a burned piston. The only consolation was that the structure of the cars did not sustain much of a beating in the short time before the car's withdrawal...

For the Dunoon-based Burmah rally hopes of a reasonable

finish were high because KDU 498N had been thoroughly updated in the same way as KDU 497N, except for the fact that Pond chose not to use the new five-speed gearbox on this event. Unhappily, Pond put the car gently off the road on the very first special stage, the Island section, and found it so bogged down that he ran out of time before he could get it retrieved – afterwards he admitted that there was no one but himself to blame.

For the Manx Trophy rally KDU 498N now ran with the same specification as its sister TR7 and Pond put up a truly stirring performance – one that brought great joy to many Triumph enthusiasts – to finish third overall, beaten only by the flying Ari Vatanen in his Escort RS1800 and Cahal Curley's Porsche 911 Carrera. Pond's only moment of drama came in mid-event when he spun the TR7, damaging the front of the car in such a way that it continued with one headlamp flipped up and the other stubbornly down!

The Lindisfarne rally, a classic British forestry-stage event, was rather less successful. On a rally dominated by Escort RS1800s, KDU 498N was always going to struggle, and indeed did so. Progress was not helped when the car clipped a rock at the edge of the track on one stage, puncturing a tyre and causing the car to handle very badly. Ninth overall was

Tony Pond struggled to ninth place in KDU 498N in the 1976 Lindisfarne rally, where the still-new TR7 showed that traction was a problem.

By the autumn of 1976, the TR7 was becoming more reliable. This is Tony Pond in KDU 498N on his way to third overall in the Castrol 76 event.

the best that could be expected after that.

At this point all the further modifications already described for KDU 497N were also applied to Pond's car and for the next event, the Castrol 76, Pond was visibly quicker and far happier. He set some storming times and finished third overall, just pipped by two Escort RS1800s.

Finally, and in a great hurry, KDU 498N was entered in the Raylor rally, a minor 18-stage event in North Yorkshire that visited many familiar forestry stages. The main purpose of this outing was to test the new high-ratio 'quick' steering rack and the disc-braked rear axle, but the latter could not be completed in time. Accompanied by Mike Nicholson, who was more familiar as Pat Ryan's co-driver, Pond faced little significant competition, although privateer Tony Drummond put up a great fight in his Escort RS1800, and won the event, setting seven fastest stage times. In fairness this was no big deal, but for British Leyland, which had suffered such a traumatic start to the TR7's rally career, it was a great relief.

After his mechanical disappointments in the RAC rally in OOE 938R, Pond hoped for better things in the first of his outings in 1977, when the four-cylinder TR7s had more powerful engines and with four-wheel disc brakes. The breakthrough came at once, when Tony teamed up with co-driver Fred Gallagher and travelled to Belgium to contest the Boucles de Spa – and won outright!

Fog, ice, snow and mud were all features of this event, which took place mainly on tarmac, but Pond found the car competitive throughout, apart from repeated trouble in getting its latest magnesium Minilite wheels to fit properly to the hubs. Once Stig Blomqvist's 16-valve Saab 99 had broken its gearbox, Tony's lead was assured. To quote a delighted Pond: 'Naturally we were thrilled to win our first European event. The mechanics were superb, but we have all got to become much more polished and professional to succeed in Europe. We learnt an enormous amount about the car...'

And that, in fact, was the end of this car's works career.

Even though the Raylor rally of 1976 was only a relatively minor one-day event in North Yorkshire, all rallying fans were ecstatic about Tony Pond's victory.

COMPETITION RECORD	
1976 Welsh	
Tony Pond	Did not finish
1976 Scottish	
Tony Pond	Did not finish
1976 Burmah	
Tony Pond	Did not finish
1976 Manx Trophy	
Tony Pond	3rd overall
1976 Lindisfarne	
Tony Pond	9th overall
1976 Castrol 76	
Tony Pond	3rd overall
1976 Raylor	
Tony Pond	1st overall
1976 RAC	
Tony Pond	Did not finish
1977 Boucles de Spa	
Tony Pond	1st overall

OOE 937R

FIRST REGISTERED	UNKNOWN
ENGINE SIZE	1,998cc
MODEL TYPE	TR7

To put into practice all the work done on the original works TR7s – on which so many indignities had been imposed – two additional new cars were completed just in time to take part in the 1976 RAC rally, which started and finished in Bath.

Both of the new 16-valve TR7s were as up-to-the-minute as

the supply of components could allow. This meant that they had Don Moore-prepared engines, five-speed gearboxes and the five-link rear suspension that worked so well towards the end of 1976. Even so, the disc-braked rear axles were still not quite ready and would not be standardised until 1977.

What followed was a rally that might almost have been designed to be difficult for the works TR7s. There were few tarmac stages for them to show off their newly improved handling, and there were so many narrower cars in the event that the ruts on the forestry tracks were worn at exactly the wrong gauge for the TR7s to be comfortable. Endurance? Not a problem for old hands like Brian Culcheth and Tony Pond, but with 76 stages to be tackled in a four-day route of two legs, it was certainly going to be a tough test.

Even so, it was not an event that brought Culcheth any joy

Brian Culcheth on his way to ninth place in the RAC rally of 1976 – the restyled front end of OOE 937R resulted from an argument with a stout fence post.

had problems – Brian was reduced to driving solely in fourth gear at one point – and even a replacement gearbox gave trouble before the end of the event. But he persevered and managed to get the car to the finish – in ninth place.

It was more than two months before these 'second-phase' TR7s appeared again, by which time Pond had already recorded his outright victory on the Boucles de Spa in KDU 498N. For the 1977 Mintex, therefore, OOE 937R got the latest version of the four-cylinder engine, but Culcheth still elected not to run with the latest rear-wheel disc-brake installation. All in all, the icy conditions of this event did not suit him and he finally struggled home in 17th position, having gone off the road at one point.

In the Welsh International, a forestry-stage event on which the TR7s had made their début exactly a year earlier, Culcheth's car struggled for pace and had plenty of troubles: a burned-out alternator, an off-piste excursion, a cracked exhaust manifold (which could not be changed) and finally a broken engine oil pipe on the Eppynt ranges that led to engine failure and instant retirement.

There was no better luck on the 24 Hours of Ypres tarmac rally in Belgium, where the handling benefited from pre-event testing in another car. But more than halfway through the event Culcheth put the TR7 off the road and it could not be recovered – co-driver Johnstone Syer was later cited for misreading the pace notes.

Nor was there better fortune on the German Hunsruck rally, a two-day event run on mixed-surfaces stages that were not advertised in advance and therefore could not be practised or pace-noted. With Culcheth again at the wheel, the TR7 suffered brake problems and punctures before breaking rear wheel studs and immobilising itself 14 stages from the end of the event.

After these non-finishes in its last three events, this TR7's lacklustre works career came to an end.

with OOE 937R. He went off the road twice on the first night, at one point falling back to 41st place overall before fighting back tenaciously. His car suffered several minor breakdowns, and a rear-suspension locating bar broke not once but twice – not even the jury-rigging of a repair, by welding a tyre lever alongside to buttress it, could solve the problem. Not only that, but the five-speed transmission also

Brian Culcheth had little luck in the snow-afflicted Mintex in February 1977, but OOE 937R nevertheless helped Leyland win the team prize.

COMPETITION RECORD	
1976 RAC	
Brian Culcheth	9th overall
1977 Mintex	
Brian Culcheth	17th overall
1977 Welsh	
Brian Culcheth	Did not finish
1977 24 Hours of Ypres	
Brian Culcheth	Did not finish
1977 Hunsruck	
Brian Culcheth	Did not finish

OOE 938R

FIRST REGISTERED	UNKNOWN
ENGINE SIZE	1,998cc
MODEL TYPE	TR7

Like OOE 937R, this car was brand new for the 1976 RAC rally, where Tony Pond got off to a fine start on the first day and gave the many Triumph enthusiasts hope that a really good result would ensue. But it was not to be, for Tony struck trouble while lying second overall.

By the time the car got to the middle of 'Killer Kielder', it had already set three fastest stage times, but on rounding a corner it encountered a big rock that had been displaced by the previous car to pass. This shattered the rim of one of the Minilite front wheels, which caught up in the steering rack and jammed. As *Autosport*'s report commented: 'With no steering he was powerless to do anything about it, sliding hopelessly off into the bushes. The crew lost about 8 minutes extracting themselves from this very sad setback.' Later in the event the car suffered from the same type of rear suspension breakages that had afflicted Culcheth's sister car and a repair was not possible – retirement was inevitable.

As part of a careful rebuild for the 1977 Mintex, OOE 938R was upgraded to run with the same specification as the earlier TR7 in which Pond had just won the Boucles de Spa – that meant an enhanced engine, four-wheel disc brakes and the improved suspension. Pond put in a scintillating performance, not even the snow and ice putting him off his fight for the lead. At one point, however, he slid off the road and clouted the rear corner of the TR7 on a gatepost, with the unexpected consequence of setting off the on-board fire extinguisher – fumes from which badly affected the crew. Nevertheless, the TR7 set fastest time on seven of the 48 stages and ended up in third place, only three minutes behind the mercurial Ari Vatanen in a brand-new Escort RS1800.

Next time out, just two months later, OOE 938R tackled the Tour of Elba in the sunny Mediterranean, where Pond was immediately and grittily competitive against works-backed Lancia Stratos and Fiat 131 Abarth models. He did not let the complete loss of front brakes perturb him too much, although it took ages for the cause to be identified. In the end he finished third overall, setting three fastest and five second-fastest stage times along the way – all of which was extremely encouraging.

Tony Pond drove OOE 938R to a magnificent second place in the 1977 Scottish rally, an event that did not truly suit the TR7.

Only a month later the same car reverted to 'British forest' specification for Pond to tackle the Welsh in high spirits. Too high, perhaps, for after only nine stages he put the car off the road after a blind brow, it rolled over at least twice in mid-air, and eventually landed over 30ft below the level of the road. Damage was amazingly slight and the car would have been able to continue if it could have been retrieved, but there was no chance of that.

What followed in the Scottish rally showed that the works

Tony Pond knew only one way to drive the TR7 in rallies – absolutely flat out. In the 1977 Mintex rally he leaned OOE 938R heavily on a pile of logs in one of the Yorkshire special stages but, unabashed, he continued and finished a fine third overall.

TR7 was now in need of more power, for Pond, despite his valiant efforts in the rebuilt OOE 938R, was outpaced by the latest works-specification Escorts. On 60 stages he could set only one fastest stage time and ended up nearly five minutes behind Ari Vatanen's Ford, but nevertheless in a splendid second place overall – a very fine performance on such a long and gruelling event.

It was, therefore, rather an insult that this, the latest of the up-to-date four-cylinder works TR7s, was then sent off to tackle the extremely rough Mille Pistes event in the south of France, where, predictably, it all ended in failure. The car retired on only the third special stage with structural failure to the rear-axle assembly, which resulted in a dislocated half-shaft. Was it any wonder that this was the car's final works appearance?

COMPETITION RECORD	
1976 RAC	
Tony Pond	Did not finish
1977 Mintex	
Tony Pond	3rd overall
1977 Tour of Elba	
Tony Pond	3rd overall
1977 Welsh	
Tony Pond	Did not finish
1977 Scottish	
Tony Pond	2nd overall
1977 Mille Pistes	
Tony Pond	Did not finish

OOM 512R

FIRST REGISTERED	UNKNOWN
ENGINE SIZE	1,998cc/3,528cc
MODEL TYPE	TR7, THEN TR7 V8

On its first outing as a V8-engined TR7 V8, OOM 512R took second place in the Texaco TV rallysprint at Esgair Daffyd, with Tony Pond loving all the extra power.

Brand new in mid-1977, with the very latest 225bhp 2-litre engine and chassis specification of that time, OOM 512R started only two events as a four-cylinder TR7 and then became the first of the works cars to appear in public with a V8 engine.

Much pre-event testing at Cadwell Park circuit with another car had resulted in a new tarmac-handling package that enthused Brian Culcheth, who was therefore under-standably astonished to discover that OOM 512R, when he débuted it in the Isle of Man, was not built to that specification. After what were first described as discussions but later developed into full-scale disagreements, Culcheth was told to drive what was there or be instantly dismissed!

The result was that Culcheth, in cold fury, but as deter-mined as he had ever been in a TR7, rose above on-event problems that included having to change front-suspension struts and even the complete rear axle. In the end he set eight fastest and 12 second fastest stage times to finish a stirring second overall – the best performance ever achieved by a four-cylinder TR7 on a British international rally.

This was a very promising prelude to the end-of-season RAC rally, where Brian was set to drive OOM 512R as one of four works TR7 entries on his last event for the works team. The car did not seem to be competitive and during the first night, in mid-Wales, wheel studs broke on the rear axle in the Pantperthog stage, near Machynlleth, stranding the TR7 and putting it out of the event.

Although this was the end of the car's short career as a four-cylinder TR7, its rebirth with a V8 engine brought an altogether more distinguished record. After overcoming a testing mishap, an engine fire that might have been disas-trous, the car was readied for its first event in the startling new red-and-blue colour scheme used for all works TR7 V8s from this point. That event was a TV spectacular, the Texaco Rallysprint, run on a 1.9-mile downhill stage at Esgair Dafydd in central Wales.

With the engine running to a conservative specification – restricted to 6,500rpm and claimed to have only 250bhp – Tony Pond was able to qualify easily for later rounds during the day, which would culminate in a head-to-head battle with Hannu Mikkola in his fuel-injected works Ford Escort RS1800. The outcome was a stirring battle, which provided extremely enjoyable TV viewing, and the big Triumph finished just 2.2 seconds adrift.

Thus encouraged, the team entered the same car in the national-status Granite City rally, which was centred on Aberdeen. Starting at No 3, Tony Pond was a firm favourite but soon discovered that there was still much to be learned about this promising new car, for he was profoundly disappointed with its handling and Abingdon's mechanics worked on the settings throughout the event to rectify things. Although the outcome was a very welcome victory, the first for the TR7 V8, it was a cliffhanger to the end. Pond set fastest time on three of the event's 17 forestry special stages and narrowly beat Nigel Rockey's works-specification Escort by only 12 seconds – the champagne could be popped at last!

Bill Price's authoritative history of Abingdon operations tells us that this car was then used for Dunlop/Goodyear tyre assessments before being sent off to compete in the Border Counties rally, which was centred on Hawick in southern Scotland. Although Price claims that Pond finished fourth, the *Autosport* report of the event does not credit it with finishing at all…

This car then contested the Glasgow-based Burmah International rally in the hands of John Buffum, an American who had been winning events regularly in his home country in a

works-prepared 16-valve 2-litre TR7. Co-driven by Neil Wilson, Buffum was making one of his very infrequent visits to Europe and must have been somewhat daunted to face a phalanx of works Ford, Fiat and Vauxhall drivers. Following the work carried out in previous weeks, the car was available with a selection of Dunlop and Goodyear tyres, and used the slightly narrower front track that Pond insisted made it easier to drive on forestry stages. John drove sensibly but was not quite on the pace, eventually finishing eighth, behind seven other factory cars.

Almost at once OOM 512R was rushed out to Canada, where Buffum drove it in the World Championship Critérium de Québec rally. Although his stage times put him in sixth place, he was disqualified after the finish. Officials had observed him driving in stages without a crash helmet: this occurred after the car lost a rear wheel when wheel studs

American rally driver John Buffum took OOM 512R to eighth place in the Burmah rally, which was based in west Scotland. It helps if a car has two good tyres on the driving wheels – note the complete lack of rubber on the nearside rear!

At the very end of 1978 the works team lent OOM 512R to Graham Elsmore to tackle his 'home' event, the Wyedean rally. On this last outing as a works car it achieved a fine second place overall.

COMPETITION RECORD

1977 Manx Trophy
Brian Culcheth   2nd overall
1977 RAC
Brian Culcheth   Did not finish
1978 TV Rallysprint (Esgair Dafydd)[1]
Tony Pond   2nd overall
1978 Granite City
Tony Pond   1st overall
1978 Border Counties
Tony Pond   4th overall
1978 Burmah
John Buffum   8th overall
1978 Critérium de Québec
John Buffum   Disqualified
1978 TV Rallysprint (Donington)
Tony Pond/John Watson   2nd/3rd overall
1978 Wyedean
Graham Elsmore   2nd overall
[1] *First event as a newly shelled TR7 V8.*

sheared and Buffum, in his haste after making a temporary repair, foolishly completed the stage without first donning his helmet.

Once returned to the UK, the car was then made ready for the BBC TV Texaco Rallysprint at Donington Park, where a mixed bag of race and rally drivers tackled races in identical Ford Fiesta 1300s and a rally stage in a variety of competitive cars. The TR7 V8 was allocated to Pond and Formula 1 driver John Watson, who was by no means expert at this sort of thing and could only finish seventh fastest behind works Escorts and the Chequered Flag Lancia Stratos. However, by winning the Fiesta race, Watson was awarded third place overall, while Pond was second overall.

This car was then fresh enough to be loaned to Graham Elsmore to tackle his local event, the one-day Wyedean rally in South Wales, with many people correctly assuming that he was being given a run to see if he should join the works team in 1979. Run entirely in the daytime over 76 miles of stages, this was an event that Elsmore was expected to win, but in the end he had to settle for second overall, just 11 seconds behind Andy Dawson's winning Datsun Violet, having set fastest time on six of the 17 special stages.

This, however, marked the end of the works career of this individual car. Reputedly with something of a 'tired' bodyshell, it was sold at the end of 1978 to Terry Kaby, who used it very successfully as a private owner.

OOM 513R

FIRST REGISTERED	UNKNOWN
ENGINE SIZE	1,998cc
MODEL TYPE	TR7

Tony Pond/Fred Gallagher in OOM 513R at '5-Ton Bridge' in the Manx International rally of 1977.

This new four-cylinder TR7 had a short and unsuccessful career, finishing only once in six events in a seven-month period, and it was never converted to V8 specification.

It did not appear until mid-1977, when Tony Pond débuted it in Belgium on the 24 Hours of Ypres. If only the 2-litre engine could have been persuaded to produce more power, the Belgian event should have been ideal for the TR7 for all of its stages were tarmac-surfaced and gradient-free. Although Tony Pond started well, setting fastest time and second-fastest time on two early stages, he could not keep up with Bernard Darniche's mid-engined Lancia Stratos. On the eighth stage a sparking plug broke up in the cylinder head, damaging a valve that therefore became burned, and retirement was inevitable.

Newly engined for the two-day German Hunsruck rally that followed, the car was strong enough for Tony Pond to challenge strongly for the lead and at the end of the first day he was fourth behind an ex-works Escort RS1800, a Saab 99EMS and Achim Warmbold's works-backed Toyota Corolla. Then came disappointment: early on the second day Pond rounded a corner on a stage to discover a large rock in the road and hit it hard, the resulting damage to the rear axle forcing the car's retirement.

For the Manx rally, for which a new suspension package to suit tarmac stages had been agreed after testing at Cadwell Park, Pond enjoyed only eight high-speed stages – and set fastest time on two of them – before trouble struck. The tendency of his car to bottom out after repeated jumping on the bumpy public roads meant that the engine sump guard became pushed up into the sump pan itself and displaced the oil pump, causing an engine oil pipe to fracture – which resulted in catastrophic engine failure.

The car was no more successful on the Tour de Corse than it had been on its first three events. Pond had to retire when his gearbox jammed in first gear only 21 miles into this Mediterranean event...

This, at least, meant that the car was still relatively factory-fresh when it was allocated to Pat Ryan for the RAC rally – his last appearance in the works team. Earlier in the year Pat had laboured successfully to produce results from a series of Group 1 Dolomite Sprints (see Chapter 8), but this was the one and only time that he would drive a TR7 on a rally. Like others who had already used OOM 513R, he had no luck at all and was not classified at the finish. The car needed a

clutch change at one point, then Ryan went off on the Croft circuit stage and hit a bank, then he left the road on several other stages, and finally the engine suffered from overheating and Ryan had to retire.

This car's final appearance came in the Yorkshire-based Mintex rally of February 1978, when many of the forestry stages were badly rutted and incredibly slippery. As a consequence, Tony Pond struggled to be truly competitive and he was sixth overall after the first 15 stages. Then came a foggy stage near Scarborough where the TR7 plunged down a fire-break and lost 18 minutes before it could regain the track, the engine having stalled and defied attempts to get it going again. A further off-stage excursion added insult to misery, the overall result a lowly 17th place overall even though the car had set three fastest and three second-fastest stage times.

COMPETITION RECORD	
1977 24 Hours of Ypres	
Tony Pond	Did not finish
1977 Hunsruck	
Tony Pond	Did not finish
1977 Manx	
Tony Pond	Did not finish
1977 Tour de Corse	
Tony Pond	Did not finish
1977 RAC	
Pat Ryan	Did not finish
1978 Mintex	
Tony Pond	17th overall

OOM 514R

FIRST REGISTERED	UNKNOWN
ENGINE SIZE	1,998cc/3,528cc
MODEL TYPE	TR7, THEN TR7 V8

Here was another oddity of registration and of usage. Although OOM 514R was a brand-new four-cylinder TR7 for Tony Pond to drive in the 1977 RAC rally, it then disappeared into the shadows at Abingdon, eventually to be reborn as a TR7 V8 – but it did not start another rally for over 18 months.

Pond was not at all happy with this car's handling on the RAC as it seemed to have over-heavy steering and too much understeer – and later it also suffered from clutch problems. Nevertheless, fighting valiantly throughout the four-day event, he lay seventh overall at the halfway overnight halt in York and finally took eighth place, having set second fastest time on one special stage.

The car then disappeared from public view, although one imagines that it was used for behind-the-scenes work, until August 1979, when the works team loaned what looked like a suspiciously 'new' OOM 514R to Graham Elsmore for him to gain experience in national and regional events of less importance than the RAC Open series. As the car remained in the ownership of Abingdon throughout, this programme qualifies as a works one.

The first event of this car's new life as a TR7 V8 was the Halewood rally, a 'third-level' BTRDA (British Trial & Rally Drivers Association) rally run on forestry stages and Eppynt. Elsmore drove it to second place, a good result, but it was mildly embarrassing that he was beaten – by just 29 seconds – by Terry Kaby in OOM 512R, the 'old nail' ex-works TR7

By the end of 1977 the four-cylinder TR7 had reached the limit of its development – these front and rear views show Tony Pond on his way to eighth place on that year's RAC rally.

V8 that Kaby had acquired at the end of the previous season.

Only a week later rallying returned to many of the same stages for the Peter Russek rally, which had a national permit, and it was here that Elsmore finally won an event in his TR7 V8, with which he was becoming more confident. On this occasion, too, he defeated Kaby, the gap over 17 stages being more than four minutes because Kaby had to stop in a stage to change a wheel after a puncture.

If ever there was a rally that showed up both the strengths and weaknesses of the TR7 V8, it was the Lindisfarne rally of August 1979. Elsmore was blisteringly fast on tarmac but floundered on the slippery forestry stages of Kielder. Eighth overall was the best he could achieve. Two weeks later it was the same story on the Tour of Cumbria, which used classic stages in the Borders and the Lake District. OOM 514R could only finish sixth, and there was a second dose of embarrassment in being beaten again by Kaby in his ex-works TR7 V8.

Although Elsmore then tackled the Castrol 79 rally in mid-Wales, without success, there was real encouragement in his reaction to the use of 15in wheels for the first time on a TR7, for he stated that the improvement in handling was 'magic'. Although he held third place for a time behind the Escort RS1800s of Ari Vatanen and Hannu Mikkola, it all came to naught when his rear axle seized following damage inflicted to the drain plug by a flying rock.

Just a week later the car went to Yorkshire to tackle the Scarborough Stages, the last round of the BTRDA series, and it performed flawlessly to take second place behind the flying Steve Bannister, who was a local hero at that time but still not well-known to the rest of the rallying fraternity.

Finally Elsmore got a chance to tackle his 'home' event in the Forest of Dean, where a renamed event called the Bovis National was held early in November as a round of the

Castrol/*Autosport* series. Despite facing a strong field, Elsmore took the lead and held it until after the halfway break, but problems thereafter forced him to have to settle for yet another second place. The car suffered a puncture, the flailing rear tyre then damaging the adjacent brake disc and caliper, and later the rear suspension Panhard rod also broke.

This was the end of this venerable old car's career, for Elsmore left the team at the end of the 1979 season.

COMPETITION RECORD	
1977 RAC	
Tony Pond	8th overall
1979 Halewood[1]	
Graham Elsmore	2nd overall
1979 Peter Russek	
Graham Elsmore	1st overall
1979 Lindisfarne	
Graham Elsmore	8th overall
1979 Tour of Cumbria	
Graham Elsmore	6th overall
1979 Castrol 79	
Graham Elsmore	Did not finish
1979 Scarborough Stages	
Graham Elsmore	2nd overall
1979 Bovis National (Tour of Dean)	
Graham Elsmore	2nd overall

[1] *First event as a TR7 V8, and on loan to Graham Elsmore.*

SCE 645S

FIRST REGISTERED	UNKNOWN
ENGINE SIZE	1,998cc
MODEL TYPE	TR7

This was a very odd 'one-event wonder' as far as its works career was concerned. Although entered in the 1977 RAC rally by the factory and with a totally authentic factory specification, it was neither assembled nor rally-prepared at Abingdon, and it was driven by a Finnish driver, Markku Saaristo, who was never again invited to be a member of the works team.

Cambridgeshire-based Safety Devices, a company that specialised in roll-cage manufacture and had links with several British rally teams, prepared the bodyshell and built up the car from a kit of parts supplied from Abingdon, and

then had it registered locally. For the RAC Saaristo was co-driven by Ian Grindrod and the car was serviced along with the other three Abingdon-built cars.

It was an undistinguished event for this scratch team, for Saaristo was never as fast as his more experienced team-mates. He rolled the four-cylinder TR7 in the Hafren special stage but damage to the bodyshell was relatively light and he was able to continue to the end of the event, finally taking 37th overall. The car was then sold off and does not feature again in this story.

COMPETITION RECORD	
1977 RAC	
Markku Saaristo	37th overall

SJW 533S

FIRST REGISTERED	23 NOVEMBER 1977
ENGINE SIZE	1,998cc/3,528cc
MODEL TYPE	TR7, THEN TR7 V8

Here is a real oddity. SJW 533SW was partly built before the end of 1977 but was not completed as a four-cylinder TR7 until the first months of 1978, after which it did only one event before receiving a V8 engine and taking on a new identity as a TR7 V8.

For its début, in the long and gruelling Circuit of Ireland in March 1978, there were two novelties. One was that this was the first of the team cars to appear in the striking red-and-blue colour scheme that would be retained for the next three years, while the other was that driver Tony Pond was joined by co-driver Fred Gallagher for the start of a very successful and fruitful partnership.

Not that this helped on the Circuit of Ireland, where the car's engine showed signs of overheating from a very early stage. Although the cause was only a radiator hose coming adrift and dumping all the water, it was enough to inflict severe internal damage to the engine, which blew a head gasket and could not be repaired.

Speedily converted to V8 specification, this car then suffered further disappointments on two British internationals – the Welsh and the Scottish. With engine power now claimed to be up to 275bhp, and with the car benefiting from all the suspension improvements that had been made to OOM 512R during the Granite City rally (see page 231), things looked promising on the Welsh. But two separate failures of the engine electrical pack ruined things, with punctures and engine overheating finally completing a disappointing weekend.

In Scotland Pond continued to struggle with recalcitrant handling and finally had to retire when the car went off the road on the Glenshellish special stage and rolled. Three starts and three retirements – surely it was time for a change of fortune? Would the rebuilding of the car into a new bodyshell help to turn things around?

In fact it did not, for the reborn car used a shell prepared by Broadspeed, not by Safety Devices, and on its first event, the Burmah rally, it proved to be less robust than required for rallying. Suspension anchorage points broke away from the shell, causing the propshaft to move out of alignment, and that led to severing of fuel lines leading from the tank to the engine bay. Four failures in four starts – would this car ever finish an event?

Not on the evidence of its performance on the Lindisfarne rally. Pond was sent to contest this relatively minor event in the north-east of England with the purpose of doing some pre-RAC rally forest-stage testing in Kielder, where this event's stages were concentrated – but it all went wrong when the V8 engine let go on the very first stage.

For the RAC rally the car was set up in the latest forest-stage form, which included a narrower front track, and was then allocated – very surprisingly – to Norwegian driver John Haugland, who had only previously driven rear-engined Skodas. Haugland was diplomatic on the subject of what he soon discovered about the car in testing, but set about getting it to the end of this very long event, which started and finished in Birmingham. He made it, 12th overall, but well off the pace.

For 1979 the corporate theory was that this TR7 V8, suitably refurbished and liveried, would become a semi-works car to be campaigned by The Chequered Flag, a London-based car dealer that in previous years had sweated blood and incurred innumerable big bills to keep a Lancia Stratos running in rallies, often without success. With the TR7 V8, Irishman Derek Boyd was set to tackle six Irish events, and – when the programme was launched – several unspecified European events. For the first two events, the Galway rally and the Circuit of Ireland, the plan was that SJW 533S would operate as a full works car.

What followed on the Galway rally was disastrous. After

Before and after. On the 1979 Galway rally Derek Boyd wrote off SJW 533S when he hit a stone wall, badly injuring co-driver Fred Gallagher.

only three tarmac stages Boyd and co-driver Fred Gallagher were in fourth place when, on the fourth stage, Boyd misjudged a fast corner and the car slid sideways at high speed, hitting a wall very hard on the passenger side. Both occupants were injured but it was miraculous that Gallagher, sitting on the side of the car stoved in by the wall, was not killed: he needed prolonged hospital treatment but thankfully made a full recovery and was able to rejoin the team a few months later. When the wrecked car got back to Abingdon, it was found to be six inches narrower...

An all-new car, in effect, was then built up around a new bodyshell using an almost entirely new kit of components – but the existing registration number was retained. Finished in The Chequered Flag's black-and-white livery, the car was allocated to a happily recovered Boyd for the Circuit of Ireland at Easter. It started the event with wider-than-usual rear wheel arches to allow the use of tarmac-specification tyres of up to 11in width. Not that this helped much, for after only six stages Boyd had to retire when he clipped a corner with a front wheel and immobilised the car with suspension damage and a broken brake disc.

The BP-sponsored BBC TV rallysprint extravaganza on the Esgair Dafydd stage turned out to be this car's final works appearance. Twelve carefully selected crews were invited to contest the stage – first uphill and then downhill – after a period of assiduous practice. Two TR7 V8s took part and, to increase the spectacle, they had side exhausts that could only be described as... noisy. Graham Elsmore, the nominated driver for SJW 533S, could only finish seventh fastest,

hampered by the side exhausts both loosening off on his timed runs, and no doubt also somewhat over-awed by the occasion. But a good time was had by all...

COMPETITION RECORD	
1978 Circuit of Ireland	
Tony Pond	Did not finish
1978 Welsh[1]	
Tony Pond	Did not finish
1978 Scottish	
Tony Pond	Did not finish
1978 Burmah	
Tony Pond	Did not finish
1978 Lindisfarne	
Tony Pond	Did not finish
1978 RAC	
John Haugland	12th overall
1979 Galway	
Derek Boyd	Accident
1979 Circuit of Ireland[2]	
Derek Boyd	Did not finish
1979 BP TV Rallysprint	
Graham Elsmore	7th overall

[1] *First event as a TR7 V8.*
[2] *First event in 'recreated' form following its accident on the Galway rally.*

SJW 540S

FIRST REGISTERED	23 NOVEMBER 1977
ENGINE SIZE	3,528cc
MODEL TYPE	TR7 V8

Brand new in June 1978 for the 24 Hours of Ypres, where all the stages were on tarmac and could be surveyed and practised in advance, SJW 540S put in a stirring performance and won. Development of this model was proceeding steadily, with British Leyland now admitting to 290bhp from the engine and using 9in wide rear wheels in order to harness all that power.

Not only did Tony Pond win the event outright, but he also set 22 fastest stage times, beating Gilbert Staepelaere's works Ford Escort RS1800 by more than three minutes and Tony Carello's works Lancia Stratos by six minutes. It was absolutely not a hollow victory, as Carello set only seven fastest stage times in what was ostensibly a superior car.

The next outing, in September on the Isle of Man, saw more success when Pond and Fred Gallagher won the 39-stage Manx Trophy rally outright. The event started with a gripping battle between the TR7 V8 and Hannu Mikkola's works Escort RS1800, but Pond was able to ease off after the Ford picked up a puncture, understeered off the road and damaged its steering. Game over, Pond cruised home ahead of John Taylor's Escort RS1800.

Having announced that he was leaving the team to drive for Chrysler in 1979, Pond's next event with the car was in Corsica for the all-tarmac Tour de Corse. This turned into an unmitigated disaster, for the gearbox shed all of its oil and seized within hours of the start. The drain plug was found to have come loose – sabotage by a rival was suspected but never proven.

With little time to spare between the Tour de Corse and the RAC rally, the car was adapted to a 'standard' forestry-stage chassis set-up for Pond to drive. Of the batch of relatively new 'SJW' team cars, this was expected to be the fastest – and so it proved as Pond settled into a significantly faster pace than team-mates Simo Lampinen and John Haugland.

Even so, things started badly. During an early special stage, in Trentham Gardens near Stoke-on-Trent, the car suffered a mechanical handbrake malfunction that caused the rear wheels to stay locked for three minutes until brute force dealt with the problem. Having dropped to dead last because of that drama, Pond then spent hours – days, even – fighting his way back into contention, and reached sixth place at the halfway stage. Going faster and faster as the event progressed, he eventually clawed his way up to fourth overall, setting eight fastest stage times in the process, but he could not split the three works-specification Ford Escort RS1800s ahead of him. A late-event drama, too, occurred when a cylinder head gasket started to leak and regular infusions of water and Radweld were needed to keep it all together.

Following Pond's departure from the team, new recruit Graham Elsmore got his first chance to drive this successful car, on the thoroughly snow-bound Mintex rally in Yorkshire in February 1979. Although Elsmore resourcefully kept it on the tracks for most of the event, he did go off at least twice in the tricky conditions, then towards the end of the very last stage his engine's big end failed. Subsequent examination showed that most of the oil had been consumed, rather than leaked away, a conundrum that was later found to be due to the use of an under-sized dry-sump reservoir made by an outside supplier.

Elsmore then had no luck on the Welsh Rally, which followed in May, when the car's five-speed gearbox gradually began to disintegrate, leaving him with only one gear in operation at the Aberystwyth halt and insufficient time for a replacement to be fitted.

This was turning out to be an unlucky car for Elsmore. On the star-studded Scottish rally in June he and SJW 540S were never truly on the pace, and when a cylinder head gasket let go before the Aviemore rest halt the enforced retirement may even have come as a relief.

That was the car's last appearance as an 'official' works

In a truly famous victory, Tony Pond and Fred Gallagher in SJW 540S beat the best of British competition to win the Manx Trophy rally outright in September 1978.

Using what became familiarly known as 'British Airways' livery, SJW 540S took a storming fourth place overall in Tony Pond's hands in the 1978 RAC rally.

entry, although later in the 1979 season it was loaned to Terry Kaby for the Manx rally and other lesser British championship rallies. Kaby competed against Elsmore in a works TR7 V8 on these events and proved to be equally as fast.

COMPETITION RECORD	
1978 24 Hours of Ypres	
Tony Pond	1st overall
1978 Manx Trophy	
Tony Pond	1st overall
1978 Tour de Corse	
Tony Pond	Did not finish
1978 RAC	
Tony Pond	4th overall
1979 Mintex	
Graham Elsmore	Did not finish
1979 Welsh	
Graham Elsmore	Did not finish
1979 Scottish	
Graham Elsmore	Did not finish

Graham Elsmore trying very hard indeed in the Welsh rally of 1979 – he had to retire with gearbox problems.

SJW 546S

FIRST REGISTERED	23 NOVEMBER 1977
ENGINE SIZE	3,528cc
MODEL TYPE	TR7 V8

New signing Graham Elsmore, a forestry specialist rather than a tarmac one, had the pleasure of driving this all-new tarmac-specification car on the 1979 Circuit of Ireland, but had no luck at all. On the 'Ring of Kerry' loop in the middle of the event, he put the car off the road on a special stage, beyond a bank, and although the TR7 V8 was little damaged there was no obvious way of retrieving it until the rest of the rally had passed through and the road had been reopened to the public.

After a rather fraught summer on rough, loose, forestry stages in other works TR7 V8s, Elsmore got his hands on SJW 546S again for the all-tarmac Manx Trophy rally in September. After careful practice in other cars, he put in a very assured performance on the 37-stage event. Although he set just one fastest time, he was always there or thereabouts and finally took third place overall behind a works Ford Escort RS1800 and a works Vauxhall Chevette HS. The only mechanical failures during an arduous weekend of rallying were to do with the transmission and two gearbox changes were required.

Two months later Elsmore used SJW 546S in the long, arduous RAC rally, but had no more luck than his team-mates in an event dominated by works Escorts. Before the halfway point punctures delayed him several times, and then he had a gear lever breakage in the last of the Kielder stages. Following the overnight halt in Chester, there were more punctures and the final result was a very disappointing 16th overall – and the end of Elsmore's works career at Abingdon.

During the winter SJW 546S was refurbished and became the first works TR7 V8 with one of the new Janspeed-developed V8 engines, equipped with four Weber carburettors and reputed to produce 310bhp. Carrying Sparkrite livery, the car was entered for the Galway rally in February 1980 and provided a TR7 V8 début for Roger Clark, who loved rallying in Ireland. But Roger had absolutely no luck. After a good start and while lying in fourth or fifth position on the bumpy tarmac stages, he suddenly had the gear lever break off and terminally over-revved the engine in searching around for another gear with the stub that remained.

There was also no luck on the Yorkshire-based Mintex rally, where Roger struggled to get the car into the top ten behind a fleet of Escorts and Vauxhall HSs. His task was not helped by two punctures but then he was sidelined with a blown engine after completing 32 of the 50 stages.

That was the end of this car's works career, Clark transferring – with his Sparkrite sponsorship – to XJO 414V for the rest of the 1980 season.

Graham Elsmore had a troubled season with the Triumph works team in 1979 but enjoyed a fine performance on the all-tarmac Manx Trophy rally, finishing third overall in SJW 546S.

COMPETITION RECORD	
1979 Circuit of Ireland	
Graham Elsmore	Did not finish
1979 Manx	
Graham Elsmore	3rd overall
1979 RAC	
Graham Elsmore	16th overall
1980 Galway	
Roger Clark	Did not finish
1980 Mintex	
Roger Clark	Did not finish

SJW 548S

FIRST REGISTERED	23 NOVEMBER 1977
ENGINE SIZE	3,528cc
MODEL TYPE	TR7 V8

Brand new for the Tour de Corse in November 1978, this car was allocated to the French driver Jean-Luc Thérier, but suffered precisely the same fate as Pond's SJW 540S in that the gearbox lost all its oil and seized, the cause a loose drain plug – and sabotage was suspected but never proven. At least this left the rest of the car quite unbattered for the RAC rally that followed.

For the RAC, the longest and toughest European event in the World Championship calendar, it was allocated to Finnish driver Simo Lampinen, who was not only a personal friend of John Davenport but also a previous winner of the event. That was all very well, but he had not regularly driven a rear-wheel-drive rally car for some years and had certainly never encountered the TR7 V8. Retirement came in mid-event on a Lake District stage when the clutch failed and could not be changed before the car ran out of time.

For the Boucles de Spa in February 1979, Thérier again drove the car and would undoubtedly have fared better if it had been more suited to the snow and ice that afflicted this Belgian event. It did not help that the Dunlop service truck, which should have been supporting the team and its tyre requirements, was very late in getting back from the Monte Carlo rally, with the consequence that the car was rarely on the best tyres for the conditions. Thérier may well have been relieved when, according to official sources, the rotor arm in the distributor broke and immobilised the big V8…

Just four weeks later Swedish driver Per Eklund got the chance to drive the car on the very snowy Mintex rally.

In February 1979 Jean-Luc Thérier drove SJW 548S on the Boucles de Spa, in Belgium, but had to retire when the engine's distributor failed, stranding him.

Despite going off the track more than once, Per called on all his winter-rallying experience and kept going to take second place overall, behind Stig Blomqvist's front-wheel-drive Saab 99 Turbo.

On the Welsh rally, held in May, it was Lampinen's turn to drive this car again and he was indeed fortunate to finish. Although not up among the leaders, Simo continued doggedly until Henri Toivonen's Escort RS1800 hit his TR7 V8 very hard up the rear at the finish of the Gartheinog stage. Considerably damaged but still driveable, the car kept going and limped to the end in 12th place.

Miraculously, the bodyshell was repaired in time for Lampinen to drive the car the following month on the Scottish rally, accompanied by Fred Gallagher, fully recovered from the serious injuries he sustained on the Galway rally in February. Never truly on the pace at all, Lampinen kept going and eventually finished 13th overall and third in the capacity class.

COMPETITION RECORD

1978 Tour de Corse	
Jean-Luc Thérier	Did not finish
1978 RAC	
Simo Lampinen	Did not finish
1979 Boucles de Spa	
Jean-Luc Thérier	Did not finish
1979 Mintex	
Per Eklund	2nd overall
1979 Welsh	
Simo Lampinen	12th overall
1979 Scottish	
Simo Lampinen	13th overall

Two details of the 1978-vintage works TR7 V8 included the British Airways sponsorship and the Triumph roundel, which denoted that, in theory at least, the car had been built at Coventry.

Ready to go rallying, but with no sign of the hefty undershielding that was often added to these TR7 V8s for loose-surface special stages.

A TR7? Yes and no. The cars were homologated as 'TR7 V8' models, although they were TR8s in all but name.

Works drivers of TR7 V8s had no lack of forward lighting at night! This was the definitive layout, complete with headlamps permanently fixed in the 'up' position.

For off-road rallying, the factory team set up the works TR7 V8s to have significant ground clearance. As is also clear from this shot, the front-end overhang was considerable.

Looking a touch battle-scarred, this is the cabin layout of a typical Abingdon-prepared TR7 V8.

Boot contains the battery, a sturdy spare wheel, a large dry-sump oil tank and the foam-filled fuel tank.

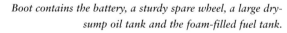

UYH 863S

FIRST REGISTERED	1 OCTOBER 1977
ENGINE SIZE	3,528cc
MODEL TYPE	TR7 V8

Abingdon produced a brand-new TR7 V8 for its brand-new driver, Graham Elsmore, to use on the Galway rally of February 1979, but his fortunes were quite overshadowed by the massive accident suffered on that event by Derek Boyd and Fred Gallagher in SJW 533S (see pages 235-236). Elsmore also crashed, in fact, when the car slid off the road on the 16th stage, clipped a tree trunk and rolled itself into a very expensive mess – not a good way to start your relationship with a new team.

An all-new car carrying the registration number UYH 863S was made ready for Terry Kaby to drive on the 1979 RAC rally nine months later. Throughout the year Kaby had been campaigning ex-works TR7 V8s, at his own expense and with great success, sometimes battling against works driver Graham Elsmore, and sometimes beating him. On the RAC, therefore, Kaby set out once again to prove that he had deserved a full-time works drive all along.

For the RAC the car was fitted with Pierburg fuel injection – this was only the second time the system had been used in a rally – and it was reputed in this latest version to deliver 318bhp, more than 20bhp above the figure usually produced

by a carburettor engine. Not that this helped much, for poor Kaby had his problems. Early on the car drowned out in the ford in the Trentham Gardens stage, while a few hours later the engine threw an oil pump drive belt and soon after that, as a consequence, the engine ran its main bearings and the car had to retire.

This TR7 V8 clearly had plenty of life left in it, but it would not be one of the team's front-line machines in 1980. After some behind-the-scenes testing and recce activity, it was brought into the open again for Tony Pond to drive at Esgair Dafydd in the *Daily Mirror* Rallysprint, a 'made-for-TV' event in which cars had two runs at the stage – one uphill, the other downhill. Of the 12 carefully selected drivers who took part in competitive rally cars, Pond was the one who blotted his copybook when he put his TR7 V8 over the edge of the stage on the downhill practice run, rolling it and taking no further part in the proceedings!

Pond's next rally was the Manx Stages, the first of two high-profile tarmac events held in the same season over closed public roads on the Isle of Man. On this occasion, to everyone's joy, Pond not only coaxed the TR7 V8 to the finish but also quite dominated the entire event, setting 12 fastest times on the 14 stages of this one-day event. There were two important aspects to this victory. One was that the engine did not miss a beat, the other that the car used Michelin rather than Dunlop tyres throughout, with conspicuous success.

Having been used in the background for further test and practice work, this now-ageing machine – by rallying standards – suddenly reappeared on the one-day Tour of Cumbria, a round of the national championship, flaunting some rather obvious visual changes and other none-too-obvious mechanical modifications. There was a modified glass-fibre nose incorporating fixed, semi-upright headlamps, which were said to be from a Vauxhall; this change, of course, was incapable of homologation because it was unrelated to any production specification. Changes under the skin

Tony Pond completely dominated the Manx Stages rally of 1980 in UYH 863S – note the ultra-wide rear wheel arches of this tarmac-specification TR7 V8.

COMPETITION RECORD	
1979 Galway	
Graham Elsmore	Did not finish
1979 RAC	
Terry Kaby	Did not finish
1980 *Daily Mirror* TV Rallysprint	
Tony Pond	Did not finish
1980 Manx Stages	
Tony Pond	1st overall
1980 Tour of Cumbria	
Tony Pond	2nd overall
1980 Castrol 80	
Tony Pond	Did not finish

included alterations to the engine installation to improve weight distribution.

Using Michelins throughout the event, which the works treated essentially as a tyre-testing exercise, Pond seemed to enjoy the car in its latest form as he set fastest time on eight of the 14 stages. He made some incorrect tyres choices in Kielder, however, and had to settle for second place to Malcolm Wilson's ex-works Ford Escort RS1800.

More 'tyre testing' came on the Castrol 80, a one-day rally centred in mid-Wales. Although the TR7 V8 was competitive, Pond setting fastest time on four of the nine stages, this outing was less encouraging because he had to retire when one puncture too many left him stranded in mid-stage and he ran out of time.

If the TR7 V8 programme had continued into 1981, there might have been a future for the developments being made on this particular car, but it was not to be. UYH 863S was not used again during 1980 and was later sold off.

TUD 682T

FIRST REGISTERED	1 APRIL 1979
ENGINE SIZE	3,528cc
MODEL TYPE	TR7 V8

This was one of the new-for-1979 TR7 V8s produced for the Circuit of Ireland of 1979. It had left-hand drive and on its début was allocated to the team's new recruit, Per Eklund of Sweden. Like the other two team cars that lined up on the same event, it had broad rear wheel arches to accommodate ultra-wide tyres on the driving wheels.

Although Eklund had much front-wheel-drive forest-stage experience, having been a successful member of the Saab team before joining BL, he was by no means a tarmac expert, yet he put in a series of sparkling times on this four-day event. Although he was fastest outright on only two stages, he was always there or thereabouts and lay fifth on the final morning. But on the very last – and very fast – stage the engine suddenly expired after a recurrence of earlier problems saw it starved of lubricant. After the event the lubrication problem, which occurred on long stages, was solved with the provision of a larger boot-mounted tank for the dry-sump system.

Out again on the Welsh, Eklund was once again very fast, but experienced delays through problems with a cylinder head gasket and the clutch master cylinder, and finally an electrical failure stranded him in the middle of the Eppynt complex. Already proving to be the fastest of the 1979 team drivers, Eklund then took this car on the Scottish rally, where he was always competitive, if not outright fastest, and finished third overall. In view of the works team's recent traumas, this was a remarkable result.

A big gamble followed on the next event – the 1,000 Lakes rally in Finland – when the team decided to put a Pierburg fuel-injected engine into this car, claiming that it was producing 20–25bhp more than any previous Weber-carburettor version of the V8. It was not a happy outing: the car suffered power loss whenever sustained full-throttle running

caused the under-bonnet temperature to rise and, as a consequence, the car never figured in the top stage times, Eklund struggling home a rather distant and dispirited eighth.

Two months later and back in carburettor form, the car was sent to a TV spectacular at Donington, where eight race and rally drivers drove several different cars over a specially constructed special stage in the infield of the circuit. The performance of the TR7 V8, which was shared between Eklund and F1 driver Alan Jones, turned out to be a complete shambles, for the V8 engine drowned out in the specially arranged water splash on both runs, the car therefore finishing last on the stages themselves. The results, if they can be called that, were complicated by the use of a fleet of near-standard TR7s for the circuit races, where Eklund and Jones did well enough to end up equal third. The rally side of the event, however, was not to British Leyland's credit.

The car then took part in the end-of-season RAC rally driven by John Buffum, who theoretically ran as a 'private' entry but had almost unlimited access to the works team's

Per Eklund took a splendid third overall in TUD 682T on the 1979 Scottish rally.

facilities and mechanics. Buffum, an American, had won many events in his native country in TR7 V8s originally supplied from Abingdon. On this occasion the car was once again fitted with Pierburg fuel injection in the hope that the colder, damper weather of the British event would suit it better than the Finnish 1,000 Lakes had done.

Everything went well in the opening hours of the event, and Buffum actually found himself leading all his so-called team-mates until he lost time with drowned-out ignition in a ford in the Hamsterley stage. Soon after he went off the road in the first stage of the Kielder complex, where, in the absence of a posse of spectators, the car could not be retrieved.

That marked the end of this car's works career, but its fuel-injected engine was retained for future use in other cars on the fleet.

COMPETITION RECORD	
1979 Circuit of Ireland	
Per Eklund	Did not finish
1979 Welsh	
Per Eklund	Did not finish
1979 Scottish	
Per Eklund	3rd overall
1979 1000 Lakes	
Per Eklund	8th overall
1979 Eaton Yale TV Rallysprint	
Per Eklund/Alan Jones	8th overall
1979 RAC	
John Buffum	Did not finish

TUD 683T

FIRST REGISTERED	1 APRIL 1979
ENGINE SIZE	3,528cc
MODEL TYPE	TR7 V8

When fully developed the TR7 V8 was a formidable rally car on tarmac stages. Tony Pond proved this with TUD 683T by winning the 1980 Manx Trophy rally – but note the damage to the nearside rear wheel arch!

Built up at Abingdon during the winter of 1978/79, this left-hand-drive car first appeared in June 1979 in the BP-sponsored televised special event at Esgair Dafydd in central Wales, where it was one of 12 selected cars to take part. An older TR7 V8, SJW 533S, was also involved and the two cars were mechanically identical, with raucously noisy side exhaust pipes fitted for the occasion.

On an event where there were only three minutes of flat-out action, it was hoped that nothing would go wrong – and in fact it did not. Driving with real flair and commitment, Per Eklund set fastest time on the first uphill run and equal-fastest on the downhill return run a couple of hours later. That was special, for the competition included Stig Blomqvist (Saab 99 Turbo), Russell Brookes (Ford Escort RS1800) and Pentti Airikkala (Vauxhall Chevette HS). Victory was sweet, even if this was a short circus act rather than a full-blown endurance event.

Still virtually new after the rallysprint outing, this car was then committed to the Finnish 1,000 Lakes rally in August. Simo Lampinen's drive was quite spoiled by two failures of the distributor rotor arm, the result being that he ran out of time and did not finish. Simo had no more luck on the San Remo rally, in October, for a rear suspension mounting bolt sheared on one of the early gravel stages, immobilising the car out of reach of service support.

By the end of the season Lampinen had decided to retire from rallying and duly announced this before the start of the RAC rally. Perhaps this was a factor in his steady and quite staid final run in the works rally team. Never on the pace, he brought TUD 683T home to Chester in a midfield 17th place.

This car's real moments of glory, however, would follow in 1980. Completely rebuilt during the winter and equipped with the Pierburg-injected version of the V8 engine, TUD 683T was allocated to Tony Pond.

Its first event, at the end of April, was the Critérium d'Alpin, which was based on the French Riviera and used many familiar ex-French Alpine stages. Pond went quickly and was lying third behind two Porsche 911s when the engine suffered valve-gear problems and could not be repaired before the car ran out of time.

Shortly afterwards everything came together at last for this car and its driver. Pond took the car, Michelin-shod, to Belgium for the all-tarmac 24 Hours of Ypres and won it very convincingly – nine whole minutes ahead of his nearest rival. Not even the very best Porsche 911s could match him, even though at one point the car required a gearbox change and the gear lever also broke off – both familiar failings.

The major success of 1980 then followed in September on the Manx Trophy event. Again using Michelin tyres, Tony fought off several formidable international rivals and won, beating Ari Vatanen's Escort RS1800 by four minutes. The car had the four-Weber engine, which was claimed to develop

Winning on the Isle of Man: TUD 683T in full flight on public roads closed for rallying.

COMPETITION RECORD	
1979 BP TV Rallysprint	
Per Eklund	1st overall
1979 1000 Lakes	
Simo Lampinen	Did not finish
1979 San Remo	
Simo Lampinen	Did not finish
1979 RAC	
Simo Lampinen	17th overall
1980 Critérium d'Alpin	
Tony Pond	Did not finish
1980 24 Hours of Ypres	
Tony Pond	1st overall
1980 Manx Trophy	
Tony Pond	1st overall

315bhp, and was geared so that Pond could reach no less than 140mph on the fastest stages! In many ways this was the copybook performance that BL had been seeking for so long, for the TR7 V8 was always in the lead and always in control of the event, despite suffering a high-speed puncture and some braking problems.

With three outright wins in its record, this car was then retired from works duties.

TUD 686T

FIRST REGISTERED	1 APRIL 1979
ENGINE SIZE	3,528cc
MODEL TYPE	TR7 V8

Although registered at the same time as its two sister cars, this car did not put in a public appearance before the 1980 Critérium d'Alpin, where the engine was fitted with the Pierburg fuel-injection installation, which was still under development. Nevertheless, Per Eklund enjoyed a really fast run and lay fourth at the end of the first of two legs. Mechanical disasters then struck, first with the need for a gearbox change, which was accomplished, and then, terminally, when

TUD 686T looks very smart before the 1979 1,000 Lakes rally, where Per Eklund drove it to a sparkling third place overall.

a rear coil spring and the engine alternator broke…

On the 24 Hours of Ypres the car ran in perfect health for most of the event and Eklund settled into second place overall behind team-mate Tony Pond. But near the end he put the car off the road and hit a concrete post, damaging the front end considerably. Amazingly, the service crew was able to patch up damage to the engine oil cooler and water radiator, but shortly afterwards a rear axle change was required and on the very last stage the gearbox failed.

Eklund drove this car again on the 1,000 Lakes rally, where it ran with a mixture of tyres, mostly Michelin but sometimes Dunlop, and was equipped with the four-Weber type of engine. Compared with the lacklustre performance in Finland in 1979, the works TR7 V8 had obviously improved considerably. Throughout the event, which featured no fewer than 48 classic high-speed special stages, Per was always among the fastest drivers and finally took an extremely encouraging third place overall.

For its last outing, the 1980 RAC rally, TUD 686T started very well, Eklund holding second or third place on the early tarmac stages, and only slipping to fourth place on the Yorkshire, Kielder and Scottish borders stages. After an enforced clutch change at the Carlisle control, however, the engine suddenly suffered a major blow-up and it was all over.

COMPETITION RECORD	
1980 Critérium d'Alpin	
Per Eklund	Did not finish
1980 24 Hours of Ypres	
Per Eklund	Did not finish
1980 1,000 Lakes	
Per Eklund	3rd overall
1980 RAC	
Per Eklund	Did not finish

XJO 414V

XJO 414V was new in September 1979 for Per Eklund to drive in the San Remo rally, where he was forced to retire after the engine consumed all its oil. In 1980 this car had a troubled season in Roger Clark's hands.

FIRST REGISTERED	1 SEPTEMBER 1979
ENGINE SIZE	3,528cc
MODEL TYPE	TR7 V8

With Per Eklund at the wheel, this car – if we go by its new registration number – made its début on the 1979 San Remo rally, where it ran in carburettor form rather than with fuel injection following the unsatisfactory performance of the Pierburg system fitted to TUD 682T on the 1,000 Lakes rally (see page 243).

Per started well, setting one fastest stage time against the might of the works Fiat and Lancia team cars, but a navigational error on one of the long transport stages in northern Italy led to the car running very late, and during a flat-out dash to regain some time the V8 engine let go; problems with the scavenge pump side of the dry-sump breathing system were again blamed.

There was no luck of any type on the RAC rally, where Eklund suffered various delays, including several punctures and the need to fix the clutch fork alignment. The final result was that he had to settle for a totally dispirited 13th overall. As the records would later show, this was not going to be a 'lucky' car.

For the 1980 Circuit of Ireland, the XJO 414V identity reappeared as Roger Clark's car, although one expert writer stated that this was his old car 'with a new bodyshell'. Since the last appearance of the 'old' car, SJW 546S, was two months earlier on the Mintex rally, there may be some truth in this! Whatever, XJO 414V once again used the Weber four-carburettor engine in its latest form.

Neither a new identity nor a new bodyshell brought any luck, for Roger failed to finish the Circuit of Ireland. With no fewer than 56 stages, this four-day event was bound to be a gruelling test of man and machine. Clark was well up with the leaders for the first half of this tarmac event and lay third at the Killarney halt, but on the 38th stage a baffle tray in the V8 engine came adrift and the oil pump belt also broke,

bringing about yet another disquieting engine failure.

For a time it looked as if Roger's luck would change on the 33-stage Welsh rally. Although his rumbling TR7 V8 could not quite match the pace of the works Ford Escorts and Talbot Sunbeam-Lotus cars, he eased his way up to seventh place overall before the final Eppynt tests had to be tackled. Then, just two stages from the end, the car suffered a fuel pump failure, the engine stopped and the car was out.

In the 45-stage Scottish rally, held in the heat and dust of June, Roger finally urged XJO 414V to an honourable finish, but his ninth place overall was some distance, and time, behind Tony Pond's fourth-placed sister car. On the high-speed Manx Trophy rally, however, the rear axle failed only six stages from the finish and immobilised the machine, Clark having been settled inside the 'top ten' of a distinguished field.

Roger's last appearance in this car came in the RAC rally, where he was not as competitive as the other works TR7 V8 drivers at first, but by smooth and consistent driving he clawed his way up to seventh overall. Then, with only a handful of special stages to go, the engine's oil pump drive

belt came adrift, all oil pressure disappeared, and that was that. It was a cruel way for a year-long effort in an unfamiliar car to come to an end.

COMPETITION RECORD	
1979 San Remo	
Per Eklund	Did not finish
1979 RAC	
Per Eklund	13th overall
1980 Circuit of Ireland	
Roger Clark	Did not finish
1980 Welsh	
Roger Clark	Did not finish
1980 Scottish	
Roger Clark	9th overall
1980 Manx Trophy	
Roger Clark	Did not finish
1980 RAC	
Roger Clark	Did not finish

HRW 250V

FIRST REGISTERED	7 AUGUST 1979
ENGINE SIZE	3,528cc
MODEL TYPE	TR7 V8

Two brand-new cars, HRW 250V and HRW 251V, were built up during the winter of 1979/80. Technically they were little changed from the 1979 cars, although for this car's first event, the Rally of Portugal, the fuel-injected version of the V8 was used. But this was little benefit to Tony Pond, who had rejoined the team after a season with Chrysler/Talbot, for the engine blew up after only two special stages, the cause a seized crankshaft bearing, which was

puzzling for the team as this was not a familiar problem area.

Things looked up on the Scottish rally, where Pond was always competitive against his main rivals – two works Escorts and Anders Kullang's Opel Ascona 400. Even so, he had to cope with a spate of broken throttle cables and a gearbox change on the first day before the car and the team settled down, allowing Pond to finish fourth overall and record his best result for some time on an international event.

Months later, in the Eaton Yale TV Rallysprint at

During 1980 HRW 250V was used in two major events and a TV rallysprint. The following year it was loaned to journalist Philip Young for him to contest the Rally of the Himalayas.

COMPETITION RECORD	
1980 Portugal	
Tony Pond	Did not finish
1980 Scottish	
Tony Pond	4th overall
1980 Eaton Yale TV Rallysprint	
Tony Pond/Alan Jones	1st overall/ 2nd equal overall
1980 Crest Forest Stages	
Harry Hockly	Finished

Donington Park, there was an intriguing contest between four rally drivers and four F1 drivers, one of the challenges being to race each other in identical Mazda RX-7s. Unlike the previous year's event, this time there was no water splash to drown out the V8 engine, and on the rally stage Pond was comfortably fastest of all in HRW 250V. Predictably enough, F1 driver Alan Jones was slower in the same car, and although the size of his deficit – eight seconds on a 90-second stage – was considerable, he made amends in the Mazda race

to end up equal second overall under the complex points scoring system. But Pond's performance on the track was good enough to give him outright victory, inspiring *Autosport* to headline its report 'Upstaging the racers'.

Only a month later the entire Triumph rally programme was abruptly closed down so the rallysprint turned out to be this car's – or should I say this identity's? – last competitive appearance as a works entry, although it was loaned to Harry Hockly for a minor event.

HRW 251V

When HRW 251V's works career was officially over, in 1980, it was retained by the factory and a year later was loaned to American driver John Buffum for the 1981 RAC rally, but he did not figure in the results.

FIRST REGISTERED	7 AUGUST 1979
ENGINE SIZE	3,528cc
MODEL TYPE	TR7 V8

Along with HRW 250V, this new car was built up during the winter of 1979/80, and for the Rally of Portugal it was allocated to Per Eklund. For this first event its specification was almost identical to that of the late-1979 models, complete with a Weber-carburettor engine.

The engine never seemed to run cleanly in Portugal and Eklund struggled, lying only eighth by the time the field arrived at Povoa de Varzim, the halfway rest halt. During the second leg his car needed a change of rear axle and gearbox, and then on the 27th of 47 special stages the SU fuel pump installation failed and immobilised the TR7 V8.

With his car refreshed for use in the *Daily Mirror* TV Rallysprint, held on the Esgair Dafydd stage in central Wales, Eklund then astonished everyone. He set fastest time in practice and was fastest on the uphill passage of the stage, but then Pentti Airikkala's Vauxhall Chevette HS overcame him in the overall standings, leaving Per second overall. But then it all went wrong on the Scottish rally, where the engine suffered a catastrophic failure before half distance.

For the 1,000 Lakes rally, held in Finland in August, the veteran Timo Mäkinen was persuaded to drive a works TR7 V8, and on this event HRW 251V ran in identical form to Per Eklund's sister car (TUD 686T), with the four-carburettor engine and a choice of Michelin or Dunlop tyres. Not as fast as Eklund on this occasion, Mäkinen was eliminated after his co-driver miscalculated how much petrol was required for a particular stage, with the consequence that the car ran dry just before the end of the test.

For the 1980 RAC rally the American champion, John Buffum, who had already won innumerable events in TR7s and TR7 V8s on the other side of the Atlantic, was invited to drive HRW 251V, which had become, to an extent, the team's spare. Buffum used BF Goodrich tyres to satisfy his existing tyre contracts and BL decided that he should run with a Pierburg fuel-injected engine. Although he put up a great show throughout, Buffum made two big mistakes in the Kielder complex, the first when he speared up a firebreak in the tree lines, the second by going off the track. These delays cost him 22 minutes, but he kept plugging on until the very last of the 70 stages, at Speech House in the Forest of Dean, where the car broke an axle shaft and was stranded.

COMPETITION RECORD
1980 Portugal
Per Eklund — Did not finish
1980 *Daily Mirror* TV Rallysprint
Per Eklund — 2nd overall
1980 Scottish
Per Eklund — Did not finish
1980 1,000 Lakes
Timo Mäkinen — Did not finish
1980 RAC
John Buffum — Did not finish

JJO 931W

FIRST REGISTERED	1 AUGUST 1980
ENGINE SIZE	3,528cc
MODEL TYPE	TR7 V8

According to the registration number, this was the very last of the works Triumph TR7 V8s, a brand-new car that theoretically came into existence on 1 August 1980, so that for marketing purposes it could use the latest 'W' suffix registration letter.

The car was allocated to Tony Pond for the RAC rally and it only tackled this one event. Stories have since circulated that JJO 931W was just a new number applied to an existing machine, but as BL seemed to change bodyshells on a regular basis this may not be at all significant.

Although Pond finished only seventh overall, he made many headlines along the way – and gained many new admirers. First there was the episode with a lions' feeding table on the very first stage! Starting from Bath, the rally went to nearby Longleat Safari Park and there it slid off the muddy track – thank goodness the lions had been temporarily accommodated elsewhere – and hit this sturdy structure, which rumpled the roof line and shattered the windscreen. This cost three minutes, which meant that Pond was instantly relegated to about 140th place and would spend the rest of the four-day event clawing his way back up the field.

With the roof approximately beaten back into shape and a new windscreen rather untidily fixed into place, the car was competitive once again. There was further incident, however, when Pond slid off the road for 15 minutes on the Calderdale stage, one of the fast Yorkshire stages, leaving him well down. Even so, he managed to get back to seventh place by the end, although nearly 30 minutes behind the winner. Along the way he set fastest time on five stages, second fastest on three stages and third fastest on no fewer than 18 stages.

If only this car/driver combination could have continued into 1981, what further honours might have been achieved?

COMPETITION RECORD
1980 RAC
Tony Pond — 7th overall

CHAPTER 10:
STANDARD EIGHT, TEN AND PENNANT (1955–59)

It would be quite wrong to complete a detailed study of works Triumphs in motorsport without covering how the 'sister' Standard marque fitted into the scheme of things. This explains why it is now time to consider the valiant and sometimes successful rally careers of the SC Standards, SC standing for 'Small Car' in Standard-Triumph project coding.

The SC was a versatile car built as a saloon, estate car, van and pick-up, and powered by a tiny 803cc or 948cc engine. It was Standard-Triumph's first all-new small car of the post-war period, for the Triumph Mayflower had used a side-valve engine inherited from the pre-war period. A great deal of investment capital was injected into the SC and its commercial success was of vital importance to the company. It was launched in 1953 as the 803cc Standard Eight and then joined by the visually similar 948cc Standard Ten in 1954.

The Eight and Ten were neat little cars but they could not be considered 'performance' models by any stretch of the imagination as they struggled to exceed 60mph! But they did

have competition careers because there were opportunities in events where technical regulations were very strict – or even where they were very lax. So it was that works Standards ran variously as much-modfied cars or as standard showroom models – whichever was best for the circumstances. It should be noted that these cars were born at a time when no one had even considered the concept of the 'homologation special'.

The first appearance of the Ten came with the entry of four works cars in the 1955 Monte Carlo rally, where close study of the regulations suggested that modified Tens might have a better chance than standard ones. This was the first of several such stratagems that Ken Richardson would employ. The main engineering department at Banner Lane carried out the engine work with much advice from Lewis Dawtrey's technical department, and there was also outside involvement from Alexander Engineering of Haddenham, Oxfordshire.

John Gott drove one of the cars, PRW 532, on the Monte in the Grand Touring category and wrote about the experience in the issue of *Autosport* dated 11 February 1955. The following extracts give interesting insight into the specification and level of preparation of his Ten.

'I was… delighted when the offer of a wheel in the Standard team not only permitted me to compete in what may well prove the turning point on the road back to the great "Montes" of pre-war, but also allowed me to prove most extensively a very intriguing little motor car.

'They succeeded… in transforming the little cars into real wolves in sheep's clothing, although no attempt was made to reduce their weight by removing trimming, upholstery, and other "comfort" equipment. Indeed, the "Monte" cars weighed considerably more, with their additional equipment, than the normal road cars would have done.

'The engines were carefully assembled, balanced and polished, and the compression ratio raised to 8.25:1. Twin SU carburettors were fitted and the camshaft slightly modified. All this raised the bhp to around 46bhp, as compared with the normal 33. Good handling was improved by roll bars, and the brakes carefully assembled and fitted with "hard" linings.

'More might have been attempted had not the strike at Standards intervened, and only many hours of hard work late into the night enabled the four cars… to catch the plane from Ferryfield [now called Lydd] on the Sunday before the start from Monte Carlo.

'It had run perfectly, the only attention required being a change of exhaust flange gasket, and had averaged just over 30mpg, despite heavy use of the gears. Maximum speed in top was 75/80mph, and in third around 65mph.'

In fact this was as exciting as it got! Standard-Triumph did not seem to be as committed as, for instance, Renault, which turned its new Dauphine into a formidable, much-modified rally car. The company dabbled with modifications such as aluminium door skins and larger drum brakes from time to

Three works Standard Tens lined up on the way to Monte Carlo in January 1955. From left are Mary Walker and Betty Haig in PRW 894, Ken Richardson and Kit Heathcote in PRW 534, and John Gott and Ray Brookes in PRW 532.

Having studied the handicap formula for the Tulip rally of 1956, Standard-Triumph entered a squad of no fewer than five perfectly standard Standard Eights. As it transpired, three of them finished second, third and fourth overall. Along with the works Austin A30 that went on to win the event overall, four of them are seen in close formation on the Zandvoort circuit test during the rally. Led by Tom Gold's privately entered example, Paddy Hopkirk is ahead of Johnny Wallwork's sister car at this moment.

All four of the new Pennants being prepared for the 1958 RAC rally. They had not then been registered, so the identity of each car cannot be clarified. In this snow-hit event, the Pennants took second overall (Ron Goldbourn), third overall (Tommy Gold), and the Manufacturers' Team Prize – yet they were never used again!

time, but not with the more worthwhile avenue of serious engine development. That could have made a great deal of difference: as the racing Spitfires demonstrated, the SC engine eventually proved capable of remarkable things (see Chapter 6).

Even so, over the next two seasons modified Standard Tens performed well and with honour, even occasionally appearing in saloon car races, but they were no faster at the end of this period than when they started out. They were, however, a useful adjunct to Standard-Triumph's TR2s and TR3s, especially in events such as the Tulip where the regulations sometimes leaned heavily against sports cars of any type.

It was in the Dutch event of 1955 that the works Standard Eight got its one and only chance to shine: a peculiarity of the regulations favoured the use of small-engined saloons and made the normal version of the Eight – not the GT – look an even more promising contender than the Ten.

After the end of the 1956 season, Standard took a back seat in the works team's activities until 1958, when new Tens were prepared to take advantage of regulations that sometimes favoured modified family cars. First of all, in the 1958 Monte, it was Johnny Wallwork's turn to pedal a little Ten, and Cyril Corbishley joined in later in the year.

That same year a successful attempt was made to scatter a little fairy dust on the image of the newly launched Pennant, which had been announced at the previous Earls Court Motor Show. The Pennant was very similar to the existing Ten in its structure and technical layout, but it was given an

extensively face-lifted nose and tail to add some customer appeal for the next two years, until the Triumph Herald became available.

Once again Ken Richardson applied some cunning and concluded that the Pennant might be a promising class entry in the Grand Touring category of the RAC rally, even though it was heavier and bulkier than the Ten. The works built up

four new Pennants, complete with the now-familiar twin-SU derivative of the 948cc engine as well as Laycock overdrive, which had become optionally available on Eights, Tens and Pennants. A Ten was also prepared for Corbishley to drive.

The performance of the little Standards on the 1958 RAC rally was quite exceptional and they came within a snow-drift's width of outright victory. This was the most rugged and demanding RAC rally yet held, partly because it was held in March and partly because the weather was unusually severe, with some roads blocked by snow and many covered in sheet ice. This was an event where rally-craft, a co-driver's cunning, careful reading of the regulations and sheer gritty experience mattered more than having a powerful car, particularly as there were many tight navigation sections in the Welsh, Lake District and Yorkshire sections. The comfortable little Pennants had a good chance of success.

As related in my individual car histories, it was only the remarkable Peter Harper and his works Sunbeam Rapier that stopped the Standards from sweeping the board, for two of the Pennants led the event at the overnight halt. Ron Gould-bourn and Tom Gold finished second and third respectively

and Corbishley's Ten finished sixth, these three cars thereby winning the Manufacturers' Team Prize.

Although the Pennants were not seen again, the Ten (TRW 607) was kept on the fleet until spring 1959 and joined by two more examples in showroom specification (VVC 675 and WWK 512) so that a team could be entered in any event with a promising set of regulations. Opportunities, in fact, were few and far between, Maurice Gatsonides' second in class in the 1958 Tulip rally – in which five works TR3As took part – proving to be the only high spot.

This was the point at which that large and genial West-countryman Ian 'Tiny' Lewis arrived on the works scene. He had already begun to win British regional events using his own Standards, first a Ten and then a Pennant, always with his personal registration number TL 5. He was given a great deal of works assistance for his Pennant on the 1959 Monte Carlo rally, and thereafter moved up to running Triumph Herald Coupés.

The smart new Heralds then took over from the Tens and Pennants, the last official outing for one of the Standards being in Gregor Grant's hands in the 1959 Tulip rally.

Maurice Gatsonides in his Standard Ten, NRW 953, on his way to fourth overall in the 1955 Tulip rally.

NRW 953

FIRST REGISTERED	6 APRIL 1955
ENGINE SIZE	948cc
MODEL TYPE	TEN

Although this Standard Ten carried an earlier registration number than the four works sister cars that took part in the 1955 Monte Carlo rally, it was registered at a later date and did not appear until that year's Tulip rally, where it was entrusted to Maurice Gatsonides. To suit Tulip rally regulations, it was prepared in absolutely standard condition, without any of the go-faster equipment fitted to the four original Tens.

It was typical of Gatsonides, the deep-thinking Dutchman, that he spent a lot of time reading the typically complex regulations in order to work out which time/handicap/class category would most likely bring success on this event, and which classes would attract the toughest opposition. Ken Richardson allowed him free rein to make his choice from Standard-Triumph's works arsenal, and was apparently somewhat surprised to be told that neither his newly successful 'GT' Standard Tens – with which Jimmy Ray had just won the RAC rally – nor his ever-improving TR2s were what Gatso wanted.

Instead the Dutchman requested an absolutely standard 'showroom-category' Ten with left-hand drive in order to compete in the up-to-1,000cc 'Standard Touring' category.

Such a car had to be 'borrowed' from elsewhere within the company and NRW 953, which had been intended for a blameless life as a demonstration car, was found.

It would take too long to explain the ins and outs of the Tulip rally handicap, so one must merely state that Gatso's pre-event calculations and forecasts proved successful. Not only did he win the capacity class, narrowly beating Rolf Mellde in a works Saab 92 by just 6.4 seconds, but he was also classified fourth overall on handicap, beaten by a Mercedes-Benz 300SL, a Bristol 403 and a Mercedes-Benz 220A. If Gatso could have been just 2.1 seconds faster on one or other of the special tests, he would have taken third place.

It was a remarkable result that inspired the works team to enter a fleet of Standard Eights in the 1956 event, with even more outstanding results. As far as NRW 953 was concerned, however, it was a 'one-event wonder' and the car soon disappeared from sight.

```
COMPETITION RECORD
1955 Tulip
Maurice Gatsonides                    4th overall
```

OOT 909

FIRST REGISTERED	NOT KNOWN
ENGINE SIZE	948cc
MODEL TYPE	TEN

Although this car was not strictly a works machine – in that it was not originally built and maintained by Ken Richardson's competitions department in Coventry – it was swept into the team for the 1956 RAC rally with its talented owner/driver Peter Cooper. A Bournemouth-based motor trader, Cooper was well worth this one-off promotion for he had shown his prowess when he finished second overall in the 1954 RAC rally in a privately prepared TR2.

For this event the existing works Tens continued to run in the 'Grand Touring' category, complete with twin SU carburettors and all the other engine modifications, while Cooper's own Ten ran as 'standard' in the 1.3-litre class. This proved to be a very wise stratagem, for he won that class very comfortably indeed as well as taking fifth overall – an excellent showing for a car with only 33bhp.

```
COMPETITION RECORD
1956 RAC
Peter Cooper                          5th overall
```

PRW 532

FIRST REGISTERED	9 NOVEMBER 1954
ENGINE SIZE	948cc
MODEL TYPE	TEN

PRW 532 was one of the four original 'Grand Touring' Standard Tens prepared at Banner Lane in December 1954 and January 1955 with the specific intention of competing in the 1955 Monte Carlo rally. Its three sister cars were PRW 534, PRW 893 and PRW 894.

John Gott, who had driven the Frazer Nash that had defeated all the TR2s in the 1954 French Alpine rally, was invited to drive PRW 532, with the implication that he might become a regular and senior team member in future. Well-known as the 'rallying policeman', Gott later became Chief Constable of Northamptonshire but still continued to go rallying as a hobby. As it transpired, this would be Gott's only drive for Standard-Triumph as he would shortly join the newly formed BMC rally team instead – it was rumoured that, as a very strong and forceful character, he and Ken Richardson clashed with each other on several occasions.

Like its sister cars, PRW 532 was equipped with twin SU carburettors. Although the power increase from 33bhp to 46bhp does not sound startling by modern standards, it was an improvement of nearly 40 per cent and this made this Ten comfortably faster than other small British cars of the period, notably the side-valve/three-speed Ford Anglia. Visually, the Ten looked standard apart from its pair of extra driving laps mounted on the front bumper, and retained its wheel covers throughout the rally. On the event Gott and co-driver Ray Brookes were dismayed to be caught out of time at several secret checks, causing them to finish way down the listings, behind two of their team-mates.

This car then missed out on the RAC rally, which followed in March, because it was destined instead for minor fame in saloon car racing when Stirling Moss was somehow persuaded to drive it in a 15-lap saloon car race at the International Trophy meeting at Oulton Park. Stirling finished second in the 1,100cc class to Tony Brooks' two-stroke DKW in an entertaining one-off drive made possible by BP fuel-company sponsorship to pay his fee.

Back in more familiar surroundings, PRW 532 was then refurbished, retaining its twin-carburettor engine, anti-roll bars and other now-proven 'Grand Touring' equipment, and

Lined up at the air ferry terminal in the UK before making for the start of the 1955 Monte Carlo rally are the four works Standard Tens with sales representative Lyndon Mills (the tall figure in the centre) and crew members (from left) Johnny Wallwork, Jimmy Ray, Betty Haig, Mary Walker, Ken Richardson, Kit Heathcote, John Gott and Ray Brookes.

sent out to compete in the 1956 RAC rally with Johnny Wall-work at the wheel. Compared with the 1955 event, which was virtually obliterated by snow, the 1956 event was held in much more favourable weather – favourable, that is, to faster, more powerful and more sporting cars! It was not surprising that the little Standard was left panting by Lyndon Sims' Aston Martin DB2/4 and Ian Appleyard's Jaguar XK140, but it still managed to win its class, the up-to-1,300cc GT category, with other works and private Tens backing it up.

COMPETITION RECORD	
1955 Monte Carlo	
John Gott	116th overall
1955 Oulton Park saloon race	
Stirling Moss	2nd in class
1956 RAC	
Johnny Wallwork	1st in class

PRW 534

FIRST REGISTERED	9 NOVEMBER 1954
ENGINE SIZE	948cc
MODEL TYPE	TEN

Team boss Ken Richardson elected to drive this car, the second of the four newly built 'GT' Tens, on the 1955 Monte Carlo rally. Like other team members, he started from Monte Carlo itself, and they all had to battle with awful weather conditions. Despite the little Ten's rather limited performance, he brought the car home fourth in its capacity class, behind a works Panhard Dyna, a works Renault 4CV and team-mate Johnny Wallwork's Ten. No one could have hoped for more.

Along with Jimmy Ray (PRW 894) and Bobby Dickson

(PRW 893), Richardson then drove the car in the RAC rally in March, all three Tens once again running as 'Grand Touring' entries. This was a typical 1950s-style 'Rally of the Tests', meandering all over Britain from starting points at Hastings and Blackpool, embracing 2,000 miles and ending up at Hastings. There was a capacity entry of 240 starters and the three works Tens started in line astern from Blackpool.

The weather was appalling, which made getting to some of the major speed and manoeuvring tests – those at Oulton Park, Cadwell Park and Prescott – more adventuresome than the tests themselves. The adverse conditions also meant that there was little chance of any car keeping to time on the night navigation sections in Yorkshire, the Lake District, Wales and the West Country.

Crashes and blocked roads were frequent, so it was miraculous that all three Tens somehow made it to the finish. Richardson and Ray were always in contention and shared most of the fastest times in their class in the 11 special tests, and in the end Richardson finished third overall, beaten only by Ray and by privateer Harold Rumsey in his Triumph TR2.

PRW 534, which had become known as 'Richardson's own Ten', then found itself a new driver for the RAC rally. Richardson had apparently promised a young Ulsterman, Paddy Hopkirk, a works Triumph drive in the 1955 Monte Carlo rally but had been unable to fulfil that promise, so his recompense was to invite Paddy to drive on the RAC rally – in a Standard Ten. As there were no spare works Tens available, Richardson stood down so that Paddy could take over his car, with regular co-driver John Garvey.

In Paddy's own words, as told in his autobiography, '...it was a bloody good car. In those days the RAC had driving tests on the promenade at Blackpool, around pylons and so on. The first few tests I cleaned up, achieving three zeroes for fastest in class, because I could use the handbrake and everything. So Ken Richardson was in a bar somewhere in Blackpool when he heard on the radio that some unknown young Irish driver was leading the rally. He nearly fell off his bar stool, and I never looked back...'

Unhappily, Paddy then made one big mistake on a night navigation section in Yorkshire. He went off the road and holed the sump (sump shields were not used in those halcyon days), losing so much time before a repair could be made that he could only be classified as a 'finisher'.

That was the end of a short but colourful career for PRW 534 but the start of an even more colourful one for Paddy, who became a regular member of the works team until 1958.

COMPETITION RECORD	
1955 Monte Carlo	
Ken Richardson	4th in class
1955 RAC	
Ken Richardson	3rd overall
1956 RAC	
Paddy Hopkirk	Finished

PRW 893

FIRST REGISTERED	10 NOVEMBER 1954
ENGINE SIZE	948cc
MODEL TYPE	TEN

This, the third of the four works Standard Tens to begin its career on the 1955 Monte Carlo rally, was mechanically identical to the other cars and finished in a sparkling third place in its class in the hands of Johnny Wallwork, who had won the 1954 RAC rally the previous year. The Ten was beaten in the class only by works Panhard Dyna and Renault 4CV cars, both of which had the traction advantage endowed by having their engines over the driving wheels.

It was not, however, a totally routine journey, as co-driver Jimmy Ray once told me. Wallwork, who collected the car from Coventry only just in time to join his team mates on the air ferry to France, got involved in a dispute with Ken Richardson after choosing to remove the blades of the engine's cooling fan, presumably in an effort to eke out a little more power. The crew also encountered problems with the front passenger door persistently coming open, cured only with a bodge using a bolt bought from a French ironmonger's shop. Finally, before the final test around the GP circuit in Monaco, Wallwork broke the rules by doing pre-event practice and was immediately arrested by the police, consequently spending the night in jail. The result was that Jimmy Ray drove in that final test but got none of the credit.

Suitably refreshed, this car was then allocated to Bobby

Johnny Wallwork (beard) and Jimmy Ray with PRW 893, the Standard Ten in which they contested the 1955 Monte Carlo rally, taking third in their capacity class.

Dickson for the 1955 RAC rally, but Dickson was apparently not as good a driver in rallies as he was in races, and his performance was disappointing. He did, however, make it to the finish, whereupon the car almost immediately went into storage, not to be used again until 1956. For Dickson, at least, there was the joy of being a member of the team that won the Manufacturer's Team Prize.

PRW 893 then became a 'Cinderella' for the rest of its

career in 1956. First of all it was loaned to Tommy Wisdom, motoring correspondent of the *Daily Herald* and an experienced rally driver, for the Monte Carlo rally. Choosing to start from Lisbon, Wisdom enjoyed an uneventful journey in the little Standard, but like the larger Vanguards in this event (see Chapter 11) he found that his little car did not have the performance or the agility to muscle its way into the final qualifiers and finished 133rd overall.

Only a few weeks later the car was handed to *Autosport*'s Gregor Grant for the Lyons-Charbonnières rally, an event in which he had performed well with works TR2s in the two previous years. Accompanied by Kit Heathcote, Richardson's assistant in the competitions department and a very capable rally co-driver, Grant was hoping for another good showing, of course, but it was not to be. Although the little car was nimble, it was quite incapable of keeping up with the timing schedule – or with sports cars such as Porsches and Alfa Romeos – on the icy roads of this high-speed winter event.

The factory did not take any works TR2s on the 1956 RAC rally, but instead entered much-modified Standard Tens. This is the line-up of four of the cars involved, taken after the finish in front of the Imperial Hotel, Blackpool: OOT 909 (Peter Cooper and Geoff Holland), XEH 224 (Tom Gold and June Gold), PRW 532 (Johnny Wallwork and Willy Cave) and PRW 894 (Harold Rumsey and Peter Roberts). Paddy Hopkirk's PRW 534 was absent.

Grant manfully kept the little car on the road in conditions that were sometimes as severe as the worst ever encountered on the Monte Carlo rally, but he could only finish a lowly ninth in class.

And with that the exploits of this fleet of modified Standard Tens came to a close.

COMPETITION RECORD	
1955 Monte Carlo	
Johnny Wallwork	3rd in class
1955 RAC	
Bobby Dickson	Finished
1956 Monte Carlo	
Tommy Wisdom	133rd overall
1956 Lyons-Charbonnières	
Gregor Grant	9th in class

PRW 894

FIRST REGISTERED	10 NOVEMBER 1954
ENGINE SIZE	948cc
MODEL TYPE	TEN

Standard-Triumph's publicity chiefs were always on the look-out for favourable mention of their products, so it can be no coincidence that Mary Walker, who had achieved some steady results during 1954 in her privately owned TR2, should be invited to join the works team to drive a 'GT' Standard Ten in the 1955 Monte Carlo rally. Along with whisky heiress Betty Haig, it was her first appointment as a works driver – and her last.

The allocated car was PRW 894, which would go on to become even more famous a few months later when it won the RAC rally outright – but not with the charming Mary at the wheel. Starting along with all her team-mates from Monte Carlo, she ran steadily until becoming badly affected by flooding along the route, suffering serious delays on her way to the time control at Vesoul, north-east of Dijon, and finally finishing a dispirited 150th overall.

With its new driver Jimmy Ray, PRW 894 then achieved lasting fame in Standard-Triumph circles by winning the 1955 RAC rally outright. As already described in the entry for PRW 534 (page 254), this was an extremely demanding event that was quite dominated by the nimble little Tens, the result being that Ray and his co-driver Brian Harrocks won the event very decisively.

There was not much money to be made from this kind of success in those days, as Jimmy later told me: 'Beforehand Ken Richardson had said that all [prize] money would be pooled – so I can't remember receiving a fat cheque – maybe £200 or so. But I do remember wanting the twin-carb kit for my own Standard Ten. I mentioned this and Standard-Triumph said, "Well, you can have those for nothing". And I think that was all.'

The motoring media was very upbeat about this result. The *Autocar*'s sports editor, J.A. Cooper, commented: 'Young

COMPETITION RECORD	
1955 Monte Carlo	
Mary Walker	150th overall
1955 RAC	
Jimmy Ray	1st overall
1956 RAC	
Harold Rumsey	3rd in class

Jimmy Ray is undoubtedly to be congratulated on his success, which underlines his position as BTRDA rally champion during the past two seasons... The products of the Standard organisation certainly had a field day... Their successes emphasise their progress in competitions during the last year or two, owing in no small degree to the work of W.K. Richardson.'

Harold Rumsey, who had come close to beating Ray in the 1955 RAC rally driving his own TR2, then got the call-up from Richardson to join the works team for the 1956 event, using the car that had defeated him! This was by nature of a 'thank you', for in the end this was Rumsey's one-and-only works drive for Standard-Triumph, in a car that was unfamiliar to him. Accompanied by Peter Roberts, Rumsey put up a fine show to take third place in the 1.3-litre Grand Touring category.

SHP 876

FIRST REGISTERED	26 MARCH 1956
ENGINE SIZE	803cc
MODEL TYPE	EIGHT

Purely because the Tulip rally of 1956 imposed a set of handicap regulations that favoured small-engined cars, Standard investigated the detail and came up with the surprising conclusion that a road-going Standard Eight would fare even better than the formidably successful TR3s that were already being built.

To his great credit, Ken Richardson persuaded his sporting-minded managing director, Alick Dick, to invest in a set of

Six totally unmodified Standard Eights ready to leave the Canley factory to compete in the Tulip Rally of 1956. The crew members (from left) are Tommy Gold, June Gold, Paddy Hopkirk, John Garvey, Dennis O'M. Taylor, Lew Tracey, Cherry Osborne, Lola Grounds and Johnny Wallwork. SHP 878 would finish second overall, with SHP 876 third and SHP 877 fourth.

Standard Eights. Dick readily agreed to the plan because he apparently thought it was all a good giggle and, if properly handled, would be a great publicity gimmick for his sales staff. The 1956 Tulip rally, therefore, became the one and only event where Standard Eights – no fewer than five of them – were entered as a works team.

The five cars – registered SHP 876, SHP 877, SHP 878, SHP 879 and SHP 884 – were prepared in something of a hurry but this mattered little because no modification was allowed. A sixth privately entered Eight, XEH 915, also took part, driven by owner Tom Gold and his wife June. The gamble was worth it for one of the works Eights so nearly won – the car driven by Johnny Wallwork was beaten only by an 803cc Austin A30 entered by a privateer who had spotted the same anomaly in the regulations.

The fortunes of SHP 876, driven by Paddy Hopkirk, were typical of three of the five works Eights. Paddy finished third overall, beaten narrowly by Wallwork and the aforemen-

tioned Austin A30 piloted by the father and son Brookes pair. All three cars were driven to the limit all the time in the speed tests, the vast majority of which were hillclimbs. The results showed that Paddy was just 46 seconds behind Wallwork after four days of pleasant low-speed motoring – and he could have done no more. The Standard 'No 1' team of Wallwork, Hopkirk and Dennis O'M. Taylor also won the Manufacturers' Team Prize.

Except for wearing out its tyres, SHP 876 seemed no worse for its European trip, although the tiny 803cc engine had probably suffered from habitual over-revving. It was never used again.

COMPETITION RECORD
1956 Tulip
Paddy Hopkirk   3rd overall

SHP 877

FIRST REGISTERED	26 MARCH 1956
ENGINE SIZE	803cc
MODEL TYPE	EIGHT

After the description of SHP 876, little more needs to be said about this car, which was built to identical specification purely for the 1956 Tulip Rally. It was driven by Dennis O'M. Taylor and Lew Tracey, who had been successful in British events in Standard and Triumphs, and were enjoying a

one-off works appearance in the absence of Maurice Gatsonides, who was busily preparing for the East African (Coronation) Safari.

By finishing fourth overall, just 27 seconds behind Paddy Hopkirk, Taylor and Tracey helped to ensure that Standard won the Manufacturers' Team Prize. Like SHP 876, nothing more was ever heard of this car, which did not compete again as a works rally car.

COMPETITION RECORD
1956 Tulip
Dennis O'M. Taylor   4th overall

SHP 878

FIRST REGISTERED	26 MARCH 1956
ENGINE SIZE	803cc
MODEL TYPE	EIGHT

As with SHP 876 and SHP 877, this was another of the 'one-event wonder' Standards with which the company flooded the Tulip rally of 1956. Johnny Wallwork drove this one and, as far as one can see, the only visual difference between this and the other team cars was that it carried two extra driving lamps whereas all the others had only one!

Wallwork, as expected, drove his heart out and ended up second overall behind the Austin A30, leading all the other

Standards home. The Tulip rally organisers were so astonished by the relatively brisk performance of the Eights (and, for that matter, the A30) that the cars were subjected to strenuous examination at the end of the event, their engines being virtually stripped down to their component parts to confirm that they were 'sporting legal' – which, of course, they were.

It was typical of Ken Richardson's irrational way of picking his works drivers that Wallwork did not receive another works invitation until the 1958 Monte Carlo rally. Was there a personal problem between the two? We will never know.

Like all of its sister cars, SHP 878 was never used again.

COMPETITION RECORD
1956 Tulip
Johnny Wallwork   2nd overall

SHP 879

FIRST REGISTERED	28 MARCH 1956
ENGINE SIZE	803cc
MODEL TYPE	EIGHT

The fourth of the new showroom-specification Standard Eights built for the 1956 Tulip rally was allocated to Cherry Osborne and Lola Grounds, the pairing who had been entrusted with a works TR2 in the 1955 event.

This time there was no cause for celebration, for on the Col de Grimone, between Valence and Monaco, the engine sump plug came adrift and all the oil drained out of the engine, which promptly blew its bearings and expired. SHP 879 was the only one of the five works Eights that had to drop out of this event.

Like the other cars in this group, it was never used again in motorsport.

COMPETITION RECORD	
1956 Tulip	
Cherry Osborne	Did not finish

SHP 884

FIRST REGISTERED	4 APRIL 1956
ENGINE SIZE	803cc
MODEL TYPE	EIGHT

The fifth standard works Standard Eight, SHP 884, was driven on the 1956 Tulip rally by Jo Ashfield and Mary Handley-Page, but had no luck at all. When Cherry Osborne's sister car deposited all its oil on the Col de Grimone, Ashfield, running immediately behind it, promptly skidded on the slick, left the road and ended up against a tree with its front sufficiently stoved for the radiator to be wrecked.

Nothing daunted, the four ladies in these two Standards exchanged condolences, rolled up their sleeves, removed the broken radiator from Jo Ashfield's car, replaced it with the healthy one from Cherry Osborne's car, and got one car on the road again, all apparently within 20 minutes. The delay, of course, ruined their chances, and they did not figure strongly in the results.

COMPETITION RECORD	
1956 Tulip	
Jo Ashfield	Finished

TRW 598

FIRST REGISTERED	29 MARCH 1957
ENGINE SIZE	803cc
MODEL TYPE	EIGHT (VANGUARD JUNIOR)

Along with two other so-called 'Vanguard Juniors' – TRW 599 and TRW 612 – a team of three utterly outclassed saloons was sent to Sweden to compete in the Midnight Sun rally in the summer of 1957. In all other respects except that of their special Scandinavian-market badging, these were Standard Eights and they had to run in near-showroom condition, which meant that they had a top speed of less than 70mph and acceleration that was inferior to that of a Austin A35 or Morris Minor 1000 of the day.

Whoever thought that these cars could be remotely competitive has never owned up to his or her delusions. Not only were the cars very slow, but none of their drivers were used to the particular Scandinavian conditions, where most of the speed tests were held on gravel-surfaced tracks with fast and sweeping profiles.

In other words, it was a waste of time and money to commit the cars to Sweden and no such expedition was tackled again.

COMPETITION RECORD	
1957 Midnight Sun	
Tom Gold	22nd in class

TRW 599

FIRST REGISTERED	29 MARCH 1957
ENGINE SIZE	803cc
MODEL TYPE	EIGHT (VANGUARD JUNIOR)

Everything written above about TRW 598 also applies to TRW 599, and Paddy Hopkirk must have thought that he could have been better employed elsewhere. As it was, of course, Standard-Triumph was not spending much on motorsport in 1957, this being the second of only two works starts for Paddy that year.

COMPETITION RECORD	
1957 Midnight Sun	
Paddy Hopkirk	22nd overall

TRW 607

FIRST REGISTERED	29 MARCH 1957
ENGINE SIZE	948cc
MODEL TYPE	TEN

Because the small fleet of existing works Standard Tens had been sold off at the end of 1956, new cars had to be built for 1958. As it transpired, two Tens were prepared in the first weeks of 1958, along with no fewer than four mechanically similar Pennants. Like the 1955/56 Tens, this new car ran in the Grand Touring category with a more powerful engine with twin SU carburettors, along with modified suspension and braking. Maybe it was not pretty, but in those pre-Mini days it was still a very suitable little machine.

TRW 607 started its short but eventful works career in January 1958, when Johnny Wallwork used it to do battle with the awful blizzard-like conditions of the Monte Carlo rally. For what looked like good publicity and marketing reasons, the new Ten started from Glasgow, along with 84 other competitors. Amazingly, in an event where all but 59 cars were eliminated before they could reach the Principality, nine of the Glasgow starters made it – one of them being the gallant Wallwork. He lay equal 24th, having lost 21 minutes in lateness before reaching Monaco. Another of the Glasgow starters to make it, incidentally, was Macclesfield motor trader Cyril Corbishley's private Ten.

It had not, however, been uneventful, as Wallwork later told me: 'Very few people got through to Monte Carlo with a clean sheet. We Glasgow starters were lucky because before reaching Chambéry [where all approach routes joined up] we went across the Central Massif – Clermont Ferrand and Le Puy – but those people who started from other points went to the Haute Savoie first and got horribly stuck.

'I failed to take a left-hand turn, used an escape road, and was rammed by Peter Bolton, who in turn was hit by Gordon Shanley. On getting out, I had to dive head-first into a snow-drift to avoid sudden death by the arrival of Ronnie Adams, somewhat out of control!

'I was competing in the same class as the Renault Dauphine that won, and it was the first time Michelin had produced studded tyres for them. The driver lived locally, so he had two advantages – the second was that his pals were out looking for the secret regularity checks to tell him in advance...'

Even so, Wallwork settled down with co-driver Tony Beaumont to seal another splendid performance from the Standard-Triumph team. Although he started the 655-mile mountain circuit in 24th place, he clawed his way up to 13th place overall and to second in class behind the eventual outright winner, Guy Monraisse in a works Renault Dauphine.

Corbishley's reward for finishing 15th overall and second in his Monte class (for unmodified saloons) to a two-stroke DKW was an invitation to drive TRW 607 on the RAC rally two months later. This time he chose as his co-driver Phil Simister, a Ford dealer in Macclesfield, Corbishley's home town. Unfortunately for Cyril, his spirited performance in the car was quite overshadowed by the hype surrounding the works Pennants on this event.

Along with his eminent Pennant team-mates, Tom Gold and Ron Gouldbourn, Corbishley kept going steadily through the snow, ice, blockages and wintry carnage of the Welsh navigation sections, establishing himself in seventh place by the halfway rest halt in Blackpool. By the end of the event, after four days and 19 special manoeuvring and speed tests, he had moved up one more place to sixth, beaten in his class only by Gold and Gouldbourn in the Pennants.

Ken Richardson, clearly pleased with Corbishley's performance, offered him another drive in TRW 607, on the French

COMPETITION RECORD	
1958 Monte Carlo	
Johnny Wallwork	13th overall
1958 RAC	
Cyril Corbishley	6th overall
1958 French Alpine	
Cyril Corbishley	Did not finish
1959 Monte Carlo	
Cyril Corbishley	Did not finish

Alpine rally in the summer of 1958. This was a difficult event through the Italian Dolomites and the French Alps, with demanding schedules, steep mountains and surfaces that were sometimes rough, but Corbishley pedalled his little twin-SU Standard Ten to great effect until it suffered a gearbox seizure very late in the event.

Six months later, in ice and snow instead of high temperatures and sunshine, Cyril tried again in TRW 607, this time in the 1959 Monte Carlo rally. While pushing as hard as he could against the clock between Chambéry and final arrival at Monaco itself, his Ten slid off the road. As one press report put it, 'At Brianconnet the Standard Ten was parked with a flat tyre, and signs of contact with a small bridge'. He had to retire on the spot with deranged steering.

TRW 612

FIRST REGISTERED	29 MARCH 1957
ENGINE SIZE	803cc
MODEL TYPE	EIGHT (VANGUARD JUNIOR)

This was the third of the three rebadged Standard Eights that competed in the 1957 Swedish Midnight Sun rally. Like the other two cars – TRW 598 and TRW 599 – it was utterly outclassed and lacking in performance.

Nancy Mitchell tried her hardest and finished the event, but cannot have enjoyed much competitive motoring. She did not drive for Standard-Triumph again and if that was her decision, who can blame her?

COMPETITION RECORD	
1957 Midnight Sun	
Nancy Mitchell	Finished

VWK 282

FIRST REGISTERED	4 FEBRUARY 1958
ENGINE SIZE	948cc
MODEL TYPE	PENNANT

By 1958 Tom Gold was becoming something of an established member of the Standard-Triumph group of drivers who were 'on call' for selected events. When the team

decided to enter four Standard Pennants for the 1958 RAC rally, he got an invitation and elected to take the experienced Willy Cave as his co-driver.

As already noted, this quartet of Pennants used the same running gear as the established 'GT' Tens, but further developed. Although the Pennant's restyled front and rear bodywork might have made the car look a little more modern, it also added weight.

As it transpired, this RAC rally came close to being abandoned because of the very wintry conditions that settled on most of the route, especially in Wales, the Lake District and the Scottish borders. Like team-mate Ron Gouldbourn, however, Gold relished fighting against the odds, something that he did on many other British rallying weekends throughout the year. He might not have been fastest on the special tests – there were 19 of these – but he kept the little car on the road, visited all the required controls (sometimes very late), and found himself second overall to Gouldbourn at the rest halt in Blackpool.

Organisationally, the second half of the event – to Hastings via the Lake District, the Scottish borders and Yorkshire – was something of a shambles. Depending on your point of view, the event was marred or enhanced – through becoming even more demanding – by the amount of snow that had settled, making access to some time controls very hazardous or even impossible because of blockages. Careful reading of

Tom Gold and Willy Cave finished third overall in their Standard Pennant, VWK 282, in the 1958 RAC rally. Here Gold tackles the final manoeuvring test on the Promenade at the finish in Hastings.

the regulations, however, showed that after incurring a penalty for missing a control it was possible to regain the marks by getting to the next control on time...

Stuart Turner, who co-drive Ron Gouldbourn in VWK 285, a sister Pennant, commented years later in his autobiography: 'Many of the hills were blocked with snow: not many crews visited every control. The marking system was screwy because even though we were not one of the 15 crews who scrambled over the Hardknott and Wrynose Passes (which meant that we missed a control up there), we still finished ahead of all but one who did.'

The 'one who did', need I say, was the car that made meteoric progress and won the event outright – Peter Harper's

works Sunbeam Rapier. In the meantime, the co-drivers of the leading Pennants, Turner and Cave, worked out all the implications and guided their drivers to the second and third overall respectively, and the top two places in their class. It was a remarkable performance and one that was never attempted again as the Pennants did not start any other major events for the factory team.

VWK 283

FIRST REGISTERED	4 FEBRUARY 1958
ENGINE SIZE	948cc
MODEL TYPE	PENNANT

Unlike her British and Irish colleagues in Pennants on the 1958 RAC rally, the French girl, Annie Soisbault, was despondent about the combination of bad weather, British-style night navigational problems to be solved en route and

the limited performance from her game little car, which had right-hand drive at that.

This just about sums up her performance on the event, which ended within 24 hours of the start. Her Pennant was the only one of the four works cars that did not make the finish – and she made sure that she would not have to drive such a car again.

VWK 284

FIRST REGISTERED	4 FEBRUARY 1958
ENGINE SIZE	948cc
MODEL TYPE	PENNANT

By comparison with the heroic drives on the 1958 RAC rally of Tom Gold and Ron Gouldbourn in sister cars, Paddy Hopkirk's outing in this Pennant, which he first tried only the day before the event, descended into farce, tempered with determination to reach the finish at any cost.

Having suffered the same sort of delays, visits to snowdrifts and heroic avoidances as his team-mates, Paddy was approaching the Scottish town of Kelso when he realised that his car's back axle was suddenly becoming noisy and, in his judgement, was about to fail. With no chance of meeting up with any factory assistance, and even less chance of getting a new axle in a hurry, Paddy summoned up all his Irish charm, called at a conveniently sited Standard dealership in the town, Tweedsmuir Motors, and persuaded them to supply a complete axle from a Ten they already had in stock!

'The staff were wonderful,' Paddy recalled, 'and fitted an axle from a second-hand Ten in the showroom, in one hour and four minutes!' Paddy promised that the factory would furnish a new replacement axle to the dealer just as soon as he could get a message back to the 'powers that be' in Coventry – and that duly happened.

Paddy then hared off up the icy roads, trying to catch up lost time, although penalised for lateness. He set several fastest test times, only for his Pennant to suffer a shattered windscreen just before the finish in Hastings.

Was it worth it? Yes, if only because Paddy, lining up later alongside Tom Gold and Ron Gouldbourn, made sure that his Pennant was one of the trio that won the Manufacturers' Team Prize.

Like the other Pennants in this batch, this was the only event that it ever tackled.

VWK 285

FIRST REGISTERED	4 FEBRUARY 1958
ENGINE SIZE	948cc
MODEL TYPE	PENNANT

Even though Paddy Hopkirk's Standard Pennant needed a complete rear axle change en route, he managed to get it to the Hastings finish of the 1958 RAC rally.

A betting man studying the weather forecast before the 1958 RAC rally would surely have put a substantial sum on Ron Gouldbourn and Stuart Turner to win it – in anything! The fact that they were driving a rather ungainly looking Standard Pennant in the appalling conditions of ice and snow would not have changed the odds.

Gouldbourn and Turner had already proved their combined worth in British rallies in privately owned TR2s and TR3, and were about to be crowned as BTRDA/British rally champions. They set out to win the 1958 RAC rally in a car that they had certainly never driven and possibly not even seen beforehand, and they did indeed very nearly win.

As already noted in the descriptions of the performances of the other Pennants on this rally, conditions were only right for a victory if the crew willed it so – and the two Potteries-based experts made it so. Leading their class from the start and leading the rally outright by the time the much-depleted field reached the rest halt in Blackpool, they were only beaten by the amazingly talented Peter Harper and his works Sunbeam Rapier.

Along with Tom Gold and Paddy Hopkirk in sister cars, they won the Manufacturers' Team Prize very convincingly indeed. The car, though, was never seen again.

COMPETITION RECORD	
1958 RAC	
Ron Gouldbourn	2nd overall

Ron Gouldbourn and Stuart Turner took second place, overall, in the 1958 RAC rally, driving this Standard Pennant.

VVC 675

FIRST REGISTERED	1 APRIL 1958
ENGINE SIZE	948cc
MODEL TYPE	PENNANT

If Maurice Gatsonides had an evening to spare before having to submit an entry for a rally, he would spend a great deal of time reading the regulations to see if he could find what could be termed 'the unfair advantage'. Thus it was that before the Tulip rally of 1958 he concluded that a standard-specification Standard Ten – not the 'GT' variety as recently reincarnated in the shape of TRW 607 – would stand a good chance of winning the 1-litre class.

Standard-Triumph was persuaded that this was so, found VVC 675 from within the company, and set the Dutchman to work. As already noted in Chapter 1 (see page 41), this particular Tulip was much more of a fast road event than before, with the difficult-to-understand handicapping system now abandoned.

On the tight road sections of the event Gatso's hunch was justified, but a smattering of speed and circuit tests was also included and here the little car could not quite keep up with the spiritedly driven two-stroke Auto Union 1000 of Madeleine Blanchoud. Even so, second in class and 15th overall was a fine performance.

This was followed by an odd entry for Gatso in the Austrian Alpine rally, which consisted of two road sections of respectively 535 and 504 miles, to be driven by one driver only. By the end, Gatso was one of 35 drivers from 71 starters who managed to keep a clean sheet on the road, and qualified for a Gold medal. No general classification, no class awards, no special prizes, nothing – it was really rather like a grown-up Pony Club gymkhana.

VVC 675 was then put into storage at Allesley for several months before being prepared, still in showroom condition, for the 1959 Monte Carlo rally, where it would be crewed by Ron Gouldbourn and Stuart Turner, who had just been crowned British rally champions for the second time. Starting from Glasgow, they arrived safely in Monaco, and were all set to tackle the final 267-mile classification test, which required regularity at time checks, some of which were secret.

This was the part of the event where local knowledge and – if you were French – a little help from the natives made it easier to keep time and to look for the secret time checks. In this respect the Gouldbourn/Turner combination, despite being formidable in British events, usually in TR3s and TR3As, could not equal many of the continental entries and ended up well down the results.

> **COMPETITION RECORD**
> **1959 Monte Carlo**
> Ron Gouldbourn   102nd overall

TL 5

> | FIRST REGISTERED | NOT KNOWN |
> |---|---|
> | ENGINE SIZE | 948cc |
> | MODEL TYPE | PENNANT |

Although this car was not prepared at Allesley and was not a member of the official factory team, in Ian 'Tiny' Lewis's hands it was granted a great deal of factory assistance for the 1959 Monte Carlo rally, becoming the third team entry alongside the Tens of Ron Gouldbourn and Cyril Corbishley. It ended up more successful in this event than any of the other works TR3As or Tens.

Starting from Glasgow, TL 5 made its way through increasingly snowy conditions in France, arriving safely in Monaco without road penalty ready to tackle the final 267-mile mountain circuit. This started and finished in the principality, taking a route up the daunting Col de Turini from the south side before making for Castellane, then swinging back to the

east, through Puget-Theniers, to complete the circuit ten hours later.

Slower than many other cars in the event and with its driver hampered by a lack of any chance to practise, on dry sections of the route TL 5 suffered six punctures caused by overheating of the studs in the snow tyres – a lesson that Dunlop would learn for subsequent years. Lewis still managed to finish 25th overall, which was a creditable performance, especially as his class included works BMC entries for Pat Moss and John Sprinzel as well as five engine-over-driving-wheels DKWs and Renaults that had the advantage of better traction on icy hills.

This was the one and only time that TL 5 received factory assistance as a Pennant, for the next time that identity appeared – in the French Alpine rally later in 1959 – it was gracing a Triumph Herald coupé!

> **COMPETITION RECORD**
> **1959 Monte Carlo**
> Ian 'Tiny' Lewis   25th overall

WWK 512

> | FIRST REGISTERED | 5 NOVEMBER 1958 |
> |---|---|
> | ENGINE SIZE | 948cc |
> | MODEL TYPE | PENNANT |

Always happy to provide cars to Gregor Grant, the long-serving founder and editor of *Autosport*, Standard-Triumph prepared a new Ten for him to drive in the 1959 Tulip rally. The car's specification was standard apart from having overdrive, which had become an optional extra.

Although weather conditions in the French Alps were often awful, the determined Scot kept it all together through fog, mud and even some snow on the higher sections.

Despite being out-gunned by a couple of factory-sponsored two-stroke Auto Union 1000s and losing five minutes on the tight road sections, he finally took a spirited fourth place in his class.

> **COMPETITION RECORD**
> **1959 Tulip**
> Gregor Grant   4th in class

CHAPTER 11:
STANDARD VANGUARD III (1956)

I hope that Standard enthusiasts will not regard this short chapter as a hatchet job. I certainly do not intend it to be, but to any true follower of rallying there never seemed to be any rhyme, reason or rationale behind Standard-Triumph's decision to enter a fleet of six new-type Standard Vanguard IIIs as works entries in the Monte Carlo Rally of 1956. In my opinion the Vanguard could never have been competitive as a rally car, and the time, resources and money would have been better spent on Standard Tens instead. The only element of logic behind the plan was that on this particular Monte the regulations banned the use of open-top cars, so the works TR2s were not eligible.

The more one studies this aberration, the more the word 'gimmick' keeps on cropping up. The Vanguard, even the commercially successful earlier models of 1948–55, had no credible motorsport history, and even though Vanguard's 'wet-liner' engine and three-speed gearbox were shared with the TR2/TR3 range, rally regulations meant that none of the sports car's hardware could be used in this saloon.

Then, of course, there was the choice of crews. Of the six nominated 'first' drivers, only Maurice Gatsonides had any record of success on the Monte, having won it in a Ford Zephyr in 1953. Ken Richardson was the team manager with no Monte success on his record, while both Peter Cooper and Peter Bolton could charitably be described as competent British amateur drivers from the motor trade.

As for the female crews, Jo Ashfield was a driver and co-driver who had competed in several events in the 1950s, but not with any outstanding success; she had at least competed in the Monte, as a co-driver in a different make of car the previous year. Cherry Osborne, who was married to the Standard-Triumph company doctor, was an amateur driver of great enthusiasm who just happened to have a TR2 of her own and was well known to Ken Richardson.

One special test held on the approach to Monte Carlo itself, in the hills behind the principality, sealed the fate of most of the team cars. This was a downhill sprint and braking test that required, above all, a fast car, a brave driver and excellent brakes. Only Gatsonides had the sort of qualifi-cations to meet such demands, and as a consequence his was the only team car of the six to finish among the fastest 90, the number of runners that would then compete in the final regularity test that followed.

After the Monte, the redoubtable Gatsonides took his car to compete in the East African Safari, where the regulations required all the special 'comfort' features used for the Monte to be replaced by standard ones. Other than that outing, the Vanguard's involvement in serious rallying ceased, which was a merciful release.

The next time large works Standard-Triumph saloons were used in motorsport was when the formidable Group 3 Triumph 2000s appeared in 1964, when, as we have already seen, they were much more effective.

Although the Vanguard IIIs were not really competitive in the 1956 Monte Carlo rally, Maurice Gatsonides and Marcel Becquart put up a spirited performance to finish eighth overall.

RVC 202

FIRST REGISTERED	7 NOVEMBER 1955
ENGINE SIZE	2,088cc
MODEL TYPE	VANGUARD III

This car had a conventional and, as far as one can see, routine run down towards Monte Carlo, but even in the hands of motor trader Peter Cooper it was neither fast enough nor nimble enough to qualify to compete in the final mountain circuit.

COMPETITION RECORD	
1956 Monte Carlo	
Peter Cooper	92nd overall

RVC 526

FIRST REGISTERED	28 NOVEMBER 1955
ENGINE SIZE	2,088cc
MODEL TYPE	VANGUARD III

Like Peter Cooper in RVC 202, Jo Ashfield had a routine run down towards Monte Carlo, except that her car suffered a puncture south of Chambéry and she lost 12 minutes changing the wheel. Like Cooper, too, she could not make her Vanguard go fast enough to qualify for the final tests.

COMPETITION RECORD	
1956 Monte Carlo	
Jo Ashfield	163rd overall

RVC 527

Maurice Gatsonides (left) with his eighth-place Vanguard III after the 1956 Monte Carlo rally – note the completely worn-out front tyres!

FIRST REGISTERED	28 NOVEMBER 1955
ENGINE SIZE	2,088cc
MODEL TYPE	VANGUARD III

It was typical of Maurice Gatsonides that he spent longer preparing for the Monte, and in getting his otherwise ordinary Vanguard to his liking, than any of his team-mates. After careful study of the routes from the choice of starting points, he elected to begin the event from Lisbon.

Along with Marcel Becquart as his co-driver, the ever-reliable Dutchman brought his Vanguard III safely through the long and tedious road section, then put up a sparkling performance on the downhill sprint/braking test. He was a remarkable 14th overall before the start of the 150-mile mountain circuit that concluded the event. Knowing all the roads around Monte Carlo quite intimately and having practised the specific route assiduously before the event, he hoisted the unwieldy car to a splendid eighth place overall. This was at the expense of the rubber on his front tyres, for the tread had completely disappeared when the car was photographed at the finish!

Not only that, but the car had also been specially prepared with the after-event 'comfort' competition in mind, which explains why it had Citroën 2CV-type front seating, with the passenger seat further re-engineered to allow it to be reclined. Although 2CV seats looked incredibly basic at the time, they were supremely comfortable. Accordingly, after being thoroughly cleaned, tidied up and given a quick 'makeover', the Vanguard went on display outside the Casino and won the Road Safety and Comfort Competition, which had gained importance at the expense of the traditional type of concours d'élégance.

Not willing to write off the Vanguard III as a complete motorsport failure, the factory then reprepared Gatso's car for him to compete in the East African Safari, which was thought to be more in favour for the big Standard because of its rough roads and the organisers' insistence that cars should be in near-showroom condition. For use in Africa, the Vanguard was reregistered locally as KFH 626 and Gatso's co-driver was Vic Gossington, who was Standard-Triumph's technical manager in the Nairobi-based import/dealership operation in Kenya.

In those early days, this fearsome event was still called the Coronation Safari, having been founded in 1953, but it was be destined to become one of the world's most famous marathons. As Gatsonides was the first Europe-based driver to tackle it, he took time to get used to the hot, dusty, 'open-road' conditions. Happily for him, he manhandled the car into third place in its class, and spoke glowingly of the event when he got back home.

COMPETITION RECORD
1956 Monte Carlo
Maurice Gatsonides	8th overall

1956 East African Safari
Maurice Gatsonides	3rd in class

RVC 529

FIRST REGISTERED	29 NOVEMBER 1955
ENGINE SIZE	2,088cc
MODEL TYPE	VANGUARD III

This was the only one of the six Monte Vanguards than ran in modified specification, for team boss Ken Richardson and his regular co-driver Kit Heathcote had twin SU carburettors on their car's 2,088cc engine and modified suspension setting.

This was, in effect, a prototype of the Vanguard Sports-man, which was due to be announced later in the year.

But it was all to no avail. On the approaches to Monte Carlo, Richardson's Vanguard slid off the road, hit a kerb and damaged its front suspension too seriously for it to continue.

The team manager's car, therefore, was the only one of the six that failed to reach the finish.

COMPETITION RECORD
1956 Monte Carlo
Ken Richardson	Did not finish

Peter Bolton, Robin Richards (of the BBC) and Arthur Slater at the end of the 1956 Monte Carlo rally.

RVC 542

FIRST REGISTERED	3 OCTOBER 1955
ENGINE SIZE	2,088cc
MODEL TYPE	VANGUARD III

For publicity purposes this entry had links with the BBC, whose motorsport reporter, Robin Richards, accompanied Peter Bolton in the car. Unfortunately Richards cannot have had much to report on: although Bolton reached the sprint/braking test above Monte Carlo without penalty, he could not then urge the car to go fast enough to qualify for the final regularity test.

COMPETITION RECORD
1956 Monte Carlo
Peter Bolton	103rd overall

RVC 544

Of the six Vanguard IIIs entered for the 1956 Monte Carlo rally, only the one driven by Maurice Gatsonides performed with honour.

FIRST REGISTERED	3 OCTOBER 1955
ENGINE SIZE	2,088cc
MODEL TYPE	VANGUARD III

Cherry Osborne's outing in the 1956 event was safe and commendable, but with such an unsuitable car she had absolutely no chance of producing a result for the factory.

COMPETITION RECORD
1956 Monte Carlo
Cherry Osborne   154th overall

APPENDIX 1:
ENGINES USED IN WORKS STANDARDS AND TRIUMPHS

Although Standard-Triumph originally had little experience in super-tuning engines for motorsport purposes, the company gradually built up a remarkable record, especially for developing high-performance endurance power units. The following, I hope, is a complete list of the engine types used in works Standards and Triumphs during the 1953–80 period.

Still used in historic rallying, this TR4, registered 6 VC, has the homologated twin-Weber carburettor installation; power output is about 135bhp from 2,138cc.

FOUR-CYLINDER, 'WET-LINER'	
TR2	1,991cc
TR3	1,991cc
TR3A	1,991cc
	2,138cc
TR4	1,991cc
	2,138cc
Standard Vanguard III	2,088cc

FOUR-CYLINDER, 'SABRINA' TWIN-CAM	
TR3S	1,985cc
TRS	1,985cc
Conrero prototype	1,985cc

FOUR-CYLINDER, SMALL 'SC'	
Standard 8hp	803cc
Standard Ten	948cc
Standard Pennant	948cc
Herald	948cc
Spitfire	1,147cc
	1,296cc

FOUR-CYLINDER, OVERHEAD-CAMSHAFT 'SLANT FOUR'	
Dolomite Sprint	1,998cc
TR7	1,998cc

SIX-CYLINDER, IN-LINE	
Vitesse	1,596cc
2000	1,998cc
2.5 PI	2,498cc
'GT6R' project	1,998cc

EIGHT-CYLINDER, ROVER V8	
TR7 V8	3,528cc

Works Spitfires – racing and rally cars – were all campaigned with twin-choke Weber carburettors, their manifolds braced to the cylinder block so that continuous vibration did not cause damage.

The World Cup rally 2.5 PIs of 1970 used specially strengthened cylinder block castings, as indicated by this cast-in 'EXP RALLY' notation.

The engine bay of this Group 2 Dolomite Sprint, SOE 8M, is well filled, with large twin-choke Weber carburettors occupying much space on the right-hand side.

For the 1970 World Cup Rally, the works 2.5 PIs had carefully reworked cylinder heads, with both the Triumph factory in Coventry and Abingdon itself having a hand in the modifications.

As homologated for use in the works Spitfires, the 1,147cc engine featured twin-choke Weber carburettors and a tubular exhaust manifold. The engine bay 'splash panels' used on road cars were discarded for the competition cars, helping air flow inside the engine bay.

On Group 2 works Dolomite Sprints the standard SU carburettors were replaced by twin-choke Webers. Bosses on the inlet manifolds were raised close to the joint with the cylinder head, so that fuel injection nozzles could be added at a later stage.

There were three phases of engine development for the works TR7 V8s: in the beginning two twin-choke Webers were used, while at the end Pierburg fuel injection was installed; in addition, as seen here on SJW 548S, the 1979–80 period also saw the use of four twin-choke Weber carburettors, which gave power output of well over 300bhp.

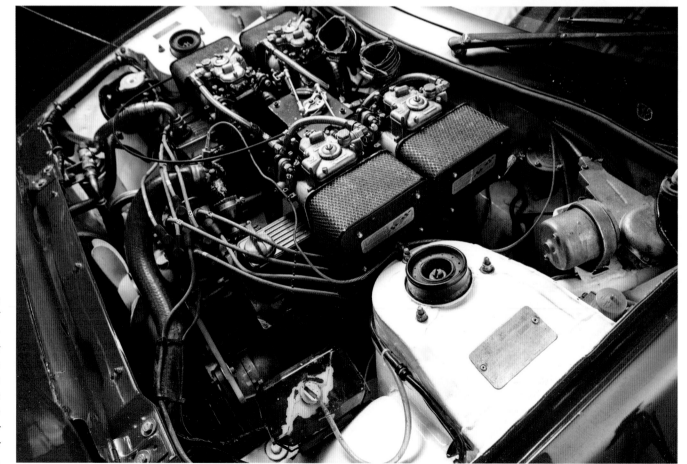

APPENDIX 2:
THE FOUR-WHEEL-DRIVE
1300 RALLYCROSS CAR (1968–69)

With British Leyland coming into existence in 1968 and with no obvious motorsport future for Ray Henderson's department in Coventry, everything went very quiet at Fletchamstead North. After the 1967 RAC rally cars had been sold off, the workshops were virtually deserted and there was no serious programme in prospect.

For a short time, Ray Henderson returned to a role that totally suited him. If there was a completely off-the-wall experimental project that was quite outside the experience of Standard-Triumph's more conventional technicians, Henderson was usually asked to tackle it. And invariably he did it very well!

According to his colleague and long-time friend Gordon Birtwistle, Ray sat down in front of his TV one Saturday afternoon in 1968 and watched the new-fangled sport of rallycross from Lydden Hill, Kent, where cars such as Lotus-Cortinas and Porsche 911s battled on a mixture of surfaces, with tarmac, mud and gravel all featuring on a single lap. As this was meant to be TV entertainment, the regulations were fairly free and easy, and the cars were certainly very varied. Gradually it dawned on Ray that not a single car had four-wheel drive, although the conditions were ideal for it.

Four-wheel drive? Why not? Could he devise a Triumph-based contender? Yes. After all, it would not need to be ferociously powerful to be competitive. The only four-wheel-drive cars on sale in the UK at the time were various Land Rovers (much too slow) and the ultra-exclusive Jensen FF (impossibly expensive). Ray, on the other hand, could already visualise a way of making a very special one-off four-wheel-drive Triumph…

Because his tiny department had nothing else on the immediate horizon and because he was in any case so well thought of within the engineering department, Ray soon got the go-ahead for his plan and was told to go away and design such a machine himself!

What sounded like a bit of a mongrel on paper was in fact an extremely well thought-out machine, a triumph of 'can-do' engineering, the sort of project that Harry Webster had always encouraged in a department that was compact by any other company's more free-spending standards.

Where did the makings of the new project come from? Firstly, there were the Triumph 1300/1300TC models, front-wheel-drive four-door saloons with an engine that was a detuned relative of the version already proven in the Spitfire Le Mans and rally cars. Secondly, there was a humble, boxy but cute four-wheel-drive pick-up truck called the Pony, which was both its project name and the name eventually given to it when it went into small-scale production in the Middle East.

The link was that the Pony used the same basic engine as the 1300 and a version of the 1300 gearbox allied to a four-wheel-drive transmission: in effect a propeller shaft extended from the back of the main gearbox to the rear wheels.

So far, so good. But no four-wheel-drive version of the 1300/1300TC had ever been built, nor even considered, and the Pony did not look a promising route because it had a live rear axle. Henderson therefore acquired a standard front-wheel-drive 1300 saloon, gutted it of its running gear, and set to work.

First he welded up the rear doors because they were redundant. Then he fashioned a bonnet scoop to encourage more

Brian Culcheth in the snow at Lydden Hill in 1969, proving that the four-wheel-drive 1300 was immensely fast.

Culcheth loved the four-wheel-drive Triumph 1300 – a fabulous low-budget project that livened up TV viewing in the winter of 1968/69.

Flying over the humps at Lydden Hill in 1969 – four-wheel drive is no use if all wheels are off the ground! The big bonnet bulge was needed to clear the much-modified engine and the deeper radiator.

fresh air into the engine bay – it looked crude but the aesthetics did not matter to Ray. Next it was time to butcher the platform in order to make space for a propeller shaft and to accommodate independent rear suspension of Triumph 2000 type, complete with semi-trailing arms and a chassis-mounted final drive.

The pièce de resistance, of course, was the choice of engine, which was to be the 1.3-litre 79X version of the 1300's normal power unit, as used in the works Spitfire rally cars in the mid-1960s. This ran on twin dual-choke Weber carburettors, produced 117bhp, and was guaranteed to turn this ungainly little machine into a real rallycross monster.

The transmission was switchable from front-wheel to four-wheel drive when the car was at rest. The only snag encountered with the installation was that it did not prove quite possible to match the ratios of the existing front differential to that of the 2000-based rear axle. The 1300's final drive ratio was 4.11:1 while that of the 2000-based unit was 4.10:1 – the difference was negligible but also noticeable, as test-driver Gordon Birtwistle confirmed: 'At all times the rear wheels wanted to go at a slightly different speed from the fronts, and I found that this essentially produced an over-steering car.' Brian Culcheth, who was later hired to drive the car in British rallycross events, found this trait eminently satisfactory, although he did note that every gearchange required some concentration because the pattern was different from standard.

The car's début, in front of TV viewers, was the unique pre-Christmas TV Autopoint event on military land in Surrey, where an amazing variety of cars raced against each other in what we might call orienteering on driven wheels. The 4x4 won the first heats, but then the engine suffered a problem. This first outing was under Ray Henderson's control, but responsibility for running the car then transferred to the British Leyland competitions department at Abingdon, as assistant competitions manager Bill Price recalls.

'It was very standard looking when it arrived at Abingdon, but we then had the steel removable panels replaced with aluminium, and the inner door mechanisms stripped out, along with the rear seats, trim, bumpers, etc. Perspex windows were also fitted to the side and rear to reduce weight: the only exterior change was the blanked-off head-lamps.' The car was also equipped with Minilite road wheels.

First time out under Abingdon's control, at a snow-blanketed Lydden Hil, onlookers could see that it was potentially a very serious project. The outing got off to a nervous start prior to qualifying, though, for it became clear that there was no anti-freeze in the engine and the team feared the worst when core plugs burst out of the cylinder block. Happily, after a bit of attention from the expert mechanics, new core plugs were hammered back into place, health was apparently restored, and the 1300 four-wheel-drive went on to become the star of the meeting.

'It took two seconds off everybody in the first 300 yards, and the handling was excellent,' said Culcheth. The car came home first overall ahead of rivals like Roger Clark's rear-wheel-drive Ford Escort, and everyone was delighted.

The following month the car appeared on TV at the Croft circuit, near Darlington, and won a demonstration race. At the same circuit a few weeks later, it was once again firmly in the lead when the gear lever broke.

Then came the final TV rallycross of the winter season at High Eggborough, near Pontefract, Yorkshire. Culcheth once again set out to establish a lead and did just that. But then a front suspension radius arm suddenly broke, that wheel immediately went on to full lock, causing the car to roll. It was a big accident but fortunately it did not inflict any injury on Brian – but the car was comprehensively destroyed.

And so, in the succinct words of team boss Peter Browning, 'That was the end of that project.'

Beginning of the end. In an event at High Eggborough, a front suspension radius arm of the four-wheel-drive 1300 snapped, the car immediately became uncontrollable, and rolled itself into oblivion. Fortunately the driver, Brian Culcheth, was not hurt.

COMPETITION RECORD

1968 London MC TV Autopoint

Brian Culcheth	1st in heat

1969 TV Rallycross, Lydden Hill

Brian Culcheth	1st

1969 TV Rallycross, Croft

Brian Culcheth	1st

1969 TV Rallycross, Croft

Brain Culcheth	Did not finish

1969 TV Rallycross, High Eggborough

Brian Culcheth	Did not finish